PENGUIN BOOKS
INDIA UNBOUND

Gurcharan Das is an author and public intellectual. He writes a regular column for the *Times of India*, *Dainik Bhaskar*, *Eenadu* and other newspapers. He also writes for the *Wall Street Journal*, *Financial Times*, *Newsweek* and *Foreign Affairs*. He graduated from Harvard University in philosophy and politics and was CEO of Procter & Gamble India before he took early retirement to become a full-time writer.

He is the author of the novel *A Fine Family*. His other literary works include a book of essays, *The Elephant Paradigm*, and an anthology, *Three English Plays*, consisting of *Larins Sahib*, a prize-winning play about the British in India, which was presented at the Edinburgh Festival; *Mira*, which was produced off-Broadway to critical acclaim; and *9 Jakhoo Hill*, which has been performed in major Indian cities.

First published in 2000, the best-selling *India Unbound* has been translated into several languages worldwide, and was also made into a film by the BBC.

Praise for the Book

'It is a wonderful book—a great mixture of memoir, economic analysis, social investigation, political scrutiny and managerial outlook being thrown into the understanding of India . . . The temper of the book is both critical as well as optimistic, and I think the combination works well. Gurcharan being happier with the world makes a difference—there is a kind of positiveness that breathes through every page'—Amartya Sen

'This brilliant work in political economy is for all young Indians, especially budding politicians and IAS probationers. It deserves to be translated in all Indian languages so that the common person can become better educated about the policies that they want for their country'—N.R. Narayana Murthy

'Having constructed a comprehensive indictment of India's economic failures, Das is optimistic about the liberalization that has opened the economy in the 1990s . . . Das writes in an engaging style, sprinkling his text with a well-chosen array of quotations. There are layman-friendly discussions of economic theories of poverty, and his arguments are leavened with a close reading of economic texts, both classic and contemporary. But what shines through is the telling anecdote, the personal example, the remembered conversation'—Shashi Tharoor, *Los Angeles Times*

'There's much to be said for this book. In the first place, it's interesting, for Das is a natural storyteller. Second, it's unpretentious—the language, while adequate, is without unnecessary flourishes. Third, it's informative—it contains a mixture of history and autobiography—which includes some essentials for anyone in business or management—and the reader glides smoothly from one to the other'—Shashi Warrier, *Indian Review of Books*

'Gurcharan Das is by any standard an amazing man . . . *India Unbound* is an education by itself. [He] goes back and forth into history, politics, social changes as and when the situation calls for, and speaks more about the world around him than about himself . . . Even when he is critical of Jawaharlal Nehru's policies he is appreciative of his sentiments'—M.V. Kamath, *The Daily Sunday*

'Gurcharan Das has written a paean to liberalization (*India Unbound*)—arguably the most readable book on the reforms of the 1990s. Gurcharan is a magical writer and a great storyteller; his account of the reforms is so upbeat that even I thought we had accomplished something'—Ashok Desai, *Business Standard*

'*India Unbound* is bound to become an essential component of the reading list for anyone interested in the contemporary Indian economy'—Sushma Ramachandran, *The Hindu*

'Gurcharan Das is a good storyteller. He weaves a series of unconnected actions into a pattern with some sort of theme. His technique is to put himself, often vicariously, as an observer, occasionally a participant, into the events he describes; in this way he gives immediacy to history'—Sudhir Mulji, *Business Standard*

'Why has a country as bountifully blessed as India achieved so little in a half century of freedom? Gurcharan Das provides a fascinating interpretation of the possible reasons in *India Unbound* . . . Not often does one come across a former CEO of a major organization . . . who is also well-read in a wide range of subjects, ranging from economics to philosophy to poetry. And if one does come across them on rare occasions, not many can wield a pen as dexterously as Das does'—V.S. Mahesh, *Business India*

'Gurcharan Das's keen eye . . . captures the panorama of the last 50 years of Indian history in his own way . . . both fascinating and interesting . . . *India Unbound* keeps your interest in top gear throughout the book'—Shunu Sen, *Business Line*

'The change in India since economic liberalization in 1991 has been astonishing, and the pace of it picks up every day. On a recent visit—after several years—I found a book which gave a vivid and persuasive explanation of the transformation all around me. *India Unbound* . . . is a mixture of memoir and social and economic inquiry, written with great energy, personal knowledge and clarity. I would firmly recommend it to any visitor to India as a key guide to its recent past'—Ian Jack, *New Statesman*

'*India Unbound* is at the top of the country's best-seller list for non-fiction, tapping into a vein of renewed self-confidence and national pride that is itself a central theme of his study. Part memoir, part history, part travelogue, part polemic, *India Unbound* dissects the failures of the country's Nehruvian socialist experiment and vividly describes the changes that are transforming the daily lives and outlooks of the country's 1 bn people'—John Thornhill, *Financial Times*

'*India Unbound* is a lively, interesting and well-documented answer—the first of its kind—to a key question: why was India rich, why is it poor, when will it be rich again? It is also full of the kind of stories which make that fascinating country come alive for the reader'—Olivier Bernier, author of *The World in 1800*

'*India Unbound* is a quiet earthquake that shook faraway shores long before its shockwave reached Britain. [Its] conclusion is that in the next two decades India will become the third-largest economy, after the US and China . . . [and] two industries, information technology and agriculture, will lift India out of poverty. It talks of an India where teenage tea-shop assistants work to save money for computer lessons . . . [and] says that if the poor get rich and a few people get filthy rich, that is better than worrying about the distribution of wealth and no one getting rich. Amartya Sen, the Nobel Prize-winner, was so impressed he asked Das to start a "secular, right-wing party" modelled on Britain's Tories in India'—*The Guardian*

'Part memoir, part journalism, part history and part management bible . . . *India Unbound* is an opinionated but insightful guide to a rapidly changing nation in which old cliches about spirituality and poverty are increasingly irrelevant . . . Das had a ringside seat at the events he describes, and the result is an engaging account that moves easily from the big picture to the telling anecdote'—*New York Times* Book Review

'The strength of [Das's] inquiry lies in its castigation of those who inherited the running of India from the British. He is commendably scathing about Nehru and his daughter Indira Gandhi, who had her father's *hubris* and contempt for businessmen but not a trace of his erudition . . . The author regards economic growth as the only way to strengthen Indian democracy . . . [and] his optimism is potent when he says, "We have good reasons to expect that the lives of the majority of Indians in the 21st century will be freer and more prosperous than their parents. Never before in recorded history have so many people been in a position to rise so quickly."'—*The Wall Street Journal*

'[*India Unbound*] could be an eye-opener to readers unfamiliar with the radical transformations currently under way in the subcontinent'—*The Washington Post Book World*

'Remarkable . . . Head and shoulders above the customary books . . . This story is so much more persuasive and effective . . . [as] Das traces his life as a journey headed in the same direction as the business life of his country, an almost literary scheme that is unusually effective . . . The issues of business vs. private enterprise [are] played against the somewhat parallel questions of modernity vs. tradition and nationalism against cosmopolitanism . . . This elegant essay has something for everyone'—*St. Louis Post-Dispatch*

'Informative, entertaining and basically correct about India's need to embrace capitalism more whole heartedly, for all the costs and risks'—*The Economist*

INDIA UNBOUND

From Independence to the Global Information Age

Gurcharan Das

PENGUIN BOOKS

For Bunu, Kim, and Puru

PENGUIN BOOKS
Published by the Penguin Group
Penguin Books India Pvt. Ltd, 11 Community Centre, Panchsheel Park,
New Delhi 110 017, India
Penguin Group (USA) Inc., 375 Hudson Street, New York, New York 10014, USA
Penguin Group (Canada), 90 Eglinton Avenue East, Suite 700, Toronto, Ontario,
M4P 2Y3, Canada (a division of Pearson Penguin Canada Inc.)
Penguin Books Ltd, 80 Strand, London WC2R 0RL, England
Penguin Ireland, 25 St Stephen's Green, Dublin 2, Ireland (a division of
Penguin Books Ltd)
Penguin Group (Australia), 250 Camberwell Road, Camberwell, Victoria 3124, Australia
(a division of Pearson Australia Group Pty Ltd)
Penguin Group (NZ), 67 Apollo Drive, Rosedale, Auckland 0632, New Zealand
(a division of Pearson New Zealand Ltd)
Penguin Group (South Africa) (Pty) Ltd, 24 Sturdee Avenue, Rosebank,
Johannesburg 2196, South Africa

Penguin Books Ltd, Registered Offices: 80 Strand, London WC2R 0RL, England

First published in Viking by Penguin Books India 2000
This revised and updated edition published in Penguin Books 2002, 2007

Copyright © Gurcharan Das 2000, 2002

All rights reserved

20 19 18 17 16 15 14

ISBN 9780143063018

For sale in the Indian Subcontinent only

Printed at Shri Krishna Printers, Noida

CONTENTS

INTRODUCTION:
THE WISE ELEPHANT

*... the causes of wealth and poverty of nations—the grand object of
all enquiries in Political Economy.*
—MALTHUS TO RICARDO,
LETTER DATED 26 JANUARY 1817

The ascent of a country from poverty to prosperity, from tradition
to modernity, is a great and fascinating enterprise. India has
recently emerged as a vibrant free-market democracy after the
economic reforms in 1991, and it has begun to flex its muscles in the
global information economy. The old centralized bureaucratic state,
which killed our industrial revolution at birth, has begun a subtle but
definite decline. With the rule of democracy the lower castes have gradually risen. This economic and social transformation is one of the
themes of this book. The struggle of one-sixth of humanity for dignity
and prosperity seems to me a drama of the highest order and of great
consequence for the future of the world. It has meaning for all of
humanity and sheds new light on the future of liberalism in the world.

The story I will be telling is soft drama. It is taking place quietly and
profoundly in the heart of Indian society. It unfolds every day, in small
increments barely visible to the naked eye, and is more difficult to grasp
than hard drama, which is more dramatic and captures the headlines.
Most people instinctively grasp the spirituality and poverty of India. But
the significance of this quiet social and economic revolution eludes
them. The change is partially based on the rise of social democracy, but

more importantly on the sustained 5 to 7 percent annual economic growth that India has experienced for the past two decades, which has tripled the size of the middle class. Although the middle class is still only 18 percent of India's one billion population, it is expected to become 50 percent within a generation. In the end, this "silent revolution" is more significant historically than the constantly changing fortunes of political leaders and parties which so absorb Indians.

I have followed, I find, the method of Defoe's *Memoirs of a Cavalier,* in which the author hangs the chronicle of great political and social events upon the thread of an individual's personal experience. However, this is not autobiography. I have decided to tell the story in the first person because I believe that one person's experience, honestly captured, even on the sidelines, not only is unique but is the only certain data of history that we possess as human beings. I did not, besides, wish this account of national competitiveness to be dry and didactic; I wished to breathe life into the clash of economic and social ideas.

When I was young, we passionately believed in Jawaharlal Nehru's dream of a modern and just India. But as the years went by we discovered that Nehru's economic path was taking us to a dead end, and the dream soured. Having set out to create socialism, we found that we had instead created statism. As a practicing manager in the 1960s I found myself caught in the thick jungle of Kafkaesque bureaucratic controls. Our sense of disillusionment reached its peak during Mrs. Gandhi's autocratic rule in the seventies. There was a glimmer of hope when Rajiv Gandhi became Prime Minister, but it quickly died when we discovered that he did not have what it takes. It was not until July 1991 that our mood of despair finally lifted, with the announcement of sweeping liberalization by the minority government of P. V. Narasimha Rao. It opened the economy to foreign investment and trade; it dismantled import controls, lowered customs duties, and devalued the currency; it virtually abolished licensing controls on private investment, dropped tax rates, and broke public sector monopolies. As a result, growth picked up to 7.5 percent a year in the mid-nineties, inflation came down from 13 percent to 6 percent by 1993, exchange reserves shot up from $1 billion to $20 billion.* As India joined the world economy we felt as though

---

*Where appropriate, I have converted the local Indian rupees to U.S. dollars at the exchange rate prevailing at a given time.

our second independence had arrived: we were going to be free from a rapacious and domineering state.

Although the reforms after 1991 have been slow, hesitant, and incomplete, they have set in motion a process of profound change in Indian society. It is as important a turning point as Deng's revolution in China in December 1978. A half century of the ballot box has also empowered the lower castes, and this means that the fruits of the reforms are likely to be better distributed. The world has, meanwhile, changed from an industrial to an information economy, and it speaks to India's advantage—our initial success in software is the first evidence. The irony is that most Indians, especially in the political class, have not yet realized it. If they had, they would invest more in education and implement the reforms much faster.

One of the intriguing questions of history is why we failed to create an industrial revolution in India. Marx predicted that the railways would transform India and usher in an industrial revolution. Indeed, by the First World War, some thought that we were ready to take off. By 1914, India had the third-largest railway network, the world's largest jute manufacturing industry, the fourth-largest cotton textile industry, the largest canal system, and 2.5 percent of world trade. It also had a merchant class hungry to become industrialists. After the war, industrialization did, in fact, pick up. G. D. Birla, Kasturbhai Lalbhai, and other businessmen made huge trading profits during the First World War and reinvested them in setting up industries. Between 1913 and 1938, our manufacturing output grew 5.6 percent a year, well ahead of the world average of 3.3. By 1947, industry's share doubled to 7.5 percent of national output from 3.4 percent. But it was not enough to broadly transform our agricultural society. Modern industry employed only 2.5 million people out of a population of 350 million. The chief problem was our agriculture, which remained stagnant, and you cannot have an industrial revolution without an agricultural surplus or the means to feed a rapidly growing urban population.

After we won freedom, Jawaharlal Nehru and his planners attempted an industrial revolution through the agency of the state. They did not trust private entrepreneurs, so they made the state the entrepreneur. Not surprisingly, they failed, and India is still paying a huge price for their follies. Instead, we experienced an agricultural revolution. Ironically, we now had an important precondition in place—an agricultural surplus—but the industrial revolution continues to elude us.

When I was in college, we talked about India as though it were an airplane and we wondered when it would take off into self-generating growth. No one asked "if" it would take off—the only question was "when." During the takeoff, economists told us, the nation's investment rate would climb to 10 to 12 percent. Well, our investment rate in India has been well over 20 percent for two decades, and yet we have not transformed our society. Why? There were at least six things wrong with India's mantra. One, it adopted an inward-looking, import-substituting path, rather than an outward-looking, export-promoting route, thus denying itself a share in world trade and the prosperity that trade brought in the postwar era. Two, it set up a massive, inefficient, and monopolistic public sector to which it denied autonomy of working; hence our investments were not productive and we had a poor capital–output ratio. Three, it overregulated private enterprise with the worst controls in the world, and this diminished competition in the market; besides, our merchant-businessmen were not "tinkerers" and they were slow to innovate. Four, it discouraged foreign capital and denied itself the benefits of technology and world-class competition. Five, it pampered organized labor to the point where we have extremely low productivity. Six, and perhaps most important, it ignored the education of half its children, especially of girls.

In part, this is a story of the betrayal of the last two generations by India's rulers. In stubbornly persisting with the wrong model of development (especially after 1970, when there was clear evidence that this path was doomed), they suppressed growth and jobs and denied their people an opportunity to rise above poverty. It is ironic that men and women of goodwill created this order and were widely admired. After all, they did succeed in institutionalizing democracy. The second irony is that in the name of the poor they refused to change course. The worst indictment of Indian socialism is that in the end it did very little for the poor. All the countries of East Asia did far better. Even China, with all its convulsions over the past fifty years, has done a better job at improving the lives of its people. Our failure came less from ideology and more from poor management.

Hence, India's per capita income is $450, which places it 162nd out of 206 countries in the *World Development Report* for 2000–2001. In 1960, it was higher than China's, but today it is half. Although by purchasing power parity India's income rises to $2,149, that lifts its global rank only marginally, to 153rd. Half the Indian people are poor by the international poverty line of one dollar per person per day, and a third of the world's poor are in India. An Indian's life expectancy is sixty-three years, lower than that in many poor countries. As many as sixty-five out of a thousand infants die, and that is too high; two-thirds of the children suffer from malnutrition and are underweight. Seventy-one percent cannot access sanitation. Four out of ten Indians are illiterate. Therefore, India is ranked 134th out of 174 countries on the United Nations Development Program's Human Development Index. India's performance is not good enough. Other similarly placed countries have done better.

To top this tale of India's lost decades, members of the Indian ruling elite—the politicians, the MPs, the senior bureaucrats, and the economic planners—are not contrite. They complacently proclaim, "After all, we have done rather well compared to the 3.5 percent Hindu rate of growth." There is no more defeatist expression in the dictionary than this fatalistic phrase. They feel no humiliation that India has lagged behind in a Third Worldish twilight while its neighbors in East and Southeast Asia have gone ahead. There is no feeling of shame that countries with a fraction of India's natural and human resource potential have created some of the most prosperous societies in the world. They have used the recent troubles of East Asia to justify our incomplete and frustratingly slow reforms. When individuals blunder, it is unfortunate and their families go down. When rulers fail, it is a national tragedy.

Indians have not traditionally accorded a high place to the making of money. The Vaishya or bania (merchant) is placed third in the four-caste hierarchy, behind the Brahmin and the Kshatriya (warrior, landowner), and only a step ahead of the laboring Shudra. Since the economic reforms, making money has become increasingly respectable and the sons of Brahmins and Kshatriyas are getting M.B.A.'s and want to become entrepreneurs. India is in the midst of a social revolution rivaled perhaps only by the ascent of Japan's merchant class during the 1868 Meiji Restoration, which helped transform Japan from an underdeveloped group of islands into a thriving modern society and economy. The commercial spirit is not limited to the cities. The smallest village has found it. On a visit to Pondicherry from Madras a few years ago, I stopped at a roadside village cafe where fourteen-year-old Raju was hustling between the tables. He served us good south Indian coffee and vadas. Raju told us that this was his summer job and it paid Rs 450 a month—enough to pay for computer lessons in the evenings in the neighboring village. For the next summer, his aunt in Madras had arranged a job for him in a computer company.

"What will you do when you grow up?" I asked. "I am going to run a computer company," said Raju. He had decided this when "I saw it in TV, where this man Bilgay [*sic*] has a software company and he is the richest man in the world."

In Bartoli, a sleepy village of six hundred families in the heart of feudal Uttar Pradesh, a government schoolteacher lamented: "Everyone has become money-minded. Even the leather workers, low down on the social scale, are removing their children from my school and putting them into this newfangled private 'English' school which opened six months ago. Can you believe it—they are willing to spend Rs 35 a month when it costs one rupee a month in my school!" They were leaving his school "because they watch TV; they want to learn English; they want to get rich. This is what happens when the 'low' castes get uppity. No one wants to work on the land."

"There is no loyalty left, sir," added Fateh Singh, who stood shyly outside the door and would not sit with us because he is from a low caste. He complained that his grown-up nephew, Vikas, wanted to set up a factory to make steel trunks in nearby Khurja rather than become a conductor in the state-run bus company like his father. Indians are slowly realizing that economic reforms are not only about tariff levels, deregulation, and structural adjustment. They are about a revolution in ideas which is changing the mind-set of the people and leading to the commercialization of Indian society.

Rich countries were supposed to specialize in the knowledge industries of tomorrow and poor countries in low-wage, low-skill industries of yesterday. This was the theory, but someone forgot to tell Bangalore (and Hyderabad, Chennai, Gurgaon, and Pune). Every day these days we read about a new success in the new "knowledge economy," and we wonder if, at last, we may have arrived. There are 325 software companies in Bangalore. Most of them have customers in America, who e-mail their needs before they leave their offices. While they sleep, Indian engineers work on their problems. By the next morning, as they bring their coffee mugs to their desks, Americans have their answers as they log on.

One of these companies is Infosys, which started out with a $500 capital; in February 2000, it was worth $15.4 billion and more than a hundred of its managers were each worth over a million dollars. Another is the National Institute of Information Technology (NIIT), which has franchised (like McDonald's hamburgers) 1,750 computer schools in Indian bazaars and in thirty-one countries. It plans to become the world leader in computer education. Over the last decade, it has created 1,750 entrepreneurs and fifteen thousand jobs. On 22 February 2000, Azim Premji had become the third-richest man in the world on *Forbes* rankings based on the market capitalization of his software company, which crossed $46 billion, or 11.3 percent of India's GDP. With his wealth, Premji could pay for India's fiscal deficit and still have change left over.

The spirit of the age is reflected in hundreds of entrepreneurial successes in the knowledge economy. Subhash Chandra used to be a rice trader in the 1980s and he has built a worldwide media empire that was worth $14 billion in February 2000; he is called the Murdoch of Asia. A tiny two-year-old company in Bangalore called Armedia achieved a breakthrough in designing a chip for digital TV in 1999; America's Broadcom bought it for $67 million and made its forty-three employees rich beyond their wildest dreams. Ranbaxy, Dr. Reddy's Laboratories, Cipla, and Wockhardt are building successful global businesses in generic drugs. Crest Communications in Bombay is one of only two studios outside North America with the expertise to make 3D animation films and it has recently won a contract from one of the Hollywood studios to make an animated feature film. Rajesh Jain's Internet sites were so attractive that Satyam Infoways bought them for $116 million—a nice return on the $57,000 that he invested five years ago. Around forty thousand Indians are employed in online "remote services"—transcribing medical records, editing books, making digital maps, doing payroll accounts for customers around the world; and McKinsey projects that this could grow to a million jobs earning $50 billion in revenues by 2010.

These entrepreneurial miracles are part of a new social contract for postreform India. The new millionaires did not inherit wealth. They have risen on the back of their talent, hard work, and professional skills. The old business houses, on the other hand, are struggling in the competitive economy created by the reforms. The dilemma of Rahul Bajaj is typical of the old companies. Bajaj is the clear leader in the world's second-largest scooter and two-wheeler market. Yet he is unable to take the next step, which is to become a global player. He has the world's lowest costs; he has successfully withstood the challenge of Japanese competitors on his home ground; he is cash rich—making more profit than all his competitors put together. But he exports only 3 percent of his output. Despite his awesome advantages, Bajaj does not have the confidence to take on the Hondas and Yamahas in the world market.

A decade ago, no one would have even thought of criticizing Rahul Bajaj for not thinking globally. Government rules did not permit him to have a foreign operation, or buy equity of a foreign company, or import components at a reasonable tariff, or expand capacity at will, or buy new technology without a lengthy approval process. Rahul Bajaj had a purely "local" mind-set of a shortage economy. He sold everything he produced, because demand was always ahead of supply—for a decade, there was a ten-year waiting period for his scooter. Thus, he never developed marketing or product development skills. Rahul Bajaj is a creature of Nehruvian socialism. The legacy of forty years of a closed economy has caught up with him. He is the symbol of the "old" India, hobbled by poor infrastructure, obstructionist bureaucrats, high tariffs and interest costs, and a "factory mind-set."

As with Bajaj, the older Indian groups are creatures of a system they did not create. They do not have the skills to succeed in the global economy. Eight years into the reforms, they are still floundering. Success in the global economy needs three things: massive investment in human resources, a passion for product improvement, and a deeply caring attitude for customers. These companies are smart and they understand this. Then why haven't they acquired these skills? The answer is that it takes time to change from doing what you have been doing successfully. But time is precisely what they do not have.

The beginning of the twenty-first century is a time of ferment. Two global trends have converged—both of which work to India's advantage and raise the hope that it may finally take off. One is the liberal revolution that has swept the globe in the past decade, opening economies that were isolated for fifty years and integrating them spectacularly into one global economy. India's economic reforms are part of this trend. They are dismantling controls and releasing the long-suppressed energies of Indian entrepreneurs. They are changing the national mind-set, especially among the young. Because we are endowed with commercial communities, we may be in a better position to take advantage of this global tendency. Merchants understand from birth the power of compound interest; they know how to accumulate capital. The Internet has also leveled the playing field, so that it seems sometimes that any mad, passionate Indian entrepreneur can write his own future.

Meanwhile, the information economy is transforming the world—this is the second global trend. We may not be tinkerers, but we are a conceptual people. We have traditionally had a Brahminical contempt for manual labor, which was relegated to the lowest caste, Shudras, who were also denied knowledge. A tinkerer combines knowledge with manual labor, and this produces innovation. Our entrepreneurs, who come mainly from the higher merchant caste, have also shied away from manual labor and technology. This may be another reason why we did not produce innovation and failed to create an industrial revolution. But this is all changed now, for the industrial age is gone and the knowledge age potentially plays to our advantage. Our success in software and the Internet is the first emerging evidence. We have wrestled with the abstract concepts of the Upanishads for three thousand years. We invented the zero. Just as spiritual space is invisible, so is cyberspace. Hence, our core competence is invisible. In information technology we may have finally found the engine that can drive India's takeoff and transform our country.

There is an old idea in economics, as old as Adam Smith, that if a rich and a poor country are linked by trade, their standard of living should converge in the long run. It makes intuitive sense, because standard of living depends on productivity, and productivity, in turn, depends on technology. When a poor nation is connected, it merely adopts the technological innovations of the rich one without having to reinvent the wheel. Thereby, it grows faster and eventually catches up. Why then has the world not converged in the past fifty years? Very simply, because the rich and poor were not joined. Two Harvard scholars, Jeffrey Sachs and Andrew Warner, studied this dilemma and concluded that only thirteen out of eighty-seven Third World countries were "open" to world trade, and they grew six times faster. Between 1970 and 1990, the thirteen open countries grew at an average 4.5 percent per capita per year compared to the 0.7 percent growth rate of the seventy-four closed countries. India was in the latter group, and not surprisingly many East Asians were in the former. Thus, convergence did take place among the virtuous few economies, and they did substantially conquer poverty.

Now the world has changed. Whereas only 20 percent of the world's people lived in open economies in 1970, today more than 90 percent do, and that is why we call it a globalized world. China and India, with more than a third of the world's population, have accelerated their growth rates in the past two decades: China 8 to 10 percent, and India 5 to 7 percent. If this is sustained and literacy keeps rising, there is a very real prospect that people below the poverty line, who live on less than a dollar a day, will decline to a more manageable 15 to 20 percent of the population from 50 percent today. This is the experience of the East Asian countries. India's poverty is a symbol of poverty on our planet, and if India can hope to make a significant dent, so can most of the Third World. China will get there probably ten to fifteen years earlier. Just ten years ago, this would have been unthinkable. Today, astonishing as it may seem, we can dare to contemplate this proposition.

The Indian state's biggest failure has been in building human capabilities. As a result, 40 percent of Indians remain illiterate. We have now realized that primary education and primary health care are the two most powerful ways to eradicate poverty. Simultaneously, there is a growing, impatient demand for these social goods from below. Indian literacy has already risen by ten percentage points in the past six and a half years, from 52 to 62 percent. It is primarily because of grassroots pressures from below as social democracy has created upward mobility among the lower castes. The push for liberal economic reforms combined with investment in human capabilities will ensure that millions of Indians lift themselves from poverty within a generation.

India embraced democracy first and capitalism afterwards, and this has made all the difference. India became a full-fledged democracy in 1950, with universal suffrage and extensive human rights, but it was not until recently that it opened up to the free play of market forces. This curious historical inversion means that India's future will not be a creation of unbridled capitalism but will evolve through a daily dialogue between the conservative forces of caste, religion, and the village, the leftist and Nehruvian socialist forces which dominated the intellectual life of the country for so long, and the new forces of global capitalism. These "million negotiations of democracy," the plurality of interests, the contentious nature of the people, and the lack of discipline and teamwork imply that the pace of economic reforms will be slow and incremental. It means that India will not grow as rapidly as the Asian tigers, nor wipe out poverty and ignorance as quickly.

The *Economist* has been trying, with some frustration, to paint stripes on India since 1991. It doesn't realize that India will never be a tiger. It is an elephant that has begun to lumber and move ahead. It will never have speed, but it will always have stamina. A Buddhist text says, "The elephant is the wisest of all animals/the only one who remembers his former lives/and he remains motionless for long periods of time/meditating thereon." The inversion between capitalism and democracy suggests that India might have a more stable, peaceful, and negotiated transition into the future than, say, China. It will also avoid some of the harmful side effects of an unprepared capitalist society, such as Russia. Although slower, India is more likely to preserve its way of life and its civilization of diversity, tolerance, and spirituality against the onslaught of the global culture. If it does, then it is perhaps a wise elephant.

PART ONE

Our Spring of Hope

(1942–65)

Some try to represent political economy as being a dry, cold abstract science, which has no warmth of feeling to spare on suffering humanity. . . . This is far from the truth; on the contrary, political economy produces feelings so intense for the removal of these evils, that it will not permit us to rest satisfied . . . but impels us to . . . discover the true causes of this wretchedness, and the mode by which it may be removed. . . .

—JAMES WILSON

ONE

Ranting in English, Chanting in Sanskrit

To everything there is a season, and a time to every purpose under the heaven. A time to be born, and a time to die . . .
— BOOK OF ECCLESIASTES (3:1–2)

I can measure the passages of my life by the nation's milestones. When I was born, we were fighting to get the British out of India. By the time I went to school, we were free and we thought we would soon enter a new paradise. During my school days in the 1950s, Nehru set about building a proud new nation based on democracy, socialism, and secularism. When I went to work in the sixties I discovered that we had become economically enslaved and socialism was leading us to statism. By the time I got married and we had children, Indira Gandhi was creating dynastic rule and leading us into a ditch. When she declared the Emergency in the mid-seventies, we knew that political freedom was gone, and paradise was lost. Mercifully, the Emergency lasted only twenty-two months, and we soon recovered our political freedom. Just before I took early retirement in the early nineties, Narasimha Rao delivered us our economic freedom. It doesn't matter who will be ruling India when I die, because democracy has got entrenched and its institutions are best run by modest men. Thanks to the reforms, we have glimpsed paradise again and are on our way to regaining it. We have climbed to a 7 percent economic growth rate, and if we grow at this rate for a few decades and keep raising our literacy level, the nation will turn increasingly middle class and the degrading poverty of India will begin to vanish.

I was born soon after Mahatma Gandhi challenged the British by launching the Quit India movement in 1942, which led to Independence five years later. My birth also coincided with a second event, the Great Bengal Famine, in which three million people perished. Both these events would never be repeated, and have become remote in public memory. They were the last examples of what were commonplace happenings during my father's and grandfather's days. In a sense, the year of my birth brought down the curtain on an age.

The Quit India movement was born of frustration. For twenty years, Gandhi and the leaders of the nationalist movement had tried to negotiate with the British. It was a nonviolent struggle, based on Gandhi's belief in satyagraha, or "truth force." Because "truth" was on his side, Gandhi believed that he would shame the rulers into giving us freedom. Twelve years earlier, on 11 March 1930, he had informed the British that he was going to violate the salt-tax laws and collect salt from the sea. On that day, in a single stroke, he aroused the whole of India. Fishermen began collecting salt; then the peasants were making salt; the housewives followed suit. Soon the whole country was breaking the law and the people began to court arrest. But how many could the police arrest? Thus, year in and year out, Gandhi provoked the rulers with civil disobedience and drove them to distraction. In the end, they just gave up and left. India won freedom without a single English casualty—and this happened in a world filled with Hitler's and Stalin's shadows. No wonder we felt that we were a nation created by saints.

I grew up in a middle-class home in Punjab in northwest India. Most of Punjab was arid, but over three generations the vision and toil of engineers like my father created a network of canals that irrigated the land and made it a granary. The lower Chenab canal was one of the first to be built in the last quarter of the nineteenth century. With it came an orderly and planned town called Lyallpur, so named after the ruling lieutenant governor of Punjab, Sir James Lyall. It was to this town that my mother's ambitious father proudly moved in the early part of this century to start a law practice. I was born there a generation and a half later. In the middle of Lyallpur was a brick clock tower where eight roads crossed and around which the town spread out in concentric circles. Our house was off one of these roads, called Kacheri Bazaar, on the way to the Company Bagh, whose gardens sprawled sumptuously over forty acres.

We were a professional middle-class family not particularly given to patriotic enthusiasms. We never thought much of Gandhi—he was merely our "liberator with clean hands." My uncle specialized in uncovering the latest scandal in our neighborhood, and that always took precedence over politics. Famines, of course, were too unpleasant to be the subject of polite conversation. Nevertheless, the famine in Bengal did intrude into our complacent world. My grandfather's nephew, Sat Pal, decided one day to help in the relief work. He took a train from Lahore to Calcutta, and from there he went on to the Bengal countryside, where he experienced the trauma of the riots and deaths that took place. On his return, he told us that he did not understand the insanity of the situation. The supply of food had declined only marginally, but its distribution had failed completely. The only thing he could say for sure was that there was a human agency involved in a criminal and nasty form. He spoke vividly of a peasant who had fallen dead on a street in Calcutta—he spoke as though he knew him intimately. When it came to explanations, Sat Pal tended to see everything in class terms, and the others would lose interest. Much to my grandfather's disappointment, Sat Pal had spurned a brilliant professional career and become a communist.

During the Great Bengal Famine entire villages ceased to exist. The tragedy of the Bengali people's suffering was equaled only by the indifference of the British authorities. It was largely a man-made event, caused not by a decline in the food available but by the inadequacy of the response. The reports of the district officers of the province and clippings from the *Statesman* reveal the progress of the tragedy: "Rangoon falls to Japan—rice imports cut off" (10 March 1942); "Cyclone hits Bengal" (4 October 1942); "Rice price doubles in Birbhum district" (6 November 1942); "Wholesale price of rice in Calcutta is Rs 13 compared to Rs 7 a year ago" (11 December 1942); "Hunger marches organised by communists" (28 December 1942); "People having to go without food" (10 February 1943); "Acute distress prevails" (26 March

1943); "Paddy looting cases have become frequent" (28 March 1943); "Major economic catastrophe in the making" (27 April 1943); "Bands of people moving about in search of rice" (12 June 1943); "Death in the streets" (12 June 1943); "Town filled with thousands of beggars who are starving" (17 July 1943); "Disposal of dead bodies . . . a problem" (27 September 1943).

Lord Wavell, the British viceroy, summed up the situation in 1944: "The Bengal Famine was one of the greatest disasters that has befallen any people under British rule and damage to our reputation here . . . is incalculable." The problem, it seems, was Winston Churchill's attitude. Mountbatten wrote in 1944 that Churchill was impossible on the topic of India and regarded sending food as "appeasement of the Congress Party." Churchill said, "I hate Indians. . . . They are a beastly people with a beastly religion." Though food was available, it was sent to Holland but not to India. Wavell noted in his diary "the very different attitude towards feeding a starving people in Europe."

Churchill's advisers frustrated Wavell's efforts to secure grain for India. One of them, Lord Cherwell, felt that the famine was a "figment of the Bengali imagination." It escaped Churchill that India had given two million fighting men for Britain's war effort. Field Marshal Alan Brooke commented that Churchill "seemed content to let India starve, while still wanting to use it as a base for military operations." The British army generals did let in some food, but much of it was diverted to their troops.

Reports of famines were familiar news to my parents and their generation. Today, famines have vanished from our memory. When the monsoon failed in 1979 and again in 1987, few people noticed. It is not only because the green revolution (to be discussed in chapter 9) has increased food supply in India. It is also because democracy and a vigorous press force politicians to act for the sake of their own survival, Nobel laureate Amartya Sen reminds us. Nowadays, the government routinely carries three to four months' supply of food grains in the national warehouses and the public distribution system. In China, on the other hand, despite higher nutritional standards, more than twenty million people died from famines during Mao's experiments in the late 1950s (though, amazingly, the world did not learn of these tragedies until the eighties). This happened partially because of the absence of democracy and an active free press. Sen's point is that merely having more food is not enough. What causes hunger is the inability of the poor to buy food. Hence, even if Wavell had succeeded in getting more food for Bengal from Churchill, he would not have saved the starving masses unless he had had a plan to create purchasing power among the poor.

The year 1942 was a watershed. The Second World War was raging in Europe and had now spread to Asia. Following their devastating raid on Pearl Harbor, the Japanese had begun to advance on British colonies in Southeast Asia. The tired nationalist movement in India had acquired a new vigor. There was an unstoppable momentum towards independence. The spectacular Japanese victories in the East had unnerved the British. The surrender of Singapore, in particular, had been a staggering blow to their prestige in India. It had also opened the Bay of Bengal to the Japanese navy. My family wondered if we should support the British in their war with the Japanese. They asked who were our real enemies— the British or the Japanese? Would the British really give up India? Would the English split the country before they left?

These questions were on the minds of many Indians in those days. Although our family was apolitical, dinnertime conversation would often veer around to politics. My grandfather used to get impatient with people who did not realize that the Japanese posed a bigger threat. My uncle would retort that we were already under alien rule, and who was to say that one foreigner was better than another? My mother would add that we should be neutral in a conflict that did not concern us. My uncle confessed that he had secretly enjoyed Britain's discomfort in the East. He had applauded the successive fall of Hong Kong, the Philippines, then Malaya and Indochina. He was amazed at the speed of the Japanese advance. It meant that the colonial empires were flimsy structures built on pillars of rotting clay.

The British sought Indian support to fight the Japanese, who were practically knocking at our eastern door. Gandhi asked for what he thought was reasonable—a commitment in principle to India's freedom after the war, and in return the Indian people would fight the Japanese. But Churchill was unwilling, saying, "I did not become the Prime Minister of England in order to preside over the liquidation of the British Empire." Even President Roosevelt, who was a great champion of Indian independence, could not persuade him. From this frustrating deadlock was born the Quit India movement.

If we hated Winston Churchill, we loved Roosevelt for supporting us. In 1942, President Roosevelt sent a personal envoy, Averell Harriman, to liaise with Churchill, and he promptly began an affair with the attractive Pamela Churchill, the wife of Winston's son Randolph. The British establishment did not seem to mind the liaison, as it might help "drag" America into the war. "To have FDR's personal representative, the man charged with keeping Britain safe, sleeping with the Prime Minister's daughter-in-law was a wonderful stroke of luck," said Lord Beaverbrook. But the establishment did resent Harriman's pressure for India's freedom. The disastrous collapse in the Far East had made Britain heavily dependent on Roosevelt, who was not amused by the irony of Churchill claiming to fight a war on behalf of freedom yet making no concessions for freedom to the second-largest country in the world.

In the end, Churchill had to resort to a lie to get Roosevelt off his back. He telegraphed Roosevelt under his famous code name, "Former Naval Person," informing him that "he had no wish to allow Indian Muslims to be governed by the Congress Caucus and Hindu priesthood when 75 percent of the Indian soldiers were Muslim." This was clearly false—the truth was that less than 35 percent of the Indian army was Muslim, and Gandhi and Nehru's Congress freedom movement was by no stretch of the imagination a Hindu priesthood. At any rate, Roosevelt was unmoved. Churchill had to agree to dispatch a political mission—the Cripps Mission—to India a few days after the fall of Rangoon. It failed and Churchill was delighted. He said to FDR, "I feel absolutely satisfied we have done our utmost." However, Roosevelt did not think so. He knew that Churchill had stacked the deck against the mission. He telegraphed Churchill to try again, saying that Britain's unwillingness "to concede to the Indians the right of self-government was at the root of failure." Churchill was so furious that he released a "string of cuss words, which lasted for two hours in the middle of the night."

One of the intriguing "what-ifs" of history is that if the Japanese had succeeded in overrunning India, we might have been tempted to follow the successful Japanese model of export-led economic development after Independence, much like the Asian tigers. At the very least, it might have been a foil to British Fabian thinking, which did us incalculable harm. One can now say with some conviction that Fabian socialism failed everywhere, and that the Japanese model succeeded everywhere (notwithstanding East Asia's troubles a few years ago). The fact, of course, is that we also inherited a democracy from Britain. If it came to a trade-off between East Asian capitalism and liberal democracy, most Indians today would still opt for democracy. However, there need not have been a trade-off. If Nehru had not been mesmerized by the Soviet Union's economic success, or if Indira Gandhi had changed course when Korea and Taiwan did and opened our economy in the late 1960s, we might have lifted our growth rate and become an economic success without in the least bit compromising democracy.

Men like my grandfather and my father were typical of a new professional middle class that emerged in the nineteenth century under British rule with the introduction of the English language and Western education. This class produced not only clerks for the East India Company but also lawyers, teachers, engineers, doctors, bureaucrats—all the new professions that were required to run a country. Since passing an exam was the only barrier to entering this class, its members came from various castes and backgrounds. Although opportunities were open to all, the upper castes were the first to seize them and hold on to them. Once they learned English, acquired an education, and cleared an exam, rewards and prestige were showered upon them. They became the new elite and closed ranks.

The rise of a new Westernized urban elite matched the decline of the landed gentry. The Mughal aristocracy was the first to be destroyed, beginning in the late eighteenth century. Then came the gradual fall in the status of the regional Muslim and Hindu nobility. To be sure, local landlords, chieftains, and zamindars continued to hold sway, but men of new learning like my grandfather and father threatened their social position. Equally, this new middle class endangered the intellectual monopoly of the Brahmins. But the Brahmins were clever. With their traditional agility, many of them took to English education, passed exams, and became part of the new middle class. Though English administrators spoke contemptuously of natives talking the language of their masters and aping the manners of their betters, as time passed and one generation succeeded another, the apparent contradiction of a Brahmin talking about equality and fraternity also became reconciled. They could now rant in English and chant in Sanskrit.

With the Congress outlawed after the Quit India movement, its leaders in jail, its funds seized, and its organization decimated, Mohammed Ali Jinnah, the Muslim leader, saw the political vacuum and seized this opportunity to create a campaign of fear and emotion among the Muslim masses. Without the sane voice of Gandhi, who passionately spoke for one India, Muslims and Hindus rapidly drifted apart. Throughout my early childhood there was growing intolerance and increasing incidents of violence between the two communities.

I was four years old when one day my aunt pulled me away from the window and closed the shutters because a Muslim mob in Lyallpur had begun to throw stones at our Hindu neighbor's house. By the end of the war, Jinnah's politics of divisiveness had succeeded and the Muslim League's demand for Pakistan had become real. Gandhi was to pay a heavy price for Quit India. Unwittingly, he had paved the way for the partition of India and the death of more than half a million people in one of the bloodiest atrocities of the twentieth century. To many, the split was inevitable. The deeper reasons were ancient, and there is no use blaming anyone for what happened. The horrendous massacres of 1947 that followed the division of the country between India and Pakistan brought to the surface the tragic history of the relations between the Hindus and Muslims ever since the thirteenth century.

Western education provided the stimulus for the most dramatic change in the minds of Indians in a thousand years. Alberuni, the Muslim traveler who came to India around A.D. 1000 in search of India's legendary philosophical and mathematical knowledge, remarked that Indians were "know-it-alls." They kept themselves aloof from the outside world, he said, and were ignorant of the arts and sciences of the West. English education changed all that in a couple of generations. Indians embraced Western knowledge with vigor. Because of their Brahminical heritage, they showed a marked preference for theoretical over practical learning. Unlike the Japanese, for example, they were more attracted to the pure sciences than to technology. As in Alberuni's time, many Indians continue to suffer from intellectual arrogance.

To my grandfather the English language was a treasured possession. He prided himself on its mastery. I was confused by his strange attachment to a foreign language, but I now realize that it was his window on the world. My uncle used to enjoy pointing out the rich irony of the British teaching us English. It introduced Indian minds to liberal ideas and the ideals of the French Revolution while the British Empire was practicing the opposite through colonial rule. Schools and colleges taught liberty and equality while the rulers practiced subjugation and inequality. After college, the same students joined the nationalist movement. By introducing English in India, the British dug their own graves. It is ironic that some state governments after Independence have done everything possible to make Indians forget English. Yet more and more Indians speak and write English today with confidence, freely mixing it with Indian words as though it were their own language.

By the time my father went to Roorkee, the premier engineering college, in 1931, there was a growing middle class that had gone through the same education system across India and had attained a general unity of vision. It had a liberal humanistic outlook which was tolerant of ambiguities and shy of certainties. It shared a community of thought, feeling, and ideas, and this partly built up a sense of Indian nationality. Freedom was its first objective. It had produced a reasonably competent nationalist leadership who wanted to socially transform India and wipe away poverty and illiteracy. Mahatma Gandhi had said on many occasions that freedom would have no meaning unless it delivered the three fundamentals—bread, clothes, and shelter. How to achieve this was not as clear.

There were two competing visions. Mahatma Gandhi had a vision of self-reliant villages, with a reinvigorated agriculture and craft production. He opposed modern urban industry because it dehumanized man. Jawaharlal Nehru had a modern scientific mind, and he was much impressed by the economic gains of the Soviet revolution; but he was also committed to democracy. He had a vision of democratic socialism with the state leading the process of industrialization. He spurned capitalism because it exploited and it created inequalities. Both Gandhi's and Nehru's dreams were flawed, however, and we have spent a long time chasing after them. Gandhi distrusted technology but not businessmen. Nehru distrusted businessmen but not technology. Instead of sorting out the contradictions, we mixed the two up. We have had to deal with holy cows: small companies are better than big ones (Gandhi); public enterprises are better than private ones (Nehru); local companies are better than foreign ones (both). They so mesmerized us that the succeeding generation, whose job was to jettison these foolish ideas, failed to do so and did us incalculable harm.

Six months after I was born, the government transferred my father to a canal colony in the wilds of Hissar district in East Punjab. He was asked to supervise the maintenance of an irrigation canal. On the way, they stopped at his guru's ashram at Beas so that their child could have the guru's blessings. My father explained to my mother that a true guru's eyes had the power to protect: his glance, alighting on the child, would give the boy an auspicious start in life. At the ashram, he placed his child at the guru's feet and requested him to give his son a name. "Since you have put him at my feet, let us call him Guru Charan Das, the servant of the guru's feet. It will remind him to live his life with humility," said the guru with a smile. He added, "It is an appropriate name, don't you think?" And he laughed at his own joke. The first two parts of my name became gradually condensed, but it did nothing to make me humble or spiritual.

Religion was closely interwoven in our lives. Depending on our persuasion, we either went to a temple, a mosque, or a gurdwara, or attended discourses of holy men. It was common to speak of truth, illusion, and the meaning of human life. People were not ashamed to intersperse their conversations with their frustration with the human situation, or truisms on the inevitability of death. They regarded man as a microcosm of the divine. "God is in man and man is in God" was the way people talked about it. Man's mind and his selfish nature were the cause of his problems, making him feel that he was separate from God. Everyone believed in karma—that actions mattered and determined what sorts of lives we would lead in future births; equally, our lives today were a result of our actions in past births. The aim of life was to achieve unity with God. Thus, day-to-day conversation had a philosophical edge to it.

As a subdivisional officer, my father was an important official of the British Raj. We lived in a brick bungalow in the Public Works Department style—whitewashed inside, with a flat roof and a wide veranda—and the canal flowing at the back. My father's mission was to maintain the canal. He made sure that water flowed efficiently through the main canal as well as the smaller distribution channels which watered the farmers' fields. He also had to provide the water fairly to all the farmers. This was difficult at times because some farmer would invariably divert his neighbor's water to his own field, and this would lead to quarrels, fights, and even murder. In such a situation, my father often became a judge.

My father provided water for the crops, and the farmers overwhelmed him with gifts from their fields. He returned them, however, because he knew that they were a bribe. So as not to hurt the feelings of the giver, he would take one piece of fruit or vegetable from a whole basket or a glass of milk from a bucketful and return the rest. The villagers were surprised at this, for some of his predecessors not only had accepted gifts but had not hesitated in asking for cows and horses.

Nine months later, the government promoted my father to a "desk job" in the irrigation department at the district headquarters at Rohtak. Whereas he had been a "big sahib" in the canal colony, here he was a "small sahib" on the lowest rung of the district officialdom. At the top of the ladder was the collector, followed by the district heads of police, medical services, railways, forestry, irrigation, and other functions. Some of these officials were English, although the Indianization of the services had advanced quite far by 1943. Whereas his colleagues were envious that he had an administrative job, my father missed working with his hands on the canal. Years later, he told me that he found it strange that Indian engineers always preferred solving conceptual design problems rather than working with machines.

My father seemed to lead two separate lives, neatly divided into two compartments. During the day, at work, he wore Western clothes, spoke English, and followed the rational, individualistic life of an official of the British Raj. In the evening he wore a loose-fitting kurta, spoke Punjabi, ate Indian food, listened to Indian music, and meditated like a good Hindu. Years later, Prakash Tandon, author of *Punjabi Century,* introduced me to the expression "cultural commuter," which, as I think about it, fitted my father and his generation quite well. However, it does not quite capture the price they must have paid and the disorientation and alienation they must have experienced.

A visit from my father's big boss, the English superintending engineer (SE), was a major occasion. The entire staff of the local irrigation department assembled at the canal rest house to "pay their respects" and garland the SE with bright marigolds. My mother found this display embarrassing ("After all, the man was here on official business"). However, this was how it had been done for two generations. The SE's staff, a dozen strong, arrived in advance to see to his comforts: two clerks, two orderlies, two guards, two bearers to serve him food, a cook, a dhobi to wash his clothes, a hamal to sweep the floors, all under the supervision of a khidmatgar. It was a brilliant spectacle, recounted my mother, to see them lined up beside the chrysanthemums, in their gleaming white uniforms, with green bands on their turbans and green cummerbunds.

After eighteen months, we were again transferred, this time to Lahore. My mother was thrilled to be finally "going to civilization," to the cosmopolitan and cultured city where she had gone to college. However, there was a severe shortage of housing, and they decided that it was best for my mother and me to go to Lyallpur until my father found a proper house. The days passed into months, and he did not succeed in finding a house in Lahore. I was now four years old. After the winter came the unbearable hot weather, and finally to everyone's relief came the rains in early July. One late afternoon in August 1946, I was in my mother's dressing room watching her comb her hair. My mother was sitting at a heavy teak dressing table. There were sounds of footsteps. They were quick and urgent, up the small staircase. My grandfather burst in. In an excited voice, he said that the British were quitting India. Mountbatten had been appointed the last viceroy to liquidate the empire. "I didn't think I would live to see the day. The British Raj is finally come to an end!" he said. My mother nervously dropped the bottle of coconut oil. She jumped with joy and hugged me. "My grandson is going to grow up in a free country," said my grandfather.

Although Indians gloss over it, the British Raj was the most important event in the making of modern India—for better and for worse. Britain gave us democracy, the rule of law, an independent judiciary, and a free press. It built railways, canals, and harbors, but it could not bring about an industrial revolution. It could not raise economic growth or lift the people out of poverty. It could not avert famines. The truth is that the Raj was economically incompetent. It just did not know how to "develop" a country. Had it known it, Britain could have gained much from having a larger market for its manufactures. It introduced modern education and helped create a small middle class, but it did not educate the mass of the people. This was its other failure and linked to the first, for development is not possible without mass literacy.

The British gave us a hundred years of peace—the so-called Pax Britannica—but they also consciously pursued a divide-and-rule policy which made Hindus and Muslims conscious of their separate identities.

This led to a tragic division of the country. Had India remained united, billions could have been saved in defense expenditures and invested instead in improving the lives of ordinary people in both countries. Whether an undivided India could have survived the Muslim–Hindu animosity is another counterfactual of history.

The Raj gave us modern values and institutions, but it did not interfere with our ancient traditions and our religion. India has therefore preserved its spiritual heritage and the old way of life continues. Many Indians despair over the divisiveness of caste and would prefer to wish it away. However, the hold of the Indian way of life is also a bulwark against the onslaught of the global culture. The British gave us the English language, which allowed us to converse with our compatriots in a country with sixteen official languages. However, English also divided us into two nations—the 10 percent elite who learned English and shut out the 90 percent who did not. Knowing English today, though, gives Indians a competitive advantage in the global economy and is an important factor in our nascent success in the information economy.

The British were different from our other invaders. They did not merge with us and remained aloof to the end. This shook our self-confidence. In school we had learned that the Indian subcontinent was a triangle with the Himalayas, the Arabian Sea, and the Bay of Bengal as its sides. The Himalayas ran from east to west and cut off the cold winds from the north. This allowed agriculture to prosper and created wealth, but it also attracted barbarian invaders from the north. It gave us a warm climate so that no one who came wanted to leave. First came the Aryans, then the Turks, the Afghans, and the Mughals. They came, they stayed, and they merged and became Indian. To accommodate them we merely created a new subcaste each time and they became part of our diversity. The British did not. But now that they have been gone for more than fifty years, our confidence is restored, especially among the young. Our infuriating diversity may also be of some value. Because we have always learned to live with pluralism, it is possible that we might be better prepared to negotiate the diversity of the global economy.

TWO

Smells of the Bazaar

The principle of competition is, as Hesiod pointed out long ago, built in the very roots of the world; there is something in the nature of things that calls for a real victory and real defeat.

—IRVING BABBITT

Like many Indians, our family did not accord a high place to the making of money. Thus, I grew up with a low opinion of commerce and merchants. Partly it was the prejudice of caste. Belonging to the Arora subcaste, we regarded ourselves as Kshatriyas, superior to the trading castes. Aroras and Khatris were the main Hindu castes of urban Punjab. Because of our administrative ability, we had been functionaries at princely courts. Despite our low opinion of commerce, we were not above moneylending. When the British came in the mid-nineteenth century to the Punjab, we were among the first to embrace the Western learning and the modern professions. Although Brahmins were superior to us in the caste hierarchy, they lost their social position because they were slow to learn English and confined themselves to Sanskrit learning and religious duties in the temple.

As a child, I remember that my grandmother used to admonish our grocer for manipulating his weighing scale. It was the same with our family jeweler, but with him she did it with more finesse. Later, my mother used to scold me for wasting my pocket money on "adulterated" ice cream. Each commercial transaction, it seems, was a challenge in our lives. It was always a case of *us*—educated, honest, taxpaying citizens—versus *them*—tax-dodging, street-smart traders.

The treachery of the English East India Company and Omichand, the banker of Calcutta, reinforced our ancient prejudice against merchants. The East India Company came to India at the end of the sixteenth century to plunder, but soon discovered that there was more money to be made in trade. With the decline of the Mughal Empire in the early eighteenth century, autonomous kingdoms had begun to replace the dying Mughal authority. One of these was Bengal, whose young nawab, Siraj-ud-Dowlah, came into conflict in 1757 with the ambitions of Robert Clive and the East India Company. By now the English had set up the trading post of Calcutta, and it attracted the most enterprising Indian merchants, especially Marwaris from Rajasthan (about whom more later). The most powerful among these was the banking house of Jagat Seth, who had played a part in installing the previous nawab.

Clive smelled an opportunity in this uncertain political climate where merchants could be kingmakers. The nawab had attacked Calcutta the previous year and Clive wanted to dethrone him and replace him with his pliable uncle by marriage, Mir Jafar, who was commander of the nawab's forces and who had promised a fortune to the British in return for his elevation. The third member of the conspiracy was Omichand, a banker close to Jagat Seth and intermediary between the nawab and the company. While Clive plotted a surprise attack, Omichand was to gull and lull the nawab, and Mir Jafar to ensure that the nawab's troops remained immobile. The battle took place on 23 June 1757 in Plassey, a village 145 kilometers north of Calcutta. Only twelve thousand of the nawab's fifty thousand troops engaged in the battle and those under Mir Jafar stood still on the field and offered no resistance. In the end, the nawab lost five thousand men, the British eighteen, and the nawab fled the field. The British had won their most decisive battle in India and changed its history. They had learned how to conquer India. Their share of the loot was £2.3 million ($1 billion in today's dollars) and Clive's share £230,000 ($140 million in today's dollars). More valuable to the British was the title they acquired to a large chunk of land around Calcutta, which later expanded to the whole of Bengal and then the entire country.

Just before the battle, Omichand hinted to Clive that he wanted a bigger share of the loot. Otherwise, he would squeal. He wanted £300,000 ($150 million in today's dollars) and he wanted it written into the secret treaty with Mir Jafar. Clive was livid and called him "the greatest villain upon the earth," but he agreed because he had no choice—the conspiracy would otherwise have collapsed. The historian Thomas Babington Macaulay says that Omichand "possessed great influence with his own race, and had in large measure the Hindoo talents, quick observation, tact, dexterity, perseverance, and the Hindoo vices, servility, greediness, and treachery." In the end, Clive was even more deceitful—he double-crossed the blackmailer. He drew up two treaties—the real one on white paper and a false one on red paper that he showed to Omichand. When the merchant came to the winner's get-together at Jagat Seth's house, he discovered the duplicity. The shrewd merchant never recovered and died after a few months. Clive went on to become Lord Clive and returned to England laden with jewels to a hero's welcome. "No Englishman who started with nothing has ever, in any line of life, created such a fortune at the early age of thirty-four," wrote Macaulay, but he also condemned Clive's deceit, for he had committed "not merely a crime but a blunder," because "nations must not be perceived to engage in duplicity."

Every Indian schoolchild knows the perfidious story of how Bengal was lost at Plassey. Is it surprising that we are suspicious of merchants and foreign companies? In contrast to these greedy and deceitful villains, we believed that saints—Gandhi and Nehru—had created our new nation in 1947. It seemed possible to believe then that India would be great because she was good.

The Indian defeat at Plassey in 1757 is similar in some respects to the Chinese defeat in the Opium War a hundred years later. They were both low-key English victories over ancient and proud civilizations. Both were mild, localized affairs, unimportant to contemporary observers. Yet both started a chain reaction of unpredictable events and opened the ancient lands to a long period of foreign subjugation, bloody conflict, and the entry of Western ideas and technology.

A small band of greedy English trader-adventurers showed to the world the impotence of two enfeebled civilizations, and how their immense wealth could be looted with ease. They proved that the natives were passive and divided, resigned to quick defeat. This humiliation of two great peoples, Indian and Chinese, left a suspiciousness of traders and foreigners and a scar of xenophobia. This explains, in part, India's antibusiness attitudes, the fear of a "foreign hand," and its absurd attachment to swadeshi, or "made in India." In China, it paved the way for a communist revolution and the persistence of an antiliberal, distrustful Chinese establishment.

We may have looked down on our banias, or merchants, but we loved money and the bazaar. The most famous bazaar in Punjab was Lahore's Anarkali, and to shop in it was the fondest wish of every Punjabi. People came from all over the northwest to taste its gaiety. All of Anarkali's women, people used to say, were beautiful, and all its men handsome. And if something could not be had in Anarkali, it was probably not worth having. For this and other reasons, they called it "a paradise on earth."

For my grandfather, a visit to Lahore was not complete without a few hours in Anarkali. One day in 1929, he remembered, there was even more excitement than usual. He was returning after briefing a barrister at the High Court, and he entered the bazaar from the Lahori Gate end. Passing by the splendid row of flower vendors on the left and the mountain of fruit overflowing in an amphitheater on the right, he stopped at the Kesari Aerated Water Company. He ordered, as he always did, a tall, refreshing glass of fresh lime juice. In his younger days he used to stop at Bhagwan Singh's for lassi, but now he found it too heavy for his liking.

Suddenly there was a buzz in the bazaar and a cry went out as a procession entered Lahori Gate. Windows sprang open, balconies filled up, and people began to shower flowers on the fine-looking Jawaharlal Nehru, who was leading the procession on a white horse. Nehru had become the new president of the Congress in the historic Lahore session of 1929. The procession stopped at Dhani Ram Bhalla's shoe store, where Nehru was greeted with a garland of currency notes—the Anarkali merchants' donation to the freedom movement. From above people yelled, "Jawaharlal Nehru zindabad, Hindustan ke be-taj badshah, zindabad!" ("Long live Jawaharlal Nehru, India's uncrowned king!"). Even my grandfather, who had a distaste for street politics, was touched by the spontaneous affection that Anarkali showered upon its future ruler.

In the confusion, however, someone in the jostling crowd collided with my grandfather and he fell down. It was one of the processionists,

who turned around and immediately gave my grandfather a helping
hand. The stranger apologized profusely. With great courtesy, he offered
to take him to a hospital. But my grandfather was not hurt. The stranger
had an impressive face, recalled my grandfather. He was slim, dressed in
a fresh dhoti and a well-pressed silk kurta and a black sleeveless Jawahar
jacket. "He didn't know me, but I knew that it was Ghanshyamdas Birla,
the Marwari magnate and Gandhi's confidant. Even though he was one
of the richest men in India, he was courteous and he spoke very softly."
Birla and Tata were the two largest business houses of India, and I recall
that throughout my childhood, they conjured the same images that
Rockefeller and Carnegie might have evoked to a young American of
their day. It was commonplace to hear, "What do you think I am—a
Birla or Tata?"

G. D. Birla invited my grandfather to join him for tea after the procession. My grandfather readily agreed, and the two drove to the comfortable home of another merchant. Amidst talk about Gandhi, Congress
politics, and business, he listened with particular fascination to GD's
account of his family. The Birlas, he learned, came from a little village
called Pilani, buried deep in the sands of Rajasthan, 650 kilometers due
south from where we lived. They belonged to the commercial Mahesh-
wari subcaste. GD's grandfather, Shiv Narain, had spurned financial
security and declined a comfortable position as accountant to the
wealthy Marwari bankers, the Ghaneriwalas, in Hyderabad.

"Marwaris are uncomfortable working for others," said GD. But
Pilani had only three thousand people and there was little challenge for
an ambitious person. Shiv Narain decided to go to Bombay. He rode a
camel for 700 kilometers, taking twenty days to reach Ahmedabad.
From there he caught a train to Bombay, where he stayed until he had
amassed a fortune trading in opium, silver, and cotton.

Shiv Narain's arrival in Bombay in the early 1860s coincided with an
event 12,000 kilometers away, on the other side of the globe, and it
transformed his destiny. The American South was infamous for slavery,
but it was famous for growing fine, long-staple cotton, which it supplied
to the textile mills of Britain. The mills converted it to cloth and sold it
around the world. Overnight, the American Civil War came and cut this
supply chain. As the supply of raw cotton dried up, prices began to sky-
rocket. Traders in Bombay smelled an opportunity. The enterprising

ones took off for the villages and convinced the farmers of western India to switch over to the particular long variety, suitable for the English mills. Soon the Indian farmers had converted, and with prices booming, a number of traders made huge fortunes in the 1860s supplying the cotton to Lancashire. Shiv Narain Birla was one of them. Some of these fortunes were reinvested in the first textile mills in Bombay and Ahmedabad in the 1870s and 1880s.

But Shiv Narain, after seven years in Bombay, returned to Pilani a rich man. There, surrounded by the sand dunes and shrub of the Aravalli hills, he built a grand haveli for his family, beside a magnificent banyan tree. He had the exterior walls painted in ocher, with riotous frescoes of parading elephants and camels and charging horses, similar in style to the Bengal Company paintings. In the inner and outer white-washed courtyards, under elaborately decorated balconies and brackets, he had artists paint scenes of merchant activity, as well as of military action and local flora and fauna. Befitting their new stature, the Birlas also acquired a luxurious bullock-chariot.

GD was born in this house and left in the care of female relatives. The men in the family were continuously away in Bombay and Calcutta, making their separate fortunes and expanding the family's wealth. GD went to a local school where there were no books and classes were held in the open air. One day the teacher disappeared without warning, taking off, it was rumored, with a local widow, and the school closed down. At nine, he was sent off to school in Calcutta, and soon after that to Bombay to learn bookkeeping and business skills, and a private tutor was engaged to improve his English. At fourteen, he returned to Pilani to get married, and a year later he had a son.

Because of the plague in Bombay, the family shifted to Calcutta at the turn of the century. They began trading in jute and opium, initially under the aegis of the enormously influential Marwari "great firm" of Tarachand Ghanshyamdas. A few years later they set up their own firm, specializing in opium futures. Opium futures fluctuated widely because of the changing value of silver—the commodity with which China paid for its opium—as well as the Chinese government's futile attempts to ban the import of the narcotic. The instability of the opium market offered great potential for speculative coups and the Birlas made many successful ones.

At the age of sixteen, GD set himself up in Calcutta as an independent trader in jute, with his own company. Thus began his first contacts with Englishmen, who were his customers. During his association with them he began to see their superiority in business methods and their organizing capacity. But their racial arrogance bothered him. He was not allowed to use the lift to go up to their offices, nor their benches while waiting to see them. He smarted under these insults and it created within him a political interest.

With the coming of the First World War, the demand for jute sacks soared and GD made a handsome fortune. So did the others in his family, and the Birla fortune quadrupled in the war years to $4 million. After the war GD wanted to invest his wartime profits in a jute factory in Calcutta, making him the first Birla to enter industry. But it was not easy to break into the stronghold of a Scottish monopoly that had governed the jute industry since its beginning. Every time GD bought some land to start the mill, the Scots (Andrew Yule, in particular) would buy land all around it and deny him access to the road.

But GD was not deterred. He knew that his future lay in manufacturing. One night he quietly bought land further south, towards Budge-Budge, along a curve on the Hooghly River. Having got the land, he needed credit. The Imperial Bank, under the influence of the monopoly, refused him a loan for the machinery. Eventually it relented, but it charged him an extremely high rate of interest compared to what it charged British firms. Transport charges too, especially for river traffic, were raised steeply, in a further attempt to stop Indian intrusion into what had been a British preserve.

Next, the jute monopolists got to the machine makers in Britain and persuaded them to quote prohibitively high prices for the machines. As a result, GD's costs ballooned and his project became unviable. In despair, he almost gave up. He agreed to sell the factory to Andrew Yule, his largest competitor. When he walked into the Andrew Yule offices to conclude the deal, the Scottish manager chided him for having had the audacity to start a jute mill. Stung, GD instantly withdrew his offer. He resolved that come what may, he would break the jute monopoly.

And he succeeded beyond everyone's expectations. After that, he was not to be stopped. Two years later GD set up a spanking new textile mill in Gwalior (in partnership with the maharaja of Gwalior) which eventually became one of the largest composite textile mills in the country. The following year he turned the tables on Andrew Yule. The Scottish company had suffered in the postwar depression and it needed desperately to raise cash to pay its debts. GD stepped forward and he proudly bought Andrew Yule's cotton mill. In 1928 he took over a confectionery company. As soon as tariff protection was extended to sugar, the Birlas set up four sugar plants between 1931 and 1933. He also went into publishing, and in a modest way into soaps and chemicals. All his investments prospered, despite the depression, and in the mid-thirties, he started an insurance company and also a large papermaking company called Orient Paper.

The Second World War provided another major stimulus to growth and Birla assets grew sixfold during the war. When my grandfather announced to my mother that the British had decided to leave India, Birla assets had grown to more than $100 million, and they were one of the top two industrial houses in India.

More significantly, GD became the largest supporter of the Congress freedom movement and a close friend of Mahatma Gandhi. They wrote to each other almost daily—their correspondence, running into four volumes, each of nearly five hundred pages, was published under the title *Bapu: A Unique Association*. GD's support to Gandhi's movement was so generous that it threatened to create a rift between his brothers. It also got him into trouble with the British. The viceroy, Lord Linlithgow, sent a "most secret and personal" letter to all provincial governors at the height of the Quit India movement in November 1942 stating that "every possible step should be taken to trace and bring home to those concerned the part played by 'Big Business' in the recent disturbance . . . [especially] by the Birla Brothers."

It was as a Congress financier that G. D. Birla had come to Lahore when my grandfather chanced upon him. Their meeting left a deep impression on my grandfather. Until that day he had not given much thought to merchants. He had certainly never believed that merchants and commerce were the lifeblood of an economy. Nor was his caste prejudice against commerce as strong as that of Jawaharlal Nehru, who expressed his bias succinctly in his autobiography: "Right through history the old Indian ideal did not glorify political and military triumph, and it looked down upon money and the professional money-making class. Today [the older culture] is fighting against a new and all-powerful opposition from the bania [Vaishya] civilization of the capitalist West."

In Nehru's case this prejudice was reinforced by his education at Harrow and Cambridge, where he acquired the English upper-class bias against trade and learned socialism from the Fabians. When he came to power in 1947, Nehru institutionalized the prejudice. Lord Wavell, viceroy in the forties, shared the bias against Marwaris. Nevertheless, he recognized G. D. Birla's uniqueness and he paid him a huge compliment by preferring him to J. R. D. Tata as Queen Mary's companion for lunch in Bombay, even though Tata was the young head of the largest and most respected business family in India. Wavell wrote:

I think Queen Mary would find G. D. Birla better company than J.R.D. Tata if she wishes to invite one of them to lunch. Tata is a pleasant enough fellow to meet, but I have not found him communicative, and as a casual acquaintance he is much the same as any other wealthy young man who has had a conventional type of education. Birla has plenty to say, and whatever one may think of Marwari businessmen and their ways, he is well worth talking to. I think Queen Mary would have a very dull lunch with Tata and quite an interesting one with Birla.

Mahatma Gandhi, a bania himself, had no qualms about accepting money from Birla or other businessmen. Nor was he contemptuous of commerce like Nehru. He came from Gujarat, which had many ports and vigorous commerce, and where the merchant was held in esteem. Gandhi believed that a businessman's wealth was not his own but held in trust for the rest of society. Although he did not persuade anyone of his naïve faith in trusteeship, he did succeed in transforming the freedom movement from an upper-caste debating society into a genuine, broad-based people's movement, challenging our middle-class conception of independence as "English rule without Englishmen." His discovery of the masses had far-reaching influence on the orientation of the intelligentsia.

But Gandhi could not change our suspicion of traders and commerce. The Japanese, on the other hand, who suspect foreigners even more than we do, did succeed in getting over their mistrust of businessmen.

The Japanese responded to the Western challenge in a vastly different way. After their humiliation by Commodore Matthew Perry in 1854, they recognized that their ancient civilization was like a paper-thin shoji door, too flimsy to defend them against the superior technology of the West. Instead of tiresomely proclaiming their own superior past, they humbly went to school during the Meiji period, in the second half of the nineteenth century. They vigorously began to acquire Western learning, skills, and ways. They were not ashamed to throw out what did not work and adopt what did. They took to Western dress, laws, methods, and technology. Unlike the ambivalent Indians and Chinese, they became so good at copying that they eventually beat the West at its own game.

The Europeans had brought to India, China, and Japan a virile new culture based on science, modern organization, and the ideas of the Enlightenment. The Japanese responded quickly and with purpose. The Meiji state sponsored a full-scale reform of the economy and society, and the people responded with discipline and teamwork. They were so successful that by 1905 they had defeated the Russians. The Chinese embarked on a more fitful and tragic path, first under the Kuomintang and then the communists, and tens of millions lost their lives in three huge convulsions between 1949 and 1974. But after Deng's economic reforms in 1979 China has blazed ahead at a blistering pace and now aspires to world-power status. In India, it took three generations of freedom fighters, liberals, reformers, and anticolonialists to create national consciousness and pride.

After Independence, democracy took root in India and gradually the masses acquired a stake in the system, periodically electing representatives even from the lowest castes. But the rulers shackled the energies of the people by adopting a socialist economic path that led us to a dead end. Indians won their economic independence only after 1991. Thus, India embraced democracy before capitalism. This makes its journey to modernity unique, and this singular reversal explains a great deal about Indian society. Among the big three in Asia, Japan won first prize in the economic race, China seems to have taken second place, and India came in last. The Japanese are probably three to four generations ahead of India. The Chinese, who were at a comparable level of development in the mid-1970s, are now a generation ahead. Why did India fail? It has little to do with our colonial past. Neither is it a problem of national character. Nor is it the fault of our "soft democracy." The chief reason for nonperformance is our wrong "mixed economy" model, which allowed our obstructive bureaucracy to kill our industrial revolution at birth.

THREE

The Train to Nowhere

They saw a Dream of Loveliness descending from the train.
—CHARLES LELAND

A t midnight on 14 August 1947 the British Raj came to an end.
On the same day Pakistan was born, carved out of Punjab and
Bengal. Sir Cyril Radcliffe did the actual carving in five weeks,
and the demarcation on the map came to be known as the Radcliffe
Boundary Award. The partition led to an unprecedented transfer of
population and rendered ten million homeless. An estimated twenty
million Hindus left West Punjab and East Bengal, and eighteen million
Muslims went to Pakistan. As a part of this mass movement, over half a
million people lost their lives; there were 22,000 reported cases of rape
and kidnapping of women; 220,000 people were declared missing.

My family had also become refugees. We found asylum at my father's
guru's ashram, which turned out to be some sixty kilometers within the
Indian border according to Mr. Radcliffe's penciled line. There we heard
Nehru's historic address to the new nation.

Long years ago we made a tryst with destiny, and now the time comes
when we shall redeem our pledge. . . . At the stroke of the midnight hour,
while the world sleeps, India will awake to life and freedom. A moment
comes, which comes but rarely in history, when we step out from the old to

*the new, when an age ends, and when the soul of a nation, long sup-
pressed, finds utterance. . . .*

Despite the suffering and the uncertainty about our future, we were
filled with emotion as we listened to Nehru's words. We heard the
national anthem of the new nation for the first time. Few recognized it.
My father was the first to stand up. Then one by one the other listeners
got up, until everyone was standing at attention. When the reference
came to "Punjab" in the song, the refugees looked at each other, help-
lessness in their eyes. Despite our travails, we realized our good fortune
in having witnessed the birth of our free nation. In what became the
most important speech delivered in modern India, Nehru went on to
say, "The achievement we celebrate today is but a step, an opening of
opportunity, to the great triumphs and achievements that await us." He
reminded his people that the task ahead included "the ending of poverty
and ignorance and disease and inequality of opportunity."

It is with this task that this book is concerned. Nehru achieved much
in the seventeen years that he went on to rule, but he failed in this task.
After fifty years the failure is staggering: four out of ten Indians are illiterate; half are miserably poor, earning less than a dollar a day; one-third
of the people do not have access to safe drinking water; only a sixth of
the villages have modern medical facilities. Even more devastating, the
system that Nehru created and his daughter, Indira Gandhi, perfected
actually suppressed growth. The irony is that this system, which was
made in the name of the poor, in the end did very little for them. As a
result, 60 percent of the budgets of the Indian governments at all levels
go to pay civil servants' salaries and 70 percent of the twenty-seven million Indian workers employed in the organized sector belong to inefficient state-owned enterprises which are bleeding the country. If a small
portion of this money had been spent wisely on education and health, it
would have delivered far greater benefits to the average Indian.

This is not to say that there hasn't been progress. Famines have been
eliminated, and the country sits routinely on a mountain of grain
reserves each year. Life expectancy has doubled from thirty to sixty-four
years; literacy has risen from 17 percent to 62 percent (although female
literacy is below 40 percent). Infant mortality has been halved. The stagnant economy, which grew by 1 percent per year in the first half of the
century, has grown by 4.4 percent a year in the second half of the cen-

tury. It grew 3.5 percent annually between 1950 and 1975; it accelerated in the eighties to 5.6 percent; and after the reforms it touched 7.5 percent for three years in a row in the mid-nineties.

At the guru's ashram, my father learned that he had been transferred to Simla, where the government shifted temporarily after the loss of Lahore to Pakistan. We took a train from Jullunder to Kalka, where we changed to the miniature train for Simla. From the window of our train we feasted on the snow-tipped crests of the world's highest mountains. The journey through the lower Himalayas to Simla in August 1947 refreshed our exhausted emotions and marked the decisive break with our bloody past. The stench of death was left far behind. On each bend of the winding journey there were green slopes with tiers of neatly cultivated terraces. Towards the south, we could see the Ambala plains far below, and the Kasauli hills in the foreground. Higher up, belts of pine, fir, and deodar punctuated the terraces. Masses of rhododendrons clothed the slopes. Northwards rose the confused Himalayan mountain chains, range after snowy range.

The train stopped at Barog, where a white car on rails went speeding by. "The rail car," explained the Anglo-Indian ticket collector, "carries the rich and the busy, who don't carry luggage and who want to reach Simla in a hurry. It used to be only the white sahibs who traveled in it. Since Independence, everyone is on it. Amazing, how quickly the brown sahibs have slid into the shoes of the departing masters!" At Shogi, we glimpsed the first wondrous vision of Simla. From afar, it looked like a mythical, green-carpeted garden dotted with red-roofed houses. Our excitement mounted. We passed Jutogh, crossed Summer Hill, turned into tunnel number 103, and finally reached Simla's Victorian railway station. It was the best train journey of our lives.

Indian Railways, one of the world's greatest railway systems, was built soon after the British crown took over the running of India from the East India Company. It was the largest single injection of British capital into India's economy, and the network went on to become the third largest in the world. Yet this massive construction was not enough to modernize and lift the Indian economy. India alone among the great railway countries remained unindustrialized. In the other railway powers—the United States, Russia, and Germany—the railway had been a dynamo of the industrial revolution. It had no such effect in India, even though the country's network by 1947 was more than 50,000 miles long, employing more than a million men, with 9,000 locomotives, 225,000 freight cars, and more than 16,000 passenger coaches.

Soon after Independence, my cousin Jeet Varma got into Indian Railways. We were all proud. At a time when jobs were scarce he had landed a coveted job in the railways entirely on his own initiative. Soon after the turmoil of Partition, he had joined an engineering college at Kashmere Gate in Delhi, where he heard that the Railways was expanding and needed engineers. He passed an exam, cleared the interview, and went off to Jamalpur for a six-year training program. Jeet was not impressed with either the colonial setting or the training program. Nor did he think much of his teachers. But he stuck it out, made a name for himself as a tennis player, and in the end was sent on his first job to Calcutta as assistant mechanical engineer in the Sealdah division. Over the years, Jeet told us many things about the Railways.

The story of Indian Railways began in London in the 1840s. The promoters were adventurous, determined men. They got in touch with Britain's merchants, manufacturers, and shipping interests, to whom they held out the prospect of a vast and opulent India. Once opened up by railways, they said, India would become a fabulous supply house of cotton and wheat and a huge consumer of textiles and manufactured products of Britain. They told the great mercantile houses that they would be able to bring coal by rail to Calcutta from the mines of western Bengal and become even wealthier. They put together a powerful coalition in Parliament and exerted great pressure on the British government. They succeeded in getting hugely favorable contracts, which allowed them to raise funds in Britain to build and manage the railway operations in India—all of it guaranteed by the government against any risk of loss. They could not have got a better deal.

The East Indian Railway Company was one of the first to get started. It built and operated a line running a few dozen miles north from Calcutta along the Hooghly River. Later it extended it to the coal mines, 100 miles northwest of Calcutta, and subsequently to the well-populated and fertile Gangetic plains. About the same time, the Great Indian Peninsular Railway Company constructed a second line running north from Bombay for thirty-five miles to Kalyan, which it expanded later over the Western Ghats into the rich cotton fields of the Deccan. Many lines followed thereafter. The cost of construction was high because the companies had a guaranteed return of cost plus five percent. They had little incentive to economize and they built carelessly and lavishly. When the work was defective, they simply rebuilt it. They erected stations in a grand style and provided luxury coaches for upper–class passengers.

These railway lines had a profound effect on millions of lives. People began to travel, and merchants began to send their goods to distant parts. New towns came up along the railway lines. However, the artisans in villages and towns began to lose their living because they could not compete with British manufactured goods that began to arrive rapidly. Earlier, the peasants had stored their surplus grains in the good years. Now the railways began to carry food and commercial crops to the ports for export. Reserves were thus depleted and in the bad years of the 1870s and 1890s devastating famines followed. If the railway companies had not thought only of British needs, and been less wasteful and conserved their resources, they might have had a more benign impact. In the end, the "spread effects" of this great investment were limited. Japan's railways, by contrast, built at the same time, had a domestic orientation, and carefully economized their limited capital. They had a more positive result. Moreover, the Indian railway network, although huge in absolute terms, was comparatively small. In 1937, India had 26 miles of railway lines per 1,000 square miles of land area. In comparison, the United States had 80 and Germany 253.3. It partially explains why the railways did not engender an industrial revolution in India. Nevertheless, it was a powerful legacy of the British Raj to independent India in a general economic landscape of backwardness. Without the railways, India would have been even less industrialized.

After our train journey to Simla we went to a little red-roofed cottage called "Pine Villa" in Chota Simla. Like many houses in Simla it resembled something in between a Swiss cottage and a Victorian villa in an English village, surrounded by a garden bursting with dahlias, pansies, and sweet peas. We loved our little house, which had been provided us by the Punjab government, and which was icy cold at night. It was situated in a handsome grove of oaks and deodars, and from our veranda we had a spectacular view of the next ridge and many ridges beyond. From the narrow veranda, we stepped onto a little lawn; from the lawn, there was nothing to step onto except fresh air for the ground suddenly dropped beneath our feet, as it often does in Simla.

Indians now slipped into English shoes naturally and with vigor. In the evenings, everyone in Simla went to the Mall, no matter what the season. Between five and seven o'clock the thing to do was to get dressed and take a stroll from the Ridge to the end of the lower Mall in order "to eat the air." It was a delightful winding stretch of about a mile along a gentle slope, with glamorous shops and smart cafes. One went there to be seen and to see others, and every evening was a veritable fashion parade where men, women, and children vied with one another in the elegance of their clothes. The colorful display of women's silk sarees was especially striking, but even the men strutted about in the latest cuts from London. The refugees from West Punjab were so happy to be alive that they embraced Simla's joie de vivre with reckless abandon. They pulled themselves up to make a new life rather than regret the life they had lost in Pakistan. The Punjabi on the Mall felt the same emotions that a fashionable Parisian must have felt when strolling on the Champs-Elysées at the turn of the century.

My father earned a modest salary, and my mother ran the house on a tight budget. Her biggest expenses were for school fees and uniforms, and milk for her growing children. She worked hard to get us into an English-speaking school, although it cost more than she could afford. It had a long waiting list because of the recent influx of refugees, and she had to apply "influence" to get us in. She made sure that we worked hard at studies and got good marks, especially in English and mathematics. She also wanted us to excel in sports. At the end of the month there was little money left for anything else.

We used to come home from school around four in the afternoon, drink a glass of hot milk, and go out to play. We returned after an hour to do homework under the watchful eye of my mother. Before dinner she would sit with us and tell us stories from the Ramayana and Mahabharata. My mother's narration from the ancient Hindu epics was deeply colored by her middle-class values. She always emphasized the virtues of thrift, hard work, courage, and a respect for elders. On the other hand, my father, who often joined us at this time, emphasized the love of God, respect for the guru, the value of meditation, and the ultimate goal of life, spiritual enlightenment.

My father was a mystic and he devoted all his spare time to meditation or to reading discourses by his guru. In the evenings he would go on a solitary walk and return to his room to meditate, when we were expected to be quiet. Because of my father's spiritual inclinations, we were vegetarian. But even those who ate meat did so only occasionally. This was partly because meat was expensive, but also because Indian vegetarian food is tasty. My father used to say that one inherited the karma of the animal that one ate and therefore one regressed in the rein-carnation cycle of births and deaths. The goal of life was to break free from this cycle and achieve unity with the Absolute. It did not make sense to eat meat and add to one's karmic burdens.

Not unlike other Indian boys, I was closer to my mother. She was clearly the dominant presence in my childhood. My father, in compari-son, was a distant figure. He seemed always occupied by his work or his spiritual quest. He was a good and kindly man, gentle and soft-spoken. He was also extremely shy and reserved, preferring his own company. If I had a problem or needed advice, I would turn to my mother. I cannot recall that she indulged me excessively, but she must have, for my early memories are surrounded by a warm glow. She wanted us to grow tough, do well in our exams, and rise in the world.

After dinner we listened to the English news on the radio, read in an authoritative manner by Melville De Mello. The news usually consisted of reports of Jawaharlal Nehru's activities and speeches. Nehru inspired in us the ideals of democracy, socialism, secularism, and world peace. We innocently believed in the United Nations and in the unique role that India was meant to play in a new moral world order.

Nehru was a hero to the nation and we had implicit faith in his Five Year Plans that would develop our country and one day wipe poverty from our land. We were proud that his government was investing in steel and power. Since my father was helping to design the irrigation projects in Punjab, we felt that we too were a part of nation building. It was an exciting time, and although we did not discuss politics at home, there was always optimism in the air. We felt as though we were creating our future based on grand ideals. The country was free at last, and it was a new and wonderful experience for my parents and their friends, who had only known colonial rule.

My mother used to say, "I cannot believe it! I wake up, pick up the paper, and I don't read about Gandhi and Nehru being arrested for sedi-tious activities. Then I pinch myself, and I say, You silly thing, we are finally free. And I feel like dancing all the way to the Mall in my night-clothes because there is no English sahib to judge my behavior."

One of my earliest memories is of our class preparing for the UN

Day. It was in 1950. We were learning how to march in single file, to salute, to about-face, and to stand at ease. Suddenly we heard that the Prime Minister was coming to town, and our class had been selected to stand along the road to cheer as his motorcade went by. There was endless excitement and our teacher was in a constant state of hysteria. On the appointed day, we trooped to the Mall. It had a festive air with a continuous stream of flags—the blue UN flag alternating with the Indian tricolor. Thousands of children from dozens of schools thronged the street. Nehru's open car arrived right on time, preceded by motorcycles and a pilot car with a siren. Nehru looked unbelievably handsome, I thought, in his Gandhi cap and long white coat, with a red rose on the lapel. All of a sudden, he threw a garland of marigolds towards us. It brushed my arm and landed on my neighbor, who became an instant celebrity. I too shared in some of the halo—after all, the garland had touched my arm.

Thinking back, I feel the garland was symbolic of all the fine things that Nehru gave us. He united a nation out of the most heterogeneous people on the earth. He nurtured democracy. More than any other individual, we owe him our present-day attachment to democratic institutions. He respected minorities and made us secular in our temperament. Most important, he injected in us the modernist ideas of liberty and equality. He gave us youthful hope and optimism. Yet I had failed to catch the garland. That, for me, came to symbolize Nehru's failed economic promises, which have cost us two generations of missed opportunities. Instead of socialism, his path led to a corrupt, domineering state which we are desperately trying to dismantle today with the economic reforms. The problems of Nehru's India began to appear soon after Independence, and my cousin Jeet discovered them on his very first day at work.

By the time he left work that day in December 1954 Jeet had created a sensation. He spotted a ticket collector (TC) openly taking bribes from ticketless hawkers as they came past the exit gate at Sealdah station. Without another thought, he sprang into action. He noted the TC's badge number and grabbed his open palm just as it was about to be greased by a vegetable vendor. With his other hand, Jeet emptied the TC's bribe-filled pocket. Notes and coins fell out.

"Thief!" shouted the TC. An understandable reaction, for the TC did not recognize him. "Thief, catch the thief!" he screamed again, and Jeet saw the whole station descend upon him. At that moment, Jeet made the best decision of his life—he ran. Followed by a menacing mob led by ticketless hawkers and egged on by the TC, Jeet sprinted towards the moving express to Ranaghat. His training as a tennis player helped him to quickly put some distance between himself and his pursuers. However, Jeet did not know that the TC was also a star footballer of Mohun Bagan, Calcutta's premier football club. As he looked back, he found the TC rapidly closing in. Providentially, Jeet reached the accelerating train and leapt in. The TC too tried to jump, but he missed and there was a loud thud on the platform. A few seconds more, and Jeet realized he would have had it. From Ranaghat he caught a train to Kanchrapara, where he arrived in time for tennis. That evening Jeet entertained the Kanchrapara club with an account of his first day at work.

The next morning the entire Sealdah division was on strike. All the trains were at a standstill. On his second day at work, Jeet was brought under police guard, and he found forty-five hundred screaming railway workers gathered on the maidan outside. The corrupt TC had instigated the trade union. Now, goaded on by trade union leaders, the workers were baying for his blood. The railway managers were anxious, under great pressure from the top brass to get the trains moving. Jeet was brought before the division superintendent (DS), who was surrounded by a dozen angry union men. The DS asked Jeet to make an apology to the TC and the whole matter would be closed. Jeet refused. He demanded, on the contrary, that action be taken against the dirty TC.

"But you abused him!" said a menacing union leader.

"No, I caught him red-handed." Jeet produced the Rs 69 that he had taken from the TC's pocket.

"Well, it's your word against his, isn't it?" said the union leader.

"And that of a hundred witnesses," said Jeet.

"Why don't you be a good chap, Mr. Varma?" said the DS in a conciliatory way. "Offer an apology; it doesn't cost you anything. And we are back in business."

Jeet stood adamant. The division superintendent dismissed everyone and called his boss. As Jeet was leaving, the DS hissed, "You realize, of course, this is going to hurt you." Ten minutes later, Jeet heard on the microphone, "Apology is done. Go back to work. Apology is done. You won't be penalized for work stoppage." Jeet was stunned. A few days later he learned that the TC had been let off with a warning, and soon the affair died. But it left a bad taste with Jeet. He thought his bosses were weak and cowardly, the unions all-powerful, and corruption unstoppable. Jeet's story brought home to me the first intimations of the rot that would settle in the monopolistic public sector. Almost everything that the government touched—certainly in the economic sphere—would turn to dust.

The state-owned railways are a miniature portrait of contemporary India, reflecting both the good and the bad. They are the people's transport. For one dollar you can travel 200 kilometers in a second-class compartment. They are cheaper than anywhere in the world because extortionate freight prices subsidize the passenger fares. Yet seventy million Indians travel every year without tickets. The railways symbolize democracy's triumph. The poorest Indian has become mobile. They are also inefficient, corrupt, hopelessly overmanned, and politicized. They employ 1.5 million people, seven times more manpower per kilometer than in the developed countries. Their powerful unions resist scaling down or modernization. The fastest train between Delhi and Bombay averages 65 kilometers per hour and it is often late. Yet Indians do not seem to mind because they have no other alternative. Private companies would not dream of transporting goods by rail, not only because of high tariffs and constant delays but because they would be stolen. Consequently, even petrol and diesel are inefficiently transported by road. Politicians make investment decisions in the railways and they bear no resemblance to commercial considerations or consumer needs. They are nationalized and there is no prospect of privatization.

I remember little from my school days in Simla, but I do recall my teacher telling us the story of one of the most famous battles fought on Indian soil—between Alexander the Great and Raja Puru (Porus, in Greek) of Punjab. I was so moved by Puru's courage that I named my younger son Puru. Later in life I returned to this encounter because it illustrated for me an important weakness in the Indian character—our lack of teamwork. Since this trait affects our competitiveness as a nation, I narrate the story at some length.

On a fine spring day in 326 B.C., Alexander marched over the Hindu Kush and descended upon India. There was the glitter of spears as long lines of mailed men passed through the Khyber Pass and emerged upon the plain about Peshawar. Having decimated the mighty Persian Empire, the "Conqueror of the World" now sought power and wealth across the river Indus. He had heard many fabulous tales of India from Herodotus—among others of giant, gold-digging ants who labored in gold-strewn deserts filled with riches.

The bazaars and palaces of Punjab had been filled with talk ever since Alexander made the Persian Empire vanish four years before. The princes of India had shivered when they heard that Persepolis had been set on fire. But the India that Alexander faced was not united. Even Punjab, guarding the northwest gateway, was divided between three major kings and dozens of free tribes who were constantly at war. Their inability to unite lost them four years during which they could have planned for Alexander.

Alexander crossed the Indus near Attock and reached the kingdom of Taxila, between the Indus and Jhelum (Hydaspes) rivers. Ambhi, the king of Taxila, from prudence or cowardice, chose not to fight. He sent Alexander envoys and presents and offered him his army, provided his kingdom was spared. Ambhi warmly welcomed the Greek invader and threw open the gates to his city, long famous as a center of trading and learning. The inquisitive crowds in Taxila watched the strange Greek figures in curious dress who milled about their streets.

Smaller chiefs from the surrounding areas brought presents, and Alexander rewarded them with generous extensions of their territories and vessels of gold and silver. The Greek soldiers performed games and sacrifices before the awestruck citizens. The Greeks were impressed by the civilized city life within the mud-brick maze of Indian streets. They visited the university and the learned men. They watched the rich townsfolk go about in linen tunics, capes, and turbans, their beards dyed white, blue, red, and purple. Some carried umbrellas, others wore leather boots. Holy men blessed the passersby by smearing their foreheads with oil.

Puru watched Alexander from across the Jhelum River. He observed the traitorous alliance struck by Ambhi, his old enemy. He saw the other princes rapidly submit to the new power, including his own Paurava kinsmen. He realized that he was up against huge odds, and he had to

fight or surrender. When Alexander's envoys came to summon him to
Taxila, Puru replied that he could meet another king only as an equal.
War became inevitable and the stage was set for one of Alexander's
greatest battles.

Alexander's army soon marched towards the Jhelum, accompanied by
Taxila's forces. When they reached the river and saw Puru's hundred elephants massed on the other bank, the Macedonian cavalry became
frightened. Not having faced elephants before, the Greeks feared them
as soldiers feared the Patton tank in recent times. Behind the elephants
stood a thousand chariots and Puru's forty thousand infantry. Although
different figures are given about the relative strength of the two forces,
they were more or less equal, with Alexander's cavalry superior in numbers. Alexander quickly realized that a direct crossing would be impossible. Meanwhile, the river began to rise, as the snows melted early in the
Himalayas. Heavy rain and storms made the river swell further. Puru's
spies brought news that Alexander had ordered vast quantities of grain,
and since nothing seemed to happen for days, Puru concluded that the
invasion had been put off for several months, till after the monsoons.

One morning at dawn, Puru was stunned to learn that boats filled
with horses had crossed twenty miles up the river. Concealed by the tor-
rential downpour Alexander had quietly moved a third of his army
upstream. He had chosen this point because it was hidden from the
other side of the bank by a wooded island. As the rain abated, Alexander
and his cavalry crossed in the first light of dawn. A single narrow boat
carried history—the king himself with his great captains, who would
one day rule vast parts of the world: Ptolemy, the future king of Egypt;
Lysimachus, the future king of Thrace; Perdiccas, the future regent; and
Seleucus, who would inherit Alexander's vast Asian empire. However,
they had not reached the other shore. They were still on the island,
which a swollen channel had completely cut off from the eastern shore
after the rains.

It was here that Puru's outposts discovered the Greeks, who had to
hurry to get across because Puru's troops would arrive any moment.
They found to their horror that the channel was not fordable: they were
caught in a trap. They made desperate efforts at various points, at all of
which the water was too deep. In that moment of panic, Alexander reas-
sured his men that they were doing all this for the sake of glory—one

day the people of Athens would talk and write about them. Eventually, they found a spot where the water was only waist-high and the men and horses struggled through.

When Puru heard that the enemy had crossed, he sent his son with a force of two thousand mounted men and 120 chariots. He did not send the bulk of his force because he did not believe that this was the main attack. Across the river, he saw the Macedonian phalanxes, the royal guard, and the Asiatic horsemen were in a state of readiness. As soon as Puru's son reached the scene, he was greeted by a hail of arrows followed by squadron after squadron of the famous Macedonian horsemen. Soon they were overpowered. Four hundred cavalry fell fighting. All his 120 chariots were captured—most of them stuck in the mud, the charioteers dead.

When Puru heard of this, he realized that the final hour of decision had come. He turned his entire force upstream. He placed himself on the largest elephant, alongside the image of Indra. Puru was a giant of a man, and his troops took courage from the sight of their powerfully built leader with the banner of the warrior god. The battle began with the trumpeting of the elephants, which terrified the European horses. Alexander's thousand mounted archers from Central Asia began to hail arrows upon the Indian left flank. The Indian archers responded, but the rain made it impossible to get a firm rest for their longer bows. When the Indian cavalry began a wheeling movement on the left wing, Alexander's horse guard charged upon them from the right. The Indian cavalry found itself outnumbered by the Greek cavalry, which had the experience of a hundred battles. Finding that they now had the upper hand, the Greeks sprang a surprise attack from the rear. Puru's infantry was thrown into confusion. The elephants, pushed back from the front, were now hemmed in from behind. Under stress, they caused a stampede on their own men. Resistance became hopeless; butchery followed. Meanwhile, the balance of Alexander's forces crossed the river, including two fresh Macedonian phalanxes, and they completed the rout. In the end, Alexander's superior cavalry had decided the battle. Among the thousands who died that bloody day were two sons of Puru and a brave neighboring prince.

Puru himself, unlike the king of Persia, did not flee nor surrender. Despite the losing battle, he kept fighting and goading his men to keep their honor. Alexander's forces were impressed, by both his size and his courage. It was only when he was hit by a dart on his right shoulder that, wounded and tired, he turned his elephant to safety. He had not gone far when he recognized the hated face of the traitor Ambhi. He turned around and hurled a lance with whatever strength his wounded arm could muster. Ambhi evaded it and turned back. Soon, two envoys from Alexander came up to him. Loss of blood had made him intolerably thirsty. He halted his elephant and got down. Alexander's envoys honored him and gave him water to drink, and he commanded them to lead him to their king.

As Puru neared the Macedonian lines, Alexander came galloping out to meet him. He was filled with admiration for his brave and proud adversary and asked Puru how he wished to be treated. "Treat me, Alexander, as you would treat a king," replied Puru. Alexander was confused and asked him to be more precise. "When I said 'a king,'" repeated Puru, "everything was said."

Alexander was pleased with the reply. He not only gave Puru back his kingdom but, much to Ambhi's chagrin, enlarged Puru's territory to all the lands towards the east. Thus, Puru accepted the Greek dominion and became Alexander's faithful and energetic ally. Puru's own people, like the Greeks, were also proud of their king. Alexander ordered a city of victory, Nicaea, to be built on the field of battle, and another at the gray spot on the opposite bank from where he had crossed the Jhelum that morning. He called the second Bucephala, after his great horse who had died that day. The Greeks then performed their sacrifices and athletic games before the admiring people of the Paurava kingdom. After this great battle of the Hydaspes River the Greeks marched on. When they reached the fifth river of Punjab, the Beas (Hyphasis in Greek), Alexander's tired army refused to go further. He ordered and cajoled them, but it was to no avail. Disappointed, he turned back, somewhere near modern Gurdaspur.

Seven years later, all trace of Greek authority had disappeared from India. The chief reason was another romantic figure, Chandragupta, who was a lesser warrior but a greater ruler than Alexander. The young nobleman from Magadha, helped by his subtle, Machiavellian adviser, Chanakya, organized an army and overcame the Greek garrisons. He established the Mauryan Empire, which ruled north India and Afghanistan for 137 years.

At the end of this saga, the main question is, why did Puru lose and Alexander win? On the face of it, the invader's superior strategy and the element of surprise clearly gave the Greeks a decisive edge. However, beneath the surface there were important differences between the two armies. Professor Stephen Rosen, the military historian from Harvard, has recently found the answer in the divisions in Indian society, which resulted in poor coordination in Puru's army. Puru's cavalry refused to aid the infantry. On the soggy banks of the Jhelum that morning, the Greek historian Arrian observed, Puru's chariots got stuck and the charioteers were unwilling to double up as infantry. Later in the day, cohesion in the Indian army broke down as the Macedonian phalanx put pressure on Puru's infantry, and the elephants pushed back and began to trample their own men. In this crisis, Rosen notes, "the Indian cavalry . . . did not assist the Indian infantry against the enemy phalanx but dealt as best as it could with the Macedonian cavalry."

In contrast, Alexander's army was a professional machine. Originally it had been, like Puru's, a tribal militia. Neither was Greek society more cohesive, but Alexander had professionalized his army and separated it from the divisions in society. When Alexander's cavalry first sighted Puru's troops, their first instinct was to charge. Alexander, however, "checked the advance of his cavalry to allow his infantry to come up with him. Regiment by regiment, they made contact, moving swiftly until the whole force was again united."

Indian military historians have also noted this aspect. Rosen attributes the lack of solidarity partially to the caste system, although he correctly points out that caste structures were not yet fully developed. Caste, he hypothesizes, divides society, encourages loyalty within the subgroup, and discourages it across caste lines. Puru's upper-caste mounted cavalry did not sufficiently support the lower-caste soldier who was on foot. Jadunath Sarkar, an authority on ancient and medieval military affairs, said that although "the Indian defenders of the Punjab were brave, each man fought to death in isolation." The soldiers were "unable to make a mass movement in concert with their brethren of other corps." The people of Punjab were disunited and narrowly self-centered, with the net effect that "divided we fell."

Puru may have lost to the greatest general of his time, but the theme of the poor teamwork runs throughout Indian history. Babur's victories at

Panipat and at Khanua (against the Rajput confederacy, led by Rana Sangha) were partly a result of the same deficiencies. Although the Marathas had more cohesive armies, they too suffered because some sub-castes armed themselves against others. The British Empire professional-ized the Indian armies, however, and after 1947 the Indian military has been "an island of discipline." Despite that, there have been problems between generals in the battlefield. In the 1962 Indo-Chinese war, the commander of the Fourth Division at Se-La confessed that "private ani-mosities, personal weakness and in many cases lack of mutual confidence among the commanders . . . led to disaster." Even in the victorious wars against Pakistan, in 1965 and 1971, there were major failures of coordina-tion, according to Generals Harbaksh Singh and Sukhwant Singh.

Poor teamwork is pervasive in India. Take any institution, scratch its surface, and one finds factionalism. Whether it is a company, a univer-sity, a hospital, a village panchayat, or a municipal board, it is beset with dissension, and it affects national competitiveness. What is the cause of our divisiveness? Is it our diversity? Is it the caste system? I am generally wary of cultural explanations, but in my frustration at not being able to find an answer, I asked my cousin, Usha Kumar, if it had something to do with the Indian personality. She is a trained psychologist from the University of Michigan, and she pointed me to Sudhir Kakar, the author of *The Inner World: A Psycho-analytic Study of Childhood and Society in India.* Kakar said that it begins with the Indian bride, who is not fully accepted in her husband's home until she produces a male child. She is so grateful when a son is born that she indulges him to excess. As the boy grows up, he remains close to the mother and distant from the father. The end result is that the boy grows up narcissistic and has a weak ego.

The adult Indian male personality that emerges from various psychol-ogists' accounts has a weak sense of the self, one that needs the support of authority figures. He is less comfortable on his own. He needs appre-ciative, older, hierarchical figures, even late in his professional life. His relationships tend to be vertical and "control oriented," and he is not good at forming horizontal, cooperative relationships with his peers. This translates into poor teamwork. In an organizational setting, such a person tends to behave in an egotistical manner. A good team player is self-confident and forms easy and healthy relationships based on equality. It is difficult to say how valid this hypothesis is in the absence of broad sociopsychological data (which, in turn, would need hundreds of senior managers, administrators, and generals on psychiatrists' couches). Nevertheless, there seems to be near-universal agreement about this Indian personality among professionals. Despite the plausibility of this explanation, I tend to shy away from value judgments based on culture, especially when comparing different societies. In the past such historical answers have been dangerous in the hands of political leaders, and psychological ones even more treacherous. I tend to be more comfortable with the economists' approach. Hence, I believe that with more competition in the Indian market, we will get better teamwork in the business world. When companies fight for survival, there is less luxury for egotistical behavior; we sink or swim together. Since the 1991 reforms Indian markets have become more competitive, cohesion should gradually increase. According to Kakar, Indian society is also changing. More women are working, and there is less time to overindulge the male child; so perhaps there is hope that the Indian male will grow up with a healthier ego and be a better team player. With more and more self-confident women in the managerial ranks, this healthy trend might even be reinforced.

Such thoughts on cooperation were the furthest from old Puru's mind when he faced Alexander, but I believe it is important to recognize that some habits constitute virtues and others vices in a nation's economic life. Honesty and reliability are virtues because they foster trust between buyers and sellers and reduce the cost of transactions. Sociability in the form of teamwork is critical because almost all activity in a modern economy is carried out by groups rather than individuals. As human beings create wealth in the market economy, they must learn to work together. And as the economy grows, new forms of organization come into being. Although we normally associate economic growth with technological developments, innovation in organizing work has played an equally powerful part ever since the industrial revolution began.

FOUR

Blind Then, Blind Now

Good intentions are useless in the absence of common sense.
                                    —JAMI, BAHARISTAN

Some men occupy one's imagination for a whole generation, and this is literally true of Jawaharlal Nehru. Young people of my generation remained under his spell for decades. I never met him personally, apart from fleeting glimpses from a distance when I was a child. I regret this, for it seems to me that to meet and to hear at a close distance someone who has meant so much must modify one's impression deeply, and make it more concrete and less unidimensional. Nehru taught us all our good and bad habits. He taught us to be liberal and tolerant (of Muslims, especially). He inculcated in us a respect for democracy and a loathing for feudal behavior. He infected us with his idealism. But he also reinforced our prejudice against businessmen and profit. We never learned about the virtues of entrepreneurship and competition and we paid dearly for this blind spot.

On the day I started school in Simla, Kasturbhai Lalbhai, a Jain businessman 1,600 kilometers to the south, in Gujarat, founded the Indian chemical industry. Kasturbhai was a Marwari like G. D. Birla, but he belonged to the older and more illustrious family of Shantidas Zaveri, who had been jewelers to the Mughal emperors. The family had migrated from the sands of Rajasthan around the time that the Mughal Empire extended its rule over Gujarat.

Gujarat had been a trading hub since ancient times. For a thousand years Gujarati traders sold Indian cottons and silk to the Arabs in return for silver and gold. Until the fifteenth century Chinese junks used to stop here to trade. In the seventeenth century the English East India Company set up warehouses on the coast, and Gujaratis became bankers to the English in their three-way trade between Europe, India, and China. Many Gujarati traders also moved to East and South Africa and the Middle East. Gujaratis were rigorous savers, and their family members worked endless hours and lived abstemiously to ensure their success. But the success of the migrants also created resentment among the locals, as it did in the 1960s in Uganda. They were expelled and hurled westwards to Britain and America, where the Gujarati Diaspora began a new phase of capital accumulation.

In the sixteenth and seventeenth centuries, during the Mughal Age, Gujarat was one of the richest centers of trade and commerce in the world, serviced by the busy ports of Surat and Cambay. This also was the time when Kasturbhai's family prospered in trade and banking in Ahmedabad. An English document of 1627, the year of Emperor Jehangir's death, described the family as "the deceased king's jewellers." Shah Jehan, who had just finished building the Taj, conferred on them a robe of honor in 1656 and a grant of villages and havelis and gardens in Ahmedabad. East India Company documents refer to them as "Chief Banians" to the Mughal court. Because of their power and influence, they acquired the title Nagarsheth, "merchants of the city."

Soon after winning the throne, Aurangzeb, the last of the great Mughals, chose Shantidas Zaveri to bring the message of conciliation to the city population. The new emperor issued a *farman* granting Palitana, its hills and its temples, to the jeweler. Shantidas used his wealth to build the gigantic Chintamani Jain temple in marble, which the German traveler J. Albert de Mandelslo described in 1638 as "without dispute, one of the noblest structures [in the world]." Aurangzeb could not tolerate that the handsomest structure in Ahmedabad should be an infidel temple and he converted it into a Muslim mosque. However, the jeweler had sufficient advantage with the emperor to have the shrine restored. Jain records in the eighteenth century tell us that the Nagarsheth family traded in Delhi, Agra, Kota, and Bengal, and possessed shops as far away as Dacca, and that it sold a variety of textiles which were "light in weight and heavy in price." For two hundred years they were the leading family in Ahmedabad, much admired by the populace for supporting Jain temples and charities.

The British rule brought the railway to Ahmedabad in 1864. With it came opportunities for the export of cotton from the Gujarat heartland to the mills of Manchester, especially after the American Civil War had cut off their supply of cotton. The British also brought modern education. The Nagarsheth family learned English and shifted from trade to industry. Between 1895 and 1905 they established two textile mills. But soon there was trouble in the family. The brothers fought and their assets were divided. Lalbhai, the head of one branch of the family, died of a heart attack in 1912. Kasturbhai, his second son, had to drop out of school at seventeen to look after their ailing Raipur mill. It was his only asset after the family division, and his family's status had plunged in Ahmedabad society to its lowest level in two hundred years. For the rest of his life, Kasturbhai was driven to regain the glory of his family.

The teenager learned the textile business quickly. Soon came the First World War. Imports were cut off and domestic demand skyrocketed. Kasturbhai was ready. He used the opportunity to turn the sick mill around and made huge profits during the war. After this, he never looked back. He invested his war profits to set up four new textile mills, and by the mid-1930s he had seven mills and had become the largest producer of textiles in India, and among the largest in the world.

When competition went into a shell during the Great Depression, Kasturbhai upgraded and expanded his mills. "If the price of textiles is low," he argued, "so is the price of textile machinery." He acquired new machines at throwaway prices in the gloomy world market and he moved upwards to make finer and higher-value-added varieties of textiles. He also began to make starch. When the Second World War came, he was again ready to take advantage. With seven modernized mills under his control, Kasturbhai began to flood the domestic and export markets with a wide range of high-quality textiles. Again, war brought him huge profits. By now, he had restored his family's place in Gujarat society. His philanthropy had also become legendary. Like G. D. Birla, he had become a major donor to the freedom movement and a national figure. Yet he continued to suffer from discontent.

With the coming of Independence, Kasturbhai, like many Indian businessmen, began to dream of glory. Having conquered the textile industry, he went in search of new businesses. He got the idea of making synthetic dyes and colors, which the textile industry needed in vast quantities. Until then dyes had been imported, mainly from Germany. Although India had once held the world's monopoly in indigo (until synthetic dyes were discovered in the twentieth century), a modern dyestuff industry was nonexistent in India, and it could become the nucleus, he thought, of a broad chemicals business.

Kasturbhai flew to New York, where he signed an agreement with American Cyanamid to design a plant and provide technical expertise for a new chemical plant. He registered the new company on 5 September 1947, the day I joined first grade in Simla. It was the beginning of a brand-new industry in India. He called it Atul, meaning "the incomparable."

Soon a spanking new town came up around Kasturbhai's plant in the wilds of Gujarat. Kasturbhai employed local illiterate villagers, whom he trained and built neat little homes for. In March 1952, when the new plant was ready, he invited Jawaharlal Nehru to open it. But Nehru refused. He had recently committed the nation to the socialist goal of central planning, and he was certainly not going to inaugurate a capitalist factory. He had persuaded the Congress Party to reject the narrow path of the capitalist West because capitalism increased inequality and cornered society's savings. It hired mainly skilled middle-class workers, excluding the vast majority of peasants from the gains of development, and benefited only those who were already affluent. Only over a hopelessly long term might capitalist development trickle down to the masses, Nehru felt, and this was clearly unacceptable.

A few weeks later, however, Nehru relented, justifying to himself that his "third way," or the Congress planning model, did not totally reject private enterprise—as long as it was under social control. Besides, Kasturbhai had been extremely persistent and had infected him with his enthusiasm. (That his own sister, Krishna, was married to Kasturbhai's sister's son, Gunottam Hutheesing, might also have had something to do with it.) One hundred ninety thousand people showed up at the opening and Nehru addressed them in his halting, sonorous voice: "Sheth Kasturbhai has set up a basic industrial unit, which will go a long way towards our industrial progress. The dyestuff and chemical industry has a special significance in our total economy. I view this project in a broader national context, the advantage it will bring to the nation, and not in terms of profits to an individual or a company set up by an individual." Despite his best efforts, the socialist Nehru's defensiveness in opening a private businessman's factory was obvious to everyone that day.

Forty-four years later, in March 1996, I spent three days in Ahmedabad with Kasturbhai's grandson, Sanjay Lalbhai. He had invited me on a consulting assignment, and I discovered that Kasturbhai never did realize his dream of creating a great chemical industry. Atul had done reasonably well, but not well enough to generate the surpluses needed to expand and build an industry. The government's antibusiness, socialist policies—extortionate taxes, which rose to 97 percent, the lack of licenses for "monopoly houses" like Kasturbhai's—were some of the main reasons for the failure. The family's textile business had also declined along with the rest of the Indian textile industry. Only in the mid-1980s did the energy return, when Sanjay Lalbhai took over Arvind Mills and turned the business around. Sanjay found the answer in denim, and he went on to become the third-largest denim producer in the world. By then, he had the world's lowest costs, and he had forged an alliance with a leading European textile company to penetrate markets in the West.

My parents read about Kasturbhai Lalbhai in the newspaper that day in 1952 when Nehru opened his chemical factory. The newspaper reports captured the expansive mood of Indian business, as well as Nehru's defensiveness and discomfort. We were living in the wilds of Bhakra-Nangal at the time. I was ten years old and my father had been transferred there to design the powerhouses at Bhakra dam on the Sutlej River. His job was to harness the energy released from dropping an awesome body of water from a 200-meter-high concrete wall, stretched half a kilometer across a jagged Himalayan gorge. Over three years half a million cubic meters of concrete were raised from the ground to create the greatest "temple of new India." There were others—Hirakud Dam on the Mahanadi River, gleaming steel plants at Bokaro, Bhilai, and Durgapur, and dozens of other big, audacious factories built by Nehru's government to fulfill the nation's image of its future as an industrial giant. Big dams are in disrepute today, but fifty years ago Bhakra-Nangal captured the nation's imagination.

It was clear to me, even at that young age, that the great dam inspired feelings bordering on ecstasy among the men who were working on it.

My father was no exception. Normally he did not talk about his work nor express undue emotion. Therefore, I was surprised to find him caught up in the fever of building the dam. He worked untiringly. Sometimes I would not see him for days together. He would leave early in the morning, before I got up, and return late, after I was asleep. Most of his colleagues did the same. They were transformed by the magnitude of the challenge.

"Earlier, we used to measure our achievement in terms of the pleasure we gave to our bosses," said my father one day to my mother. "Now I feel differently. Here at Bhakra, I measure my work in terms of the results that we produce and the pleasure that we get."

It was dusty work. He would come home covered in mud, and even his files were laden with dust. "Before, I used to be a slave to my files," he told my mother. "Here, in this huge project, where no one knows the answers, we take quick and clean decisions on the spot. We have never built a dam like this before, with ninety thousand people working on it. So we have to take chances and the morale is important." It was the idea of achievement—the new spirit of a rising nation—that generated the morale. Bhakra was a great dream, and it became a reality before our eyes.

I recall one especially difficult week. They were blasting tunnels in the rock to divert the water of the Sutlej and nine workers were caught in a landslide. My father and his colleagues tried everything they could but without success. When they had given up all hope of saving the men, a junior engineer came up with a desperate plan on Sunday evening. They worked all night and by the morning they had succeeded in rescuing the men. When my father returned home with his colleagues, he was weeping like a child. The others started crying as well. My father and his colleagues embraced the junior engineer in turn. All of them wept like children from happiness and excitement. I shall never forget that moment.

On a fine morning in 1954 I sat proudly beside my father, along with thousands of workers, and we listened with reverence to Nehru's words: "Probably nowhere else in the world is there a dam as high as this. . . . As I walked around the site I thought that these days the biggest temple and mosque and gurdwara is the place where man works for the good of mankind. Which place can be greater than this, this Bhakra–Nangal?"

Nehru spoke at length about his vision of India. He talked glowingly about the new state-owned companies, calling them the "temples of modern India," an expression which drew applause from his audience. He wanted to build a just and casteless society with a socialist pattern where the inequalities of wealth would diminish. Since there were few resources in the private sector, only the government could make these huge investments. At the same time, he explained, he wanted to preserve democratic freedoms; he did not want India to become a communist society like Russia and China. Thus he called his system a "mixed economy," which would combine the best of socialism and capitalism.

Nehru was a handsome man, and we all fell in love with him. Everyone in my family was proud of him. All our neighbors admired him. My parents' friends never tired of talking about him. The Indian middle class had bought his dream wholesale. And why not? It was a good dream. It captured the ideals of the modern age, founded on the equality of all human beings. Nehru was especially attractive to women and was also attracted by them. He was sensitive to their needs, and courageously he pushed through Parliament the Hindu Code bill, which liberated women and gave them an equal share in family property. It was not unfashionable in the 1950s for either the old or the young to admit to idealism. Unlike the tired, old, and devious nations of Europe whose "realism" and "balance of power" had brought on two world wars, we in India felt that we could build a nation on moral principles and on nonviolence. Had we not won our freedom based on Gandhi's nonviolent principles? In contrast, the passage of the other two great nations, China and Russia, into modernity had been based on violent revolutions. We thus had permission to take the moral high ground. (In our minds, the violence that accompanied Partition did not seem to count.)

An odd thing happened that morning as Nehru was nearing the end of his speech. One of the engineers in the front row got up to go to the toilet. Nehru was distracted and he stopped in the middle of his sentence. He became annoyed, went off on a tangent, and began to rant about discipline and courtesy. The poor engineer was mortified. My father later told my mother that it was strange for a man so acutely conscious of his place in history to have been diverted by trivia.

Decades later, when I think back to that morning, I am filled with sadness. Nehru's "mixed economy" turned out to be a gravely flawed image of our future. It was Nehru's fault, partly, that we never learned to value the dreams of Kasturbhai Lalbhai and G. D. Birla. But how was an innocent, starry-eyed ten-year-old boy to know that Nehru's intellectual blueprint of state-directed industrialization, based on publicly owned heavy industry and insulated from international competition, was fundamentally wrong? Nor could he have predicted that the state would so emasculate the textile industry with controls that it would be as good as destroyed. Had a hundred Kasturbhais been encouraged rather than discouraged we might have had a different India. When ordinary human beings err, it is sad, but when leaders do, it haunts us for generations.

FIVE

If We Were Once Rich,
Why Are We Now Poor?

The greatest thing since the creation of the world, except for the incarnation and death of Him who created it, is the discovery of the Indies.

—FRANCISCO LÓPEZ DE GÓMARA

Years later, my grandfather admitted that he was a little sad to see the British go. He raised himself on his elbow and called up to me as I was trying to sleep on the upper berth of the Frontier Mail, "It is certainly nice to feel the fresh breeze of freedom, but you must remember, my son, that India had been the best-governed country in the world for a hundred years, and Punjab had been its best-governed province. Why, Britain itself was not as well ruled because it was, after all, a messy parliamentary democracy, and it was not run by the Indian civil service." As his words sank in, I peered out of the window at the dusty wheat fields of Punjab rushing wildly by in the light of the full moon. After a pause, he added, "Yes, the English were arrogant, but it was a cheap price to pay for a hundred years of peace, good government, railways, irrigation canals, and the best law and order in the world. You may call me antinational, but this is how I feel."

"If the British were such good rulers, why was India so poor?" I asked. Clearly, he had not connected governance with prosperity. After a long pause, he admitted that he did not know. "For that you must speak to your uncle, Sat Pal."

By now my father had been transferred to Delhi, along with the design offices of Bhakra Dam. We lived in the heart of New Delhi, in a spanking new whitewashed neighborhood called Kaka Nagar, under the shadow of Purana Qila, the old fort of Mughal emperor Humayan. We were surrounded by other families of engineers, colleagues of my father's in the design office of the dam. Slowly, however, other families of government technocrats and professionals moved in and the colony expanded. The government had decided to solve the problem of housing its expanding bureaucracy by building spacious but simple and monotonous apartments on two levels. Those who lived on the ground floor had a pocket garden; those on the upper level got the roof terrace above, which was needed in those days before air-conditioning because we slept outside in the 100-degree heat of the summer nights. The colonies themselves were nicely laid out with playing fields and grassy squares, even if they were standardized constructions of the Public Works Department.

Soon after we arrived in Delhi, my mother's first priority was to get us into a good school. After some quick research, she decided that it was going to b. Modern School on Barakhamba Road. It had the right mix of the traditional and the modern, but most important, it had high standards. It was not as Westernized as our school in Simla. She felt that we needed to become stronger in Hindi and mathematics, which had been the weak spots in our earlier education. The question was how we were to get into Modern. We did not have money or influence. But my mother was determined. She went to the school first thing Monday morning. The principal would not see her. She waited until lunchtime. She returned on Tuesday morning, and the same thing happened again. She came back home feeling defeated and she cried all afternoon. On Wednesday morning, she tried again. Finally, on Thursday the principal took pity and called her in. He was skeptical of our ability to cope with the tough standards of the school, but she persuaded him to test us. We did reasonably well in the tests and he reluctantly agreed to let us in on a trial basis. As it turned out, all of us did exceptionally well in our first exams. Grudgingly, the principal admitted to my mother that he had been wrong to treat her as he had.

Today every middle-class parent in India goes through my mother's anxiety and humiliation. It is worse now because the middle class has grown and the demand for good private schools has outstripped supply. The story of education in free India is a sad one. The government created a vast number of schools, practically free, after Independence. But they were so uniformly bad that the middle classes shunned them and scrambled for places in a few private schools. Thus there arose a situation of scarcity, and you needed either money or contacts to get in. If this is the plight of the middle class, the situation of the masses is tragic. The state has failed to provide both the quantity and quality of education.

I n our history class at school we learned that Columbus went in quest of the riches of India and discovered America. Thinking that he had found India, he called the natives "Indians." The name stuck and so has the linguistic confusion. What captured my imagination in school was that India had once been fabulously wealthy and this had set the Europeans on their great voyages of discovery. In the European mind, the name "Golconda" became the symbol of the haunting wealth of India. Famous for his diamonds, the king of Golconda was the richest prince in India after the Mughal emperor. Today his fortress lies in ruins, six miles west of Hyderabad. As the Europeans got to know her, India's wisdom also attracted them. G. W. F. Hegel, the great German philosopher, wrote, "From the most ancient times downwards, all nations have directed their wishes and longings to gaining access to the treasures of this land of marvels, the most costly which the Earth presents; treasures of Nature— pearls, diamonds, perfumes, rose-essences, elephants, lions, etc.—as also treasures of wisdom. The way, by which these treasures have passed to the West, has at all times been a matter of world-historical importance, bound up with the fate of nations."

The Portuguese were shocked that Spain, their enemy, had won the prize of discovering America when it could have been theirs. It took them five years to get over the humiliation, and in 1497 they sent Vasco da Gama the other way, with a flotilla of four ships to go around Africa and find the real India. The two-year voyage was not a commercial success and they lost 116 of the 170 crew members. When they arrived near Calicut, on the Malabar Coast in southwest India, someone asked, "What brought you here?" A member of the crew replied, "We seek Christians and spices." However, the Indians were not interested in European trinkets and clothes. They made far better fabrics and trinkets themselves. But da Gama brought back something more important. He told King Manuel of Portugal of "large cities, large buildings and rivers, and great populations." He spoke about spices and jewels, precious stones and "mines of gold." He believed that he had found the legendary wealth of India. In the words of Adam Smith, "The discovery of America and the passage to the East Indies by the Cape of Good Hope are the two greatest events recorded in the history of mankind."

The English got to this wealth more than a hundred years later, at the beginning of the seventeenth century. By then the kingdoms of Spain and Portugal were united through marriage. The English were at war with this formidable empire, and miraculously they had repelled the seemingly invincible Spanish Armada in 1588. The English first came to the Indies to plunder rather than to trade. They avoided the Portuguese on the west and went east to the Coromandel Coast, where they set up at Madras. Discovering that the fruits of trade were better than plunder, they turned back to the Malabar Coast. Carefully skirting the Portuguese, they set up a trading post in Surat, the rich Gujarati port of the Mughal Empire. Next, they gingerly came downwards and established on an empty island what became the flourishing commercial city of Bombay. On the eastern coast they moved northwards and set up another commercial city, Calcutta.

The English found that India produced the world's best cotton yarn and textiles and in enormous quantities. India's textile industry was "unbeatable for quality, variety and cost. This industry not only satisfied the large domestic demand but exported roughly half its output throughout the Indian Ocean and indirectly to South Asia and China. To this huge market, they brought in the beginning of the seventeenth century, the huge stimulus of European demand," according to David Landes, the Harvard economic historian. Thus, by the end of the seventeenth century India controlled a quarter of the world trade in textiles. "Indian cottons transformed the dress of Europe. . . . Lighter and cheaper than woolens, more decorative (by dyeing or printing), easier to clean and change, cotton was made for a new wide world. Even in cold climes, the suitability of cotton for underwear transformed the standards of cleanliness, comfort and health," adds Landes. The English learned about cotton textiles from India and soon they turned the tables. English textiles brought an industrial revolution to Britain but destroyed the lives of millions of Indian weavers.

During the Mughal Empire, at the end of the sixteenth century, India's wealth sustained more than a hundred million people. With plenty of arable land, India's agriculture was "not in any way backward when compared with other contemporary societies, including those of Western Europe," according to the historian Irfan Habib. Its productivity too was comparable. Even the subsistence-oriented peasant got a good return. India had a vigorous and large skilled workforce that produced not only cotton but also luxurious products for the rich landlords, the courts, and the aristocracy. Consequently, the economy produced a fabulous financial surplus. "The annual revenues of the Mogul emperor Aurangzeb (1659–1701) are said to have amounted to $450,000,000, more than ten times those of (his contemporary) Louis XIV. According to an estimate of 1638, the Mogul court of India had accumulated a treasure equivalent to one and a half billion dollars." The economic surplus was used to support the vast and growing Mughal Empire and finance spectacular monuments like the Taj Mahal.

My uncle and the nationalists were correct in saying that India was the leading manufacturing country in the world in the early eighteenth century. Manufacturing, of course, meant handloom textiles and handicraft at that time. India had a 22.6 percent share of the world's GDP, according to economic historian Angus Maddison. Paul Bairoch confirms that it had a 25 percent share of the global trade in textiles. "More important, there was a large commercialized sector with a highly sophisticated market and credit structure, manned by a skilful and in many instances very wealthy commercial class." Indian methods of production and of industrial and commercial organization could stand comparison with those in vogue in any other part of the world. It had developed an indigenous banking system. Merchant capital had emerged with an elaborate network of agents, brokers, and middlemen. Its bills of exchange were honored in major cities of Asia. It is not surprising, then, that English travelers to India found an economy that was dynamic and commercial, not stagnant or backward.

Given the enormous financial surplus, large exports, plenty of arable land and people, an agricultural productivity equal to the best in the world, and a large artisan workforce, the question is, why didn't a modern industrial economy emerge in India? Why did India become instead one of the most impoverished countries? Despite a dynamic and a growing commercial sector which responded to market forces and extensive foreign trade, the truth is that eighteenth-century India was significantly behind Western Europe in technology, institutions, and ideas. Neither an agricultural revolution nor a scientific revolution had occurred. "The competitive strength of Indian manufacturers in overseas markets was based on a ruthlessly inequitable system of distribution . . . [and] in the long run the manual skill of the Indian artisan could be no substitute for technological progress." Even with his expanding trade, the Indian merchant was unable to change the local supply structure in order to improve the quality of his exports or to improve his logistics. This sort of flexibility in attitude would have required the application of a scientific mind.

Notwithstanding the surplus and the trade, the peasant was extremely poor. François Bernier, a French physician who spent twelve years in India, wrote about the poverty of the masses. He described their decrepit houses, their humiliating lives, and the dramatic inequality between the rich few and the impoverished many. Because the rapacious Mughal state took away something like half the agricultural produce, there was little incentive to improve the land. Despite their vigorous trade, the merchants hid their wealth for fear of the tax collector.

There is no easy answer to the problem that the country was prosperous and the people were poor. One obvious explanation is that in an overpopulated country there is plenty of cheap labor. When the supply of labor is elastic, it always seems more economical to hire people than to invest in machines. This was true in the eighteenth century and it is true today. An English observer wrote in 1807, "In India it is seldom that an attempt is made to accomplish anything by machinery that can be performed by human labor."

Having said that, it is important to remember that 250 years ago there did not exist the great disparities in income that exist today between nations. According to Paul Bairoch, the difference in income between

Europe and India (or China) was 1.5 or 2 to 1. The economic fortunes of England and India began to diverge in the nineteenth century. India remained slow and England experienced an industrial revolution. This is not because India was a colony of England but because England had achieved the preconditions for industrialization—it possessed a variety of social, political, and economic institutions, attitudes, and values which permitted it to respond to technological opportunities.

Thus, I return to the original question: If we were once rich, why are we now poor? Following my grandfather's advice, I went to meet my uncle Sat Pal. He had always been my grandfather's favorite. He came from Ramnagar, the village where the English forces had won the decisive battle against the Sikh army in 1849, paving the way for a hundred years of British rule in Punjab. Sat Pal went to our local Dayanand Anglo-Vedic School and later to the Government College in Lyallpur, where he won all the prizes. My grandfather used to dream of a brilliant career for him until one day, to his horror, he discovered that Sat Pal had become a Marxist. It was a great blow to our family, whose bourgeois hopes of prestige and wealth were shattered.

After Independence, Sat Pal became a respected labor leader in Cheharta, near Amritsar. He was loved by the workers and feared by industrialists. Welcoming me into his austere two-room home, Sat Pal painted the most devastating portrait of British colonial rule. The English began by robbing and plundering soon after they took over Bengal in 1757, he said. Their Lancashire mills crushed our handloom textile industry and threw millions of weavers out of work in the nineteenth century. As a result, our textile exports plunged from world leadership (before the start of Britain's industrial revolution) to a fraction of what they had been. Simultaneously, the indigenous banking system, which financed these exports, was also destroyed. Since the colonial government did not erect tariff barriers, Indian consumers also shifted to cheaper English mill-made cloth and millions of handloom workers were left in misery. In the process, British colonial rule "deindustrialized" India, and from an exporter of textiles, India became an exporter of raw cotton. Sat Pal quoted Sir William Bentinck, a contemporary observer, who had noted that "the bones of the cotton weavers were bleaching the plains of India."

I was about to interrupt my uncle when Vimla, his attractive Kashmiri wife, entered the room with two steel tumblers of buttermilk. She too was an ardent activist, and was now a member of the state legislature. They had met in Lahore during their heady student days in the 1940s. In their charmed leftist circle, Vimia was admired for her good looks, her deep convictions, and her glamorous background. Her father worked for the BBC. Her mother had been trained in Italy in the Montessori teaching system, and taught at Sir Ganga Ram College. They used to meet at the India Coffee House and listen to the poetry of Iqbal and Faiz Ahmed Faiz. It was something of a coup, I thought, that he got her to marry him when she must have been coveted by so many.

As we drank our buttermilk, Sat Pal turned to agriculture. Britain taxed the Indian farmer heavily. It changed the old land revenue system to the disadvantage of the farmer, who had to pay revenue whether or not the monsoon failed. Agriculture lost its capacity to generate savings, and a series of famines followed in the bad years in the last quarter of the nineteenth century. The worst one, in 1896–97, affected ninety-six million people and killed an estimated five million. Food also declined in areas where jute, indigo, cotton, tea, and coffee plantations were set up by the Europeans. Although these cash crops were profitable, the surpluses remained with the Europeans, who transferred them to England. The railways commercialized the food crops by moving them over long distances, and the enlarged national market sucked away the surpluses, which the peasants had earlier stored for the bad years. Thus, agricultural production remained stagnant for a century.

After paying the cost of its huge imperial establishment in India, the British government transferred its surplus revenues back home. Since India consistently exported more than it imported in the second half of the nineteenth century and early twentieth century, Britain used India's trade surplus to finance its own trade deficit with the rest of the world, to pay for its exports to India, and to cover capital repayments plus interest charges in London. According to Sat Pal, this represented a massive drain of India's wealth—8 percent of our gross national product was transferred to Britain each year. Thereby, Britain impoverished the Indian masses, and we financed its industrial revolution.

"In that case," I said, "now that we are free and England has lost its colonies, India will become richer and England will become poorer. Is that right?" He nodded. My uncle had put forth the classic nationalist

case for India's poverty during the colonial period. It was compelling.
Sat Pal and Vimla's selfless life of integrity and simplicity also left a deep
impression on me. After lunch, Vimla brought out an album of pho-
tographs of their younger days. One of the pictures was taken in a Bengal village. It showed Sat Pal and Vimla, two idealistic faces, helping out
during the terrible famine in 1943. Another photograph showed Vimla
in Prague in 1947, where she had gone to attend the first World Youth
Festival as leader of the All India Students Federation. There was triumph in her eyes because she had been elected vice president of the
World Federation of Democratic Youth. Her face conveyed the wonderful confidence that she must have felt as a youth leader at the peak of
the international communist movement. At that moment she had every
reason to believe that right was on her side and communists would rule
the world one day. I thought of that spring day in 1968 when Soviet
tanks had moved to crush freedom in Prague as I looked again at Vimla's
happy face in the picture.

My meeting with Sat Pal and Vimla spurred me to read economic
history and I found that the scholars mostly confirmed my uncle's classic
analysis of India's poverty. Britain's trade policies, they agreed, had
encouraged the import of manufactures and the export of raw materials. And by heavily taxing the farmer, Britain contributed to the stagnation of Indian agriculture.

As the years went by, however, a new generation of historians
emerged who began to challenge the classic picture. These serious scholars expended great time and effort interpreting the historical data. One of
them concluded that the land tax had not been exorbitant—by 1900 it
was only 5 percent of the agricultural output, which was less than half
the average per capita tax burden. Another agreed that there had been a
"drain of wealth" from India to Britain, especially in the nineteenth century, but it was only 1.5 percent of GNP every year. The revisionist historians argued that India's payments to Britain were for real military and
civilian services and to service capital investments (which increased
India's wealth). Also, the overhead cost to maintain the British establishment—the so-called home charges—was in fact quite small. If India had
maintained its own army and navy, it might have had to spend more
money. They conceded that India did have a balance of payments surplus
which Britain used to finance its part of its deficit, but they said that India

was partially compensated for it through the import of gold and silver into India. Only a part of that precious metal was minted for coinage and most went into private Indian hands. Indians have always been mesmerized by gold and silver. Even the Roman Pliny had observed this, and had called India the "sink of the world's gold."

The revisionists' most serious challenge was to the nationalist thesis that Britain had deliberately deindustrialized India. They agreed with my uncle that Indian industry declined in the nineteenth century. They calculated that India enjoyed 17.6 percent of the world's industrial production in 1830, while Britain's share was 9.5 percent. By 1900, India's share had declined to 1.7 percent while Britain's had grown to 18.6 percent. But this decline, they argued, was caused by technology. The machines of Britain's industrial revolution wiped out Indian textiles, in the same way that traditional handmade textiles disappeared in Europe and the rest of the world. Fifty years later Indian textile mills would have destroyed them. India's weavers were thus the victims of technological obsolescence.

Handlooms all over the world gave way to mill-made cloth, and weavers everywhere lost their jobs no less than in India. Unfortunately, there were more weavers affected in India because India was the largest maker of textiles in the world. This is not to take away from the great misery and enormous suffering caused by their impoverishment. If the British Raj had been sensitive to their plight, it might have erected trade barriers in India. This might have cushioned the impact and Indian handmade textiles might have survived for a period. (It is true that the British government did put up barriers in eighteenth-century England against Indian textiles.)

After 1850, Indian entrepreneurs began to set up their own modern textile mills. By 1875, India began to export textiles again and slowly recaptured the domestic market. In 1896, Indian mills supplied only 8 percent of total cloth consumed in India; in 1913, 20 percent; in 1936, 62 percent; and in 1945, 76 percent. Both British and Indian capitalists made large profits during the First World War. While the British businesses remitted their wartime profits to England, Indian businessmen reinvested theirs in new industrial enterprises after the war. Thus, Indian industry began to grow rapidly after the war. G. D. Birla, Kasturbhai Lalbhai, and a dozen other entrepreneurs built significant industrial empires in the interwar years. Manufacturing output grew 5.6 percent per annum between 1913 and 1938, well above the world average of 3.3 percent. The British government finally provided tariff protection from the 1920s. This helped industrialists to expand and diversify. The Birlas went beyond textiles and jute into sugar, cement, and paper. Hirachand, the construction magnate, diversified into shipping; Shri Ram, in the north, went into sewing machines; and Tatas, in Bombay, started an airline which later became Air India.

By the Second World War, the pre–First World War supremacy of British business was broken and Indian entrepreneurs were now stronger and in a position to buy out the businesses of the departing foreigners. The share of industry in India's GNP doubled from 3.8 percent (in 1913) to 7.5 percent (in 1947). The composition of India's trade also changed— the share of manufactures in its exports rose from 22.4 percent (in 1913) to 30 percent (in 1947), while the share of manufactures in imports declined from 79.4 percent to 64 percent. Industrial employment, however, did *not* grow in tandem. Modern industry could not make up for the loss in jobs suffered by handloom weavers.

Indian nationalists have exaggerated the economic importance of India to Britain. They thought that the Indian empire was hugely profitable. They got the idea from Cecil Rhodes, the great imperialist of the nineteenth century, who used to say, "The Empire is a bread and butter question . . . [we] must acquire new lands for settling the surplus population of the country, to provide new markets for the goods produced in factories and mines." Churchill was a leading exponent of this view in the twentieth century. Conservatives certainly believed it, but even the left wing of the Labour Party thought so. Bevin told the House of Commons: "If the British Empire fell . . . it would mean the standard of life of our constituents would fall considerably." The truth is that the Indian colony was not terribly profitable to Britain. After the crude period of exploitation in the eighteenth century was over, Britain's rising prosperity in the next century owed more to its free trade with the "new world" and to its investments in America. If there was a "drain," it was by the transfer of dividends by English companies from America. Certainly, a few Englishmen became very rich from India—the owners of the tea and indigo plantations, the shareholders of the East India Company and other commercial firms, the employees of the managing agencies, the railway builders, the civil and military personnel, and others connected with India. But the profit to Britain as a whole was meager.

My uncle's prediction also turned out to be wrong. Britain did not become poorer after losing India. Instead, it enjoyed shocking prosperity in the 1950s and 1960s, at the very time that it was losing its colonies. So did France, Holland, and other colonialists. The fact is that Britain's colonial prosperity was not founded on the exploitation of India. In the end, whether Britain impoverished or enriched India is really an academic question. What is more relevant is why the forces of global capitalism in the second half of the nineteenth century and early twentieth century did not release widespread growth and development in India, as they did, for example, in Japan. The rapid building of railways and canals and the simultaneous expansion of foreign trade should have acted as a strong engine of growth. India had an experienced merchant class which had begun to develop modern industry.

By 1914, India had the world's largest jute manufacturing industry, the fourth-largest cotton textile industry, the largest canal network, the third-largest railway network, and 2.5 percent of world trade. Fifty years earlier, Karl Marx had predicted that the introduction of railways and modern factories into India would transform the subcontinent. Why didn't it happen? India remained largely nonindustrial and extremely poor at the time of Independence. Modern industry contributed only 7.5 percent of national income at Independence, and employed barely 2.5 million people out of a population of 350 million. Why didn't an industrial revolution occur?

My father's English boss and other colonial officials used to blame India's poverty on the otherworldly spirituality of Hindu life and its fatalistic beliefs. Max Weber, the German sociologist, who admired the richness of India, attributed the absence of development to the caste system. Swedish economist Gunnar Myrdal found that India's social system and attitudes were an important cause of its low productivity, primitive production techniques, and low levels of living. According to Myrdal, poor work discipline, contempt for manual work, lack of punctuality, alertness, and ambition, low aptitude for cooperation, and superstition were the result of inhibiting attitudes. These were compounded by unfavorable conditions, such as a debilitating land tenure system, low standards of efficiency and integrity in public administration, weak participation of the people in local affairs, and a rigid and unequal social structure. Myrdal believed that these premodern attitudes and institutions had to be attacked directly, primarily through education, and India could not wait to erase them as a by-product of growth and income. The only agent that could break the forces of stagnation, he felt, was the Indian state. But the Indian government would not be able to do it, he concluded, because it was a "soft state." It would not be able to impose the social discipline that this required. He said this in 1967, and the Indian state has become even "softer" since then.

Max Weber is often criticized for saying that Asian societies could not become capitalist. But the criticism is unfair, for he was addressing a different issue: he was trying to understand why modern capitalism, as well as other aspects of the modern world such as natural science and the rational mastery of nature, arose in Protestant Europe and not in traditional India, China, and Japan. After all, China's level of technology was higher than that prevailing in Europe in 1500, as Joseph Needham and others have shown. But China lacked what the West later developed—the scientific method of experiment and empirical observation which helped Europe to conquer nature. The scientific method came about by an intellectual temper which sought the causes behind physical principles through abstract reasoning.

Capitalism developed in the East when India, China, and Japan confronted the technology and social prowess of the West and shed some of their inhibiting institutions. China got rid of political Confucianism and its imperial system with its mandarin class of gentleman scholars. Japan dropped its old class divisions and redirected its samurai warrior ethic towards the market. India shed its Brahminical contempt for modern learning and critically re-examined its traditional institutions in the nineteenth century. Thus, capitalism developed in the Eastern countries only when they came into contact with the West and its ideas of economic modernity.

Deepak Lall, another economist, has similarly explained economic stagnation in terms of a low-level "Hindu equilibrium" around the caste system which bought stability in the context of political warfare, monsoon failure and climatic uncertainty, labor shortage, and an undervalued merchant class. Lall argues that "India's social organisation and agriculture system were a second-best Pareto-efficient response to its specific environment." David Landes, the economic historian at Harvard, has recently reopened the politically incorrect controversy relating to geography and the weather. He blames India's enervating heat. For this reason, rich countries lie in temperate zones and the poor in the tropics and semitropics. Although air-conditioning and tropical medicine, he says, have leveled the playing field somewhat after the Second World War (and made possible the prosperity of the American South), the unpleasant truth is that "nature like life is unfair, unequal in its favors" and "geography brings bad tidings."

I am always skeptical of easy cultural or geographic explanations. In my experience, successful Hindu entrepreneurs can be both extremely religious and aggressive in business. The Indian farmer responds quickly to market-based incentives, as the green revolution demonstrates. Brahmins will plow their own land in traditional Uttar Pradesh if they have to, and conservative Rajput Thakurs in Rajasthan will shed their feudal ways for the sake of a commercial opportunity. Moreover, there are substantial non-Hindus in India and these communities have also been stuck in the same rut of stagnation. Other Asian countries such as China and Indonesia were equally backward, but they had no "Hindu equilibrium" to explain away their stagnation. Tropical, enervating Singapore has achieved Western levels of prosperity despite the unfairness of nature. I cannot help but conclude that these cultural stereotypes, and the dirigiste prescriptions that flow from them, stem from a paternalism bordering on contempt for the masses of the Third World. How could these wretched and ignorant peasants behave like rational consumers and producers of classical economics? But they do behave in that way, as empirical evidence has shown beyond doubt. The 1982 Development Report of the World Bank points out, "All farmers—small, medium, and large—respond to economic incentives. Far from being 'tradition-bound peasants,' farmers have shown that they share a rationality that far outweighs differences in their social and ecological conditions."

Economic historians no longer seek explanations of India's economic backwardness in culture—the otherworldly values of the Hindus or the immobilizing effects of the caste system or the conservative habits of the merchant caste. They look to economic factors that motivate a businessman to invest in a business—the size of the market, the capability of suppliers, the costs of production, the distribution hurdles, the availability of technology, and the state of competition. Amiya Kumar Bagchi argues that it was lack of effective demand that limited business opportunity. Indians were just too poor, he says, to buy modern goods and services. With weak purchasing power the market remained tiny, and this prevented entrepreneurs from investing. I am not convinced, however, that the lack of demand provides a sufficient cause. If the domestic Indian market was small, the entrepreneur could have supplemented it by producing for overseas markets. Morris D. Morris, the economic historian, says that backwardness is the result of supply constraints. An Indian entrepreneur, he feels, was beset by formidable uncertainties because of a shortage of technology, skilled labor, and capital—all of which raised his cost of production. According to the Calcutta historian Rajat Ray, the Indian businessman did not export because he could only make inferior-quality products, which were not acceptable to the world market. And he did not have the technology to make superior products. In his view, the single biggest failing lay in the technological backwardness of Indians. Ironically, a hundred years later, the same situation persists.

Thus, there is no easy answer to India's backwardness. Unlike the nationalists, I do not believe that there was a British conspiracy to deliberately underinvest in India, or to sabotage Indian business interests (despite G. D. Birla's difficulties with the Scottish jute lobby). The nationalist thesis is weak because British business was not a homogeneous force. Bombay's textile mills in the nineteenth century were built with credit, technical assistance, and machines from the British textile machinery makers even when these mills were a competitive threat to Manchester's mills. Burn and Company, a full-blooded European company, had no hesitation to start making steam vessels in India when it found it cheaper than importing them from Britain. Businessmen invest whenever and wherever profit is to be made, and their decisions have little to do with nationalism or racial considerations. Companies only look to their bottom line and do not fly the flag of their parent countries.

What then is the verdict on British rule in India? Did the British impoverish India? There is no question that in the eighteenth century the British plundered and looted India's wealth, as all conquerors have done in history. The more important historical question is if Britain systematically exploited its colony by creating ongoing institutions that were to India's detriment. This has to do with the nature and theory of colonialism. I have already said that the British did not deliberately dein-dustrialize India. It was the industrial revolution that threw millions of weavers out of work. It would have happened anyway when the new technologies reached India. British government policy could have cush-ioned the impact by erecting trade barriers, but protecting handlooms would have been a temporary palliative at best.

Odd as it may seem, Britain did not "exploit" India enough. Had it made the massive investments in India that it did in the Americas, India would have become prosperous and a much bigger market for British goods. An impoverished India was certainly not in Britain's economic interest. The tragedy is that the failure to develop India was a great loss for Great Britain as well as for India; a richer India would have been even a better customer, a better supplier, and a firmer basis of Empire. Our nationalists have failed to comprehend that capital is a progressive and positive force, however exploitative it may appear. Marx understood this. He knew that capitalism is the only efficient way to accumulate capital, make investments, raise output, and increase productivity. Even today, many Indians, with their phobia of multinationals, do not under-stand this.

Britain's main failure was to remain detached when it came to devel-opment and economic growth. Unlike the Japanese government follow-ing the Meiji reforms after 1868, which actively promoted the country's development, Britain neglected India. It was an imperial power and had little interest in the people of India. It did not actively encourage invest-ment either by Indians or by Englishmen. It did not try to educate the Indian masses—83 percent of Indians were illiterate at Independence. The British education system in India produced only a thin upper crust of extremely well-educated Indians. The Japanese and the Koreans, at the same time, concentrated on making their masses literate. By 1950, more than half of Japan's and Korea's populations were literate. Although it built railways and canals, Britain made no effort to provide credit to entrepreneurs or farmers in a capital-starved country. Nor did it suffi-ciently protect the infant Indian industry that came up in the nineteenth century (although it did from 1921 onwards). Then "no colonial power helped its colony to industrialise," says the wise economist Arthur W. Lewis. The crude fact is that Britain did not understand how to make an economy grow. It only knew how to keep the budget balanced.

Indian nationalists have overestimated Britain's impact on India's wealth and poverty. To be sure, there was a "drain" of wealth from India to Britain, especially in the nineteenth century. They used our export earnings to finance the transfer of our wealth to Britain rather than reinvesting the trade surplus in India. It is also true that India progressively became an exporter of raw materials and importer of manufactured products. India's leaders took this to mean that foreign trade and foreign capital were responsible for our poverty, and closed our economy and pursued a policy of self-sufficiency. In the process, they wasted an opportunity. They forgot that India had a centuries-old tradition of trading before the British came, and that it had once enjoyed enormous prosperity through exports and imports. For these and other reasons, we became pessimistic about our ability to compete in the world economy and regain our historic preeminence as a great trading nation. We closed our doors. And our share of world trade declined from 2.4 percent in 1947 to 0.4 percent in 1990. We learned the wrong lessons from history.

How to make a poor nation prosperous is a more difficult question. The answer seems to lie in technology and institutions. Since Britain's industrial revolution in the late eighteenth century, not only has there been for the first time in recorded history a continuous flow of inventions, but they have been absorbed commercially as profitable innovations. History teaches that a nation's ability to absorb these innovations and create an industrial revolution depends on having the right institutions in place—for example, property rights, enforcement of contracts, roads to reach products, schools, and stable governance. In the second half of the twentieth century, Asian tigers demonstrated that it can be done—a poor nation can become rich, and very quickly. They took less than thirty years to transform their societies, whereas the West needed a hundred. Latecomers too are sometimes blessed.

SIX

The Paper Route

In democracies nothing is more great or more brilliant than commerce: it attracts the attention of the public, and fills the imagination of the multitude; all energetic passions are directed towards it.
—ALEXIS DE TOCQUEVILLE

Our family moved to Washington, D.C., in the mid–1950s when the Indian government posted my father as a part of a small team of engineers to negotiate the division of the Punjab rivers with Pakistan. The World Bank had offered to mediate the water dispute because it was funding development of river basins. We arrived in America during the heyday of the Eisenhower age. The country was in the midst of unparalleled prosperity. The American middle class was absorbed in the serious business of collecting bigger appliances and bigger cars for its bigger homes in the mushrooming suburbs. I was put into a typical American high school a short bus ride away from our apartment hotel on Sixteenth Street. My school was 80 percent "white" when I arrived and 80 percent "black" when I left three years later. Each day I used to lose a white classmate and gain a black classmate, and I witnessed the profound demographic revolution that led to the destruction of the American city and the triumph of suburbia.

Like many American kids, I got a job delivering newspapers before school. Each morning I would walk my route, distributing the *Washing-*

ton Post from house to house. I had to get up at 5 a.m., and in the freezing cold of winter, that required a lot of willpower. But I knew that my customers depended on me. There were other things that I had to bear in mind. When it rained or snowed, I had to cover the newspapers so people didn't have to struggle with wet pages. I had to hold my tongue even if they didn't pay me on time.

My paper route taught me that the customer is the most important person in America. No matter how big you are, you have a customer. I also learned that America was truly the land of opportunity. Not only because there were jobs available but because a hardworking person could hope to rise to the top in every field. Almost everyone believed that the best person would get ahead (except, that is, some of my black classmates who lived on Twenty-fourth Street). Americans were positive and optimistic. They did not think, as we did in India, that you had to snatch something from your neighbor in order to succeed. Both could get ahead, for there was enough to go around. The consistently high growth of the economy since the end of the war had reinforced this belief. Americans were thus less "political." In contrast, middle-class Indians at this time had to put up with enormous scarcities of public and private goods; they were forced to cultivate "contacts" and "influence" for their most basic needs. They had to become "political," for either my neighbor's son or mine would get into a good school—there were not enough desks for both.

In my school in Washington I was surprised that we had to attend a class called "shop." The classroom was filled with lathes, tools, and machines, and we learned to work with our hands. We learned to repair a window, make a table, or unclog a sink. At the end of the year, we had lost our fear of technology. We had understood Bronowski's dictum that the world is understood through the hand, not the mind—the hand is the cutting edge of the mind. It explains why many Americans are "tinkerers." This is a powerful idea for India, where we have traditionally had contempt for manual labor because of our caste system.

Three years later, my family returned to India, as the river dispute was settled peacefully across the table. The successful outcome was in part due to the farsightedness of the World Bank and its major donors, who agreed to finance irrigation development in both countries. It was a rare experience for the two hostile countries to resolve a conflict without a war. Since I was in my final year in school at the time, my parents agreed to let me stay behind. Just as I was getting ready to go back home six months later, I heard to my happy surprise that I had won a scholarship to Harvard University. So I stayed on.

My most vivid memories of Harvard are of encounters with ideas rather than persons. Over time the memory of persons has grown paler, whereas the ideas have grown and become richer. One of the first ideas I encountered at Harvard was that the "nation" was a relatively new concept in human history, although countries had existed for a long time. The United States, I began to realize, was the first modern nation, the country where the notion of modernity had originated. For the first time, a people had consciously decided to become a nation. The French, during their great revolution, followed the American example. However, they had to deal with a past. So did every other country that decided to become a nation in the past two hundred years. The Americans did not have a past. But Americans were also unique because they lived only for the future. We in India got the American idea of founding a nation via England; but our inspiration was American. This may sound odd to many Indians who contemptuously dismiss America as the land of Coke and McDonald's. Indian seekers of Hindutva and swadeshi should pause and reflect that their search for nationality is as American in its intellectual origins as the dreaded Kentucky Fried Chicken.

The more I lived in America, the more I learned about India. Unlike Americans, our project of nationhood, I realized, has to deal with the difficult terrain of our "golden past." It is particularly exhausting because we do not have a homogeneous history. It is a diverse past of many religions, many regions and languages, and many peoples. The Americans solved their problem of diversity by throwing their numerous immigrant communities into the "melting pot." Their ethnic immigrant minorities did not form separatist movements; they eagerly embraced the English language and the American way of life in order to get ahead in the land of opportunity. In India, we have historically dealt with our problem of diversity through the caste system. Each new minority became a subcaste. This solution worked well except when it came to the Islamic immigrants, who were the product of a proud universal religion and were unwilling to be assimilated as a subcaste.

If America is a melting pot, India is a mosaic. A good mosaic has a unity of style, and India's civilization and its way of life has a stylistic unity. Modern India is a product of Hindu tradition, the religion of Islam, and Western civilization. The search for a modern Indian nation has been the overwhelming obsession of the educated Indian for more than a hundred years. And it continues to this day. The first seekers were liberal products of Macaulay's education policy, just as the modern Japanese were products of the Meiji education policy. They critiqued the past; they helped reform society (both Hindu and Muslim); they gave birth to the political movement for independence, and they brought about a national consciousness and ushered in an optimistic, modern India.

Soon after arriving at Harvard, I was caught up in another sort of optimism. It had to do with the future of the poor countries, and for a change even the usually gloomy economists were hopeful. They had begun to think that the poor nations could rise out of poverty—and quickly at that. There was even a new and cheerful course in college called Development Economics which tried to capture their hopes. Paul Rosenstein-Rodan and Ragnar Nurkse were among the gurus of this new discipline. Rosenstein-Rodan diagnosed the problem of poverty as a failure of investment. When businessmen failed to invest, he argued, it was clearly the state's job to do so, and he advocated a massive plan of investment by the government to achieve what he called "balanced growth." Albert Hirschman, on the other hand, argued that it was better for the state to offer incentives to businessmen to invest rather than do so directly. He had acquired rich, hands-on experience of development in Latin America, and he was reluctant to let the government get into business. Limited protection, such as higher tariffs and cheaper credit, were the sort of incentives he had in mind to induce businessmen to invest.

What caught everyone's fancy in those days, however, was the well-known Harrod-Domar model, which regarded the problem as one of raising the savings in society and investing them wisely. The model was simple and elegant: growth was a function of the savings ratio divided by the marginal capital-output ratio. Thus, a poor country could accelerate its development if it could raise its savings by means of taxes or foreign aid—no one thought of foreign investment in those anticolonial days—and invest them in such a way that it got the most production out of its savings. India was the favorite laboratory among economists because it seemed to be following the prescription of Rosenstein-Rodan and Harrod-Domar. Intellectual opinion throughout the academic world held that the state could raise domestic savings and invest them in public-sector companies to accelerate economic growth and achieve what everyone called the "takeoff." Walt Rostow had recently introduced this expression in a book called *The Stages of Economic Growth*. It was the point when domestic savings reached a self-sustaining level. The "takeoff" remained a fashionable buzzword throughout my college days.

In India, I later realized, we primarily focused on the numerator, that is, how to raise savings, thinking it to be the essential problem. We ignored the denominator—capital productivity—and it turned out to be our Achilles' heel. Indian policy makers naïvely assumed that once the government made the investments, the returns from the capital would come automatically. Their innocent faith in state companies turned out to be altogether misplaced, for the output from the capital invested in the public sector was unacceptably low. There were many reasons for this, the chief ones being the lack of training, autonomy, and accountability of the senior managers in the public enterprises. It was a management failure. A little more realism and a lot more humility among our leaders might have helped in those early days. They could have instilled a stronger bias for profit and efficiency and this would have made all the difference.

Ragnar Nurkse suggested that there was "disguised unemployment" in the countryside, which represented "hidden resources" of surplus labor waiting to be tapped for investment projects. Albert Hirschman added that as the economy gained momentum, latent entrepreneurship would emerge and technological breakthroughs would occur in the marketplace, representing a different sort of hidden resource. C. N. Vakil and P. R. Brahmanand in India, partially inspired by Ragnar Nurkse's "disguised unemployment," formulated their "wage goods" model of development, which Indian policymakers tragically ignored.

Most development economists at the time had an implicit faith in the ability of economic growth to ameliorate poverty. Growth would provide jobs, raise incomes, and "pull up" the people from poverty, said Jagdish Bhagwati in *The Economics of Underdeveloped Countries*. Despite their optimism, it is surprising that the economists were pessimistic

about the ability of poor countries to export. Nurkse argued that the era
of export-led growth was over and trade could not be an "engine of
growth." Raúl Prebisch, the influential economist in Latin America,
insisted on import substitution because the terms of trade did not favor
poor (Latin American) countries. The number of Indians who were
taken in by Prebisch's "dependency theory" amazed me. This unfortunate proposition of the Argentine economist, which swept the Third
World in the 1960s, argued that the poor countries were permanently
imprisoned in a state of dependency to the rich countries because of
unequal terms of trade. The price of the manufactured goods of the
rich countries would continuously rise, Prebisch argued, while the
prices of the agricultural commodities would continuously go down.
Thus, there was no hope for the Third World. With the rise of the East
Asian countries, the world rightly discarded Mr. Prebisch's second-rate
theory.

There was a mild, noncombative student of economics in Cambridge, England, named Manmohan Singh, who argued for greater
openness in trade and for a less controlled economy. He wrestled against
Nurkse, saying that even "the initiation of the process of balanced
growth" in Nurkse's closed economy would entail an increase in import
requirements which would have to be paid for by exports. He went on
to rebut the prevailing pessimistic view about the poor countries' export
prospects by means of detailed empirical data. He showed that India's
"stagnation of export earnings was partly a consequence of faulty economic policies," and not because of "dependency theory." In the intellectual climate of the early 1960s, this low-key plea for reorienting the
underdeveloped economies towards exports was lost as an aberration.
Japan was the only example at the time of consistent rapid growth
through exports among developing economies. Experts said that it too
had practiced import substitution for a long time, and that too with
extensive government intervention.

Thirty years later, the same mild-mannered economist got a chance
to practice what he had preached. In 1991, Manmohan Singh found
himself finance minister of India, where he acquitted himself brilliantly,
using his low-key approach to his advantage, and ushered in the far-
reaching economic reforms.

The Far East countries proved the tribe of development economists of the 1950s and 1960s wrong. Beginning with Japan, and followed by the four dragons—Korea, Taiwan, Hong Kong, and Singapore—East Asia embarked on a strategy of penetrating world markets with the export of low-cost manufactures, and they were gloriously rewarded by the enormous expansion in world trade in the fifties and sixties. Brazil too seized this opportunity and prospered in the process. However, the rest of the Third World missed the bus. The economists, it seems, turned out to be hopelessly optimistic about the ability of poor countries to transform their economies through investment in import-substituting manufactures and overly pessimistic about their ability to export.

The economists also made the great blunder of believing that the state could become an entrepreneur. India and much of the Third World created state-owned companies which turned out to be hopelessly inefficient. These companies did not provide adequate returns and they did not add to the stock of domestic savings. Instead, they began to lose huge amounts of cash and became a drag on the economy. Import substitution led local businessmen to reinvent the wheel, resulting in the manufacture of poor-quality, high-cost goods without any reference to comparative advantage. At the same time, severe controls were placed on the private sector in many Third World countries. The desire for balanced growth and the need to ration scarce foreign exchange motivated the governments. However, this vastly reduced competition. Ironically, these and other state interventions ended in making the poor countries wasteful of capital. The investments did not pay off, their capital-output ratio was poor, and massive corruption was an unfortunate side effect.

In the end, the hope of rapid economic growth did not materialize. True, economic growth rates were better than they had been before the Second World War. After the war, the developing countries did grow— on average around 4 percent per annum—when they had been virtually stagnant in the first half of the century. This rate was also better than the 1 to 2 percent growth of the Western countries in the nineteenth century, at a comparable period of their industrial revolution. But the 4 percent growth was neutralized by population growth of 2.5 to 3.5 percent, leaving around 1 percent as real growth. This certainly was lower than what everybody dreamed of, and it was much lower than that of the Far East economies, which grew in excess of 5 to 6 percent (net of population growth) in the 1970s and 1980s.

The experience of Japan and the Far East countries turned out to be far more hopeful. They showed to the world not only that they could grow rapidly but also that they could ameliorate poverty at the same time. Their secret lay partly in their investments in education and health, which helped to create the initial conditions of greater equality as they undertook rapid industrialization. They understood that primary education (especially of girls) and primary health care do more for the poor, not only because they put a brake on population growth but because they place them in a better position to take advantage of the job opportunities that come with economic growth. Thus, prosperity is better spread across the population. Amartya Sen has propagated this idea of investing in human development with a missionary zeal; it may have won him a Nobel Prize, but it has not spurred the Indian state to act. The neglect of primary education remains our single biggest failure.

Like most of my classmates at Harvard, I was an unrepentant liberal. In the 1960s, liberals favored government intervention to fix market failures, create jobs, control prices, and create a welfare state. My liberal classmates were enthusiastic supporters of FDR's New Deal and Kennedy's vision of a compassionate society, which Lyndon Johnson took over after Kennedy's assassination. In Europe, liberals of our persuasion were socialists or social democrats. Liberals were left of center in America, but in the India of the sixties, we were smack in the center. We embraced wholeheartedly Nehru's vision of state-led industrialization, redistributive taxation, controls on the private sector—all this eventually to wipe out poverty.

One of our liberal heroes at Harvard was John Kenneth Galbraith. Galbraith was lean and tall, witty and provocative, but he was also dogmatic and arrogant. He was already a celebrity, having captured America's imagination with *The Affluent Society,* but I found him a bad teacher. He used to mumble unintelligibly in class and did not care for his students. Serious economists ignored him, but his ideas held sway over my classmates and the liberals of our generation.

Galbraith used to dwell on the failings of market capitalism. Competition was at best imperfect in the real marketplace, he would say, and consumer sovereignty was a myth. Large companies set prices, contributed to cost-push inflation, and manipulated consumers through advertising to buy needless products. Giant corporations, with an army of skilled experts, exercised vast economic and social power, not in the community's interest but in their own. This made contemporary Western society rich in private goods but poor in public goods such as mass transport, public health, and low-cost housing and good schools for ordinary people. The remedy for these ills was an enlightened and interventionist government whose duty it was to fill the gap in public goods, thus ensuring a more balanced society that served the common good rather than the corporations and the rich.

John F. Kennedy appointed Galbraith ambassador to India after he became President, and I went to meet him in the summer of my sophomore year when I came home to Delhi on holiday. He generously invited me to lunch, along with several other young people. I was awed by the grand dining room of the opulent American embassy, recently designed by Edward Durrell Stone. I had expected Galbraith to be happy at the prospect of living in a country that was practicing his ideas. Instead, I found him gloomy and ambivalent. During lunch, he expressed serious concerns about excessive state controls on the Indian economy. He confessed that it might be better to have more private enterprise in a country at India's stage of development. His own ideas, he felt, were more suited to an affluent society. Galbraith's grim remarks that afternoon reinforced my growing doubts about Nehru's socialism, and the innocent lunch became a turning point in my thinking.

The celebrated issue of "planning versus the market" had been intensely debated around the world in the 1930s and 1940s. The worldwide consensus that emerged in the next decade supported enthusiastically India's experiment in planning. The most famous debate had taken place, curiously enough, among a bunch of Austrian economists. Those supporting planning, Oskar Lange and Abba Lerner, had pointed to the failures of the market and its inability to ensure perfect competition. They had argued that by planning, and with the use of computers, they could ensure that the right products were produced in the correct quantities and thus stimulate perfect competition. Their critics, Friedrich Hayek and Ludwig von Mises, however, had retorted that the most powerful computers of the planners would never be able to acquire the billions of pieces of information on constantly changing consumer needs and preferences and marry them to the resources of society, the production processes, and the technologies. Even if they got the information, they would not be able to react to it as speedily as the market. Moreover, in a planned economy, the factory managers would not have the incentive to provide truthful and rapid information to the planners. Since they were evaluated based on how much they produced, they would try to corner raw material to ensure that their production targets were met (to the detriment of other factories). As such, the planned economy would have enormous waste and inefficiency compared to the market. Human self-interest in the market economy eliminated this inefficiency.

The development of the poor countries is an emotional subject that inspires much breast-beating. In the end, the medley of theories of the development economists turned out to be no different. They were disappointing. Together they constituted what Deepak Lall calls "dirigiste dogma," seeking to justify massive government intervention and supplant the workings of a market economy. They concluded, among other things, that classical nineteenth-century liberal free trade was not valid for the developing countries; they argued that normal market-based growth was not appropriate for alleviating poverty but needed governments to redistribute assets through price and wage controls. Their many theoretical fads—"foreign exchange bottlenecks," "unequal exchange," "basic needs," "dual economies," "inexorably declining terms of trade"—were not harmless curiosities. Tragically, they were translated into policies, with poverty-stricken peoples as guinea pigs. And so we discovered that "bureaucratic failures" are far more common and worse than "market failures."

Like all undergraduates, I read John Locke, Hobbes, and Mill in abundance, and I found my interest turning to philosophy. After reading Hume's *Treatise of Human Nature,* I switched my major to philosophy at the end of my sophomore year. I was quickly rewarded with the elegant lectures of Quine on logic. More than the famous names, I was drawn to a shy and lanky professor named John Rawls who had recently arrived at Harvard. It was rumored that he had won tenure on the basis of a single, five-page paper called "Justice as Fairness," having been preferred by the selection committee over many famous and established philosophers whose bibliographies ran into dozens of pages of books and scholarly articles. Rawls went on to become the most influential moral and political philosopher of his generation. His five-page paper became a famous book called *A Theory of Justice* which transformed the debate on equality, liberty, rights, and the role of the state. His selection was as much a tribute to Harvard's ability to take risks with unknown but potential greats. Rawls also changed my way of looking at the world. His lectures made me question my beliefs, especially my uncritical acceptance of Marx's notion of equality.

Rawls walked into class one day and asked us to play a thought game. We were to imagine that we were living in a hypothetical state of equality. We were to assume that we were all free, rational, self-interested people who were ignorant of our place in society—of our class, income, and status. Nor did any of us know our fortunes in nature's distribution of assets and abilities, such as intelligence, strength, and beauty. Lastly, we were to assume that none of us suffered from an excess of envy. With this "veil of ignorance" we were asked to agree to a set of principles of justice with which we would build and appraise our institutions. Rawls contended that we would agree to two principles: first, that each person should have the maximum liberty compatible with equal liberty for others; second, we would opt for equality unless the inequality helped everyone, including the worst-off, and everyone had a chance to reach to the top.

Having agreed to the two principles in the hypothetical circumstances of a social contract, one practical consequence of his second principle is that in practical terms, as a worker I would consent to the president of the company earning more than me as long it motivated the president to earn more profit for the company and I got a bigger bonus or a higher salary as a result. The greater benefits earned by a few could be justified, I realized, if the inequality improved the situation of the worst-off. Although Rawls's starting point was egalitarian, he had found a moral basis for inequality. His great insight was that free individuals would voluntarily consent to inequality in certain circumstances. This was a far more morally satisfying basis for inequality than Bentham's or Mill's utilitarian appeal to improving the common good or on grounds of efficiency (the company's performance). A moral justification based on consent seemed to me superior to one based on "the greatest good for the greatest number." In an oversimplified sense, Rawls had strengthened the foundations of a market-based liberal democracy, which strives for an equality of opportunity but not an equality of result. In my eyes, Rawls had diminished the attractiveness of socialism.

Most of us had become socialists because we were repelled by the inequality of capitalism. Having said that, it is important to remember that Rawls's model only works in a genuinely open society. In the real world no society (not even America) is completely open. The key is to try to ensure that everyone has an equal start in life and can hope to rise to the top. Thus, an "open" primary school system is essential. Amartya Sen and others have also pointed out that equality is good in itself; there are other reasons to have it, such as individual self-esteem.

Despite my concerns with distributive justice, I have come to believe that alleviating poverty is more important than achieving equality. Improving the income distribution in a society should be an instrument for enabling the poorest and the most unfortunate to rise above the poverty line rather than achieving equality per se. My experience in an American high school has taught me that a decent public (nonprivate) education system, open to the poorest child, will do more for equality in society than all of Nehru's socialist programs. Capitalist America has done more in a practical sense for equality—by providing equality of opportunity—than many socialist or even social democratic Western countries. Even in an elitist place like Harvard, half my classmates were on scholarship and came from ordinary backgrounds. Surveys show that half the presidents of the largest American corporations come from modest backgrounds. Every family in America, from the richest to the poorest, believes that it belongs to the middle class (with the notable exception of African Americans living in the inner city). Inequality has grown in America over the past twenty years, but opportunities have not diminished.

I have found it frustrating that Indian intellectuals and political leaders are so anti-American that they are unable to perceive these qualities of America. The American education system has many flaws, but it is far fairer (and more creative) than most systems. Every time I suggested looking at the American education system, Indian intellectuals and policy makers dismissed me. This was also one of Nehru's blind spots.

Although Americans think of themselves as individualistic, they have historically had a rich civil society. One of the best books I read at Harvard was Alexis de Tocqueville's *Democracy in America,* which opened my eyes to the vibrancy of community life in America. I had also experienced it as a schoolchild in Washington, when my parents had to attend the Parent-Teacher Association meetings. At these PTA meetings, my parents got to know their neighbors. They talked about how to improve the school. Their talk soon turned to garbage on the streets, the local bus service, the condition of the roads, and other community concerns. I witnessed local democracy in action. Social scientists refer to this as "social capital." Tocqueville, a Frenchman who visited America in the 1830s, wrote that Americans were "joiners": they joined all manner of local organizations (unlike the Europeans), and this was the strength of American democracy. They have a dense network of voluntary organizations: churches, professional groups, charitable institutions, neighborhood clubs, and so on. (However, this rich associational life has weakened in the last generation as family life has deteriorated.)

In contrast, the social life of Indians revolves around the family or caste. It does not encompass the whole community. Perhaps this is why our streets are dirty when our homes are spotlessly clean. Mahatma Gandhi understood this, and he tried to instill civic sense in his fellow citizens, but he failed. We finally amended our Constitution in the 1990s to usher in local democracy. Although state governments have been reluctant to give up power, panchayati raj has increasingly become real. ("Panchayat" refers to the ancient village assembly of five wise persons, and the name has been revived to designate the elected village council.) We now have periodic elections in villages, and today we have three million local legislators in our half a million villages (and one million are women). Madhya Pradesh has among the most vibrant ones, where Digvijay Singh, the chief minister, has pushed responsibility of schools down to the local panchayats in the manner of the American school district.

The great thing about an American liberal education is that it allows an undergraduate the freedom to explore many subjects. In my junior year I was drawn to Harvard's well-known Sanskrit department, which had produced the great Harvard Oriental Series, consisting of more than a hundred volumes of Sanskrit scholarship and translations by the world's leading scholars, similar to F. Max Müller's *Sacred Books of the East*. Filled with reverence and awe, I was examining a leather-bound set on the shelves of Widener Library when I met Daniel Ingalls, the legendary professor of Sanskrit. He was reputed to be aloof and crotchety, but he agreed to let me join his elementary Sanskrit class, warning me that it was not going to be easy. We raced through Panini's elegant grammar rules in the first six weeks, using Perry's primer and Whitney's grammar, and soon began reading selections from the *Kathasaritsagara,* the *Hitopadesha,* the Rig Veda, and the *Manavadharmashastra* from Lanman's reader. We were half a dozen students, and the class used to meet in Ingalls's Widener office, where he presided like an old schoolmaster. He used to scold and insult us each time we broke one of Panini's rules. When we were good, he would reward us by reading from his forthcoming translation of Vidyakara's love poetry. As he read, his mood would change. He would start to smile, and occasionally his eyes shone with a lover's guile.

Ingalls was right. It turned out to be a difficult course, and I discovered that I could either read Sanskrit or do all my other courses. Reluctantly, I dropped Sanskrit after the winter semester. Ingalls was angry, saying that he had wasted three months on me. He tried to paint a romantic picture of the life of a Sanskrit scholar, but I was unmoved. My parents, on the other hand, were relieved that I had given up my love affair with Sanskrit. The idea of their son going all the way to Harvard to study Sanskrit was too bizarre.

If Ingalls fed my illusions about India, Henry Kissinger pricked them. I had replaced Sanskrit with Government 180, which was the basic course in international relations. Henry Kissinger was not as famous at the time, but he was already a provocative name and his lectures attracted a hundred undergraduates. Kissinger taught us that the pursuit of national self-interest was the only legitimate course for a nation in its relations with other countries. When all nations pursued their interest it resulted in predictability, balance of power, and eventually peace in the world. There was no room for morality or altruism. Metternich was Kissinger's hero and model, and because of him and Talleyrand, Castlereagh, and Czar Alexander at the Congress of Vienna in 1815, the nineteenth century had been a "century of peace." The rules of the game were governed by realpolitik and political leaders played by these rules. Kissinger taught us that diplomacy was best conducted in secret, because media and parliaments in democracies tended to confuse the issue with moral considerations, and this led nations to take irrational positions that did not necessarily further their own interests.

For innocent and idealistic American undergraduates, especially during Kennedy's presidency, this amoral lesson was difficult to stomach, especially as it came from a "wily European." (Kissinger's thick German accent was particularly hard on us, and it emphasized his Europeanness.) To my discomfort, Kissinger used Nehru as an example of how *not* to conduct international affairs. He felt that Nehru injected a dangerous element of morality and idealism in international affairs. Besides, he said, moralizing was not pleasant to behold—no one liked being lectured to—and this was why India was not popular among the practitioners of power, although Nehru was a hero to the postwar world. Nehru was irresponsible, Kissinger said, in not promoting his own country's interest and in leaving India vulnerable. I wasn't sure what he meant. If he meant that India was too trusting of the Chinese, I think he was right. And history would soon prove him correct. If he meant that India's interest lay in aligning itself with America and not remaining nonaligned, that is a debatable issue. Kissinger concluded his lecture by saying that "it is dangerous to put dreamers in power."

Henry Kissinger went on to become secretary of state and to greater glory. He had the rare fortune of being able to practice what he had preached as an academic. But he was not good for India. At the best of times the relationship between the two largest democracies had been prickly, but in the early 1970s it plunged to its depths with Nixon and Kissinger's notorious "tilt" towards Pakistan, which further pushed India into the chilling embrace of the Soviet Union.

As I look back on my four years at college, I am shocked that we were so concerned with the distribution of wealth in those days that we ignored the whole subject of wealth creation. Perhaps it was because the Western economies were in the midst of unprecedented expansion, and everyone assumed that wealth would keep growing. But India's problem was different—to create wealth in the first place. India's intellectuals and policymakers, many of whom had been trained in the West, suffered from the same blind spot. Caught up in the Western fashions, I did not read the great Austrians, Joseph Alois Schumpeter and Friedrich A. Hayek and Ludvig von Mises. Thus, I missed the excitement of the capitalist revolution and the romance of "creative destruction." It was overshadowed by Marx's brilliant critique of capitalism, which I read in plenty. Even Max Weber's *Protestant Ethic and the Spirit of Capitalism* sounded more like a critique than a celebration. Most of my teachers at

Harvard also had an antibusiness bias, which reinforced my own prejudice. As undergraduates in arts and sciences, we looked with contempt
at the Harvard Business School across the Charles River. All of us
wanted to be scholars and dedicate our lives to the dispassionate pursuits
of "truth, beauty, and justice" like Socrates. It is, of course, vastly different today, I realize. Today's undergraduates, both in India and in the
United States, don't seem to suffer from our hang-ups and our idealism.
They have the opposite problem. If the spirit of those times came in the
way of building upon the lessons that I first learned as a thirteen-year-
old boy from my paper route, today's youth sometimes need to be
reminded, I think, that there is a great world out there beyond money.

SEVEN

Capitalism for the Rich,
Socialism for the Poor

Those who have given themselves the most concern about the happiness of people have made their neighbours very miserable.

—ANATOLE FRANCE

While I was studying in America, India had begun to implement with much vigor the ideas and theories of the development economists. I got a first taste of where we were headed when I came home during my summer vacation. I spent several weeks in Ludhiana, in East Punjab, where my grandfather had settled as a refugee. Ludhiana went on to become famous for creating a small-scale industrial revolution in the fifties and the "green revolution" in the sixties. When I visited my grandfather, I found that he would spend the entire morning reading the *Tribune* in his courtyard, and complain to anyone who would listen that Nehru was recklessly wasting the taxpayers' money. He felt that Nehru's state-owned companies were being managed by civil servants, people who had no training in running commercial enterprises. Nor were they asked to make a profit. They were recklessly hiring workers without any thought to performance. He angrily pointed to a front-page news story in which Nehru had resolutely defended their losses in Parliament, saying that their job was not to make a profit but to meet social objectives. "The public sector has become the politician's cow—to be milked forever," he groaned. He was no economist, but he could tell when common sense was defied. His lawyer's sensibilities were also wounded by Nehru's disregard of private property. The government had nationalized a number of industries without adequately compensating the owners.

Grandfather was ahead of his time. All his friends and neighbors thought his views odd, because everyone was hopelessly under the sway of Nehru's ideas. He predicted that the bureaucracy's growth would spread like cancer, lead to corruption, and threaten liberty one day. He did not think that Nehru had his feet on the ground; his talk of social-ism put him off, just as my uncle Sat Pal's Marxism did. Nehru defended himself by saying that he admired the Soviet Union for having trans-formed a backward peasant economy into a world power, but he did not approve of Stalin's methods. His ideas were closer to those of the Fabians and other English intellectuals between the wars, who advocated the rationality of central planning within a parliamentary system that pro-tected civil liberties and democratic rights.

In those early years, there was, in fact, a competing philosophy to Nehru's. It belonged to Mahatma Gandhi. It was a vision of a republic of self-sufficient villages employing indigenous technologies, materials, and talents. Gandhi's guiding principle was to achieve self-reliance, in the village for the basic needs of the people—food, clothing, and shel-ter. Such an approach, Gandhi felt, would avoid mass migration to the cities, with the attendant problems of unemployment, homelessness, and crime. Nehru thought Gandhi's vision hopelessly idealistic, but he agreed with him about rural development, and he created a community development program in the 1950s, funded partly with American aid. Begun with great fanfare and enthusiasm, the program soon became hopelessly bureaucratized. Like many other well-intentioned programs, it failed because Nehru did not have the patience, the managerial skills, or the passion to implement it. Nor was it Gandhian in spirit—it was "top down" rather than "bottom up."

Surprisingly, Indian businessmen also supported Nehru's ideas on central planning. They were seduced by the thought that piecemeal growth based entirely on market forces might not bring about rapid development. They too believed that free trade and the laissez-faire policies of the British Raj had been at the root of the country's economic problems. Moreover, they had benefited from the Raj's interventions in the interwar years. They had gained enormously from high tariffs on imported goods since the 1920s, and it was natural that they should want them to continue. However, they resented Britain's neglect of India's power, roads, and other infrastructure.

In 1944, India's leading capitalists came together in Bombay and crystallized their vision for a modern, independent India. They included the giants of Indian business—J. R. D. Tata, G. D. Birla, Lala Shri Ram, Kasturbhai Lalbhai, Purshotamdas Thakurdas, A. D. Shroff, and John Mathai—and they produced what came to be known famously as the "Bombay Plan." The Bombay Plan argued for rapid and self-reliant industrialization. Although the industrialists recognized the need for foreign capital and technology, they wanted it to be under the strict control of the state. They preferred foreign debt or loans rather than equity or entrepreneurial investment, and they wanted foreign ownership to be prohibited in essential areas like banking, insurance, power, and aviation. Where it existed, they wanted it nationalized. Ominously, they were willing to accept "important limitations on the freedom of private enterprise," and they agreed that "rights attached to private property would naturally be circumscribed." Even more disastrous was their acceptance of a vast area of state control—in fixing prices, limiting dividends, controlling foreign trade and foreign exchange, in licensing production, and in allocating capital goods and distributing consumer goods. Without realizing it, the Indian capitalists had dug their graves. Indian businessmen must thus share the blame for misreading history.

During the last decade of the Raj, the government's involvement in running the economy had grown. With the coming of the Second World War, rationing, price controls, and other bureaucratic interventions had become necessary. They now provided the politicians and bureaucrats with ready instruments to control the economy of independent India. While in other countries these controls were gradually dismantled by the end of the war, they continued in India.

India was not unique in wanting to develop and industrialize rapidly through the agency of the state. All the countries that became independent after the war shared this ambition. They followed India's example, although India was unusual in wanting to do so by democratic means.

Who was responsible for taking India on the path of democratic social-ism? Nehru certainly, but also the extraordinary Bengali Brahmin, Pras-anta Chandra Mahalanobis, who was the central intellectual figure of the 1950s. He symbolized a distinctive feature of the Nehru era: to bring the rationality of technocrats, economists, and scientists to bear on deci-sion making. Professor Mahalanobis was the éminence grise at the Plan-ning Commission, which was situated only three kilometers from our house in Kaka Nagar. Throughout the 1950s the Planning Commission enjoyed unparalleled prestige. Mahalanobis was a man of science, but he was also a philosopher, literary critic, and Sanskrit scholar. He had stud-ied mathematics and physics at Cambridge, and had founded the Indian Statistical Institute in two rooms at the Presidency College, Calcutta, from where he published *Sankhya,* a journal on statistics, which later became the influential house journal of Indian planners. Not only was he a close associate of Rabindranath Tagore, he also knew more about the canon of the poet's early writings than the poet himself could recall.

It was Mahalanobis's deep commitment to rationality that attracted him to Nehru. He believed that the characteristic mark of the modern age was a scientific temper, which "subjects natural phenomena to ratio-nal explanation and human control, and provides the great breakthrough of the human intellect." Mahalanobis wanted India and other backward countries to place men and women of scientific outlook in positions of responsibility. He regretted that India's caste-based society did not encourage a spirit of rational inquiry. We used to have a great tradition of respect for the Brahmin, as a teacher, he used to say, but now we needed to build a tradition of appreciation for science and scientists. The idea that science could provide the answer to raising India's economy appealed to Nehru. Mahalanobis suggested to Nehru that statistics could become a powerful tool for economic planning. Although he was not an economist, Mahalanobis quickly mastered the new subject and began collecting statistical data on national income in 1949. Such was the power of his mind and personality that he soon became the central focus of policy making and began to dominate the planning process.

Mahalanobis had a profound effect on Nehru's thinking, although he held no official position. His title, "Honorary Statistical Advisor to the Government of India," certainly did not reflect the extent of his influ-ence. His biggest contribution was the draft plan frame for the Second

Five Year Plan, possibly the single most important document in the 1950s and "possibly one of the most important documents in the world at that time." In it he put into practice the socialist ideas of investment in a large public sector (at the expense of the private sector), with emphasis on heavy industry (at the expense of consumer goods) and a focus on import substitution (at the expense of export promotion), besides other follies which were inspired by the USSR and China. No wonder he became the darling of the left.

The plan frame proposed "a two-pronged attack on the problem of breaking through India's static economy: the creation of a large machine-building industry as a basis for the expansion of secondary industries; and decentralised cottage industries to create jobs for India's army of unemployed." The latter was expected to produce consumer goods at a low cost and create employment with minimum social dislocation. "Once a machine-building industry was established the hand-loom would be replaced by the power-loom, and low cost cottage industry would be able to compete with factory manufactured goods."

The Gandhians loved the protection for cottage industry. Socialists welcomed the emphasis on a heavy industry and the expansion of the public sector. However, the business community was dismayed by the drift of the country towards socialism and Soviet-style planning. Neither did civil servants warm up to the "socialist tendencies" in the document, although secretly they must have been pleased, as they would be in charge. The finance minister, C. D. Deshmukh, was distressed that there was insufficient discussion of the plan frame's ideology in the cabinet. But the thinking elite was electrified by the document. Intellectuals abroad were euphoric. J. B. S. Haldane, the distinguished albeit committed scientist, expressed the sense of excitement among intellectuals overseas:

> *Even if one is pessimistic, and allows a 15 per cent chance of failure through interference by the United States (via Pakistan or otherwise), a 10 per cent chance of interference by the Soviet Union and China, a 20 per cent chance of interference by civil service traditionalism and political obstruction, and a 5 per cent chance of interference by Hindu traditionalism, that leaves a 50 per cent chance for a success which will alter the whole history of the world for the better.*

Taya Zinkin, a British journalist, pointed out that there was a socialist revolution by consent under way in India that would make "communism look both old-fashioned and barbarian by comparison. It was a revolution without class wars, heretics or victims, and its weapons were a series of tedious legal acts." Nehru was anxious to explain his policies to the masses and give them a sense of participation in economic and social development. He made a long string of speeches in the winter of 1954 to educate the people about his vision of a socialist society. This culminated in his landmark resolution at the Avadi session of the Congress Party in January 1955, which committed the nation to "the establishment of a socialist pattern of society where the principal means of production are under social ownership or control." It gave legitimacy to Nehru's intellectual joint venture between Keynesian macroeconomics, Stalinist public investment policy, and Gandhian rural development. Thus, it was in the spirit of high adventure and profound confidence following Independence that India embarked upon the program of planned development to lift the economy out of centuries of backwardness.

Mahalanobis believed that steel was central to the revolution. "The production of steel probably has the highest correlation with national income in different countries," he argued, and "we shall . . . use the steel to produce more machinery to produce more steel and tools; and also to produce machinery to make more consumer goods." The logic was clear. But to get started India needed a heavy dose of investment and technology from abroad. India had only two relatively small steel plants at the time, making barely a million metric tons a year. Given his socialist bias, Mahalanobis ruled out private foreign investment; nor did Indian entrepreneurs have the massive funds, he felt, to fulfill the bold vision. The government thus reached out to foreign governments who could build the plants based on foreign aid. The West Germans agreed to give a loan to build a plant with the famous Krupp technology in Rourkela in Orissa. The British offered a loan to their equipment makers to set up a plant at Durgapur in West Bengal. The Soviet Union came forth with a plant at Bhilai in Madhya Pradesh. Together these three plants added only 2.3 million metric tons, and India still imported a million metric tons a year at a cost of $200 million in the early sixties. The Indian government now approached the United States for the fourth plant at Bokaro. John F. Kennedy, the President, was a friend of

India and he readily agreed to champion the project. It was to be the biggest plant, and it had the biggest price tag—roughly a billion dollars, to make four million metric tons of steel. Despite a friendly President and supportive ambassador (Galbraith), the plant was spiked in the U.S. Congress. That day I was among the vast number of Indians who were deeply disappointed with America. India was again pushed into the Soviet embrace to finance the plant, and Russia had to finally set it up.

In the 1950s, there was an alternative vision to that of Mahalanobis. It belonged to the Bombay economists C. N. Vakil and P. R. Brahmanand. It was neither as glamorous nor as technically rigorous as Mahalanobis's, but it was more suited to the underdeveloped Indian economy. Its starting point was that India lacked capital but had plenty of people. There was huge disguised unemployment in the countryside. The thing to do was to put these people into productive work at the lowest capital cost. The Bombay economists suggested that we employ the surplus labor to produce "wage goods," or simple consumer products—clothes, toys, shoes, snacks, radios, and bicycles. These low-capital, low-risk businesses would attract loads of entrepreneurs, for they would yield quick output and rapid returns on investment. Labor would produce the goods it would eventually consume with the wages it earned in producing the goods. They were called "wage goods" because the wage earner would create the demand for the goods that he produced. The idea was similar, in a sense, to that of Henry Ford, who paid his workers generously so that they could afford to buy his cheap, mass-produced cars. This Bombay strategy was exactly opposite to Mahalanobis's vision of huge state-controlled, capital-intensive steel plants, employing few people and delivering low returns over long gestation periods. The "wage goods" strategy would have pushed investments into agriculture, rural infrastructure, agro-industry, and simple consumer manufactures for both the home and export markets. It would have meant postponing the ambitious projects in capital and heavy industry. We would have imported the capital goods in the near term, and the foreign exchange for their import would have been earned from the export of simple consumer manufactures—the sort of products that Japan and the Asian tigers started with. The result would have been high economic growth, high employment, rising exports, and prosperity.

Bombay is known for Alphonso mangoes, its deep natural harbor which is ideal for shipping, and its famous stock exchange. But not for its economists. Economists largely grow in Calcutta, and when they are ripe they are sent off to Delhi. It is no wonder that Bombay's vision was ignored. It was too practical and sensible—much like Bombay's citizens. It is a great tragedy of history that no one paid attention to Vakil and Brahamand's strategy, certainly no one in the government. The Indian intelligentsia was mesmerized by the apparent success of the USSR. It wanted big steel plants and not small factories which made clothes, shoes, toys, and bicycles—the sort of things that the masses could use. In those days, anyone in India who advocated greater investment in agriculture was branded an American agent. When American foreign aid experts had recommended that we invest in agriculture instead of steel, Indians had seen it as a sinister plot to keep India backward.

Mahalanobis and Nehru made two other strategic errors, which we discovered only later. They assumed that there were no opportunities for rapid export expansion. Some years later we would find out that tiny Hong Kong earned more from its exports than the whole of India. They also despised competition. Painfully, we would learn that there could be no improvement in productivity without it. Nehru thought competition wasteful; in a letter to his daughter, Indira, he said that individual planning without coordination results in squandered resources. Private enterprises, he wrote, attempted "to overreach or get the better of other individual concerns. Naturally, this results in the very opposite of planning; it means excess and want, side by side." From this failure sprang many weaknesses—apart from low productivity, lack of innovation, poor-quality products, low investment in human resources. Nehru failed to appreciate that robust competition is the best school in which industry learns to succeed. It creates demanding customers who continually push companies to innovate and improve product quality. Competition also forces companies to invest in employees and upgrade their skills. Eventually a nation's prosperity grows out of its industries' ability to gain competitive advantage in the global market, based on technological superiority and the skills of its workforce. India's failure on the world economic stage is in great part due to the lack of competition in its domestic marketplace. As a result of this and other errors, India would begin to fall behind its more dynamic rivals and slowly lose its reputation.

It was India's interventionist licensing, however, that turned out to be an economic cancer. Mahalanobis's thinking on the Second Plan was logically extended to the damaging Industrial Policy Resolution in 1956, which reserved seventeen industries exclusively for the public sector. The reserved industries included iron and steel, mining, machine tool manufacture, and heavy electrical plants. Although it left the door open for private entry into the reserved list, in practice the door was closed for thirty-five years, and the reservation became sacrosanct until the reforms of 1991. The logic behind "reservations" was that these were industries of "basic strategic importance" and "required investment on a scale which only the state could provide." It was flawed logic. In the 1950s, perhaps an industrialist did not have the resources, but in the 1960s many did (when G. D. Birla, for instance, was refused a license to set up a steel plant).

It never did make sense to close an industry to the private sector—it was tantamount to discouraging entrepreneurship and competition. It was prejudice, pure and simple, against the market. The successful countries of the Far East, in contrast, practiced the opposite policy beginning in the 1960s. In Korea, for example, the government offered cheap credit to private business when it did not have the resources necessary to set up strategic and basic industries. The Japanese miracle was based on the brutal competition in its marketplace. The Tatas made 119 proposals between 1960 and 1989 to start new businesses or expand old ones, and all of them ended in the wastebaskets of the bureaucrats. Aditya Birla, the young and dynamic inheritor of the Birla empire, who had trained at MIT, was so disillusioned with Indian policy that he decided to expand Birla enterprises outside India, and eventually set up dynamic companies in Thailand, Malaysia, Indonesia, and the Philippines, away from the hostile atmosphere of his home.

Even more damaging than placing the public sector at "the commanding heights of the economy" were the creeping controls on the private sector. The most bizarre and damaging was the licensing system. It began with the Industries (Development and Regulation) Act of 1951, which required an entrepreneur to get a license to set up a new unit, to expand it, or change the product mix. The purpose of licensing was (a) to create the planned pattern of investment, (b) to counteract monopoly and the concentration of wealth, (c) to maintain regional balance in locating industries, (d) to protect the interests of small-scale producers and encourage the entry of new entrepreneurs, and (e) to encourage optimum scale of plants and advanced technology. All these were good intentions, but the way that the bureaucracy went about administrating the licensing system created a nightmare for the entrepreneur.

An untrained army of underpaid, third-rate engineers at the Directorate General of Technical Development, operating on the basis of inadequate and ill-organized information and without clear-cut criteria, vetted thousands of applications on an ad hoc basis. The low-level functionaries took months in the futile microreview of an application and finally sent it for approval to the administrative ministry. The ministry again lost months reviewing the same data before it sent the application to an interministerial licensing committee of senior bureaucrats, who were equally ignorant of entrepreneurial realities, and who also operated upon ad hoc criteria in the absence of well-ordered priorities. Once it cleared the licensing committee, it was sent to the minister for final approval. After the minister's approval, the investor had to seek approval for the import of machinery from the capital goods licensing committee. If a foreign collaboration was involved, an interministerial foreign agreements committee also had to give its consent. If finance was needed from a state financial institution, the same scrutiny had to be repeated afresh. The result was enormous delays, sometimes lasting years, with staggering opportunities for corruption. By the time the backbreaking process of moving files from office to office was completed, many an entrepreneur had lost heart.

Large business houses set up parallel bureaucracies in Delhi to follow up on their files, organize bribes, and win licenses. Since the system was based on first come, first served, "the bigger houses realized that they could corner a considerable amount of targeted capacity by putting in multiple and early applications for the *same* product. Thus, they could "foreclose capacity," without any intention of implementing the successful licence application." If the entrepreneur did finally get started and made a success of his enterprise, he was again in trouble. It was an offense punishable under the law to manufacture beyond the capacity granted by the license. We became the only country in the noncommunist world where the production of goods sorely needed by the people was punishable by law.

Tragically, the system ended in thwarting competition, entrepreneurship, and growth, without achieving any of its social objectives. It fostered monopolies and encouraged uneconomic-scale plants employing second-rate technology in remote, uncompetitive locations. The endless delay in clearing applications discouraged the entry of efficient and honest entrants and rewarded wily, inefficient producers who could manipulate the system. In many cases the basic entrepreneurial decisions, such as the choice of technology and the size and location of plants, which impacted on costs and prices, were taken away from risk-taking businessmen and were made by bureaucrats who did not have a clue about the basics of running a business. Thus, licensing was an unmitigated disaster. It raised costs, brought delays, arbitrariness, and corruption, and achieved nothing. We killed at birth any hope for an industrial revolution.

The responsibility for instituting the nightmarish controls clearly lies with the bureaucracy. I. G. Patel, the distinguished economist who was closely associated with the government in senior positions, confessed that Nehru's "acceptance of controls came through the influence of civil servants (and economists) who had gone to the same kind of schools and who spoke the same kind of English and with whom, as a result, he came to have a special kind of rapport." There was probably no more distinguished group than the top civil servants Nehru had gathered in economic decision making at the time. There were Rama Rau and H. V. R. Iyengar at the Reserve Bank, H. M. Patel and M. V. Rangachari at the finance ministry, L. K. Jha and K. B. Lall at commerce and industry, Tarlok Singh at the Planning Commission. Like Nehru, they were honest, well-intentioned people.

B. K. Nehru, the Prime Minister's cousin (who also played an important role in economic decision making at the time), admitted in his autobiography that "with the benefit of hindsight it seems totally absurd that a country wanting to develop its industry should prescribe for its establishment conditions which were guaranteed to strangle it." He confessed that there was hardly any experience in the government of how industry was actually run. Prime Minister Nehru merely desired that "the commanding heights of the economy" should be in the public sector. Beyond that, the Prime Minister left it to the civil servants to create a framework to regulate private enterprise. The underlying assumption remained that business was dishonest, and that "to ensure honesty and eliminate profiteering, private business should operate under strict government control."

The one person who could have stopped the growing regulatory monster was the powerful T. T. Krishnamachari (TTK), who had the implicit trust of the Prime Minister. He was a cabinet minister in charge of commerce and industry between 1952 and 1956, of iron and steel in 1955–1956, and then served as finance minister in 1956–58 and 1963–65. He was a businessman who understood how the economy worked. He was afraid neither of Mahalanobis nor of ideology. He was one of the ablest members of the cabinet, and he was impatient to get on with the job. He didn't bother if investment was public or private. He encouraged both. He constantly met private industrialists and goaded them to invest. He helped the Tatas to expand their steel plant and set up their truck-making project. He set up major financial institutions for providing cheap credit and financing to the private sector. He pushed for the speedy erection of the three public-sector steel plants. He chided the Gandhians for wanting to go back to the village. He was critical of the socialists, saying, "greater emphasis on State enterprises [will] merrily lead to a dead end."

TTK worried about the organizational setup of the public-sector enterprises: "The one enterprise which I took over (in the public sector), the Hindustan Steel Ltd, would, I am afraid, if publicly scrutinised, condemn forever the creation of a public sector." Despite the brave words, TTK turned out in the end to be merely a wily politician, and his convictions ran only skin-deep. His power depended on the trust that Nehru reposed in him. Nehru's confidence in him depended on TTK's enthusiastic support of the Prime Minister's socialist policies. Because it was politically correct, TTK cogently defended Mahalanobis's Second Plan in Parliament. He nationalized insurance. He was the author of the Industrial Policy Resolution of 1956, which put industry into a complete straitjacket. He also presented the infamous budget of 1957–58, which added Kaldor's wealth tax, expenditure tax, gift tax, and capital tax, *on top of* an 87.5 income tax rate, and thereby he killed the stock market.

How a bright and able businessman destroyed the future of private industry in India can only be explained by TTK's thirst for power. Instead of resisting controls, he cheerfully added to them, because he thought it would consolidate his popularity with Nehru. The business class, who should have been the first to protest, was too timid. In the years after Independence, people had been hard hit by inflation because of postwar dislocations and the partition of the country. As the prices of food rose, it was natural for the middle class to blame the usurious merchants in the neighborhood, calling them "profiteers and black marketers." Hence, businessmen were defensive.

Neither did the international experts complain. During the 1950s and 1960s, a galaxy of world-renowned economists came to India. Among them were Rosenstein-Rodan, Arnold Harberger, Jan Tinbergen, Ragnar Frisch, Ian Little, Richard Eckaus, Max Millikan, Nicholas Kaldor, Richard Goodwin, Oskar Lange, Brian Redway, Alan Manne, and James Mirlees. Most of them were full of praise for Nehru's bold experiment to combine the social justice of socialism with democracy's freedom.

Criticism against controls finally came from the Swatantra Party in the early 1960s. Led by the respected figure of C. R. Rajagopalachari, the party championed the cause of free enterprise in India. He gave the name "License Raj" to Nehru's socialism. But the party did not survive because Indian businessmen found it easier to get what they individually wanted (licenses, permits) from staying on the right side of the Congress Party. Neither have Indian businessmen been ideologically committed to free competition. They are forever ready to seek protection from foreign imports and foreign capital. Moreover, they genuinely believed that Britain's laissez-faire policies had aborted India's industrialization, and they were willing to put up with an interventionist state. The Swatantra Party was ineffectual because there was insufficient intellectual support for free and competitive markets in India. In a society steeped in feudal traditions and generations of economic stagnation, it is difficult to think of positive-sum results. Everyone is programmed to think that "my success can only come at the expense of your failure," and "I can only get more land by taking it from you." The government is "mother and father," protecting me from my rapacious brother. In such a society the madness of governmental controls—License Raj—was a natural development.

With all that was going for India in the 1950s, what went wrong? Where did science let us down? How did the development experts fail?

Despite the gloss of science, despite the acclaim of the international economists, the fact is that our fundamental ideology was flawed. We adopted Nehru's "mixed economy" because we believed that it was superior to both capitalism and communism. By "mixed economy" Nehru meant a mixture of socialism and capitalism in which the state would take a leading role in industrialization. We grew up in the smug belief that although the mixed economy was inefficient, it was better than capitalism because it preserved democratic freedoms. This turned out to be wrong in practice.

The mixed economy ended in combining the worst features of socialism and capitalism—the "controls" of socialism with the "monopolies and lobbies" of capitalism—and we got the worst of both worlds. The "controls" suppressed growth by subduing the innovative energies and animal spirits of capitalism. Nor did the mixed economy deliver social justice and welfare, which at least the socialist countries did. Instead of delivering quality education and public health to the masses, it delivered subsidies, which usually went to the better-off.

The problem of the mixed economy was of performance, not of faith. It was a noble vision of Nehru's which led to oppression by the state. Indians later learned from painful experience that the state does not necessarily work on behalf of the people. It works on behalf of itself—the politicians, bureaucrats, and the interests which directly support them. State employees went on to become a powerful vested interest that was responsible to no one, and they often believed that they did not have to work.

There were at least five flaws with our socialism. We adopted an inward-looking, import-substituting path rather than an outward-looking, export-promoting route, and thus we did not participate in world trade and the prosperity that trade engendered in the postwar era. We set up a massive, inefficient, and monopolistic public sector to which we denied autonomy of working. We overregulated private enterprise with the worst (case-by-case) controls in the world, and this diminished competition in the home market. We discouraged foreign capital and denied ourselves the benefits of technology and world-class competition. We pampered organized labor and that led to extremely low productivity.

Ultimately, we paid a heavy price for our skepticism of the market's ability to allocate resources wisely. We did not trust profit to reflect economic efficiency. Neither did we think that Indian entrepreneurs had the will or the resources to make the investments needed to transform the country rapidly. We felt that only the state could assume this role. We were under the spell of the Soviet economic miracle and this led to a bias towards heavy industry and against agriculture and light consumer industry. We assumed that India could not export and would always be short of foreign exchange. Therefore, we had to depend on substituting imported products, especially capital goods. These assumptions turned out to be wrong.

It was a failure both of ideology and management—the latter more than the former. Many believe that if Sardar Patel had become our first Prime Minister rather than Nehru, our future may have been different. Patel was not only less ideological, he was a superb manager.

Let us not forget that socialism was attractive to any sensitive person in the idealistic 1950s. The country had become free after two hundred years, and there was a sense of hope. The class with money and influence was tiny and came entirely from the upper castes. It had monopolized power and privilege and the few scarce facilities for education, health, and infrastructure. It naturally wanted to preserve its privileges. The rest of the population had been left out in the cold. It was natural for the ordinary Indian to expect that independent India should intervene on behalf of the masses. We must not forget that Nehru too was the product of a certain society and age. The spirit of the times offered socialism as the answer. The leaders, for their part, who had fought for decades for freedom and who were now in power, were also in a hurry. They could not wait for the benefits to "trickle down" from a market-oriented strategy. However, the socialism that emerged was "a rather weak and hollow reed in which one could blow almost any kind of music."

PART TWO

The Lost Generation

(1966–91)

The people are happy when the king is far.
—CHINESE PROVERB

EIGHT

Bazaar Power

Commerce is the art of exploiting the need or desire someone has for something.

— EDMOND AND JULES DE GONCOURT

I arrived on the island of Bombay on a wet monsoon day after eight years in America. The damp streets shone from the rain and the city's air was dense with wetness. The yellow and black taxi drove me through soggy quarters, carelessly bouncing over puddles. It was an early evening in August and the streetlights glistened on the asphalt. That night I saw fifteen-foot-tall waves of the Arabian Sea shatter thunderously against the rocks below my window. The southwest wind whistled through the cracks between the shutters as the rain advanced from the deep sea like the disciplined forward phalanx of an army. The next morning I reported for duty at Vicks's Indian subsidiary. The office turned out to be a tiny rented space on the third floor of a run-down but quaint old building called Queens Mansions in the Fort area, with a dozen employees. This felt like a real comedown from the company's swank New York offices in midtown Manhattan, where I had been hired and trained for three months.

After graduating from Harvard, I was confused. I missed home. Although I had several scholarships to pursue postgraduate studies in philosophy, I was less and less inclined to become an academic. Yet I did not know what else to do. I couldn't return home empty-handed. My parents would never have understood. In desperation, I wrote to several dozen American companies with operations in India asking them for a job in their Indian subsidiary. I did not think I wanted to make a career in business, only that it might make a nice break for a couple of years from the academic life. Only one company responded. It was Vicks, the makers of VapoRub and other over-the-counter medicines. After several interviews in New York, Surin Banta, the general manager of the Indian subsidiary, called Richardson Hindustan Ltd, who happened to be visiting from Bombay, offered me a job. He explained that the company was relatively new in India, and this was my chance to get in on the ground floor. And so, I was in Bombay.

I was given a desk and a chair in a room with two other marketing people and designated "trainee" at a salary of Rs 750 per month. My boss was the advertising manager, a pleasant Gujarati from Ahmedabad, who welcomed me with a warm smile. At eleven o'clock tea was brought to me on a tray, which confirmed my status as an "officer." The clerks and the secretaries received pre-prepared tea in a cup and saucer. My job was to learn to market Vicks remedies for coughs and colds in the Indian market. But by noon on the very first day, I was already in trouble. Around eleven-thirty I had been summoned by the sales director. He began to brief me on the sales and distribution structure of the company. Since I knew nothing about business, I asked the most elementary questions. I wanted to know why things were done the way they were. He thought I was being insolent. No one, it seems, had questioned the basic system. In my defense I said that I was merely trying to learn by questioning. He got angry and complained to Banta. He said that the company had made a wrong decision in hiring me.

"Why?" asked Banta.

"He asks too many questions!" said the sales director. "He won't survive. We had better let him go." Banta said that he would ask the advertising manager to talk to me. "He can talk as much as he wants. But I know a rotten egg when I see one. He won't fit here."

That afternoon the advertising manager called me into his room. He looked at the fluorescent light overhead and then at his olive-colored steel desk. There was a long pause. Finally, he cleared his throat and began to speak uneasily. It took him a while to get to the point. He asked me what had gone wrong at my meeting with the sales director. "Nothing," I said.

"Well, he wants to fire you." I was shocked.

The problem seemed to be my attitude. "He thinks you ask too many questions."

"Is it wrong to ask questions?"

"Yes, if it shows a lack of respect. You are no longer at the university. First, you must learn how things are done. Then there will be time enough to ask questions. We'll give you one more chance. But remember, I won't be able to save you the next time."

I was devastated. When I went back into the hall, I thought all the clerks were staring at me. It seemed everyone knew that I was in trouble. Instead of going back to my desk, I went out into the street and wandered aimlessly toward the harbor, feeling defeated. It was a funny world, I thought, where you couldn't ask questions. I looked at the gritty, impossible city. I passed a row of warehouses and soon reached the great natural harbor, with its miles upon miles of deep, sheltered water. A dozen merchant ships were moored there, waiting to unload. It was a clear day and the mainland of India was visible in the distance, under the brilliant monsoon sky, but the vast scene was colored by my unhappiness.

As the days went by, things seemed to improve. Both Banta and the advertising manager realized that my problem was that I was "excessively curious." The sales director, however, continued to be hostile and I tried to avoid him. This was not easy since he would barge into our room three times a day. All three of us were expected to jump to attention when he entered, and speak only when spoken to. It fed his ego, but I thought it a most inefficient way of working, particularly since he spent hours haranguing us, wasting his time and ours.

I had a cousin in Bombay and one evening he invited me for dinner. He worked in a big British company with many factories, thousands of employees, and plush multistoried marble offices. He asked me many questions about my job, my company, my title, and my place in the hierarchy. After listening to him, I felt small and ashamed to talk about my office and my job.

"How many factories do you have?" he wanted to know.

"None," I said.

"How many salesmen do you have?" he asked.

"None," I said.

"How many employees?"

"Twelve."

"How big are your offices?"

"A little smaller than your house," I replied honestly.

Years later, I realized that what had embarrassed me that night turned out to be my company's strength. All twelve of our employees were focused on building the Vicks brand without the distraction of factories, headquarters staff, sales forces, industrial relations, and dozens of departments. Boots, an English drug manufacturer, made our products under contract. A distributor, Muller and Phipps, who had a hundred salesmen spread around the country, distributed them under contract. Our external auditors had arranged for someone to do our accounting, and our lawyers took care of our government work. We were lean, nimble, and all of us were building the business, attempting to create loyalty among the chemists and the consumers. We were also very profitable.

All my cousin's talk that night revolved around office politics, and all his advice was about how to get around the office bureaucracy. It was not clear to me how his company made decisions. But he was a smart man, and I sensed that with all his pride in working for a giant organization, he had little respect for its bureaucratic style. It seems to me now that if persuading the customer to buy a product is ultimately what leads to business success, then it is logical that a company should spend all its time and energy on ways to enhance customer satisfaction and employ outside suppliers to do everything else. It should spin off as many services as suppliers are willing to take on and leave everyone inside the company to develop and improve products and create, retain, and satisfy consumers.

There is a concept in Yoga called one-pointedness (from the Sanskrit *ekagrata,* which means to direct and concentrate one's energy at a point). All twelve of us in those days were one-pointedly focused on making Vicks a household name in India. As I look back on my early days on the job, I certainly learned the value of a one-pointed focus on one's core competence. In a consumer product company, this means that product development and marketing are the only skills that need to exist in-house. All the other jobs can be contracted. I learned this lesson because

I was constantly put face-to-face with the consumer. It would have taken a lot to learn this lesson in a glass tower in Manhattan.

As so often in life, however, by the time I could apply the lesson I had learned, our company had a thousand people, several factories, a national sales force, and many departments that were having a lot of fun fighting over turf. I believe that tomorrow's big companies may well consist of hundreds of small decentralized units, each with a sharp focus on its particular customers and markets.

Like every northerner, I did not like Bombay at first. It seemed crowded, noisy, and chaotic after the open spaces of north India. I had to learn to negotiate the tangled traffic, the beggars, and the pavement sleepers. I found it all squalid and dismal. The smoke from the mills in Parel was like exhaust fumes, especially in the rain. Amidst the harsh nakedness of industrial India, I sorely missed the India of my childhood—the Himalayan birds, the trees, and the grassy spaces with which I had grown up in Simla and Delhi. When I looked at the mill workers, I saw empty faces, without any expression of life. There was no beauty visible to me in the lives of the industrial masses.

From the local train I could see the urban stain spreading, eating away at peaceful old villages, driving back the coconut trees, smothering the once calm lives in lazy bungalows with chemical fumes and dotting the shores of creeks with slums. Because it is an island, joined at the top with the mainland, Bombay's dormitory suburbs lay to the north; on the other three sides there was only water. The northern reaches of the city were mile after mile of urban sprawl, with sordid apartment blocks, dirty and crumbling, though only recently constructed. In between I caught a glimpse of a green field here and there, scattered palm trees, an occasional blue mountain. But more often the view was of shanty towns with mud huts pushing one against the other, covered with tin or plastic sheets, sometimes only with rags. Exposed suddenly to this horror, I felt ambivalent about industry and "city living." I imagined the island city one day being swamped by a dangerous tide of humanity and crumbling into the sea.

After the initial shock wore off, the city slowly began to grow on me. The breeze from the Arabian Sea, sent as if by Bedouins, had the power to banish all uncomfortable thoughts and soothe the body. I delighted in the entrancing view of the sea, shining like a brilliant turquoise stone. I walked on full-moon nights in the dazed air of Hanging Gardens, alongside the gulmohar trees. Even negotiating the gales on Marine Drive during the monsoon was an adventure. The city gradually won me over. I admired it for its great heart. Bombay was a miniature India which opened its arms to people from all over the country. It contained an infinite number of social worlds, intricately woven yet separate.

My ambivalent feelings about industry gradually underwent a change as I was slowly caught in the romance of the commercial world. I worked in the heart of the business city, surrounded by the port, the stock exchange, and the commodity markets. On my way to work, I passed warehouses, business houses, and shipping agents. Gradually I adopted Bombay's heroes as my own. My eyes would grow misty when talk turned to the merchant princes like the Sassoons, Wadias, Tatas, and Birlas. Instead of viewing industry with disdain, I began to see it as the nation's lifeblood and a symbol of prosperity. I began to understand that if the engineering industry had not succeeded the old textile industry, and if petrochemicals and chemicals had not succeeded engineering, Bombay would not have retained its energy, nor its position as the premier employer and taxpayer of the country. But I was bothered by the fact that squalor seemed to grow as fast as prosperity.

A month after I joined the company, Surin Banta handed me a brown salesman's leather bag and a train ticket and sent me "up-country." A man of the old school, he believed that you learned marketing only in the bazaar. So I spent ten of my first fifteen months on the road and saw many up-country bazaars. Despite the heat and the dust, and the seedy traveling salesmen's hotels, I enjoyed my field training and meeting new people. Every day I worked diligently from morning to evening and learned to outsmart wily traders. I grew accustomed to the narrow, congested streets full of bullock-carts, bicycles, handcarts, and garbage dumps. After visiting the local stockist who was the exclusive wholesaler of our products, I would call upon the major retailers in the town, accompanied by a "poster man" and a deliveryman on a tricycle filled with my company's products. While I took the order, the tricycle driver delivered stock and collected cash, and the poster man plastered the shop with advertising. The stockist provided the delivery and poster men. It was an efficient division of labor, although the poster man sometimes stuck the posters upside down. Overall, I was amazed by the sophistication of trade, the seriousness of purpose of the merchants, and the enormous wealth that it was capable of producing. In contrast to the rich patterns of commercial life, the routine in an Indian government office struck me as dull and decadent, even barbaric.

Early one winter morning I arrived at Ratlam, a rail junction in Madhya Pradesh, on the main line between Bombay and Delhi. A coolie carried my bedroll and trunk a hundred yards to Sri Krishna Lodge. The pink and green ten-room hotel was popular with salesmen and commercial travelers. As it was full, I had to share a room on the first floor. I was grateful for a bed, and did not mind the flies or the open drain outside the window. I walked out to the small balcony and looked down the street. The movie theater diagonally across seemed forlorn. A cyclerickshaw pulled up at a tea stall. Its driver, with a red scarf around his head, lit up a cheap cigarette. Another rickshaw passed, top-heavy with half a dozen schoolchildren perched precariously. I turned around and walked along the corridor stained by betel juice to wait my turn outside the wet bathroom. I bathed noisily out of a metal bucket, using a brass mug to pour water over my head.

My first call was on our stockist, Messrs. Malwa Traders, the leading wholesaler of patent medicines in town. For a 5 percent commission, it served as our stock point for the local retailers and wholesalers who catered to rural clients. I was greeted by the dust-covered and unshaven proprietor, Kewal Ram. He was cleaning his teeth with a neem twig, and had not changed from the lungi he'd slept in. The shop was equally dusty. His open jute bags of grains and chilies sent me into a fit of sneezing.

Kewal Ram ordered tea from the tea stall in front of his shop. I got busy checking our stock. Over tea, we chatted about wholesale rates. "The market is depressed," said Kewal Ram mournfully. Noticing that I was a novice, Kewal Ram decided to take me under his wing, and lectured to me on the devious ways of the market. Meanwhile, two salesmen arrived from a thread-making company. Kewal Ram was their wholesaler but not their stockist. They sat down and tea was again ordered. They too were new men. Shyly, they opened their order books and took an order. Soon they were ready to leave, but the tea had not yet arrived. They asked to be excused as they were in a hurry.

"Ah, but you must have tea," insisted Kewal Ram.

"No, no, heh, you are so kind."

"No, you must have tea!"

"Well, if you insist. But we have to catch the noon train, and many shops still to cover."

"What happened to the tea?" Kewal Ram roared at the tea stall, lifting his finger indignantly. "Bring two glasses of your best special. And quickly." After waiting ten minutes, the salesmen got restless and wanted to leave, but their host was insistent. Again, he shouted across the street, admonishing the tea shop with his finger. Soon the salesmen left, while Kewal Ram continued to curse the tea shop. When they were gone, another cup of tea arrived promptly for me.

Later that evening at the hotel, my "roommate" threw light on the tea episode. "Kewal Ram is both a stockist and a wholesaler," he explained. "His policy is to serve tea only to the salesmen of companies who have appointed him stockist. However, he does not want to appear less hospitable to the others. Therefore, the lifted finger is an old, established signal between him and the tea shop. If he orders tea with a lifted finger, it is understood that tea is not to be served. The old-timers know his ways, but these thread people must have been new. Anyway, everyone gets caught the first time." I wondered how Kewal Ram benefited from this foolish tea policy, which must lose him the goodwill of his suppliers.

On the road, I would typically meet our trade customers in the mornings and consumers in the evenings. In the afternoons, everyone slept. Lunch was always a leisurely meal, since the bazaar closed for the afternoon. I could not get used to sleeping in the afternoon and would read a book instead, sitting on my hotel bed under a fan. Usually I read history, especially about the region that I was visiting. In the evening I would meet consumers, and at night, if I didn't have to catch a train for the next town, I would walk down to a nearby cinema, "check" the advertising commercials of my company, and watch the latest Hindi melodrama. Occasionally I would be expected to hire and supervise schoolboys and girls to sample and demonstrate our products either in the bazaar or at schools and public gatherings. These demonstrations were in accordance with the promotion plans laid down by the advertising department in Bombay, and they supplemented the meager reach of mass media in small towns. The stockist usually contributed part of the cost of these promotions.

By and large my fieldwork went off uneventfully, except in a little trading center called Katni, near Jabalpur, where I was bitten by a poisonous snake. The hostel staff carried me off, not to the local hospital, but to a Parsee cloth merchant. "Stand!" shouted the Parsee as I wobbled before him. While I tried to stand erect, the grave merchant recited a mantra.

"Stamp your foot!" bellowed the Parsee.

I obeyed and again the Parsee repeated the mantra.

"Stamp your foot, twice!" A few minutes later I walked out of the merchant's shop without a limp, fully cured.

In the evenings, the merchants were too busy to talk to me. I used the time to visit the homes of our consumers and write elaborate reports to the advertising manager about my "market research." One day in Surat I learned the most important lesson of my business career.

Surat is a busy trading town 360 kilometers north of Bombay. It was the busiest port and banking center of India before the British built Bombay. In the seventeenth and eighteenth centuries, the bankers of Surat had financed the East India Company's trade to the Far East. I knocked on the door of a Surat home one evening. The woman of the house reluctantly opened the door. After a few preliminaries, I asked her what her family did to treat coughs and colds. Her eyes lit up and her face became animated. She told me that she had discovered the most wonderful solution. She asked me in, went into the kitchen, and brought back a kettle. I thought we were going to have tea. However, she explained that she used this particular kettle for treating her family's colds. "Here, let me show you," she said.

Before I could say anything, she had disappeared into the kitchen. Soon she returned with the kettle full of boiling water. She poured a spoonful of Vicks VapoRub into the kettle and together we inhaled the medicated vapors from the spout. Instead of drinking tea that evening, we inhaled Vicks. When she discovered that I worked for the same company, she was in raptures. She said that her whole family had been raised on Vicks, and to express her gratitude she offered me a box of sweets. As I walked back from her home, I too felt intoxicated. She had infected me with her enthusiasm. More important, I had finally discovered that it was she and millions of mothers like her who paid my salary. From that day onwards I acquired a new respect for my work, which also did a lot for my self-esteem. On returning to Bombay, I quickly persuaded the company to put her ideas in our advertising. Till then I had believed that my salary came from the payroll clerk, who also doubled as Surin Banta's secretary. Therefore, I was especially nice to her. She was also pretty and I enjoyed doing little favors for her. Now I knew better. It was the same lesson that I had learned on my paper route in Washington.

The bazaar continued to reinforce the message. Every time I ate in a roadside cafe or dhaba, my rice plate would arrive in three minutes flat. If I wanted an extra roti, it would arrive in thirty seconds. In a saree shop, the shopkeeper showed me a hundred sarees even if I did not buy a single one. After I left, he would go through the laborious and thankless job of folding back each saree, one at a time, and placing it back on the shelf. In contrast, when I went to buy a railway ticket, pay my telephone bill, or withdraw money from my nationalized bank, I was mistreated or regarded as a nuisance, and made to wait in a long queue. The bazaar offered outstanding service because the shopkeeper knew that his existence depended on his customer. If he was courteous and offered quality products at a competitive price, his customer rewarded him. If not, his customers deserted him for the shop next door. There was no competition in the railways, telephones, or banks, and their employees could never place the customer in the center.

After two years, I was promoted. I became the first brand manager in the company and I was given our most important brand, Vicks VapoRub, to manage. The first thing I noticed was that my product was growing strongly in the south but having trouble in the north. I asked myself whether I should try to fix the north or capitalize on the momentum in the south. I chose the latter, and it was the right decision. I later discovered that north Indians don't like to rub things on their bodies, but the more important lesson I learned is that it is usually better to build on your strength than to try and correct a weakness. It is wiser to listen to the market than to try to impose your will on it. South Indians were quite happy to rub balms for headaches, colds, body aches, insect bites, and a host of other minor maladies. This made it a large market. However, we also had a big and successful competitor in the south called Amrutanjan balm, which offered relief for all the symptoms mentioned above. My first impulse was to try to expand the use of Vicks VapoRub to other symptoms besides coughs and colds in order to compete in the large south Indian balm market. Banta quickly and wisely put a stop to that. In an uncharacteristically loud voice, he explained that VapoRub's unique function was to relieve colds. "Each object has a function," he said. "A chair's function is to seat a person. A desk is to write on. You do not want to use a chair for writing and a desk for sitting. You never want to mix up functions."

Over the years, I learned that a great part of VapoRub's success in India was because of its clear position in the consumer's mind. It is cold relief in a jar, which a mother rubs on her child's chest at bedtime. Balms are quite the opposite. Adults rub balms on themselves mainly for headaches during the day. VapoRub was succeeding precisely because it was not a balm; it was a rub for colds. Every brand manager after me had to learn that same lesson. It is important to know who and what you are. This did not prevent us from building a successful business with adults, but as Surin Banta used to say, "Adult colds, that is an armchair. But it is still a chair and not a desk."

When I first became brand manager, we were spending most of our advertising budget to promote our products in the winter. It had worked in North America and in Europe, where people caught colds mainly in that season. However, our monthly volume data stubbornly suggested that we were shipping a lot of VapoRub between July and September, the hot monsoon season. So I got the advertising manager's agreement to bring forward a good chunk of our media money to promote the product in the monsoon months, and we were rewarded with an immediate gain in sales. I followed this up by getting our advertising agency to make a cinema commercial (we had no television then) showing a child playing in the rain and catching a cold. We even coined a new ailment, "wet monsoon colds." Eventually the monsoon season became as important as the winter in terms of sales.

Moves like these made us hugely successful and leaders in market share. But instead of celebrating, Banta seemed to grow depressed. He called me into his office one day and asked how fast the market was growing.

"Ten percent," I said.

"Is that good?"

"The market's been growing 10 percent but our sales have been growing almost 15 percent, and that's why we have become number one in India," I said with pride.

"That's good, but we are still fishing in a small pond. That pond has to become a lake, and then an ocean. You have to grow the market. Only then will we become number one in the world." Banta was right, of course. Despite our success, Vicks VapoRub was still a middle-class product. Although our 19 gram jar sold for only Rs 3.50—cheaper than in any other country—it was still too expensive for the masses. The problem in selling a smaller size was the high cost of a glass jar. Plastics had not yet come of age. Banta pushed us hard to come up with a smaller size. We pushed our suppliers, and one of them came up one day with a 5 gram tin and it eventually provided a major breakthrough.

At first, it was not successful. We took the risk and lowered its price to 10 cents, with the result that it became cheaper to buy four 5 gram tins than one 19 gram jar. The trade thought we had gone crazy. Why would anyone buy the more expensive jar? They would trade down to the tin. However, it did not happen. Why? Because we had positioned the tin for the working class. We were right in believing that the middle class would stay loyal to the middle-class size. The main lesson I learned from wrestling with sizes was that even when you are number one, your job is still to grow the market. You must always benchmark yourself against the best in the world, not just against the local competition. Eventually, the Indian subsidiary became the largest producer of Vicks VapoRub among 130 countries in the world.

We could not have succeeded in building the Vicks business in India without the support of local traders like Kewal Ram. They took our products deep into the hinterland, to every nook and corner of a very large country. We were often tempted to set up an alternative Western-style distribution network. Fortunately, we never did. Instead, we chose each time to continue relying on the indigenous wholesaler system. We appointed the largest wholesaler in each major town to become our exclusive stock point and direct customer, and called him our stockist. Kewal Ram was one such stockist. One of our salesmen visited the stockist monthly, as I had done during my field training, going from shop to shop redistributing our products to the retailers and wholesalers of the town. Over time, the stockists expanded their functions. They hired local salesmen who provided interim coverage of the market between the visits of our salesmen, and also visited satellite villages and helped us penetrate the interior. They conducted local promotions and advertising campaigns, and they became our ambassadors to the local community. The stockists performed all these services for a 5 percent commission, and they paid us promptly—our receivables averaged six days of sales outstanding. This system allowed us to take Vicks products deep into villages and the smallest towns in the country, and at a very low cost. Too often foreign companies do not value low-cost local infrastructure. They think they have to fashion everything according to a preconceived model.

I never did go back to the academic world. I discovered that I liked the rough-and-tumble of the business life. A few years later my company sent me to our New York headquarters. I also worked in Mexico and Spain for a number of years. In 1981, at the age of thirty-eight, I became head of the Indian company at a time when we were up against a wall. The chemists and pharmacists had united nationwide and decided to boycott our products in a fight for higher margins from the entire industry. Because of price controls, the government did not permit us to raise consumer prices. Thus, we faced a severe profit squeeze if we gave in to the demand of the trade. We decided to fight it out. Those were depressing days as our sales plummeted to zero. Eventually a settlement was reached, but by then all our profits were gone for the year and we had to declare a loss in our annual accounts.

Adversity, however, has it uses. On an especially dreary morning during the crisis, the answer to our problems came as a flash of insight from one of our brilliant Gujarati managers, Bharat Patel. As though he was thinking aloud, he asked, "What if our products were classified as Ayurvedic rather than as Western medicines—how would that help?" Our R&D manager, a Tamil Brahmin named Dr. T. Rajgopalan, decided to humor him. "If Vicks VapoRub and our other Vicks products are all natural, herbal formulas, why can't we reclassify them as Ayurvedic?" Our Bengali finance manager, S. Bhattacharya, picked up the thread: "If that were possible, then we might escape price control." Our Marwari company secretary, Mansukh Bangard, added another brick to the castle in the air: "We might also escape from the clutches of the chemists and distribute our products in all sorts of stores." We looked at each other in disbelief. Dr. Rajgopalan got so excited that he ran to the Ayurvedic library at Bombay University to check if the ingredients in our products could be found in the thousand-year-old Ayurvedic texts. Bhattacharya and Bangard rushed to our lawyers to confirm if the Ayurvedic system of medicine enjoyed special patronage from the government, and if we could change our registration from Western medicine to Indian medicine. If so, could we expand our distribution to food shops, general stores, and street kiosks and thus reduce dependence on the pharmacists?

To our amazement, the answer from the library and the lawyers was "yes." We tried to suppress our excitement; there was a lot of work to be done. Our lawyers thought that our solution was "perfectly legal, although innovative," but they added, "It seems too good to be true." They confirmed that a change in registration would get us out of both price control and distribution control. A new registration would allow us to set up a new plant in a tax-advantaged "backward area," where we could raise productivity by means of improved technology, better work practices, and lower labor costs. We then went to meet some friendly and objective bureaucrats in Delhi, who were informed that all the ingredients of VapoRub's formula appeared in the ancient texts. They too felt that the government could not stop us legally. We promptly applied to the local Food and Drug Administration (FDA) office. The regulators at the FDA could not find a single fault with our case and, to our delight, gave us a new registration.

All our troubles seemed to be over at a stroke! Our sales force heroically and rapidly expanded the distribution of our products to the non-drug trade, tripling the outlets that carried Vicks to roughly 750,000 stores. Our dependence on chemists eventually came down to 30 percent. Consumers were pleased that they could buy our products at every street corner. We quickly built a new plant near Hyderabad which had no union and whose productivity turned out to be six times higher than that of our Bombay plant. With higher prices and better costs, we began to invest aggressively in marketing and advertising. Our after-tax profits rose from 1 percent to 12 percent of sales, and we became a blue chip on the Bombay stock exchange as our share price rose from Rs 30 to Rs 400 within eighteen months. We were careful not to ruffle the government or get too greedy. Technically, the Ayurvedic classification also permitted us to pay a lower excise tax. We deliberately continued to pay tax at a higher rate.

The last installment of this story took place when we decided to return the compliment to the Indian system of medicine. I flew to the

United States to try to persuade our headquarters to let us establish an R&D center to investigate other safe and natural Ayurvedic therapies. When I first mooted this idea, our senior managers in Connecticut—we had shifted from New York—practically fell off their chairs. Slowly, however, they became comfortable with the idea. I appealed to their sense of history and destiny. To a member of the Richardson family, who owned a major stake in the company, I said, "Your ancestor in Greensboro, North Carolina, discovered the formula of Vicks from his study of Eastern medicine in the 1890s. Today, a hundred years later, he would be proud of our attempts to do the same." After much debate, I got their agreement, and a check for two million dollars.

We set up our Ayurvedic labs in Bombay under the leadership of Dr. T. Rajgopalan, who had studied in the United States under a Nobel Prize winner and had worked in the Ciba labs at Basel in Switzerland. He began by creating a computerized data bank of herbs and formulas from the ancient texts; he invented a "fingerprinting" process to standardize herbal raw materials with the help of computers; he organized clinical trials in Bombay hospitals to confirm the safety and efficacy of the new products. His team developed two products, which we sold for many years in the Indian market—Vicks VapoSyrup, an all-natural cough liquid, and Vicks Hotsip, a hot drink for coughs and colds. The lab later became part of Procter & Gamble's global research network when it bought Vicks in 1986. Unfortunately, the two products never achieved commercial success, and the efforts of the lab were gradually redirected to solve P&G's global health care agenda. Dr. Rajgopalan went on to win much acclaim and many awards and patents.

The story of Vicks in India illustrates how companies create global brands. There is a popular misconception among managers that you merely need to start with a brand name, create a standardized product, packaging, and advertising, push a button, and bingo—you are on the way to capturing global markets. Marlboro, Coke, Sony, and Levi's are cited as examples of this strategy. However, if it is so easy, why do so many powerful brands flounder? Without going into the standardization vs. adaptation debate, the Vicks story demonstrates at least one essential ingredient for global market success: *the importance of local conviction.* If local managers believe a product is theirs, then local consumers will believe it too. Indeed a survey of Indian consumers a few years ago showed that 70 percent of Indian housewives believed Vicks was an Indian brand!

In the United States, where the Vicks business started, managers in the 1970s became persuaded that Vicks VapoRub was old-fashioned "grandmother's medicine." Sure enough, the consumer began to feel the same way, and business began to decline. When I moved in 1992 to P&G headquarters, I challenged this assumption. Some managers argued that America had become such a rushed society that mothers no longer had the time to apply a bedtime rub on their children. In the end, they agreed to invest in the brand and they were rewarded, as hundred-year-old VapoRub began to grow again.

Managerial basics, I am convinced, are the same everywhere, in the West and in the Third World. However, you need to do more than push a button on a powerful brand name with a standard product, packaging, and advertising in order to conquer global markets. The key to success is a tremendous amount of local passion for the brand and a feeling of local pride and ownership. Globalization does not mean imposing homogeneous solutions in a pluralistic world. It means having a global vision and strategy, but it also means cultivating roots and individual identities. It means nourishing local insights, but it also means reemploying communicable ideas in new geographies around the world. The more human beings belong to their own time and place, the more they belong to *all* times and places. Today's best global managers know this truth. They nourish each "blade of grass."

It would be wrong to conclude from the Vicks story that managing a global brand is purely a local affair. On the contrary, the winners in the new borderless economy will be the brands and companies that make the best use of the richness of experience they acquire from their geographical diversity. Multinational companies have a natural advantage over local companies because they have talented people solving similar problems for identical brands in different parts of the world, and these brand managers can learn from each other's successes and failures. If a good idea emerges in Egypt, a smart brand manager in Malaysia or Venezuela should at least try it.

The Surat lady's teakettle became the basis of a national campaign in India. "One-pointedness" emerged from a hole in the wall in Bombay, but it became the fulcrum on which we built an excellent business over a generation. Advertising for colds during the hot monsoon months seems highly parochial, but it taught us the importance of advertising year-round in other countries. The stockist system found applicability in Indonesia and China. Even the Ayurvedic system of medicine might plausibly be reapplied in the form of a safe and efficacious herbal remedy for common, self-limiting ailments in other countries. The Ayurvedic story also taught me that overregulation has bizarre consequences. Great businesses are built through discontinuous ideas, and a good manager, who is one-pointed, knows when to seize them.

Oddly enough, I learned the most valuable lessons about effectiveness in business from Kamble, our security guard at Richardson Hindustan. One evening around seven-thirty, as I was leaving the office, Kamble asked me to check the envelope on his desk. He did not think it was addressed properly and the courier would be there any minute to collect it. He was right. In fact, it was an important tape that our marketing people wanted to rush to the television studios for airing the following day. We quickly telephoned the advertising agency, corrected the address, and repaired the damage.

As I drove home, I recalled that this was not the first time Kamble had saved the situation. He had come to us four years earlier as a "temporary guard" and quietly become indispensable. First, he had learned to operate the telephone switchboard on his own initiative. Next, he had learned to use our complicated photocopying machine. Then, he began to send faxes. Finally, he became expert in fixing any number of things. He knew who was staying late, who was traveling, how to reach anyone's home. It had got so that if anything was needed after hours, our reaction was, "Where is Kamble?"

When our telephone operator went on maternity leave, Kamble offered to take her place for six weeks. We soon discovered that our telephone service had improved dramatically. Our business associates asked what had happened. For years, they had complained that our phones would ring and ring, and they had resigned themselves to a long wait. Now, to their surprise, our telephones were being answered on the second ring. I asked Kamble. "Well, there might be a customer at the other end," he replied, "and we might lose an order." Kamble was too perceptive not to know that our business did not generally come over the telephone, but it was his attitude that mattered.

I asked myself how we could get all our employees to act like Kamble. How could we get everyone in the company to answer their telephones as though there was a customer at the other end? This is the challenge before all managers. How does one get ordinary employees to care for the business as though they are owners, and do extraordinary things? The trouble is that most employees do not see customers when they come to work in the morning. They only see other employees. They see directors, middle managers, junior executives, secretaries, office boys, but they do not see customers. So they get busy in office politics. Directors get absorbed in building empires; middle managers spend their time comparing the size of their office with those of their peers; junior executives are concerned with locating their name on interoffice memos to gauge whether they are rising or falling in the office hierarchy. The irony is that a company makes all its money outside the company— when the customer buys a product—but the employees spend all their time inside, usually arguing over turf.

The answer was clear—we had to take our employees closer to our customers. This might also help to give more meaning to their work. At the next management committee I suggested to our senior managers that all our employees ought to spend two days a year in the bazaar meeting ten consumers and ten retailers, and write a report offering their suggestions. The committee responded enthusiastically and we decided to implement the idea. A year later we discovered that less than a quarter of the people had actually gone to the market. From those who had gone, we got some excellent suggestions on how to improve our products, our work processes, and our behavior. However, among the majority there was great lethargy to break the office routine. The following year we made the visit to the bazaar mandatory—the personnel department withheld salary increments unless it received a copy of the "bazaar report." Thus, market visits became an annual habit. Once they got to the bazaar, I think most people liked it. They understood why we were in business, and the company got some good suggestions in return.

The point of this symbolic exercise was to drive home the point that one exists because of one's customers. Once people start to believe this and it becomes widespread in the company, it is translated each day into hundreds of small activities that improve customer satisfaction. The greatest benefits of this belief come from scientists in product development. If scientists visit the bazaar frequently and early in their careers, they realize that they are working not for "science" but to improve the lives of ordinary consumers. Once the consumer drives R&D efforts, rewards begin to come rapidly. Product improvements acquire urgency. As we stand at the threshold of the new WTO-mandated global economic order, I think this is an important lesson for Indian companies. The only certainty now is that markets are going to become even more competitive. Only companies that are close to their customers will survive.

Kamble was a product of the absence of rigid rules in our small company. The more rules there are, the less people will do on their own, and the more effort they will spend in getting around the rules. Most organizations—whether they are companies, hospitals, schools, or NGOs—operate on the basis that an employee will do something wrong, given half a chance. I have always believed the opposite. The ordinary person will generally do the right thing, left to his or her own devices. The important thing is that people believe that only results will win them rewards. Our personnel department, however, was suspicious of people and it constantly tried to make rules. I, on the other hand, liked ambiguity. Kamble had succeeded precisely because no one knew where his job started and where it ended. If only results matter, then I think ordinary employees will surprise managers by doing extraordinary things.

Everybody in our company used to play a board game during lunch hour. For decades desktops would get emptied between one and two o'clock and our office became a loud youth camp. It bothered our personnel department and it tried to put a stop to this unseemly behavior. I had to gently intervene and explain that playing at lunch might well be the tonic and relaxation that people needed. Perhaps the louder they shouted, the more creative they became. Who really knows the source of human creativity? If you worry too much about appearances, you end up with employees who will give you good appearances. If you only care about results, then employees will give you good results.

It is important not to direct people too much and to let them find their way. It might bring out their creative urges. This is not to say that one abdicates responsibility to train employees. A manager must train his subordinates all the time, and with a passion. But he or she must refrain from controlling them. The best thing a manager can do is to provide clear, ambitious objectives and monitor the work of his subordinates against these objectives. If one trusts people and makes them feel trusted, they will respond. People behave according to the way they are treated.

It is vital that all employees share the company's mission and objectives. Most companies tend to be secretive and fear that competitors will steal their secrets. Thus, they avoid telling employees the most basic things. They forget that information, especially about goals and performance standards, is a powerful way to motivate employees. In a large organization, people desperately need to feel that there is meaning to their work. There is a story that one day Shah Jehan wanted to know how the Taj Mahal was progressing. To find out, he disguised himself as an old man and went to the site by the Yamuna River. There he came across a stonecutter, whom he asked, "What are you doing?" The stonecutter was annoyed by the disturbance and said, "Go away old man, don't you see that I am busy?" The stonecutter's dedication impressed Shah Jehan. He went to the next stonecutter, and he asked the same question. The second stonecutter was equally impatient and he told the disguised emperor, "Cutting stone is a great art, old man, and I can't be answering questions and practicing my art." Again Shah Jehan was impressed; from his body language he could tell that the man was proud of his professional skills.

Finally, the emperor went to the third stonecutter, to whom he put the same question. "I am building the Taj Mahal, old man, and if I keep answering idle questions, I shall never be able to complete the most beautiful monument on earth." Shah Jehan returned to his palace much pleased. Clearly the third stonecutter had given the best answer. The first worker represented dedication to work—an honest day's work for an honest day's pay. The second showed professional excellence. The third symbolized the power of a shared vision. Too often at the workplace we falter because employees do not share a common goal and pull in different directions. I have found that ordinary people can do extraordinary things when they all focus on a common goal. After the oil shock in the 1980s, Nissan in Japan was able to cut its costs by 30 percent in nine months because all its employees pulled together to achieve the goal. Good managers, I have found, are one-pointed towards a goal. They do very few things. But they make sure that these are the right things. Then they execute them brilliantly. They also seem to have fun doing them.

NINE

Lerma Rojo and
Taichung Native No. 1

*There is life in the ground: it goes into the seeds; and it also, when it
is stirred up, goes into the man who stirs it.*
— CHARLES DUDLEY WARNER

M y mother remembers fondly her visits to my great-aunts
once a year in the country. It was the big event of her childhood, taking weeks of planning and coordination. There
was excitement and bustle in our Lyallpur house for days together. The
entire family went by train from Lyallpur to Gujranwala, and along the
way, at different stops, many relatives would join the train. By the time
they arrived, it had become a great big clan party. At Gujranwala station,
they piled onto tongas, and amidst much merrymaking, they would
head for the village to enjoy the generous hospitality of our country
cousins.

Even at that time, my mother tells me, there was a sharp divide in
attitudes between town and country. My mother's family considered
themselves superior, even though they were not as wealthy as their
landowning cousins. This was primarily because they lived in a town,
were better educated, and spoke English. My mother tells me that she
used to feel squeamish about the hygiene and bathroom arrangements at

the farm, but she was very conscious of their money and their generosity. Lyallpur was a "model town" in British India—what Le Corbusier's Chandigarh would be to Nehru's India. It was orderly, rationally planned, and reflected a spirit of modernity. Our Lyallpur family was part of India's educated, urban upper-caste elite—that is, professionals with status and voice but with little money and economic power. My grandfather used to say that the policies of the Raj, especially learning the English language, had divided us from our Gujranwala family and the rural elite. We held the status but they had the money.

Agrarian power was different across India's geography, but it rested everywhere with those who controlled the land and its produce. Many of the rural landowners were themselves the creation of British rule. Our country cousins, for example, had acquired wealth because they had shifted to Gujranwala after the building of the canal. In other parts of the country many families came up with the colonial land policy, introduced first in Bengal in 1793 and then extended in haphazard fashion to other parts of the country. It assigned ownership to local landlords in return for rents paid to the East India Company. From these settlements emerged a class of wealthy landlords called zamindars in the east and the north, and smaller tenurial cultivators, the ryots, in the south and the west. Many zamindars, of course, traced their position to the pre-Mughal days. However, in Punjab zamindars were fewer because land was tilled by independent and vigorous landowning peasant castes such as the Jats.

Landowners had profited from the peace and stability of British rule and they were not anti-British in their views. For this reason, the nationalist struggle did not engage them particularly. Indian nationalism was a product of urban stirrings among the educated intelligentsia, men like my uncle Sat Pal. Typically, nationalists were successful lawyers like Motilal Nehru. Mahatma Gandhi's great achievement was to lay a bridge after 1920 between the town and the countryside, but social differences and attitudes were never reconciled. These differences remain to this day and explain a great deal about Indian politics. The partition in 1947 changed the circumstances of our cousins and cut our tenuous connection with the countryside. They lost their lands because Gujranwala went to Pakistan and they became poor. Like my grandfather, they too settled down in Ludhiana in 1947, and after a few years the government partially compensated them for their lost lands, but they never quite recovered their old glory. They could not get going primarily because they were uneducated.

I grew up without any organic link with the village, where two out of three Indians still live. I did not visit an Indian village until I was in my early twenties. My boss wanted me to find out how we could sell more Vicks VapoRub in villages and he packed me off on a tour of rural India. I spent a month in Madhya Pradesh, Gujarat, and Tamil Nadu. It was not a good year to go to the villages because the rains had failed and there was enormous anxiety and misery. On my return, I wrote a longish report saying that getting our products to villages would not be a problem because of a highly developed network of wholesalers. We would need to subsidize our rural vans until they became self-paying. However, we had to create demand, and for that I recommended advertising in traveling cinemas, and I took the initiative to negotiate rates and logistics with cinema owners in the districts that I visited. In my report, I also wrote extensively about the condition of the peasants, and my boss began to worry that he might have an unpleasant radical in the company.

I was struck by the self-sufficiency of the village economy. The typical village was functionally integrated between agriculture and handicraft industry, with some communal ownership of land, and well-defined social responsibilities for the different castes. I found agriculturists, craftsmen, astrologers, tanners, carpenters, barbers, priests, smiths, petty retailers, musicians, record keepers, headmen, and so on. I counted thirty-two occupations, although not every village had all of them. For the first time, I began to understand Mahatma Gandhi's dream of building modern India along the lines of self-governing village republics. Marx too, curiously enough, had talked about the independent nature of the Indian village, with its blend of agriculture and industry. Marx, among others, had said that the Indian village is self-sufficient because it "contains within itself all the conditions of surplus production" that guarantee an independent economy to each village. But this independence also made it stagnant and resistant to change, he felt. It bred in the peasant an indifference to politics, making him susceptible to despotic rule, and doomed him to conquest by foreigners. Marx thought that Western technology would change all that. The destruction of their handicrafts was the price Indians would have to pay for becoming modern and joining the flow of world history.

Although I found this self-sufficient community romantic and attractive, Marx had condemned it as closed, stagnant, and a victim of nature. In a vitriolic passage he said, "These idyllic village communities . . . had always been the solid foundation of oriental depotism . . . they restrained the human mind within the smallest possible compass, making it the unresisting tool of superstition, enslaving it beneath traditional rules, depriving it of all grandeur and historical energies." Although Marx denounced British rule in India, calling it "swinish," he approved of its modernizing influence. British machine-made textiles might destroy Indian handmade cloth, but they would undercut India's stagnant village economy and society. "By blowing up the economic basis of India's villages, Britain was produc: ·g the greatest, and to speak the truth, the only social revolution ever h ·rd of in Asia," he said. Marx predicted that "modern industry, resulting from the railway system, will dissolve the hereditary division of labour upon which rest the Indian castes, those decisive impediments of Indian progress and Indian power."

Mahatma Gandhi had the opposite prescription for the Indian village. He wanted a revival of village handicrafts and industries. Only thus would the villager attain gainful employment and dignity. He admired the simplicity of village life and did not wish to alter its basic character by multiplying the villager's wants. He sought, therefore, to promote hand-spinning, handweaving, hand-pounding of rice, hand-grinding of corn, and traditional oil pressing. "The traditional old implements, the plough and the spinning wheel, have made our wisdom and welfare," he said. "We must gradually return to the old simplicity. . . . The railways, telegraphs, hospitals, lawyers, doctors—all have to go. . . . You cannot build non-violence on factory civilisation; but you can build it on self-contained villages." Unfortunately, Gandhi was going against history. He could not stop the advance of industrialization. His followers, however, made a heroic effort after Independence to implement his ideas. "Rural uplift" and "community development" became extremely fashionable words for a long time, but in the end, Gandhian programs failed and probably did more harm than good because they made us ambivalent. Most Congress men ritually wore handwoven clothes and performed their quota of spinning, but they did not believe in it. They put their faith behind Nehru and the world of machines and a factory civilization.

On 27 May 1964, I was roaming the wilds of Madhya Pradesh when I heard on the radio that Jawaharlal Nehru had died. I remember it vividly. I was in our stockist's van that day, going from village to village in Sagar district. Everyone seemed to be in a daze. Many retailers had closed. A shopkeeper told me, "Son, you want to sell me Vicks when I have lost my appetite for life. My love has gone and left me." Not since Mahatma Gandhi's death did the nation grieve as it did that day. Every American who was old enough then remembers where he was when President Kennedy was shot. The same, I think, is true for Indians of my generation when it comes to Nehru's death, or my parents' generation when it comes to Gandhi's.

Since the late 1950s we had asked persistently, "After Nehru, who?" Foreign correspondents had regularly predicted India's descent into chaos after Nehru's death. Now the moment had come and we were worried. I was on a train on 2 June when I heard that the Congress Parliamentary Party had unanimously elected Lal Bahadur Shastri as Nehru's successor in the Central Hall of Parliament. The same afternoon President Radhakrishnan invited Shastri to form a new government. With that, the succession was complete. Everyone in our train compartment was relieved. Some applauded; others smiled. The prophets of doom had been proved wrong. Even Indians like myself, who had been optimistic that the succession would be orderly, were surprised by the mature and dignified transfer of power. We were proud that we had passed an important test of democracy.

In the late 1950s, Selig Harrison of the *Washington Post* had argued, most plausibly, that India would disintegrate. But this has not happened. The dangerous decades have come and gone. There have been regional tensions to be sure, but India remains intact. Nobody, I think, would seriously offer such a thesis today. Those who glibly argued that India was a creation of the British, or a "geographical expression," as Churchill used to say, were plainly wrong. Clearly, we underestimate the historical unity of India and the strength of its cultural, social, and even economic bonds. Amartya Sen once told me to read the first volume of *The Cambridge Economic History of India* in order to appreciate the extent of social and economic integration that obtained in India before the British.

Lal Bahadur Shastri inherited an economic crisis. There was terrible scarcity of food. Prices had risen, bringing misery all round. Agriculture had been stagnant. Industrial growth had slowed and unemployment was growing. Foreign exchange reserves were virtually down to nil. Worse, there was a crisis of confidence both in the Congress Party and outside. It was not the best setting for a new leader. The Congress Party bosses had selected Shastri because he was nonthreatening: a modest and unassuming man who was also homegrown—in short, the complete opposite of Nehru. He was less ideological and far more pragmatic. Feeding India was his first priority.

Shastri was aware that agriculture had been neglected. Although he was guilty of ignoring it, Nehru periodically expressed his frustration with the food situation. In 1957, Nehru confessed with his usual candor: "It is a painful thought that after ten years of Independence, an agricultural country cannot feed itself. It would be wrong for us to blame the gods or the stars or floods and drought. We must recognise that there must be something lacking in our approach which has led to this relative lack of success." Honest words, indeed. Alas, Nehru's ability to act and manage did not equal his verbal capabilities. If Nehru had wanted to focus on agriculture and food and had brought the weight of his office to bear on it, he could have made a difference. For years, the Americans had been gently suggesting that we pay greater attention to agriculture. However, on each occasion the ideologues around Nehru had shot these proposals down, seeing in them an evil American plot to keep India poor and underdeveloped. This despite the fact that America's foreign aid program to India—over $600 million a year—was at the time the largest in the world.

India had begun regularly importing wheat from the United States in the early 1950s. The Americans were overproducing and had piled up huge stocks in old Second World War freighters. Behind the surplus was the farm vote. Against common sense and their religion of the market, the Americans guaranteed their farmers a support price, which invariably turned out to be higher than the market price. As a result, the government was stuck each year with unsalable wheat, which had to be stored at huge expense. As a result, they were left with the choice of having to burn it, dump it in the sea, or give it away to a country like India. Since getting rid of it actually saved them money, the United States passed a law called PL-480, which allowed sales to developing countries in local currencies—it being understood that these were "blocked funds" and would not be used. In his fine autobiography, B. K.

Nehru, a former ambassador in Washington, describes this subterfuge as being necessary because of opposition in the U.S. Congress. "The representatives of the people had objected to giving away the taxpayers' money to the foreigner. They had relented only when they were told that the proposal was not to give away anything but to sell it on credit." The congressmen were satisfied with this explanation. The American wheat came in especially handy when the monsoons failed in 1957–59 and scarcity reached a danger point. However, we became addicted to PL-480. Between 1960 and 1964, India imported a massive quantity—16 million metric tons. Because of these imports, India began to be seen as a "basket case" in the world's eyes, especially in Washington.

As usual, Indians were divided on the issue. At one end were the leftists who argued that there was no food shortage—the scarcity was caused by traders and middlemen who were holding back the food in order to let the prices rise and thereby reap huge profits. Their solution was to nationalize trading in food grains, have statutory rationing, and put the errant traders behind bars. At the other end were rightists—men like S. K. Patil—who said that the shortage was real and caused by state intervention. Yes, wheat was being hoarded by two million peasants (as well as traders), but it was because they lacked confidence in the government. Traders and farmers were scared by the draconian talk of state trading. Their answer was a completely free market. Let prices rise for the farmers, who would then be encouraged to produce more. In between these two extremes was a range of opinion held by economists and commentators, who blamed the "food zones" artificially created by the states, the disincentive to farmers from large-scale American imports, and a variety of other factors. Very few among the Indian elite were grateful for America's generosity; nor did we mute our criticism of American involvement in Vietnam. The problem, in fact, got much worse in 1966 and 1967. We had two consecutive droughts and a real famine threatened. Starvation was prevented only by the arrival of ships from the United States with over 14 million metric tons of grain worth more than a billion and a half dollars. At the peak, grain ships were leaving American ports at the rate of one every ten minutes.

B. K. Nehru was responsible for the logistics of this massive operation. He recalls that suddenly one day the ships stopped. BK panicked. He "rushed around like a headless chicken"—to Dean Rusk, the secre-

tary of state, to Orville Freeman, the secretary of agriculture, to David
Bell, the head of USAID, but to no avail. No one knew why the ships
had stopped. New Delhi was in a panic and bombarded its ambassador
with telegrams. The media got hold of it and the *New York Times*
viciously attacked the administration for this inexplicable behavior. It
turned out that President Johnson himself had given the order. He later
told B. K. Nehru that his daughter Lucy had said to him, "What are you
doing, Daddy? You can't let the Indians starve at Christmas." "I told her
not to worry," said LBJ, "no Indian was going to starve at Christmas."
The next day the ships started moving again. B. K. Nehru speculated
that it might have had to do with Johnson's displeasure over the joint
communiqué issued by the Indians and the Soviets, which was critical of
U.S. policy in Vietnam. More likely, though, he thinks, it was LBJ's way
of "reminding us of the consequences if we failed to pursue with vigour
our new agriculture policy."

When Shastri took over, he rightly felt this could not go on and agriculture reform became his top priority. One of Shastri's first and best
moves was to place C. Subramaniam, a dynamic and intelligent man, as
minister of food and agriculture. He had a modern mind and could be
counted on to be independent and bold. He learned that Norman Bor-
laug, an American scientist, had developed a remarkable dwarf wheat in
Mexico which could dramatically raise output. He had found his
answer. Quietly and patiently, he negotiated with the states for several
months. Once he had won their support, Subramaniam announced a
dramatic new agricultural strategy. It gambled the nation on this new
wheat.

C. Subramaniam was a man in a hurry and he chartered several Boeing 707s and flew in 16,000 metric tons of seed of this miracle wheat. To
support his gamble, he organized massive fertilizer imports and invited
foreign private investment in fertilizer plants. The rest is history. This
dwarf wheat went on to create the famous green revolution and make
India self-sufficient in food. Punjabi farmers still speak lovingly of Mexico's Lerma Rojo, one of the earliest varieties to take root in their soil.
Indian democracy is not used to bold action by its leaders. Not unex-
pectedly, there was great criticism in Parliament and the media. Fortunately, the intellectual elite trusted Subramaniam, who also defended his
policy with great skill and credibility. Subramaniam also impressed Pres-

ident Lyndon Johnson. "That Subber Mainyam of yours. He's a good feller," Johnson told B. K. Nehru. The American President was interested in India's food minister because India had been importing huge quantities of food grains every year, which affected American farm policy, and this in turn had a great impact on politics in America. It is ironic that America was preaching capitalism to the world while engaging in such a vast socialist program at home. Even more ironic is the history of official attitudes and prickly relations between the two largest democracies in the world. It is individuals who make history rather than the other way around, and no two men did more harm to this relationship—setting it on a sour path for fifty years—than John Foster Dulles, the American secretary of state in the 1950s, and Krishna Menon, Nehru's leftist confidant and India's representative at the United Nations at the time. After the bitter experience of British colonialism, India wanted to be neutral (or nonaligned) in the Cold War, but Dulles declared, "You can either be our friend or our enemy." Krishna Menon compounded the folly by regularly lecturing to the world about evil American capitalism and imperialism, which naturally set the U.S. State Department on edge. No one in subsequent years had the courage to reverse the stance on either side, and the relationship has remained strained ever since.

Subramaniam continued to face enormous opposition from within the cabinet and the Congress Party. T. T. Krishnamachari, who was cabinet minister again in Shastri's government, fought hard against the proposal to raise wheat prices by 15 percent. But Subramaniam was adamant. He insisted that the farmers needed an incentive to take the risk and adopt the new high-yield wheat. He understood that if the new technology was not supported by right policies on prices, fertilizers, land ownership, water, and credit, it would not work. He saw it as a package deal.

Thanks to Shastri and Subramaniam, and supported by M. S. Swaminathan, a technocrat, and Sivaraman, a bureaucrat, India implemented the new strategy with vigor. The rewards came quickly. Indian agriculture was finally placed on a growth path, and the stagnation of the colonial period decisively broken. Wheat production rose 5.5 percent a year for a whole decade from 1967 to 1977. By 1980, official U.S. documents—the *Report of the Presidential Commission on World Hunger*—

quoted India as being the "only developing country in the world which has built a solid system of food security." In the 1980s India was in a position to donate food to relieve famine in Ethiopia and give a wheat loan to Vietnam. Food grains production has risen from 54 million metric tons in 1950–51 to 200 million metric tons now, a growth of 3 percent a year, and ahead of a 2.1 percent population growth. In contrast, food grains output had grown less than 1 percent between 1905 and 1945.

On the negative side, the green revolution has mainly benefited the irrigated wheat areas of the northwest, and it has led to widespread disparities with other parts of the country. By 1985, the three northwest states accounted for 83 percent of the surplus and Punjab alone accounted for 50 percent. Some people worry that one region has become the breadbasket for the whole nation, and they think this is bad for national unity. I disagree. I believe that this is how it happens in nature, and man should learn to accept nature's limitations. Even industry has a habit of clustering in regions. There is new evidence that the green revolution has moved eastwards to the poorer states and has also included rice, although with less dramatic impact than wheat. Wherever it has gone, the revolution has shown great appetite to absorb surplus labor. This partially explains why 65 percent of Indians still live in the rural areas, although agriculture's contribution to the GDP has now declined to 25 percent. This is despite increased mechanization and the adoption of labor-saving practices. In the beginning of the green revolution, it was the larger farmers who took advantage because they had the capital and the ability to take risk. Gradually, it caught on with the smaller farmers, and in course of time, it has expanded to the poorer regions. Hence, regional disparities in wages also started declining from the mid-1970s. The poor have gained not only because of jobs but also by the decline in the *relative prices* of food grains.

Despite this bright spot in an otherwise depressing economic scene, it is odd that Indian intellectuals, especially the powerful left, have been consistently critical of the green revolution. Newspapers in the 1970s, I remember, used to call it a "sellout to America." For years, academics wrote serious essays in the *Economic and Political Weekly* condemning the revolution. Some of the essays were by committed radicals whose hope for a peasant revolution was cut short. They had hoped for the Marxist process of "immiserizing growth," which would radicalize the lower peasantry and landless labor. At its root, I am certain, their opposition to the green revolution is on account of their hostility towards markets, profit, and capitalists. They rightly saw the transformation as promoting capitalist agriculture. Even Ashok Rudra, normally a balanced economist, wrote, "The task of developing agriculture is being entrusted to the greed and the acquisitive spirit, which motivates capitalists. *In traditional Indian agriculture greed was located and condemned in the professional moneylender, the speculative trader. . . .*"

During the late 1960s, I met Daniel Thorner, an extraordinary American economist who had traveled extensively in Indian villages, and I learned much from him about the green revolution. Daniel and Alice Thorner came to India in the 1950s partially to escape from the witch-hunts of Senator Joseph McCarthy in the United States. Because Thorner refused to save his skin by naming his leftist friends, he lost his job and a government-funded fellowship for a research trip to India. Undeterred, he and Alice borrowed money from their parents and came to Bombay. They quickly built a large circle of friends and admirers. Sachin Choudhary asked Thorner to write on agricultural questions in the *Economic and Political Weekly;* V. K. R. V. Rao invited him to lecture at the Delhi School of Economics; P. C. Mahalanobis, the czar at the Planning Commission, gave them a research project to refine the concepts relating to the 1961 census.

When I first met Thorner, in 1966, it was after one of his long trips to the countryside. He looked tanned and relaxed as he spoke about capitalist stirrings in rural India. He enthusiastically described a boom in agriculture in many parts of India. He painted a hopeful picture of thousands of farmers, big and small, investing in new hybrid seeds, new tube wells, tractors, pump sets, and fertilizers. Not all the investors were farmers, however. He described a visit to the agricultural officer in Karnal district of Haryana, where he met a short, chubby, gray-haired man in his fifties. Although he looked a sedentary sort, he turned out to be the prize cultivator of the area. This model farmer told Thorner that he had been a moneylender. But he gave up this occupation after the elaborate regulations of 1938. After showing him round his fields, he took Thorner across the road to see new plots of Taichung Native No. 1 hybrid paddy. There Thorner noticed another man, short and wiry, who

came up to them in bare feet. He was wearing only an undershirt, draw-
ers, and a wristwatch. Thorner asked, "Is this your supervisor?" Back
came the reply: "Oh no, this is Lalaji, my neighbour." Lalaji, he discovered, owned both a tube well and a tractor. "For the life of me, I could
not recall ever having previously seen an affluent man of mercantile origin out in his fields so scantily clad, taking personal charge of the agricultural work." Thorner saw the same thing in Meerut and Bara Banki
in Uttar Pradesh, in Gujarat and coastal Andhra, where many farmers
who had earlier given their lands to sharecroppers were now beginning
to farm them on their own with help of a tractor, a tube well, and even
a power tiller.

I had not realized until I met Thorner that the development of a
technologically advanced, profit-oriented village agriculture was a very
recent phenomenon. In the years down to 1947, large landholders had
contented themselves for the most part with giving out small parcels on
tenancy. "It was rare to come across in the days before Independence a
genuine capitalist producer who worked his land with hired labour to
produce crops for sale at a profit and re-invested his gains in intensifying
production or enlarging the scale." There was a revolution under way.

Thorner's observations confirmed what I had also seen on my visits to
the Terai region of western Uttar Pradesh, which lies between the plains
and the hills. I had gone there for my company to assess if farmers would
be willing to grow mint of a particular variety (called *Mentha arvensis*).
From this mint we hoped to distill oil and eventually make menthol, a
decongestant which went into Vicks VapoRub. Alongside peasants, I
found many retired military officers who had cleared the wasteland and
reclaimed it. They were enthusiastic and scientifically inclined. Because
our mint was potentially a "bonus" third crop for them, after the winter
rabi wheat crop, they became "early adapters" and set an example for
the smaller, more conservative farmers. These farmers had also been the
first in the area to plant the Mexican varieties of wheat. When I met
them in 1968, they proudly showed me Lerma Rojo, which had created
such a sensation on the farms the previous year.

Thorner said that the same thing had happened with grapes in
Hyderabad, Bangalore, and a number of places in Maharashtra. I recall
that grapes were a rare luxury in our home in the 1950s, but by the 1970s
there had been a veritable revolution in the Deccan. Prices dropped year

after year, and it became a common fruit on middle-class tables. The same happened to strawberries in the early 1990s. As an early witness of the green revolution, Thorner saw the emergence of an advanced capitalistic sector in agriculture that was similar to the advanced sector in industry. He saw landowners who had never tilled the land take advantage of government subsidies and begin to work on the land themselves after the technological breakthrough with Mexican seeds.

While leftists complained of the growing inequalities, Thorner predicted that these capitalist farmers would one day solve India's food problem. He was right. Wherever it went, the green revolution also brought huge purchasing power to millions of small farmers and provided a tremendous boost to the entire economy with "multiplier effects" upon the output of tractors, tools, fertilizers, consumer goods, banking services, and so on. Whereas the left focused on the failures of the government, especially in land reform, Thorner spoke about the success of capitalist farming. He conceded that there had been widespread evasion of land reforms, but he continued to focus on the positive picture. He wrote that the "decade after 1947 witnessed an impressive series of land reforms. A sizeable number of landlords, particularly among the absentees who had made their homes in the cities, lost much of their land in favour of their tenants in the villages. Many millions of cultivators who had previously been weak tenants or tenants-at-will were enabled to become superior tenants or virtual owners." The land reforms, such as they were, had the effect of inducing landed proprietors to undertake cultivation, or, at the least, to make a show of cultivating, if they wished to hold on to some of their ancestral lands.

Thorner had no illusion that landless laborers would obtain land through these reforms, but he found that they benefited through rising opportunities for employment as the new hybrid varieties were more labor-intensive. As yields rose with the Mexican varieties, the farmers experienced labor shortage. Wages rose and they began to import casual workers from other parts, especially Bihar, during the harvest season. Within two years the labor rate doubled from one to two rupees a day (in 1995 it had crossed Rs 50 per day in Punjab and western Uttar Pradesh). Although the chief beneficiaries of this revolution were the owner-cultivators, Thorner contended that rural labor had also shared in this prosperity. "For many months of the year in Punjab, Haryana, central Gujarat and coastal Andhra agricultural labourers managed to eat two and a half to three meals per day. In the lean seasons they may have to do with a scanty breakfast, some scraps at mid-day and only one proper meal, usually in the evening. . . ."

How times have changed! In the 1960s we were a "basket case." Now, India comfortably sits on a grain mountain year after year. Stocks in the central pool typically swell to 35 million metric tons by June every year. This is not a good thing either, because it blocks a colossal amount of taxpayer's money and burdens the nation in avoidable inventory-carrying cost. Although we have become a surplus nation, we continue to suffer from a scarcity mentality.

Where do we go from here? Experts believe that we are on the verge of a second green revolution. With our large area of arable land and plentiful sunshine, India can become a major global power in agriculture. First, we must change our "poor starving country" mentality and regard the World Trade Organization and the global economy as not enemies but allies. Second, we will not conquer the world through peasant farming, but through technology and capital. Remember, the first green revolution was a technological revolution. Third, technology is now with international companies and they will have to play an important role. All the talk about terminator technology is rubbish. We heard the same talk about Mexican wheat in the 1960s. Fourth, we have to liberalize agriculture and remove needless controls.

Ashok Gulati, the agricultural economist, has spelled out a clear reform agenda. He has demonstrated that India has a global competitive advantage in a dozen commodities. Among these are cotton, wheat, rice, horticulture, and dairy products. We should allow them to be freely exported and imported and link them to world prices. Consumers will benefit from lower world prices and farmers from a larger market. Let us begin by liberalizing one commodity—for example, cotton. We have definite comparative advantage in longer staple, labor-intensive cottons. Once cotton exports explode, we will gain the confidence to make reforms that are more sweeping.

Liberalizing agriculture is not going to be easy because the price of food is politically sensitive. Today, the government controls both the consumer and producer prices. Although agricultural growth slowed somewhat in the 1990s, the economic reforms have changed the terms of trade in favor of agriculture. With the opening of the industrial economy, the relative prices of manufactured goods have declined and agricultural prices risen. Consequently, farmers have increased their investment in agriculture. Freeing some farm exports has also benefited farmers. On the negative side, public spending on agriculture and irrigation has declined. Because the treasury is bankrupt, subsidies on power, water, and fertilizers will soon have to go, but politicians will have to be kicked and dragged before they free agriculture prices.

Agricultural expansion is not enough to conquer poverty. Amartya Sen has repeatedly reminded us that what causes hunger in India is the wide prevalence of poverty. It is the inability of a large number of people to buy enough food, or, as Sen would put it, "to establish entitlement over an adequate amount of food." He is rightly harsh against dubious claims that the problem of poverty is adequately addressed through the green revolution. He has vividly demonstrated that just raising food output does not solve the problem of undernourished people in India. He has shown that undernourishment is higher in India than in sub-Saharan Africa, especially among the children. The problem relates to the endemic poverty of the Indian masses. Africa is more susceptible to periodic declines and transient famines, but India has a larger proportion of persistent undernourishment and endemic hunger. Although this does not in any way undermine India's agricultural achievement, it is a sobering corrective to our thinking.

The six billionth child was born sometime in October 1999. There were plenty of scare stories in newspapers around the world, accompanied by the usual neo-Malthusian breast-beating about the population explosion. This happens periodically, but the Malthusian nightmare has not happened. Total food output has consistently outstripped population growth, and per capita income of the world has risen since 1945. Malthus was wrong, and food has won the race. Amartya Sen also settled the question of famines long ago by showing that famines are caused by income failures rather than harvest failures. If the government launches a sensible "work program" to create purchasing power among the poor, famines can be avoided. If the six billionth child is born in India, there is a 50 percent chance that it will be malnourished. But there is every likelihood that its life will improve as it grows older.

All in all, the green revolution is a good story of contemporary India. There is another equally exciting story. It is of a "white revolution" in milk—about how a terribly deficient India has become the largest milk producer in the world. Again, it was one man. Dr. Verghese Kurien, who created this miracle, which in many ways is unique because it is the success story of cooperative farming in a country where cooperatives have miserably failed. The lesson I have learned is that only individuals make history, and often unknowingly, without understanding the eventual consequences of their deeds. The British would not have possessed India without Clive's stubborn wish to teach Siraj a lesson. India would not have become surplus in food or be sitting on a mountain of grain today were it not for C. Subramaniam's willfulness and the unfailing support of Prime Minister Shastri.

TEN

Caste

*Distribute the world as you will, the principal question remains inex-
orable—who is to dig it? Which of us, in a brief word, is to do the
hard and dirty work, and for what pay?*

—JOHN RUSKIN

People everywhere want to feel superior to others, and all societies
have some sort of hierarchy. But this doesn't mean that they have
a caste system. In India hierarchy has been institutionalized, carried much further and lasted much longer. Indian tradition separated the
social classes and did not tolerate marriages between them. Neither did
it allow them to change occupations, nor permit some to sit and eat
together. The question is whether India's deep-rooted obsession with
ranking has suppressed our capacity to grow and develop.

The caste system seems to fragment India's social and political life, but
does it influence modern economic life? To what extent does caste
affect the ability of Indian firms to compete in the world economy?
Clearly, having traditional merchant castes that know how to accumulate capital would seem to confer an advantage. Merchant families have
also proven the ability to shift from trading to industry. And some
younger sons of the merchant castes are showing capabilities to move
from industry to information technology (although the big success stories in software and information-based services seem to have come so far

from the nontrading castes). But caste rigidities may also be responsible for our lack of cohesiveness and inadequate technological innovation—both of which might have contributed to our weak performance in the industrial economy. On the other hand, our Brahminical proficiency may be a reason for our emerging success in the new information economy. Finally, how has democracy changed the caste system? These are some of the questions I examine here.

When I was growing up, I was not as aware of caste as other Indians. This was either because we were an urban middle-class family or because we came from Punjab, where caste had weakened from centuries of foreign invasions and the influence of Islam, Sikhism, and Hindu reform movements like the Arya Samaj. Whatever the reason, caste divisions were not ubiquitous, nor did they structure our everyday life. Our differences were religious. Later, when I began to travel in rural areas for Vicks, I realized that caste indeed was the central organizing feature of social life in the countryside, even though the educated middle and upper middle classes in the cities tended to gloss over it. Caste seemed to divide Indian society into groups whose members did not intermarry and usually did not eat with each other, their status decided by who would and would not take water from the other's hand. Everyone within a caste was a brother, and outside it a stranger. Caste varied by region, and the relative position of the castes differed from village to village. But everywhere caste rules were rigid, and there was little room for individuality.

In Hindu society the Brahmin (priest, teacher) is at the top of the four-caste hierarchy, followed by the Kshatriya (variously landholder, warrior, ruler). The Vaishya or bania (businessman) comes third, and the Shudra (laborer, artisan) is last. Below the four are casteless "untouchables" and tribals. The three upper castes constitute roughly 15 percent of India's population, and have ruled the country for three thousand years. About half of India is laboring or Shudra caste, divided in turn into hundreds of subcastes. Some are occupational—cobblers and carpenters, for example—others are geographic. More than 20 percent of the population are the casteless or "untouchables" and tribals for whose uplift Mahatma Gandhi worked all his life. The remaining 15 percent of India belongs to other religions: 11 percent Muslim; the rest Sikh, Christian, Parsee, etc.

The common mistake is to confuse the four broad castes *(varnas)* of the ancient literary and religious texts with the thousands of local sub-castes or *jatis* which really matter in people's day-to-day lives. There are about three thousand such jatis, and their members broadly identify themselves with the four historical varnas. Some are social in origin; others are occupational; some are territorial. People of one jati often share a traditional vocation, and will not marry or dine outside the jati. As they become prosperous, jatis also rise in the social scale from one varna to another. For example, oil-pressers in Bengal upgraded themselves a couple of generations ago. Carpenters in one district of Punjab enhanced their status. Low-caste Ganthis became textile traders in Surat. Curiously, the conversion to Buddhism, Islam, or Christianity does not necessarily liberate one from the caste system. In the villages, Muslims and Christians carry on as before as Muslim and Christian untouchables.

Diversity is India's most vital metaphor. Apart from caste and religion, linguistic states also divide it. It is thus a multinational nation. In a sense, it is what plural Europe would like to be—a united economic and political entity in which its different nationalities and minorities continue to flourish. India's diversity is the result of historic migrations and wanderings of many peoples and tribes who came here over thousands of years and made it their home. An anthropologist described the subcontinent of India as "a deep net" into which various races and peoples of Asia drifted over time and were caught. The tall Himalayas in the north and the sea in the west, east, and south isolated this net from the rest of the world and this led to the development of a unique society and is the origin of the caste system. It has made it possible for such a vast variety of people to live together in a single social system over thousands of years. It has proved capable of absorbing new intruders.

Observers have often noted the tolerance of Indians. They are surprised that people of such diversity can live together in reasonable harmony. The answer may well lie in the caste system. In this system "a group's acknowledged differences . . . become the very principle whereby it is integrated into society. If you eat beef, you must accept being classed among the untouchables, and on this condition your practice will be tolerated." Some academics have argued that caste is an artificial category, invented by imperialist Europeans to simplify the character of Indian social life for the purpose of legitimizing colonialism and to establish

European cultural and political supremacy. It is true that some nineteenth-century scholars (like James Mill) did paint an overly simplified and rigid picture of caste in India that is plainly inaccurate, but to conclude that caste is a social construct of the imperialist West, and must therefore be dismissed, is silly. Travelers to India—from the Chinese to the Arabs, in ancient and medieval times—consistently observed and described the caste system. Indian nationalist leaders inveighed against the evils of caste for a hundred years. Indian and foreign anthropologists and social scientists made detailed studies of caste. Plainly, caste is indigenous. But it is an evolving institution; it varies from one part of the country to another—more unbending in some areas and flexible in others—and it impacts modern life in different ways.

In recent years, sociologists have challenged the old stereotype of the caste system as closed and rigid, since it did not allow individuals to change their hereditary occupations. G. S. Ghurye showed that administrative and military jobs were always open to all castes. So was farming, except to Brahmins, who were not expected to touch the plow. He pointed to evidence that "untouchables" like chamars had entered traditional jobs such as weaving. He studied a village in Maharashtra (which his students restudied after a twenty-year gap in 1954) and showed that all the low castes in the village had taken to modern occupations. André Béteille proved in 1965 that the caste of an individual in a Tamil village no longer inhibited him from adopting a modern occupation. Other sociologists have confirmed that "untouchables" have often given up their menial jobs in favor of carpentry, blacksmithing, and white-collar occupations.

Adrian Mayer studied the same village, Ramkheri, in central India in 1954 and 1992. He found that most of the artisans had changed their occupations, except carpenters. Many lower- and middle-caste farmers had become commuters to the neighboring town of Dewas, where they had found jobs in textile and engineering companies, in the State Electricity Board, and also become teachers, bus conductors, and security guards. Others have found new occupations in the village as repairers of pumps, televisions, and bicycles, and also become agents of cattle feed, seed, and fertilizer companies.

There are at least two cultures in India. The first is primarily rural and is dominated by traditional Hindu beliefs; the second is an urban elite culture, more modern and national in its outlook. It is often not easy to separate the two, but I have always assumed that caste is the last thing on the minds of modern professionals who manage India's companies. Yet Indian business is overwhelmingly family-run. The business families are socially conservative and have tended to hire employees from their own community and caste. The Birla companies are filled with Marwaris. Even in the Tata companies—the most professionalized group—it is surprising to come across a disproportionate number of Parsees. The reasons are understandable. Business requires trust, and a kin or a familiar name from one's caste is likely to be more trustworthy. Traditionally, Indian merchants engaged in trade cover vast distances, and a caste member, whether an employee or an agent or a business partner, adds to one's comfort. The Marwari "great firms" in the nineteenth century had business networks in China and Central Asia and transacted vast sums merely on the merchant's word. Naturally, they looked to their own.

Between 1960 and 1990, when labor became militant, some business families began to hire workers from their own community, thinking that one's caste brethren would be less hostile and more pliable. In the pro-labor socialist environment of the 1970s, a superintendent in a Bombay company said that he preferred to recruit new workers through reliable channels. "The man coming from the employment exchange is a total stranger to us. Newspaper advertisements are all right in the case of officers' and engineers' posts. But in the worker's case our experience has been that it is safer to take in a person coming in through a person we know," he said.

Loyal employees from their caste also helped industrialists to negotiate the onerous rules of the License Raj. Many companies used to pre-empt competition by filing multiple applications in the name of trusted employees. "They needed trustworthy managers who could keep their firm's secrets." The socialist system ensured that every businessman would break some law or the other every month. Hence, it was important to have members of one's caste and kin in sensitive positions. With liberalization in the 1990s, the situation has changed, however. Competition has become fierce and survival is at stake. Business families increasingly look outside their caste for talent. In some functions, like marketing and product development, there is now a veritable scramble for professionals, and salaries have multiplied manifold. Caste loyalties seem now to be diminishing as businessmen recognize that they must have the best person for the job, no matter what his or her caste.

The managers in my company came from different castes and different parts of the country. While hiring a new employee, we were unaware of his or her caste. We recruited the best person for the job. I discovered that no two senior managers on our management committee came from a single state, nor did they share a single regional language. Hence, all our work was in English. Most of our managers were Hindu, but we also had Muslims, Christians, and Parsees. Other multinationals in India share this diversity. So, in fact, does the government. Government jobs have always been based on competitive exams. The same is true in banking, medicine, law, engineering, and jobs in colleges and universities.

Despite this, however, most managers and professionals in India come from upper-caste backgrounds. The artisan castes seem to dominate the supervisory and skilled workers categories, and unskilled workers are mainly drawn from the lowest castes. Sociologists call this "caste clustering." Caste is especially important for underprivileged low-caste workers because they lack the education and other resources and must depend on their caste linkages to get a job. The reason is simple. The upper castes were the first to seize the opportunities to get educated, and with education came jobs in the modern professions. This has been true since my grandfather's time. There has never been a significant "caste barrier" to entry in modern jobs, despite the myth perpetuated by backward-caste politicians. Education has always been the answer to raising the backward castes, and not reservations and quotas, as the political movement of the backward castes has been fighting for. Yet not a single backward-caste politician talks of primary schools. A more vigorous rural education thrust by the government would certainly have ensured greater equality of opportunity.

Sentiment against caste has been gathering among modern Indians for more than a hundred years. Nationalists railed against the caste system and wanted to eliminate untouchability. It was partly because caste hindered economic advance. But it was mostly a humanitarian desire to improve the lot of the low castes and to send a clear message to the agrarian high castes that this system is inconsistent with a modern society.

Once India became politically free in 1947, our liberal-minded leaders lost no time in abolishing untouchability and making its practice a criminal offense. Wide-ranging affirmative action programs were launched and roughly 20 percent of seats were reserved in colleges, universities, and jobs in the public sector and the government. The "untouchables"—who now call themselves Dalit, meaning "the oppressed"—were given generous scholarships, and efforts were made in all states to ensure their political representation. In this manner, the new nation attempted to atone for centuries of injustice.

However, one cannot legislate away thousands of years of bad behavior, and prejudice persists. Barriers are breaking down and fading in the cities, where the modern economy requires a high degree of interdependence across occupations, but in rural areas competitive politics have created "vote banks" and strengthened instead the consciousness of caste. During elections, caste has been aggressively used to gain power and promote the rise of the lower castes, especially in the Hindi-speaking north. It has also led to clashes and violence between the castes. There is an ongoing caste war in backward Bihar, in which massacres of both Dalits and upper castes take place periodically. Everywhere the privileged tend to protect their turf and try to keep the oppressed down. In Bihar, the upper-caste farmers have created a private army called the Ranvir Sena, which burns down the homes of the Dalits every time they rise in support of their rights.

Curiously, this competition between castes may actually be destroying its fundamentals. The caste system was based on interdependence and acceptance of one's status. Once the lower castes believed that they could rise and be enriched through the competitive politics of democracy, they no longer accepted their lower position and their traditional relationship of dependence in village society. Now they are in competition with the higher castes and the old equilibrium is disappearing. They have formed caste associations and deliberately use caste to enlarge their territorial reach in order to increase their power. They have begun to behave like modern interest groups, competing for spoils in a democracy.

After the abolition of untouchability in 1950, the most dramatic development relating to caste occurred in 1990. Vishwanath Pratap Singh, the aristocrat turned politician (and able finance minister under

Rajiv Gandhi), needed an electoral platform to differentiate himself from other politicians. Socialism had run out of steam. Mrs. Gandhi's populism had been discredited. The Bharatiya Janata Party had appropriated the religious platform. The old Gandhian path no longer had much appeal. Corruption was not a sustainable competitive advantage because voters believed that *all* politicians were corrupt. V. P. Singh looked for a gap, and he found it in the backwardness of the "other backward castes" (OBCs). These were the laboring Shudra majority, fully half the country's population—barbers, carpenters, cobblers, goatherds, other artisans, and farm labor—who had lacked a political voice. In comparison, the Dalits had already found a voice in politics and there were programs in place to lift them, and the upper castes had always looked after themselves nicely for three thousand years.

V. P. Singh now made the most desperate move of his career. He dug up a government report by a man called Mandal that justified affirmative action for the "other backward castes" and he promised reservations for them. The OBC movement spread like wildfire in the north Indian heartland. The upper castes were horrified. Suddenly, another 50 percent of government jobs and places in colleges might be denied to them. With 20 percent of the jobs already reserved for the Dalits, they realized that if the OBC demand succeeded only 30 percent of future seats would be available on merit. It was an invitation for a caste war. And it came. Thousands of upper-caste students led demonstrations, and dozens burned themselves in public. In the end, their sacrifice was to no avail. The logic of the ballot box was too strong. None of the political parties dared support the students. After a few months, the rebellion died and students went back to classes. V. P. Singh, as Prime Minister of a coalition government, tried to fulfill his election promise, but his attempts to increase reservations became mired in the courts. However, the succeeding Congress government of Narasimha Rao seized the opportunity to win the OBC vote. It enacted legislation raising the reservations of OBCs by 30 percent. Thus, 50 percent of government jobs and seats in colleges are today based on criteria other than merit.

For the first time in history, India has begun to extend justice to people lower down. There is no doubt that the Dalit and OBC movements are bringing about a social revolution in north India. The 1996 general elections showed that power was rapidly shifting from the upper castes to the backward castes, especially in populous Uttar Pradesh and Bihar. Rajasthan and Madhya Pradesh are unlikely to remain insulated from this social churning. In the south, the social revolution is much further along, where social and political power passed from the upper to the lower castes decades ago.

After fifty years of reservations, Dalits still suffer great social discrimination, but the old untouchability is virtually gone. Elections have put them in Parliament, and reservations have given them jobs in the bureaucracy, the police, and the public sector. They now have their own political parties. The President of India is a Dalit. So are a number of ministers. Other backward castes are no longer a persecuted minority; they are the majority. Earlier, they suffered caste oppression, but now democracy has converted their advantage in numbers into enormous political clout. As a result, there is continuous clamor for more quotas. The original aim of reservations was to accelerate the rise of the backward castes. It is now a sectarian tool used by backward castes to demand a share of the patronage. Having said that, the fact remains that half a century after Independence the Dalits and some of the backward castes are still the most wretchedly poor, the most illiterate, the most exploited, and the most disadvantaged in India. The answer to their plight in the long run is education and the market. The state has done its bit by giving them protective discrimination through quotas. But quotas are at best a temporary palliative. For jobs in the future are not going to grow in government and the public sector but in the market economy. The middle class is appalled that they have thrown up politicians like Laloo Yadav, the former chief minister of Bihar who is under investigation in a "fodder scam" involving Rs 1,000 crore. Today India is ruled by dozens of corrupt politicians. In the words of V. S. Naipaul, "You can't get people from Bihar behaving beautifully. When the oppressed have the power to assert themselves they will behave badly." He thinks that it will require at least a couple of generations—once the lower castes begin to trust institutions—"before people in that situation begin to behave well. Meanwhile, we have to live with messiness."

On the face of it, caste ought to kill enterprise. It segments human experience for generations and fragments society. Its inherent conservatism ought to destroy creativity and experimentation. It gives the monopoly of knowledge to Brahmins and the monopoly of risk taking to banias. It delegates manual work to the lowly. In such a society, how can innovation and capitalism flourish? Karl Marx believed that caste would come in the way of modernizing the Indian economy. But he also predicted that caste would eventually die out because "modern industry, resulting from the railway system, will dissolve the hereditary division of labour, upon which rests the Indian caste." That did not happen, but neither did an industrial revolution.

Max Weber, the German sociologist, also concluded that caste would have a negative effect on enterprise. He argued that "India's caste order formed an obstacle . . . [A] profound estrangement usually exists between the castes, and often deadly jealousy and hostility as well, precisely because the castes are completely oriented towards social rank." Weber contrasted India's caste society with the class differences and tradesmen's guilds in premodern Western Europe. The ethic of Christianity, he argued, united European society into a social and religious fraternity, and this led to a common civic life. This in turn helped create a capitalist society, and the classes and guilds did not prevent the flowering of mercantile towns. In India, however, the Hindu religion sanctioned the divisions of the caste system. These divisions, he believed, would prevent cooperation and lead to poor cohesion in Indian society.

Although both Marx and Weber were wrong in their conclusions, Weber raises an important issue with regard to teamwork. Modern economic activity depends vitally on interdependence. That Indians do not combine well is well known, but is the caste system somehow responsible for our inability to cooperate? With all our triumphs at my company, Richardson Hindustan, I failed to build a cohesive management team. Poor teamwork at the top had the most devastating consequences on our younger managers. Like most companies, we were functionally organized, with top managers heading the key departments—marketing, product development, finance, sales, production. Because the heads of the departments were intent on building empires, there were constant and futile battles over turf. The younger managers would often get caught in the crossfire and become victims. Worse, they would emulate the damaging behavior of their seniors. We conducted a series of "team-building workshops" which had a positive effect on behavior, but the effect was temporary. After a few months of good conduct, we would begin to fight again.

55555

I felt disheartened. I thought I had failed as a leader, and I had the most terrible doubts. Perhaps I was incapable of building a team. I talked to other heads of companies in Bombay, and to my surprise, I discovered that most of them faced the same problem. Temporarily, I felt consoled: at least I was not the problem. But the issue would not go away. During the twelve years that I led Richardson Hindustan and Procter & Gamble India, poor teamwork was a festering, chronic disease.

Since leaving P&G, I have been consultant to half a dozen Indian companies, and I have concluded that most Indian enterprises suffer from this problem, some more and some less. I am concerned that this problem may be a serious source of national competitive disadvantage. It is not limited to the commercial world; it infects all sorts of organizations. Whether it is a university, a hospital, a village panchayat, or a municipal board, it is beset with dissension. To a lesser extent, even the armed forces seem to suffer from poor teamwork.

The paradigmatic story concerns two Indians who meet in New York and decide to form an Indian Association. When a third arrives, they form a Tamil Association; with a fourth comes the Bengali Association. And so on until there are fifteen regional associations and the old Indian Association is forgotten. One day someone has the "brilliant idea" to join the regional associations into an Indian Association. It's a funny story, and it makes us laugh, but it also illustrates our divisive character. A Swiss manager of a multinational company told me that a sure way to inaction is to put two talented Indians on a global task force. They will never agree and brilliantly argue the proposal to death.

What is the cause of our divisiveness? Is it our diversity? Is it the caste system? Oscar Lewis, the noted American anthropologist, studied a Jat village near Delhi. He found that the village was more or less permanently divided along rival caste lines. The more powerful group was led by the dominant caste, but supported by clientele recruited from its dependent castes. The factions seemed to be constantly fighting each other. Other sociologists have confirmed that discord and factionalism pervade village life almost universally in different parts of the country.

However, caste alone cannot explain dissension. I have noticed that in the most homogeneous Marwari companies, brothers and nephews incessantly fight with each other. To some extent, jockeying for power exists, of course, in every company everywhere. It is natural for directors to build empires, quarrel over turf, and squabble in boardrooms. However, in good companies around the world these conflicts are contained so that they do not hurt competitiveness. In India, they tend to spill out, and when they do the effect is devastating.

In the nineteenth century, British colonialists used to blame our caste system for everything wrong in India. The nationalist leaders followed suit in the twentieth century. Mahatma Gandhi constantly told Indians that they were undeserving of independence unless they reformed their society and rid it of untouchability. I was taught as a child that caste was evil, and responsible for our backwardness. Now I have a different perspective. Instead of morally judging caste, I seek to understand its impact on competitiveness. I have come to believe that being endowed with commercial castes is a source of advantage in the global economy. Bania traders know how to accumulate and manage capital. They have the financial resources and, more important, financial acumen. They have an austere lifestyle and the propensity to take calculated risks. They have proven their flexibility of mind as they have graduated from trading to industry. These constitute significant strengths. Joel Kotkin demonstrates these strengths in the case of Palanpuri Jains, who have used their caste and family networks in wresting half the global market for uncut diamonds from the Jews.

After the economic reforms, our business houses have acquired new respectability and are on the rise socially. More and more people in our society want to emulate them and become entrepreneurs. Making money has become respectable. There is a huge change in people's attitudes, and intellectuals call it the "baniaization of Indian society," after the bania trading caste. The children of the Brahmins and Kshatriyas no longer view the civil service as the career of choice. They want to get an M.B.A. and go into business. Indeed, business schools are one of the biggest growth industries. Money and not power is what motivates young people. I once heard the high priest of a south Indian temple say that this unholy mixing of caste occupations is "deplorable. . . . [It is] the beginning of the end of Hindu society." As mentioned earlier, it is similar to the redefinition of Japan's merchant class during the 1868 Meiji Restoration, which led to Japan's transformation from an underdeveloped group of islands into a prosperous and modern society. India is also in the midst of a social revolution, and our new entrepreneurs in software, e-commerce, pharmaceuticals, and other knowledge industries are predominantly emerging from the noncommercial castes.

The commercialization of society will indeed bring prosperity to India as the middle class grows. But it will also exact social costs. It will entail megacities, overcrowding, atrocious working conditions, and environmental disasters. Bourgeois life tends to become consumerist and banal, and the individual is alienated from his surroundings. Mobility, weakened family bonds, decline in religion, and loss of community life accompany industrialization. Caste will weaken, but commercialization could threaten the old Indian way of life.

In the competitive market some will gain and others will lose. Even if the winners greatly outnumber the losers, in a country like India the losers will be considerable. But it has to be that way in a society with a young population that needs to absorb an increasing labor force. One should be aware of the downside of capitalism, but one cannot morally stop the yearning of the underprivileged and the poor to rise to a better standard of living. With education and time, Indians too will learn to come to grips with their environmental problems. India will also have to balance growth in a framework of social order. Nobody knows the ideal social mix. The West certainly does not offer a model, for its tendency to excessive individualism has had a corrosive effect on family and society. Individualism is clearly vital in the economy of information and innovation, but the West has learned that individuals need a supportive society as well. Indians will also have to confront the problem of how to blend society and the market and try to achieve a better balance between career, family, and society than has the West.

It is no good hoping that Indian values and the Indian way of life will survive intact. With all the triumphant talk of "Asian values" that we have heard over the past decade, it is now becoming clear that they may not offer a robust alternative. Critics have said that Asian values are indistinguishable from Victorian values (strong family, strong state, strong nationalism). In everything from industrialization to democratization we are following the well-trodden historical path of development. Modernization has its positive and negative consequences, and we have to live with them.

Many Indians blame the caste system for our industrial failings. As already discussed, Brahmins monopolized learning and looked down on Shudra artisans, who worked with their hands. Since Brahmins were role models, these attitudes (including contempt for manual labor) filtered down to the other castes. Thus, the worlds of knowledge and labor remained separate and inhibited technological innovation. It is true that when it comes to product development and innovation, Indian companies have clearly failed. Our goods are shoddy, and our businessmen rarely know how their product works. Their standard response to product improvement is to try to buy technology or hire a scientist. Unless Indian companies overcome this historical weakness, they are not going to survive the new competitive environment of the post–1991 reforms period.

The Japanese, despite their current troubles, can teach us many things. The Japanese businessman is obsessed with product improvement. Japanese entrepreneurs have had great interest in technology since the Meiji times. It is, of course, true that the Japanese mania for product superiority is spurred by a more competitive home market. Whatever the reason—caste prejudice or lack of competition—the Indian business class deserves scorn for its record of innovation. Equally, the artisan is blameworthy for not improving centuries-old products and practices. Indian roads are filled with cycle-rickshaws that break the driver's back and primitive motorized three-wheelers that pollute the air. From the household broom to the bullock-cart, no object of daily use has been improved for centuries. The Japanese, too, had a four-tiered caste system, but it does not seem to have stopped them from achieving the miracles of industrialization. Warriors, or samurai, were the highest caste in the Japanese system; they were a highly trained fighting machine, organized and orderly, loyal to their code. However, Japan's caste system was more fluid than India's. A Japanese commoner could move into the samurai class by adoption or marriage. Although the position of household head was passed from father to eldest son, the role of eldest son could be played by an outsider, provided he had been legally adopted. Rich moneylenders often bought samurai status for their sons by marrying them to the daughters of the samurai during the shogunate. According to one study, 39.3 percent of samurai families had adopted sons in the nineteenth century. When the feudal economy changed into an industrial economy, the new entrepreneurs and the conglomerates, or zaibatsu, became the adopted sons-in-law of the state. Many samurai, who took charge of Japan's industrialization, were combative and competitive, and they helped to make the Japanese domestic market fiercely competitive. This is an essential difference from India. As noted, India's policymakers, and especially Jawaharlal Nehru, dampened the competitive spirit of India's entrepreneurs. Nehru once innocently asked, "Why do we need nineteen brands of toothpaste?" While he thought competition wasteful, the competitive spirit has turned out to be an important factor in Japan's success.

If our caste system slowed our response in the industrial age, it may actually have positive consequences in the knowledge age. Ever since Indians began to succeed in Silicon Valley and Bangalore, people have wondered why we have been more successful in software and information-related business than in the old smokestack industries. My hypothesis, as I have already suggested, is that Brahmins have had thousands of years of experience in dealing with abstract philosophical and spiritual concepts of the Upanishads. This may explain why Indians are especially good at mathematics and theoretical physics (as opposed to experimental physics). Indians invented the zero. The information age thus plays to our strengths. After all, cyberspace, like spiritual space, is invisible. Our core competence may well be invisible. It is not surprising that an unusually large number of information technology entrepreneurs, both in Silicon Valley and in south India, come from the Brahmin caste, not from the traditional trading castes. Hence, I believe that we may actually skip the industrial revolution and leap right into the information revolution.

Today India's caste system is in a state of transition. A half century of democracy has raised the status and esteem of the lower castes. Periodic elections have created vote banks, the lower castes have used politics to rise socially, and there is a social revolution under way, especially in the backward northern states. Its biggest prize is that half the government jobs and places in colleges are now reserved for the lower castes. What democracy has done for caste in the twentieth century, capitalism will do in the twenty-first. At the beginning of the twenty-first century, India is one of the fastest-growing economies in the world, and there is little to stop it from continuing to grow between 6 and 8 percent a year for the next couple of decades. At this rate there will be unprecedented new jobs, and this will create new opportunities for everyone. The better jobs, it is true, will go to the better educated. But as the lower castes begin to realize that the better jobs are in the private sector rather than in the government, they will turn, one hopes, to education rather than to reservations.

Caste certainly does not pervade modern economic life in the way that it structures rural social life. The diffusion of economic growth will further weaken the old caste—occupation link. The old stereotype of village occupational rigidity was never entirely accurate. Lower castes had always shown the capability of "moving up" or changing occupation. Modern organizations in the cities have usually hired people based on merit and exams. As markets become more competitive—as they have since the 1991 reforms—this trend will hasten and caste should diminish further. One day, perhaps, as the great scholar of caste M. N. Srinivas predicted before his death, caste will become symbolic of ethnicity rather than hierarchy.

ELEVEN

Multiplying by Zero

*Though those that are betrayed
Do feel the reason sharply, yet the traitor
Stands in worse case of woe.*

—WILLIAM SHAKESPEARE

Lal Bahadur Shastri died suddenly of a heart attack on 11 January 1966, nineteen months after he became Prime Minister. He died in the fabled city of Tashkent after signing an agreement with Pakistan giving up significant territorial gains in the victorious autumn war, including the strategic Haji Pir Pass, gateway to the Kashmir valley. I was at my parents' home in Chandigarh when we heard the news, and like the rest of the country, we were in a state of shock. Shastri had begun to grow on us. Although we did not want him to part with the pass, we felt that he had displayed qualities of statesmanship. What endeared Shastri to us was a disarming absence of ego, and this had also made him an effective leader.

A great deal died with Shastri that day. Contrary to what most people think, Jawaharlal Nehru's death did not end an era. It was Shastri's death that did. Although he had been a cabinet minister for many years in the 1950s, he was poor when he died. All he owned at the end was an old car, which he had bought on installments from the government and for which he still owed money. He had set high standards. He was the only

railway minister who resigned from office following a major train acci-
dent as he felt compelled to own moral responsibility. After Shastri's
death, values departed from our political life and governance became
amoral. A new personalized style of politics came into being. Institutions began to erode, the biggest victim being the Congress Party. More
than values, Shastri's early death lost us the opportunity for pragmatic
policies in our economic life. Had he lived, our nation would have done
far better and more people would have risen out of poverty. Alas, he did
not, and what might have happened must remain a counterfactual of
history.

There was high drama in the Congress Party over Shastri's succession.
Rumors flew and fortunes changed by the hour. The barrel-chested,
taciturn president of the Congress Party, K. Kamaraj, turned out to be
the kingmaker. He was a brilliant strategist but his strength lay in the
absence of ambition—he did not want to be Prime Minister. We respect
that in a man. Neither did he know Hindi or English—he spoke only
Tamil—and he must have realized that this would be a terrible handicap.
He had another quality unusual in a politician—he did not speak. He
could spend hours listening without saying a word, and people thought
him wise. Again, Morarji Desai was the leading candidate. We did not
like Morarji because he was rigid, authoritarian, aloof, with countless
silly fads. Neither did the powerful Congress bosses, known as the Syndicate. However, they had different reasons. They wanted someone pliable, whom they could control from the back room.

To stop Morarji, the Syndicate tried to draft Kamaraj. He stood firm.
Morarji wanted to have a proper election among the Congress members
of Parliament. The Syndicate was afraid that Morarji might actually win
a contest and kept stalling a poll. In its defense, it kept saying that it
wanted a unanimous candidate, and charged Kamaraj with determining
who that would be. We may not have liked Morarji, but we liked the
Syndicate's methods less. We supported Morarji's democratic right to an
election. From these machinations Indira Gandhi's name emerged. The
political bosses favored Jawaharlal Nehru's daughter because they
thought a frail and inexperienced woman would turn to them for
advice. We disliked her candidacy because it smelled of dynasty. In the
end, after endless consultations, Kamaraj revealed his hand—he proposed Mrs. Gandhi's name as the "unanimous choice of the party."

Since she had the aura of the Nehru name, he said, she offered the best chance of delivering victory to the party in the coming general election. However, Morarji remained firm on an MPs' poll. Kamaraj then swung into action and began to build pressure. He got the state chief ministers to come out publicly in her favor. This created a bandwagon effect. Finally, a secret ballot was held on 19 January in the domed Central Hall of Parliament among the Congress MPs and Indira Gandhi won 355 to 169.

Lal Bahadur Shastri had been full of common sense. He had come to feel that our elaborate system of controls had become heavy and self-perpetuating. For every control that failed, we needed two more to shore up the original one. In the complex, nonmonolithic government that India had become, controls were causing delays, waste, and enormous harm. He thought it was time to loosen up, and he entrusted the task to L. K. Jha, his principal secretary. The *Times of India* ran a story on the front page in early December 1965 saying that the government was contemplating liberalizing some of the less useful controls—this was the first time I came across the word "liberalization." Four days later, there appeared another story in the same paper. Unfortunately, a month later Shastri died, and with him died the prospects of liberalization. Mrs. Gandhi, who was ideological like her father, brought in her leftist advisers. She replaced L. K. Jha with P. N. Haksar. Mohan Kumaramanglam, the former communist, began to play a decisive role in policy making. They quickly buried the liberalization initiative. Many years later, L. K. Jha confirmed the veracity of the *Times* report—he said that there had been a serious attempt to deregulate the industrial economy under Shastri.

It had become clear that Nehru's economic path was delivering neither growth nor equity. Shastri had done some fire fighting, particularly in freeing agriculture, and he had tried to shift the tone towards the market. But he died before he could change course. We persisted on the wrong path in the 1970s and 1980s even when we knew that we were failing and the "mixed economy" was leading to a dead end. In fact, Indira Gandhi's government became even more rigid, introduced more controls, and became bureaucratic and authoritarian. It nationalized banks, discouraged foreign investment, and placed more hurdles before domestic enterprise. Some East Asian countries, in the meantime, began to make a decisive break with the past and adopted export-oriented policies that did not distort market prices.

Modern India's tragedy is not that we adopted the wrong economic model in the 1950s, but that we did not reverse direction after 1965. Industrial growth (not economic growth) plunged from 7.7 percent a year between 1951 and 1965 to 4 percent between 1966 and 1980. India withdrew further from world trade, raised tariffs and taxes even higher, and became one of the worst-performing developing countries in the 1970s. Rakesh Mohan, the head of the National Council of Applied Economic Research, has conservatively estimated the economic cost of Mrs. Gandhi's follies at 1.3 percent lower per capita GDP growth per year. Put another way, the per capita GDP would have been at least 80 percent higher in 1990—$550 instead of $300. With some modest liberalization in the eighties, industry did begin to grow, but experts agree that "1966–1980 is effectively the dark period for the Indian economy." Ironically, Mrs. Gandhi ruled in the name of the poor—"garibi hatao" ("End poverty") was her winning slogan during elections. But in the end, she suppressed economic growth and destroyed the chances for the poor.

Experts came up with different answers about what was going wrong and why growth was decelerating. Indira Gandhi's apologists argued that the terms of trade had changed in favor of agriculture after the green revolution. This is patently incorrect, for these terms did not change until the 1991 reforms. Others said that inequalities had grown and the market for mass-consumption products had shrunk. Hence, overall demand was the problem. This hypothesis, too, seems false, for the Gini coefficient, which measures income inequality, does not support it. A third explanation was the lack of capital. This too cannot be true, for the most dramatic change in the post-Independence economy has been the rise in savings rate and capital formation. India's savings rate rose from about 6 percent in 1950 to 14 percent in 1960, 18 percent in 1980, and to 23 percent of income by 1990. The investment rate also rose from 17 percent in 1960 to 23 percent of national income in the 1980s. This compares well with the advanced countries, although it may not be as high as that of the Asian tigers. Thus, shortage of capital was not the reason for our failure.

The blame lies squarely with the productivity of our investments, as well as their capital-intensive nature. Although we saved and invested, the returns were poor. Economist Isher Ahluwalia estimates that the productivity of Indian manufacturing declined half a percent a year between 1960 and 1985. Capital–output ratio deteriorated because we got poor returns from the inefficient, heavy-industry-based public sector. The private sector did not perform because we had emasculated it with massive controls. Ironically, we had created state-owned companies in part to raise our savings rate. We thought they would give good returns and this would augment the nation's savings. But they failed and ended up destroying our savings. The growth in savings actually came from private households.

Infrastructure was the other reason for our poor performance. Power, railways, coal, telephones became bottlenecks. Anyone who lived in India in the 1970s and 1980s felt the horrendous shortages. There were constant blackouts as power was unavailable. Railway freight suddenly started declining. There were shortages of coal, cement, steel. One seemed to feed on the other. For example, once railways started doing badly, then coal did not get taken from the coal mine to the thermal plant that made electricity from coal. If enough electricity was not generated, then coal could not be mined. If coal and electric power suffered, then the railways could not run. Why the bottlenecks developed was a subject of constant study but insufficient action. A combination of declining productivity and slowing investment was the problem. All infrastructure was state-controlled and not subject to market forces. Even cement was heavily controlled. This meant that politicians and bureaucrats set prices and decided when and where to build a new factory. A strong politician could get away with building a power plant in his area even when the shortage was in another area. Or he might build a railway line to please his rural voters when the more industrial areas needed it. He justified it in the name of equity and regional balance. Mismatches quickly came about, for the rules of demand and supply were not followed. Hopelessly low prices meant that the state power companies became bankrupt and did not have the funds to invest in new plants or expand existing ones.

Trade unions became powerful because politicians were unwilling to displease their large vote bank. Trade unions wanted to hire more workers, and existing workers to work less. This suited the politicians, for it meant that they could create jobs and please the voters. According to the law, no one could fire a worker for not working. As the work ethic declined, productivity plummeted. Managers of the state enterprise complained, but no one listened. Workers would loiter on the job and often not show up, and the managers could do nothing. Many power plants ran at half their efficiency. Linesmen of the power companies made private deals with small industrialists and stole a third of the power; they "fixed" the power meters so that their crime could not be detected. A mafia operated in the coal mining area of Bihar and became a law unto itself. Finances of the government rapidly deteriorated and there was no money for new investments. The result was shortages. The amazing thing is that the system did not completely break down.

Our company's salesman in Bengal was a bit of a hero during the 1980s because his sales were consistently rising. One of the reasons, he said, was his excellent performance from Haldia, where a state fertilizer plant had been set up. Thousands of well-paid workers had lifted the demand for our products. A sparkling new township had come up with bungalows for managers and nice flats for workers. There were wide roads, bright lights, a school, a dispensary, and a hospital, even a subsidized store for the employees. The capital budget of the plant had paid for this middle-class dream. However, the factory never produced a kilo of fertilizer! And this went on for years. The cleaning crew kept the factory clean, the mechanics kept the machinery in good order, and the workshop supplied spare parts. The managers and workers came to work, and the personnel department marked attendance. Everyone was paid, including a bonus, and even overtime in some cases. However, they had no work because soon after the factory was built it was discovered that the company was unviable. If they had produced, they would have lost masses of money. It was cheaper not to produce. Yet they could not close down. Not only was it bad politics to close, the law did not permit it.

The plight of Haldia was extreme, but there were other examples. Another firm, Scooters India Ltd., in Lucknow, was still paying wages to three thousand workers in 1992, although it had not built a scooter for ten years. By the end of the eighties three-quarters of the state-owned companies were losing money. To pay for these losses the subsidy to state enterprises rose from 3 percent of their income in 1970–77 to 26 percent in 1980–81. It was 20 percent in 1988–89.

Prakash Tandon, who wrote the classic memoir *Punjabi Century,* relates a fascinating tale of public and private sectors. Each year he used to take his family on holiday to Kashmir by road from Bombay. One year, he noticed a petrol station had come up on the highway beyond Nasik. About the same time a large public-sector factory had also come up twenty kilometers beyond the petrol pump, complete with wide, tree-lined boulevards, spacious homes, schools, hospitals, and sports amenities. The next year, Tandon noticed that the petrol pump was doing good business and a mechanic's workshop had come up alongside. The following year, he found that a roadside restaurant had also come up whose food was especially popular among truck drivers. A cigarette and paan vendor followed; then a fruit seller; next came a tailor and a general merchant. In less than a decade, a flourishing little town emerged. Meanwhile, the state company began to lose money, and in the same period its losses had grown colossal.

The contrast is instructive. In one case, wealth was created organically. A lonely petrol pump attracted entrepreneurs, and they offered services that people wanted. They reinvested their profits and they expanded. Their profits attracted others. In the end, society's wealth was generated from within and it supported a flourishing population of a thousand families. It had all started with a petrol pump! Twenty kilometers away, the state also created a town. However, with one difference—the state destroyed society's wealth.

During these unfortunate decades the number of people who depended on the state expanded enormously. Fully 70 percent of the employees in India's "organized sector" (that is, firms employing more than ten workers) received their paychecks from the government. If one excludes civil servants and the government bureaucracy, 55 percent of the Indian industrial workforce was on the rolls of public-sector companies in 1990. Yet the public sector's share of production was only 27 percent in 1990. By contrast, China's state-owned firms employed 40 percent of its industrial workers. The very rapid growth of private enterprise in the eighties following China's reforms means that India's economy is now more socialist than China's.

By 1990, India's planning process had created a large rentier class of state employees in the public enterprises and the bureaucracies of the central, state, and local governments. This class exercised great power. It mediated every significant decision. It directed society's resources—it decided what to produce, at what price; who would get subsidies, who would get credit; who would get licenses. This gave this new class enormous authority over ordinary citizens and the ability to extract "rents"—the economist's term for corruption and bribery. Since nothing happened without some sort of exchange, there also emerged a group of power brokers who cultivated the ruling class and utilized their contacts for personal gain.

After 1967, India withdrew further from world trade. Our products became shoddier and more expensive as we raised tariffs dramatically. Actual duties collected went up from 21.2 percent of total imports between 1960 and 1965 to 54.8 percent in 1985–90, while exports stagnated around 5 percent of GDP. We protected our industry with draconian controls that we administered in a ridiculous "case by case" manner. Ironically, these heavy-handed controls were created to conserve foreign exchange; yet we were in balance-of-payment difficulties in twenty-nine out of thirty-five years from 1956 onwards. Despite these enormous defects, industry did manage to grow at a little over 6 percent a year over the forty years from 1950 to 1990, and its share in the country's income doubled from 11.8 percent in 1951–52 to 24.6 percent of GDP by 1990–91. But it was not enough for the economy to take off. Although we saved and invested, the returns were poor. Our expenditure on the bureaucracy far outstripped the growth in the nation's income. Predictably, India's position declined in the world and among similarly placed countries. Based on John Page's broad comparative data for the Third World, Rakesh Mohan concluded that "India was amongst the worst performers among developing countries between 1950 and 1982."

I sometimes wonder how we could have gone so wrong when we had such brilliant economists. The Delhi School of Economics had acquired a formidable and well-deserved international reputation as a center of excellence. It had Jagdish Bhagwati doing seminal work on trade; A. L. Nagar was engaged in pathbreaking work in econometrics; Sukhamoy Chakravarty was one of the authorities on planning models and one of the first persons to employ Pontryagin's mathematical principles in economics; Tapan Raychaudhari and Dharma Kumar had formidable reputations in economic history; Amartya Sen and Prasanta Pattanaik were world-renowned in social choice theory—with Amartya Sen going on to win the Nobel Prize. However, Professor Jagdish Bhagwati was the only Indian economist of note who tried to rouse Indians to the danger of Nehruvian socialism. His book (with Padma Desai) *Indian Planning for Industrialisation* was the first comprehensive study of the variety of ailments caused by our left turns of the 1950s and 1960s. As the intellectual climate worsened, rather than bang against the wall of intellectual intolerance erected by Indira Gandhi, Bhagwati left to teach first at MIT and then at Columbia University in New York. Amartya Sen also went away to the London School of Economics, then to Oxford, and finally to Harvard.

Apart from fine theoreticians, there were some outstanding practitioners. One of them was I. G. Patel. After important roles in the finance ministry in the 1950s, he became the governor of the Reserve Bank in the Janata government of 1977, and later was head of the London School of Economics. I. G. Patel set high standards of behavior. At the Reserve Bank, he resisted loan and debt write-offs and did not allow the banking system to deteriorate. However, he became increasingly uncomfortable during Mrs. Gandhi's second regime. Just before the 1972 elections, L. N. Mishra, Mrs. Gandhi's minister, and his friends rang him up frequently asking for clearances, which he invariably refused. Later, in 1980, when IG was at the Reserve Bank, politicians lobbied to give a license to the notorious Bank of Credit and Commerce International (BCCI), the Middle Eastern bank which grew rapidly in the seventies and collapsed in the early nineties. IG suspected BCCI and refused it a license. However, the minister of state at the time called for the BCCI file, overrode IG and approved the license. When IG heard about it, he rushed to Delhi and asked to meet the Prime Minister. Because of that meeting, the license to BCCI was withheld. After Mrs. Gandhi returned to power, IG began to feel uncomfortable and he resigned. There were two other Oxbridge-educated economists—Manmohan Singh, who served in important roles in the 1970s and 1980s, succeeding IG as governor of the Reserve Bank, and Montek Singh Ahluwalia, who was in various economic ministries throughout the eighties. Manmohan and Montek later became famous for ushering in India's 1991–93 economic reforms. The troubling question is why these outstanding people did not blow the whistle. They kept serving a bankrupt system for years, providing it with intellectual respectability and support.

My leftist friends were euphoric that day in 1969 when Mrs. Gandhi nationalized India's fourteen largest banks. They had always been critical of our banking system. They regarded the banks as "monopoly capitalists," controlled by a handful of big business houses, who made loans only to their affiliated companies or to their cronies. Mrs. Gandhi's purpose in nationalizing the banks was to reorient credit flows to the neglected areas—agriculture, small-scale industries, and small borrowers. She wanted banks to open branches in small towns and villages and bring the average Indian into the banking system. All worthy goals, which she succeeded in achieving. In the next two decades bank branches rose from 8,262 in 1969 to 60,190 in 1991—half of them in rural areas—and the average population served by a bank declined from 65,000 in 1969 to 11,000 in 1991. Bank deposits soared from 13 percent of GDP in 1969 to 38 percent in 1991, and loans expanded from 10 percent to 25 percent of GDP in the same period.

That was the good news. The bad news was that the efficiency of the system sank. Productivity and profitability of banks plunged. By 1990, the banks' gross profits dropped to 1.1 percent of working funds (without counting their bad debts) and their establishment expenses rose to 2 percent of working funds. Bad debts—what is euphemistically called "nonperforming assets"—rose to 20 percent of the credit outstanding. Consequently, most of the public-sector banks are bankrupt, especially the rural banks. They have been "captured" by their employees, the unions, and politicians, and it takes my wife half an hour to make a deposit or withdraw money from our local branch.

I once chanced to meet the manager of one of the rural branches of a nationalized bank. It was on the night train between Delhi and Amritsar. We shared our dinner like friendly travelers, and before I settled down to read for an hour prior to going to bed, he told me a few things about running a rural branch. He was a sincere young man, deeply concerned, and he wanted to unburden himself about his day-to-day problems. Neither he nor his staff, he told me, decided who qualified for a loan. The local politicians invariably made this decision. The loan takers were invariably cronies of the political bosses and did not intend to repay the money. He was told that such and such a person was to be treated as a "deserving poor." Without exception, they were rich. When the loan turned bad, the political bosses disowned any knowledge of the loan or the recipient. Therefore, at the time of the default it was the bank manager's head on the chopping block. Periodically he received instructions from headquarters to roll over the loan when it was against the rules to do so. These too were delivered orally. He dared not ask for written orders, because the only order in writing would be his transfer to an even remoter location. In contrast, when he or his office gave loans to genuine small farmers and traders, they invariably paid them off. There might be delays, but he always knew the reasons, and he was certain that the money would come back as soon as the crop was harvested.

Even more frustrating was the behavior of his staff. He did not run the office. The trade union representative decided who did what, who was to be promoted, and who transferred. He tried to promote a female clerk who was doing exceptionally well. But he was vetoed by the union leader. "Of what use am I?" he asked me sadly. I deeply empathized with his situation. I went to bed thinking what I might have done in his place. However, I could not find an easy answer. At least in my company I did not have to put up with this nonsense. The next morning, as we were getting off at Amritsar, I suggested to him that he find another job.

Because of nationalization, genuine entrepreneurs have had a harrowing time getting loans. Amrik Singh, whom I met in Bombay, was fed up with the routine of his job and decided to become a hog farmer. An enthusiastic electronics engineer, he had looked at a number of alternatives, but the rural life appealed to him. His friends tried to discourage him. However, he felt that "fourteen years in electronics is a lifetime." Being a serious person, he vigorously began studying pigs and soon became quite knowledgeable. He acquired property in a village 105 kilometers away and gave it a nice name, Arcadia Breeders. Having got the land, the next step was to find capital. For that he approached the nationalized bank in his village for a loan. The bank manager refused. Amrik Singh then asked him for a "no-objection certificate" (NOC), which would qualify him to approach another bank. The bank manager would not issue him an NOC either. After numerous visits, he at last got the manager to relent. "Submit a report," he said. "I will reject it and issue you an NOC." Amrik Singh protested, "But if you reject it, no other financial institution will touch it." Many follow-ups and seven months later, Amrik Singh finally succeeded in getting his prized NOC from the bank manager. He had learned his first lesson: had he bribed the bank manager, he would have received the loan.

After getting the NOC, he applied to another nationalized bank for a loan. This took eleven months, and only because of a chance meeting with a classmate at the rural refinance bank, which pushed his case. Meanwhile, his costs shot up and he worried if his project was still viable. Finally, he shifted to the village and began constructing sheds for the animals. A month later, the tehsildar, or village head, came by and ordered him to stop construction because he could not build on agricultural land. Amrik Singh argued that hog production was an agricultural activity like poultry, and sheds were permitted for the animals. The tehsildar refused to listen. He approached the deputy director of animal husbandry and requested him to clarify in writing that hog farming was an agricultural activity. The deputy director also refused to help. Three months later, he threw in the towel and decided to convert his land for nonagricultural use. For this he required a no-objection certificate from four different departments. Soon he became discouraged, running from one office to another. Giving up, he hired a middleman, who promptly bribed the different departments and got him the conversion in less than a month. The same tehsildar signed the order. By now he had lost six months, the monsoon had arrived, and he could not begin construction because the labor was deployed in paddy growing. He finally resumed construction after a year's delay.

Amrik Singh also qualified for Rs 100,000 seed capital under a government scheme to encourage entrepreneurs in rural areas. He promptly applied for a loan from the Development Corporation of Konkan. Again, after repeated follow-ups, he got the loan sanctioned after ten months. However, he received only Rs 69,000, because the corporation had run out of money. It seems a large part of the corporation's funds had been spent on the officers of the bureaucracy and on the traveling expenses of politicians. Consequently, the government shifted the power of giving loans to the district industries commission. Two and a half years later, when he had still not received the money, he lodged a complaint with the ombudsman, the Lokayukt of the Maharashtra government. Eight months later, he received the balance amount.

The experience of my pig farmer is no different from that of thousands of young entrepreneurs. In other countries, the entrepreneur's battle is with competitors. In India, the main enemy is the government bureaucracy. Bank nationalization has made matters infinitely worse. The bureaucrat has figured out that an entrepreneur has limited resources; he faces the pressure of time because interest costs mount by the day. So the government functionary attempts to delay every decision. It is true that many entrepreneurs fail because they are crooked or incompetent, but a large number do not succeed because they cannot cope with the bureaucracy. I am convinced that entrepreneurship in India will not flourish until we get rid of "Inspector Raj." As a citizen, I too have had to seek permissions from the government on various occasions. The last time was when we made the mistake of remodeling our house in Delhi. It took two years, thirty-eight visits, and hundreds of phone calls to the New Delhi Municipal Council and related departments before we got the permission to do so.

To the socialist mind of the 1960s, business families had a bad odor. Most people believed that they ran their businesses only for their families' welfare, without any concern for the consumer or outside investors. They thought that business houses were crooked—they did not pay their taxes, they underinvoiced their sales, and they siphoned money out of the business. Parliament was also obsessed with the "monopoly power" of business houses. Between 1964 and 1969 the government appointed four committees to examine the affairs of big business. They looked into seventy-five business families and did not like what they saw. Each year the Department of Company Affairs collected information on the growth of assets and sales of the seventy-five houses and placed it obediently before Parliament.

I am convinced that much of the findings were true. Some families defended themselves in private, saying that government controls and a 97 percent tax rate were responsible for their acts. The defense was also true. The License Raj did indeed make businessmen crooked. They cornered industrial licenses (meant to broad-base enterprise) and perpetuated the control of markets. Their products were shoddy because there was little or no competition. Shareholder returns were not the reason to do business—only control and ownership mattered. The way to do business was to get a "friendly bank" to give you a loan for the capital cost of your project. You recycled 15 percent of this loan and it became your equity contribution in the company. Then you siphoned out money from the business by giving your uncle commissions on purchases and your nephew commissions on sales. You could also grow by buying up cheaply the plantations and trading businesses of the departing English companies. By financing the elections of a dozen MPs, you could buy protection.

This was the scene when Indira Gandhi made her next major socialist move after bank nationalization. She enacted the Monopolies and Restrictive Trade Practices (MRTP) Act in 1969 and crippled private industry for a generation. When Parliament was debating the MRTP bill, I got the opportunity to meet the legendary J. R. D. Tata. Every citizen of Bombay knew that he controlled the largest industrial empire in India. He was the uncrowned prince of the only city in India where commercial power is esteemed above political power. Although the house of Tatas was at the top of the monopolies list, everyone respected JRD for his integrity. The Tata companies were thought to be squeaky clean and not to have indulged in questionable practices.

Piloo Mody, my fat and generous friend and a Swatantra Party MP, drove us to a shaded bungalow surrounded by a spacious green compound in the heart of the concrete jungle. We had come to JRD's home, The Cairn. We walked along a long, winding passage, interspersed with dozens of steps, past faded public rooms that seemed rarely used but were filled with flowers. Eventually we arrived in JRD's study. When he got up to receive us, I realized that he was smaller than I had imagined. I sat on a gray sofa and looked around the simple, lived-in room. The portrait of Jamshetji, the founder of the Tatas, caught my eye. So this was the daring man, I thought, who had defied colonial prejudice to set up a steel plant in 1907 and one of the greatest hotels in the world—the magnificent Taj Mahal Hotel—because he was not allowed to stay in the one beside it at the Gateway in Bombay.

JRD looked at me and said, "Yesterday in Parliament, they called me a monopolist with 'great concentration of power.' I wake up each morning and I am supposed to say, 'I have great concentration of power. Whom shall I crush today? A competitor or a worker in my factory, or the consumer?'" I did not quite know what to say.

"No, dear boy, I am powerless," he said. "I cannot decide how much to borrow, what shares to issue, at what price, what wages or bonus to pay, and what dividend to give. I even need the government's permission for the salary I pay to a senior executive." He smiled sadly. "Let's have some tea, shall we?"

Turning to Piloo, he said, "Now, let's see what your Swatantra Party can do about this bill—it is such an ineffective party! You do know what this new legislation means, don't you? Henceforth, I will not be allowed to start a new business or even expand an older one. What do they expect me to do?" There was an uncomfortable pause. "Sit here and wait till I die, I suppose." His face was again filled with sadness.

"But that's precisely why I have come, Jeh—to fight this bill in Parliament," said Piloo. "I need your comments on the draft memo for the Select Committee." Wearily, JRD opened the drawer and pulled out the draft. "I have corrected it in several places. Do you think it will do any good? She has the votes, you know."

Behind him in the cupboard I saw the famous reports—*The Mahalanobis Committee, 1964; The Monopolies Inquiry Commission, 1965; The Hazari Committee, 1966;* and *The Dutt Committee on Licensing, 1969.* He saw me looking at them and he said bitterly, "I have read them all." He handed Piloo the memo and we got up to go. On the way home, Piloo said, "You did not see him at his best, and this new bill has been the last straw. Things started going downhill with the nationalization of Air India sixteen years ago. He is a pilot at heart, and ever since they took Air India away, he has not been the same."

"He seems to live very simply for a man in his position," I said.

"He doesn't care about money," said Piloo. "He is not wealthy. All the Tata shares are in trusts. Whatever he inherited personally, he has also put that into a trust. In any case, he pays ninety-seven percent of his earnings to income tax; then, he pays wealth tax, and this takes his tax rate to over one hundred percent. His entire income goes in taxes, and he has to sell some assets each year to live on."

Despite their great efforts in Parliament, the Swatantra Party could not stop the MRTP bill. In the end, Mrs. Gandhi had the votes. No one read JRD's carefully drafted memorandum. A different sort of MP had come into power, one who had no use for such information. Tata's methods seemed to belong to a different era. The MRTP Act turned out to be one of the most damaging in modern Indian history. Any group with combined assets above Rs 20 crore was declared a monopoly and effectively debarred from expanding its business after 1969. A single company, with assets above Rs 1 crore, puny by world standards, was similarly placed under "antimonopolistic supervision and control." Freddie Mehta, a director of Tatas, told me in 1989 that the Tatas made over a hundred proposals for new business projects or to expand existing ones over the twenty years since the MRTP law. All of them were rejected. In the mid-1980s, Rajiv Gandhi's government raised the MRTP asset limit fivefold to Rs 100 crore. Finally, in September 1991, the Narasimha Rao government scrapped this ridiculous law.

For all their difficulties from a hostile government over the past fifty years, Tatas' core businesses were strong and they were still the largest industrial group in 1997 with a sales turnover of more than Rs 35,000 crore ($10 billion). India's first political and commercial families, the Nehrus and the Tatas, had been family friends since Motilal Nehru first brought his two children, Jawaharlal and Vijaylakshmi, to JRD's father's home in the 1920s. This friendship had continued through the years. At Jawaharlal's request, JRD had sent a parcel of mangoes to the Mountbattens in the summer of 1949. For years, Indira Gandhi used to accompany her father to JRD's shack on Juhu Beach in Bombay, or they met when JRD was invited to Nehru's home in Delhi. Both Nehru and JRD had spent their impressionable years in Europe and acquired a rational, scientific temper. Even their vision of modern India was the same. Yet JRD continued to feel a sense of personal defeat until the end—he was not able to make Nehru or Indira appreciate the value of private enterprise.

JRD tried a number of times to engage Nehru, but each time he was rebuffed. Once, before lunch in Delhi, JRD innocently mentioned that the public sector ought to be making a profit. Nehru snapped back, "Never talk to me about profit, Jeh, it is a dirty word," and he turned to look out of the window, a well-rehearsed sign that Nehru was not interested in listening. To make amends, Nehru quietly took JRD to see his giant panda. Indira had a different manner, but she could be equally impolite. Every time JRD tried to discuss economic policy with her, she would begin to doodle or open her mail. Once when this happened, JRD whispered to his colleague, Sharokh Sabawalla, "She's not interested. We are boring her." Mrs. Gandhi looked up. "No, no. I'm not bored. I'm listening, Jeh."

JRD used to urge Mrs. Gandhi to give more autonomy and accountability to the public sector. At a lecture he once said, "I am convinced that a prime cause of the inefficiency and high cost prevailing in most public enterprises does not lie in the quality, competence, or dedication of their management and staff, but in the continuing denial to them of the degree of managerial freedom of action essential to the efficient management of any large undertaking." Thus, JRD summed up the failure of public enterprise in modern India. I agree. The blame squarely lies with the bureaucracy, which has done serious harm by consistently interfering with state enterprises on a day-to-day basis. The bureaucrat and the politician have slowed decision making to such a pitiful pace that morale and discipline have been crippled. In the beginning, it may have been natural for the ministries to keep a watch on their creations. However, in time, it should have given way to managerial autonomy, as in European public enterprises.

The Gandhians compounded the follies during Mrs. Gandhi's raj. They forced the government to protect traditional industries, like handloom textiles, even when it was obvious that we were throwing good money after bad. They were hostile to modern industry, especially large industry, because it did not create enough jobs and it destroyed traditional industry. They did not understand that unviable companies must die. They felt that once capital and employment are created, they must be protected at any cost. This brand of thinking came to be called Gandhian socialism, and it became especially popular during the Janata Party's rule. Gandhian socialists succeeded in reserving 863 industries for the small sector. This meant that only entrepreneurs who invested less than Rs 60 lakh could enter one of these industries, and thus they eliminated competition from large or medium enterprises. Small firms lost the incentive to improve their products, update production techniques, reduce costs, and introduce new technology or new designs. Underlying the Gandhian socialist philosophy was a distrust of the competitive market, and the belief that whatever could be produced by small industry was inherently better, no matter what the cost and quality.

Abid Husain's committee showed in the mid-1990s that small-scale reservation was responsible for our miserable export performance, and wanted it scrapped. The Gandhian socialists were unmoved. The committee argued that the success of Japan and East Asia had been built on the competitive export of simple manufactures—toys, shoes, garments. In India these were precisely the products reserved for the small sector.

Competition would have improved our products and their potential as exports, but socialist thinking has sunk into our bones so deeply that the very subject is now a holy cow. We continue to hold the view that the small and the weak must be protected at any cost. Because of this thinking, our labor legislation makes it impossible to remove a worker on any grounds. Eventually, managements in the 1990s stopped recruiting labor and began to "farm out" manufacturing to smaller companies, who were not governed by the same stringent laws or were able to bribe labor inspectors. Labor in the organized sector stopped growing. My company did the same. We asked several entrepreneurs, one near Ahmedabad and another near Hyderabad, to manufacture Vicks throat drops on our behalf. We gave them supervisors to ensure quality, and our costs dropped significantly.

<center>~~~~~~</center>

One day in the hot summer of 1975 I came home early. I had learned that the Supreme Court had confirmed that Indira Gandhi was guilty of corrupt election practices and would have to resign. I was shocked. "How can they do it for something so trivial? It is like removing the Prime Minister for speeding in traffic," I said. The Allahabad High Court had found her guilty of using a government employee in her election and state machinery to put up rostrums and mikes during her campaign. I felt it was a minor impropriety, not an offense. Mrs. Gandhi had won by 100,000 votes, and this could not have affected the outcome.

Instead of resigning, Indira Gandhi declared an Emergency. Before dawn the next morning, police parties acting under her orders woke up political opponents and locked them up. In the next thirty-six hours, India had changed from a democracy to a dictatorship. We were angry but our anger did not last long. We were not excessively political in the commercial city of Bombay, and like millions of Indians, we slowly got absorbed in our work and our daily lives. Because of press censorship, neither did we know what was happening. The one thing we did notice was that public life began to improve visibly. Clerks began to work in government offices, trains and planes began to run on time, labor in factories became more productive, public officials became courteous and responsive. People began to say that if this was what it would take to get India going, perhaps the Emergency was not such a bad thing. Even Gandhi's great disciple Vinoba Bhave called it Anushasan Parva, a period of discipline.

It was too good to last, however. Gradually the discipline began to decline. Indira Gandhi's rule was replaced by her son's tyranny. Sanjay Gandhi was only twenty-eight, but as far as his mother was concerned, he could do no wrong. A dropout from the prestigious Doon School and an apprentice motor mechanic with Rolls-Royce in England, Sanjay Gandhi had won his mother's confidence by giving her the slogan that won her the 1971 elections—"End poverty." As Sanjay began to rule with his coterie, we heard that every chief minister and cabinet minister had become his sycophant. Once Sanjay's slipper fell, we heard, and three chief ministers ran to pick it up. They followed his most ridiculous and most criminal orders without hesitation. All our institutions were infected by the virus. The police, the judiciary, the civil service, the state chief ministers, the cabinet, the presidency—all went into decline. Corruption became rampant and the cult of sycophancy became the ruling ideology as the number of political opponents in jail reached 100,000.

Despite press censorship, we began to hear horrendous tales. Sanjay Gandhi had the laudable thought that India's expanding population needed to be controlled. He hit upon the idea of sterilizing the male population of India. With his usual frenzy, he threw himself into this project. Anyone with more than two children would be mandatorily sterilized. He gave quotas to petty bureaucrats, but he did not lay down safeguards. There was no regard for age, whether a person was married or single, or how many children he had.

We wondered how did Indira Gandhi, who had grown up in one of the most cultivated homes in the country and was privileged to meet the best minds of the age, allow this to happen? How could the daughter of such a principled and idealistic father have done this debased deed? Some said that the answer lay in her contradictory childhood. Her mother had died when she was young; her early years had been lonely when her father was constantly away in jail; she was left in the care of her two tough aunts, Nehru's younger sisters. Hence, she had become introspective and withdrawn. This had been compounded by an unhappy marriage with Firoze Gandhi, who died young in 1960. Ever since his death, they said, she depended only on her two sons, Rajiv and Sanjay. Whatever the reasons, we were staggered by the insolence of her action.

Mercifully, the Emergency lasted only twenty-one months. Mrs. Gandhi made a blunder in thinking that she was still popular and could win an election. After all, even a dictator needs legitimacy. She called and lost the election. Morarji Desai, now a part of the Janata opposition, finally got what he had always wanted. He became India's fourth Prime Minister on 24 March 1977.

Between 1965 and 1991, instead of changing course as many countries did, we tightened our system, making it more rigid and bureaucratic. Even China changed course in 1978, letting in competition, and set out on a historic path of growth. India continued to eliminate competition because it regarded it as wasteful. We made modest reforms in the 1980s, but it was far from what was needed. For example, we partially lifted controls on cement, and within two years we went from terrible scarcity to plenty. The only loser was the cement controller. But we did not learn from this and decontrol other industries as well.

It is easy to blame Jawaharlal Nehru. Although he initiated the wrong economic policies, they represented the wisdom of his age. As the failure became apparent, many developing countries changed course in the early 1970s. India did not. One *has* to blame Indira Gandhi, who ruled India during most of this period. In another sense, the entire Indian ruling class is guilty. We cannot trust ourselves unless we understand how well-meaning professionals, steeped in a modern scientific outlook, could further such an insane economic tyranny. I feel a chill when I think that it was our brightest economists and administrators (some of whom later became reformers) who were in positions of power and who defended and acted on behalf of this tyranny. "India's misfortune," says Jagdish Bhagwati, "was to have brilliant economists."

More and more young Indians insistently ask how we could have created these terrible things. And why did so few protest and demand economic freedom? The reason is that the victims were unorganized private citizens—farmers, businessmen, the unemployed, consumers. Businessmen are fine producers of goods and jobs, but they are cowards and do not speak out. One of them, Rahul Bajaj, did finally speak out at a hearing of the Monopolies Commission. The court asked him why he should not be prosecuted for producing more scooters than his licensed capacity. Bajaj replied, "Sir, my grandfather went to jail for my country's freedom. I stand ready to do the same for producing on behalf of my motherland." The MRTP inquiry was quietly dropped. In those dark days I used to worry myself silly that we had produced Vicks VapoRub beyond our authorized limit during a flu epidemic. Our legal manager spent months working with lawyers to prepare a defense in case we were hauled up. We lived in the same fear when it came to our profits. During good years, our profits had marginally exceeded the government's profitability limit as laid down by the Drug Price Control Order.

Most people remember the Emergency because it represented a generalized loss of liberty. They do not understand that by suppressing economic liberty for forty years, we destroyed growth and the future of two generations. For the average citizen it was a great betrayal. Lest we forget, we lived under a system where a third of the people went hungry and malnourished, half were illiterate while the elite enjoyed a vast system of higher education, and one of ten infants died at childbirth. Our controls and red tape stifled the entrepreneur and the farmer, and the command mentality of the bureaucrat, which fed the evil system, continues till today to frustrate every effort at reform.

TWELVE

Merchants of Marwar

No matter who reigns, the merchant reigns.

—HENRY WARD BEECHER

M arwaris have never got the respect from Indian society that
they have always yearned for. The average Indian thinks of
the Marwari as either a small-time shopkeeper who is also a
moneylender or a ruthless tycoon. Yet theirs is a fascinating story of how
a tiny community from the desert sands of Rajasthan spread out to every
corner of north, east, and central India, settling in thousands of villages
and towns in the ninteenth century. With their enormous appetite for
risk, Marwaris seized control of India's inland trade. Gradually they
turned to industry after the First World War, and today they control
roughly half the nation's private industrial assets. What made them so
successful? And why were they not able to create an industrial revolution and broadly transform the country? I shall explore these questions
first in the context of the historical emergence of Marwaris and later in
the story of Aditya Birla, the grandson of G. D. Birla, during the License
Raj.

Indian industry originated with the old merchant castes and they
continue to dominate till today. Fifteen of the twenty largest industrial
houses in 1997 were of Vaishya or bania trading castes. Eight were Marwaris. (Similarly, in contemporary Pakistan, most of the twenty-two

families who reputedly own half the nation's wealth are Kutchi Memons, the leading Muslim trading caste of undivided India.) In the latter half of the nineteenth century, the trading communities started the first cotton textile mills in Bombay and Ahmedabad. There were Parsees, Khojas, and Bhatia traders in Bombay and Jain banias in Ahmedabad. Although the Marwaris came late, after the First World War, they became the most successful. The Marwaris come from Marwar, the old Jodhpur state in Rajasthan. The most successful families come from the small Shekhawati region in the old Bikaner and Jaipur states. They are all bania by caste and either Jains or Vaishnav Hindus by religious persuasion. Of the 128 Marwari subcastes in Rajasthan, only five became big and prominent in national commerce—Maheshwaris, Oswals, Aggarwals, Porwals, and Khandelwals.

For centuries Marwaris had been bankers and helped finance the land trade between the East and the West, as the great trade route passed through northern Rajasthan. During the Mughal days, they were financiers to many princes, including the emperor's family. Kasturbhai Lalbhai's family was one of them. Jaget Seth, a Marwari Oswal, was banker to the nawabs of Bengal. Not only was he a nawab-maker, he was also a friend of Clive's and played a part in the conspiracy at Plassey. Colonel James Tod, the historian of Rajasthan, noted that in 1832 "nine-tenths of the bankers and commercial men of India are natives of Maroo des, and these chiefly of the Jain faith." As the British created a national market during the nineteenth century, there was a huge migration of Marwari traders into the smallest and remotest villages of India. The migrants began as petty shopkeepers (often with capital advanced from a wholesaler from their own community) and slowly graduated to moneylending, then moved up to finance farmers for their commercial crops, such as opium and cotton. The railways accelerated the process.

Some Marwaris became hugely successful and created large and famous firms, such as Tarachand Ghanshyamdas, with which the Birlas were proud to be associated when they first came to Calcutta around 1900. It had branches at the major seaports in Bombay and Calcutta, on the river ports along the Ganges, and throughout the opium- and cotton-growing areas. The firm took deposits, gave loans, engaged in the wholesale trade of commodities, transferred funds for clients to distant cities, cashed bills of trade, insured shipments, and speculated on commodity futures when the opportunity arose. In such a firm, trading and banking were closely interlinked and every firm was a moneylender. Some firms were exclusively bankers; they were called "shroffs." These "great firms" also lent money to the princely families. For example, Bhagoti Ram Poddar, the founder of the "great firm" Tarachand Ghanshyamdas, was banker to the royal families of Jaipur, Bikaner, and Hyderabad.

The Marwaris achieved their biggest successes in the British trading post of Calcutta. They smelled the chance for big money and they flocked there to become brokers and agents to the British (who called them "banians"). Ramdutt Goenka was a typical example. He came to Calcutta in 1830. Starting as a clerk to a Marwari firm, he gradually became a broker to the major English firms. Nathuram Saraf began as a clerk in Ramdutt Goenka's firm and he graduated to become a banian to other British firms. He opened a free hostel for migrants from the Shekhawati area, and G. D. Birla used to say that this hostel spawned many entrepreneurial careers. At night, the young apprentices would exchange stories of their commercial exploits of the day and draw lessons from them. Some of these stories became legendary. Passed on by word of mouth for generations, it was their version of Harvard Business School cases. The arrival of the Delhi–Calcutta railway in the 1860s quickened the migration to Calcutta, and by the turn of the century Marwaris had become dominant in the jute and cotton trade. During the First World War they made fabulous profits speculating in cotton, jute, and hessian, and these profits laid the foundation for many industrial careers after the war.

Why the Marwaris turned out to be so spectacularly successful had a lot to do with their wonderful support system, explains Tom Timberg in *The Marwaris*. When a Marwari traveled on business, his wife and children were cared for in a joint family at home. Wherever he went in search of trade, he found shelter and good Rajasthani food in a *basa*, a sort of collective hostel run on a cooperative basis or as a philanthropy by local Marwari merchants. G. D. Birla's grandfather, Shiv Narain, settled in a basa when he first came to Bombay in the 1860s. When the Marwari needed money, he borrowed from another Marwari trader on the understanding that the loan was payable on demand, "even at midnight," and that he would reciprocate with a similar loan. At the end of the year, they tallied and settled the interest. He could count on community banks to insure his goods in transit and collect his dues when the goods arrived. His sons and nephews were apprenticed to other Marwari traders, where they earned their salary through profit sharing, learned business skills, and accumulated capital to start their own business when they were ready.

Why some groups in society become entrepreneurs and others do not is an old question. I am not sure that there is a satisfactory answer, but I find that merchants everywhere seem to become the first industrialists. This is not surprising. They possess capital and access to credit; they have business skills; they are used to taking risks; and they are close to the market and understand the nature of the demand. The Marwaris, in addition, have always had a powerful support system within the community. To a lesser degree, this applies to other Indian trading castes. But the Marwaris score over the others because they appear to have a stronger stomach for risk. Many Marwaris made their fortunes during the First World War in extremely speculative trading in futures. Their abilities as businessmen make their competitors fear (and admire) them.

The British businessmen of Calcutta disliked G. D. Birla because he took control of the jute market and forced up prices to the European mills. At the same time, he and other Marwari shippers (Bangur, Goenka, Bajoria) undersold the Europeans in the baled jute market through cut-rate exports by hedging in the *futka* (futures) bazaar. Dalmia, who made his fortune in the Calcutta bullion market in 1917 by speculating on the rise of silver prices in London, also destroyed many English rivals. Nationalist historians interpreted the reaction of British business as an "anti-Indian feeling." In fact, the British rivals behaved like competitors anywhere and did what any businessman would have done to stop competition.

After Independence, Aditya Birla, more than anyone, symbolized the Marwari ethic. In the early eighties I used to see Aditya off and on at the badminton courts of the Bombay Gymkhana Club. He wore thick-rimmed, square glasses over his square face. We used to greet and smile at each other but never became friends. I found him exceedingly reserved, almost ascetic. I had first met him in Boston, when he was a student down the river at MIT and I was at Harvard. He used to stick with his two roommates, and I remember that we shared a passion for Guru Dutt's films, songs from which he played all the time on his hi-fi.

Aditya Birla was shy and it was difficult to believe that he was G. D.

Birla's grandson and the inheritor of one of the largest family fortunes in India. And that amazing wealth had been in his family for more than a hundred years. However, stark simplicity had been part of his family tradition. Behind the shy exterior, there was an attractive quality in Aditya which drew me to him. I was also fascinated by the breakneck speed with which he was building hugely successful companies in Southeast Asia—in Thailand, Malaysia, Indonesia, and the Philippines. By the early 1980s, he had built an empire of a dozen companies in the Far East, which had become global leaders in the manufacture of viscose staple fiber, palm oil, textiles, and carbon black.

Aditya and I were both twenty-one years old when we returned after studying in America. Whereas I joined Vicks as a trainee in 1964, he got busy planning an industrial empire. His grandfather had been keen that he join one of the large family companies (either Gwalior Rayon or Hindustan Aluminium), where he would personally train him, but Aditya politely declined his offer. GD was disappointed, but he also understood Aditya's desire to strike out on his own. After all, had he not done the same at the age of sixteen? Just before the First World War, he had started his own trading company, which became the foundation of his great empire. His son had followed his example and built an independent group of companies. Indeed, his own grandfather, Shiv Narain, had defied his father in the 1860s and set out on his own (rather than join the firm of Ghaneriwalas in Hyderabad). Aditya was merely following a family tradition. Aditya told GD six months before leaving MIT that he wanted to "create something really BIG."

Realizing that Aditya was determined not to join any of the family businesses, his father, Basant Kumar Birla, gave him an unusual graduation gift. He presented him with an industrial license—one of the most coveted pieces of paper at the time. It was for a cotton spinning mill. When giving him the present, the father offered his son the following advice: "This permission is just a piece of paper. If you are interested, take it. If not, tear it up. The entire responsibility, from start to finish, will be yours."

Along with the advice came some seed capital to get started. Without losing a day, Aditya began to look for land to locate the mill; he hired people; he sent out inquiries for machinery. He wanted only the latest technology. He found a piece of land near the Calcutta airport. Before he knew it, he was working fourteen hours a day, shuttling between his home and the factory site forty kilometers away. He also plunged into learning *parta* accounting: he knew this ancient ledger bookkeeping system was critical to success.

His parents now began to think of his marriage. Aditya had been engaged to an attractive Marwari girl, Rajshree Fomra, since he was fourteen and she ten. Now she was seventeen and in a local college in Madurai in the south. They had met only once. They were soon married, in January 1965, in the sprawling gardens of the family bungalow in Calcutta. True to character, Aditya chose Ranchi, a sleepy provincial town in nearby Bihar, for the honeymoon, and he invited several dozen friends and relatives to come along. The decision raised eyebrows, for he was, after all, "America-returned," but Aditya thought the presence of relatives and close friends would help smooth the early relationship between the couple.

On returning from his honeymoon, Aditya was besieged by problems at his textile factory. He found that he had hired the wrong executives. The 1965 Indo-Pakistan war had begun to delay deliveries and his project costs were out of control. He was mortified. He had also broken an article of family faith—a Birla plant always started on time. However, Aditya learned from this experience: it was the first and last time that he failed to construct a factory on time (and he built seventy factories in his lifetime!). The plant started in October 1965 with twelve thousand spindles and six hundred employees, and by 1967 it had turned in its first profits. Aditya was now ready for his second company. Around this time, the Birlas were offered a "sick company" by the respected Morarjee Vaidya family of Bombay. It was a large firm called Indian Rayon, employing thousands of people. Because of mismanagement, it had run up huge losses. Since it was well known, the asking price was also high. The family did not like the proposal, but Aditya saw in it untapped potential, valuable assets—and a challenge. He argued persuasively and convinced the family to take it over.

Aditya was thrilled to have a second company. But his joy was short-lived. The workers in the plant near Bombay soon went on strike. A few months later a fire broke out. The blaze continued all night, and when Aditya arrived the next morning, the plant was a shambles. He worked day and night, and within weeks he got the production started. Slowly and painfully, with a lot of time, effort, and money, he turned the company around. Gradually, he pushed up quality and productivity; he pioneered colored yarn. Eventually, Indian Rayon became one of the largest and most profitable Indian companies. By the decade's end all three generations of the main Birla branch—GD, Basant Kumar, and Aditya—owned flourishing, independent businesses. It was also the time that Indira Gandhi was consolidating her hold on the Congress Party with a series of populist moves—nationalizing banks and enacting draconian controls on private investment. Her socialist acts clearly dampened Birlas' attempts to expand, to build world-size plants (with economies of scale), to bring in world-class technology, or even modernize old plants. In the end, she crippled them.

Mrs. Gandhi's damaging policies were a clear signal to Aditya Birla that his future did not lie in India. The thought depressed him no end. At MIT, he had been excited by the way the capitalist world did business—there were transparent regulations rather than licenses and quotas, and there were reasonable taxes. Having turned around Indian Rayon, Aditya now hungered after bigger challenges. If he could not do it in India, he would have to go outside. His thoughts turned eastwards. He sent one of his managers to Bangkok, who brought a positive report saying that there was a growing market and the Thai government was hospitable. This was it, thought Aditya. He decided to set up a synthetic fiber plant. Although there was a war raging next door in Vietnam, Aditya felt that it would end one day and he began to wrestle with the problem of funding the Thai venture. How would he get the currency for a factory when the Indian government prohibited foreign exchange even for travel, medical emergencies, or for a cup of tea abroad? He hit upon an ingenious idea: he would form a joint venture—he would get Indians abroad to invest the cash while he funded his equity by exporting machinery and materials from India. This was fair and legal. He invited Vijay Mehta, a diamond merchant in Antwerp, and Amarnath Sachdev, a Bangkok textile trader, to become his partners. Aware of the legendary Birla name and management skills, they quickly agreed. The Thai venture commenced production in September 1970, on time and within budget, and was soon a great success.

The Thai venture became the model for a spate of foreign companies that Aditya Birla set up in Southeast Asia in the 1970s. The following year he set up a textile plant in Thailand, then a rayon plant, followed by a textile plant in Indonesia, a carbon black plant in Thailand, a spinning mill in the Philippines, the world's largest palm refinery in Malaysia, a viscose rayon fiber plant in Indonesia, a polyphosphate plant in Thailand, another carbon black operation in Egypt. He became the world's largest producer of viscose staple fiber, palm oil, and insulators, and the world's sixth-largest maker of carbon black. In India, his group became the largest producer of rayon filament yarn, flax yarn, caustic soda, rayon grade pulp, and aluminum (in the private sector), and among the top three makers of cement. When he died suddenly in 1995, his group had thirty-seven companies with sales close to $5 billion and after-tax profits of $450 million. More than a third of his business was overseas. He was rightly called a "human factory-making factory." At the time of his early death he was completing an oil refinery, a copper smelter, a hot-rolled coil steel mill. He was planning a petrochemical complex, a 1,000 megawatt power station, and an entry into telecommunications.

With all his successes, there were heartbreaks galore. One of them was the Mangalore refinery, which Delhi's bureaucrats took eleven years to clear—a record even by the standards of the Indian bureaucracy. While both of us were waiting for a court to open up at the Bombay Gymkhana one day, I asked Aditya Birla what had led him to invest abroad. He had no choice, he said, in his deep, unaffected voice. There were too many obstacles in India. To begin with, he needed a license, which the government would not give because the Birlas were classified as "a large house" under the MRTP Act. Even if he did get one miraculously, the government would decide where he should invest, what technology he must use, what was to be the size of his plant, how it was to be financed—even the size and structure of his public issue. Then he would have to battle the bureaucracy to get licenses for the import of capital goods and raw materials. After that, he faced dozens of clearances at the state level—for power, land, sales tax, excise, labor, among others. "All this takes years, and frankly, I get exhausted just thinking about it."

Aditya told me that he produced staple fiber in Thailand from pulp that he bought in Canada. He sent the fiber to his factory in Indonesia for converting to yarn. He exported the yarn to Belgium, where it was made into carpets, and finally, the carpet was exported to Canada. "Here is Aditya Birla," I thought, "an Indian, and yet India does not figure in this global value-added chain." It did not because India had closed its economy. By closing it, it denied its citizens the chance to participate in the enormous expansion in global trade in the second half of the twentieth century. It denied its people jobs, technology, knowledge, and new ways of organizing. Thus, it deliberately suppressed economic growth.

Domestically too, India did itself enormous damage. For example, Gwalior Rayon, GD's flagship company, of which Aditya was later chairman, wished to expand its viscose staple fiber plant in 1978. It applied to the government for permission. Despite weekly follow-ups by the Birla managers with the ministry of industries, the approval did not come because of the MRTP rules. Nor did the government reject the application. Fed up with waiting, Gwalior Rayon decided after eighteen months to transfer the project to Indonesia. Indonesia welcomed the investment and the jobs and India's loss became its gain. It is hard to imagine the absurdity of our rules. Aditya wanted to be director of his foreign company, and he applied for permission. Since the approval did not come for nine months, he went to meet the officer concerned. The official told him maliciously, "Mr. Birla, we could even prosecute you if you accepted the offer to become the director of a foreign company." Aditya had to face embarrassment with the foreign company's board of directors, who were unable to comprehend why it should take anyone nine months to accept a directorship. Finally, after hard lobbying by Birla executives, the permission came, but only after a heavy drain of precious management time.

Having achieved so much in a lifetime, Aditya Birla was left uneasy. He thought it ironic that the Indian ruling class should have such a low opinion of the Birlas. Throughout his life, his family had been under attack in Parliament, by the bureaucracy, and in the media. To many Indians, he had become a symbol of the license-permit nexus between politicians, bureaucrats, and businessmen. They thought his success was the result of a cozy relationship with the powers that be. When the economic reforms came in 1991, they said that his companies would not survive in the competitive climate. The truth is that Aditya Birla felt a huge load lifted when licensing came to an end. The critics did not realize that it was the government that had been his biggest problem. After the reforms, he was a happy man and he plunged again into fourteen-hour days to improve the performance of his Indian companies and to execute his petrochemical complex and other major projects. His Indian businesses responded after 1991 and prospered like never before. But he never got a chance to prove his critics definitively wrong. For on 1 October 1995 he died of prostate cancer, not yet fifty-two years old.

With all his triumphs, and those of his father and his brilliant grand-father, Aditya Birla had to live down the poor image that Indians have of Marwaris. Perhaps that is why Aditya and the entire Birla clan have been shy and reclusive—almost secretive. The Birlas suffered heavily from the fallout of the Hazari Committee report on monopolies in the 1960s. Hazari had pointed a finger at the Birlas for preempting 20 percent of all licenses awarded by the government between 1957 and 1966. From twenty companies in 1945, Birla companies had grown to almost 150 by 1962. To many Indians this smacked of monopoly. It confirmed their image of Marwaris as ruthless businessmen who did not stop at anything to get what they wanted, who did not pay taxes if they could get away with it.

A certain amount of antipathy to business exists in all societies. But Aditya Birla could not understand why the public chose to target his family. It pained him that the Birlas represented the ugly face of big business in the public mind. He thought it unfair. After all, they had sup-ported the nationalists' movement for independence. They had invested huge sums in charities and philanthropy. They had maintained a simple and quiet lifestyle and reinvested their entire surplus rather than con-suming it. In Aditya's mind they had come closer than anyone else to practicing Mahatma Gandhi's idea of trusteeship—that the business-man's wealth belongs to the community and he is merely a trustee of this wealth during his lifetime. In fact, GD had offered the following advice to Aditya at MIT: "Eat only vegetarian food, never drink alcohol or smoke, keep early hours, marry young, switch off lights when leaving the room, cultivate regular habits, go for a walk every day, keep in touch with the family, and above all, don't be extravagant." Aditya thought that his grandfather's counsel symbolized the ethic of the Indian merchant. Its defining tone was restraint and austerity, not dissimilar to the ethic of Protestant, Jewish, or Chinese business families. It captured the spirit of conservation that leads eventually to accumulation.

In business, Birlas were always regarded highly (and feared by com-petitors), but they never enjoyed the social status that they yearned for throughout the forty years of the socialist raj. As for the contention that they were the great beneficiaries of the License Raj, I disagree. I believe, on the contrary, that the Marwaris lost touch with the market during the socialist period. By eliminating competition, socialism distorted their behavior and suppressed their business skills. Competition is the school in which companies learn to perfect their skills. By closing the economy and discouraging competition, socialism made Indian business houses complacent and insensitive to customer needs. They lost the incentive to improve their products and acquire marketing skills. When the economy opened in 1991 and markets became increasingly competitive, the old businesses were in trouble. Hence, a decade after the economic reforms, the old Marwari houses, including the Birlas, are floundering.

THIRTEEN

Dreams in Kabutarkhana

Boldness in business is the first, second and third thing.
—THOMAS FULLER

D hirubhai Ambani was a master gamesman who managed the License Raj to his advantage and he came out on top. Against all odds, he created within a generation an outstanding company called Reliance, which grew at a scorching pace to become India's largest company and among the world's top five producers of petrochemicals, such as polyester, polypropylene, PTA, and polyethylene, the world's largest maker of paraxylene and PET, and at the end of the century set up the world's largest multifeed refinery. In the process, Dhirubhai made a mockery of the decaying and corrupt control regime of Indira Gandhi. He became an inspiration to hundreds of young entrepreneurs, and the darling of the Indian stock markets. By 1995, he had 2.4 million shareholders—more than any other company in the world—so many that it had to hold its annual general meetings in a football stadium. To its critics, he became a symbol of everything that was wrong with the License Raj.

At the time that I was wandering around the bazaars of Bombay in the mid-1960s learning to sell Vicks VapoRub to wholesalers and retailers, Dhirubhai Ambani was hustling nearby in Bombay's Mulji Jetha wholesale market. He was peddling imported nylon yarn, which he had acquired through the export of rayon fabric. He worked from a tiny borrowed office in Bhaat Bazaar, but he spent most of his day trudging in the muggy, teeming yarn markets of Pydhonie, chewing paan and drinking endless cups of tea. There was little to distinguish Dhirubhai from other traders. They were all sharp and had learned to operate on razor-thin margins. He lived in the bowels of Bombay's bazaars, in one room with his wife, his brother, his mother, and his two sons in Kabutarkhana in Bhuleshwar. It was a fifth floor walk-up, pigeonholed among five hundred families.

"Kabutarkhana" is literally a place where pigeons live, but no one is quite sure how it got its name. There is a temple next door where everybody goes and prays, and throws *chana* to the pigeons. Kabutarkhana is also home to Bombay's milkmen, and there is a milk market nearby in Pinjrapol. Strange companions to the milkmen are Bombay's embroiderers, who include the famous retailer, Maganlal Dresswalla. Everyone agrees that there is a lot of hustle and bustle in Kabutarkhana.

Like other traders, Dhirubhai used to take his family by bus to Chowpatty Beach on Sundays, where they permitted themselves two treats per person—a snack and a drink or two snacks. Sometimes on a Sunday he took his boys to watch hockey at Churchgate and followed it up with idli-sambhar at an Udipi cafe. "Sunday was an important day," remembers his son Anil Ambani. Only a short distance away from Dhirubhai's world was the upper-middle-class leisurely life of gymkhana clubs, comfortable jobs, spacious flats, and Saturday evening parties.

What set Dhirubhai apart from other Gujarati traders is that he had vision, and he understood the minds of men. He realized that synthetics were the future fabric of the Indian middle class, although the government regarded them as a luxury and taxed them at extortionate rates. Sense would prevail one day, thought Dhirubhai, as he plowed his trading profits into a small but technologically advanced textile mill that he set up near Ahmedabad with a paid-up capital of Rs 150,000. From this beginning, Dhirubhai followed an audacious but classic business strategy over the next twenty-five years: beginning with trading in synthetic fabrics, he integrated backwards to make the fabric; after manufacturing synthetic textiles, he went backwards to make its raw material, polyester fiber, and fiber intermediates; then further backwards to make polymers and chemicals, until he reached the basic raw material, petroleum.

When he got there, he built the world's largest ethylene gas cracker and oil refinery. Not content, he finally began to explore for oil off the shore of western India.

Dhirubhai is proud to belong to the "zero club," because he started with nothing. He was born to a schoolteacher in Chorwad, a village in Junagadh district in Gujarat. The nearest town was Porbander, where Mahatma Gandhi was born and raised. Dhirubhai was one of five children, and like all families of village schoolmasters, they were poor. He was of Modh bania caste and even as a boy was irrepressibly driven by the smell of business. "During Mahashivratri Dhirubhai got his friends together and sold *gathia*, a Gujarati savory, at the fair," recalls his older brother. He "was a familiar sight, cycling from village to village," adds a contemporary from Chorwad. "All he needed was an opportunity and he was off to book orders." He went to high school in Junagadh in a yellow stucco building which had been built by the nawab of Junagadh in 1902. Because he was poor, they admitted him as a "free student," and he lived in a boardinghouse supported by the Modh bania community. The nawab of Junagadh at the time was famous for only one thing—his 150 dogs and an equal number of dog handlers. He is supposed to have spent Rs 20 lakh on the wedding of his favorite canine pair and given his 700,000 subjects a public holiday on that day.

Too poor to go to college, Dhirubhai went off to Aden, then a British colony in the Middle East. His first job at seventeen was filling gas as an attendant in a Shell petrol station. Soon he found a better job as a shipping clerk in Besse & Company, an affiliate of Shell. Oil was the only business in Aden, and he became fascinated by it and dreamed of creating an oil business of his own one day. He was good at his job and he rose quickly. Soon he had a car and a flat. He came home on a holiday, married a Gujarati girl from his village, and took her back to Aden. He had achieved the middle-class dream, yet he suffered from discontent. He was not happy to remain a functionary in an insignificant subsidiary of a multinational giant. After work, he tried to divert himself by trading in the souk. Eventually, he quit and returned home to start a business of his own.

He settled in Bombay and with a capital of Rs 150,000 became a trader in synthetic yarn. The problem for a yarn dealer in Pydhonie was not to find buyers but to get supplies. Our system of industrial licensing and import controls and quotas ensured scarcity. As a result, there was massive smuggling of nylon, viscose, and polyester cloth. The major source of supply for Dhirubhai was through import or replenishment licenses (called REPs) which were issued to exporters, allowing them to import a portion of their export earnings. Strictly speaking, many of these licenses were not transferable, because one had to be an "actual user" to import. Nevertheless, a market had developed for them. Since Dhirubhai was a bigger risk-taker and willing to pay a higher price for the license, he soon became "the king of REPs." His dominant position allowed him to control the supply of yarn and he made huge profits. Periodically there were reports in the press that "actual users" licenses had been misused; there were raids by customs officials; the market would dry up. Soon the crisis would pass, and things would get sorted out. Dhirubhai was never implicated.

In order to have greater control over supplies, Dhirubhai decided to invest his trading profits in a new factory to manufacture synthetic textiles. To become an industrialist, however, he needed a license. To get a license he needed connections. He had learned by now that it was paramount to have friends in Delhi. Indira Gandhi was the Prime Minister and she had a trusted private secretary named Yashpal Kapur. Dhirubhai became a friend of Yashpal's, and later of his nephew and successor, the formidable R. K. Dhawan. He also got to know the excellent T. A. Pai, a minister in Indira Gandhi's government, whose family had owned the Syndicate Bank before it was nationalized. Like a good banker, T. A. Pai could smell a smart entrepreneur, and the Syndicate Bank agreed to finance his textile mill.

Soon Dhirubhai had become a proud manufacturer. However, he continued to be plagued by raw-material scarcity—basic filaments and yarns for making synthetic fabrics. He resisted breaking the law and smuggling in supplies (as some did). Instead, he persuaded T. A. Pai to authorize official imports of polyester filament yarn (PFY) against exports of nylon fabric. It became known as the High Unit Value Scheme and it made Dhirubhai a fortune. Even if it meant exporting the fabric at a loss, it was hugely profitable to import PFY because the Indian price of PFY was six times the world price. Dhirubhai admitted in a *Business India* interview in April 1980 that he accounted for 60 percent of the country's imports and exports under this scheme. He began to export like a maniac—to Russia, Poland, Africa; he sold synthetic sarees to Indians in Southall in London; he conducted high-profile fashion shows. His quality was excellent, his marketing was innovative, and his deliveries were reliable.

In 1977, Indira Gandhi was swept out of power. The succeeding Janata government canceled the High Unit Value Scheme and Dhirubhai's exports became unprofitable. He decided to enter the domestic market. In order to compete, he realized that he needed a brand name, one that would stand for his consistently high quality. He decided on Vimal, and launched one of the most memorable and swish advertising campaigns of the era—"Only Vimal"—and he backed it with the biggest advertising budget of the day. Soon Vimal had become a household name. However, he had a problem with distribution. He met with resistance from wholesalers in the traditional cloth markets whose loyalties were with the older mills. He solved the problem innovatively by bypassing the wholesalers and setting up exclusive Vimal showrooms in the main shopping centers of the country. He was able to franchise his name and showrooms to more than five hundred retail shops across India.

By 1980, Dhirubhai had become the leader in the textile business and he was again restless. In line with his strategy to integrate backwards, he now decided to make polyester fiber, the raw material for synthetic textiles. However, the government did not allow individuals its manufacture at the time because it still believed that synthetics were an elite product and not suitable for the masses. Mrs. Gandhi was now back in power and his friends were back in their jobs. Although he had friends in high places, he still had to patiently and tirelessly lobby for months with policy makers, demonstrating with figures the experience of other countries and the volume of synthetics smuggled into India. At last the government opened its doors. He and forty-two entrepreneurs applied for a license, and he was among three who won. His rivals screamed bloody murder and Bombay was abuzz with rumors of payoffs to politicians.

In order to be the lowest-cost producer, he wanted his polyester plant to be of world-scale capacity and of the latest technology. Only then would he be able to sustain cost and quality advantages. He also wanted to be able to continuously upgrade his technology. These ideas were too novel for the regulators. Until now, most Indian plants had been puny, of a "safe size," based on calculations of a reasonable market share in an economy of shortages. No Indian industrialist had thought boldly in terms of exploding markets, of latent demand, of competing against world players, of discontinuous technologies. The conservative bureaucrats refused to listen to him—despite his connections.

Again, Dhirubhai's people lost months trying to educate the regulators. Eventually they succeeded, but his rivals again yelled "payoffs." Once he had the coveted permissions, his organization went into high gear. They worked at a furious pace to put up the polyester plant in eighteen months. Dupont, which provided the technology, was amazed. "In our country it would take us not less than twenty-six months to erect and commission such a project," said the director of Dupont. As a result of such efficiencies, Dhirubhai's conversion cost of the yarn came down to 18 cents a pound in 1994, compared to 34 cents of Western Europe producers, 29 cents in North America, and 23 cents in the Far East. Once the polyester plant was up and running it quickly became a success—within two years its sales and profits outstripped the textile business. With plenty of domestic supply of polyester yarn, Indian textile mills switched to making synthetic textiles.

Having tasted success in the first phase of backward integration, nothing could now stop Dhirubhai from moving ahead with the rest of his dream. In 1986 he announced plans to go backwards to produce the petrochemicals terephthalic acid (TPA) and paraxylene, as well as the detergent intermediate, linear alkaline benzene (LAB). In 1988 he ventured into polymers and floated Reliance Petrochemicals. By now his two sons, Mukesh and Anil, with MBAs from America, had taken over the day-to-day running of operations. They were unusual for the second generation because they had their father's hunger, talent, and discipline. Reliance was moving at such a blistering pace that people talked of his "owning" the government. Otherwise, they said, how could he get the licenses and clearances to move ahead?

In 1991, the government's economic reforms unshackled Dhirubhai. They scrapped licensing, and he decided to build the world's largest refinery. He raised money from stock markets for Reliance Petroleum. People asked, isn't there a glut in the market with excess refining capacity? Dhirubhai replied that the rapidly growing Indian middle class had

an insatiable appetite. Both Coke and Pepsi, he pointed out, had converted to plastic bottles and crates, and this had led to an explosion in
Reliance's polyethylene and PET markets. Plastic furniture was replacing wood, and this would ensure a demand for Reliance's polypropylene. Two-wheelers were growing 35 percent a year, and India had
already become the world's second-largest market.

What captured everyone's imagination was the way Dhirubhai went
about single-handedly creating an "equity cult" among the Indian middle class. Because the banks would not lend him enough capital, and
because he was unwilling to kowtow to the public financial institutions,
he turned to the public. In 1977, he first offered his shares to the public
on the Bombay and Ahmedabad stock exchanges. Painstakingly, he went
around the country, mobilizing funds from small investors. Thanks to
him, Indian shareholders increased from one to four million between
1980 and 1985. Of these, one in four was a Reliance shareholder. He
succeeded because he delivered what he had promised—steady appreciation in their shareholding. By 1983, a Reliance shareholder had
achieved a 75 percent annual compound rate of return; by 1986, it was
still an impressive 45 percent. By the mid-nineties Dhirubhai had 2.4
million shareholders. He had become a legend in small towns, where
people who had never thought of investing in the stock market had
learned to buy shares, to read the financial pages of the newspaper, and
to monitor the value of their investment. Dhirubhai single-handedly
energized the Indian capital market.

With its millions of investors, Reliance was forced to conduct its
annual general meetings in a football stadium in south Bombay. I had
bought some shares of Reliance in 1982, and I too showed up at the
1995 meeting at the Cooperage football ground. Surrounded by 12,000
shareholders, I was fascinated by the three-hour extravaganza, which
was skillfully packaged to entertain and enlighten us. "My investors are
my biggest bankers," Dhirubhai declared at the meeting. A senior executive of a foreign bank sitting next to me whispered, "Reliance is actually a bank masquerading as a petrochemical company!" The next day's
Financial Times reported in London that it was the largest company
AGM ever held.

What is Dhirubhai's secret of success? He succeeded in part because
he stuck to his knitting. Other Indian business houses, in contrast, were

diversified hopelessly in dozens of business activities. Reliance focused on adding value to a single product's vertical chain—petroleum. Personally too, Dhirubhai concentrated on his business and shunned leadership positions in chambers of commerce and other social distractions. From the beginning, he strove for global competitiveness, and he benchmarked himself with the best in the world. Today, his leading competitors are large multinationals—Dupont, ICI, and Shell—and not Indian companies. Finally, he managed brilliantly the tough environment of the License Raj; instead of complaining, he was not shy to engage in the nitty-gritty of negotiation. He played the archaic licensing system to his advantage. For this reason, many people thought that after the 1991 reforms, he would collapse in a freer, competitive environment, and the Reliance bubble would burst. The opposite happened—his performance has improved year after year.

Today, Dhirubhai's two sons are single-minded and they put in long hours. So single-minded, in fact, that Anil Ambani took a direct flight home to Bombay four hours after completing his final exam at Wharton. After he had shaved and showered, he was taken to the office within an hour of his arrival. Within days, Anil was sent to Naroda, near Ahmedabad, to look after the textile plant. As he was leaving for Naroda, Anil asked, "What about a holiday?" Dhirubhai replied with a smile, "Naroda is your holiday, son." I met Anil Ambani in the late 1980s when he came to sell us LAB for our detergents at Procter & Gamble. I was impressed by his foresight. We had not yet decided to enter the detergents business, and I told him so. He gave me five good reasons why we should. I thought to myself, "Here is a good salesman—he is telling me how to run my business."

The Reliance story is an inspiration to many young people across India. The start of his refinery in July 1999 sent a powerful message to all Indians with global amibition that dreams could become real. In the year 2000, Reliance's sales exceeded $10 billion. It is common, especially in Bombay, to hear youngsters say, "If only there were ten Dhirubhais." However, there is another side to the story. Dhirubhai faced terrible difficulties. Everyone tried to stop him. Especially celebrated was his spat with his powerful rival Nusli Wadia, which filled the pages of the *Indian Express* for months together. His real enemy, claim his sympathizers, was the government. His critics contend, on the other hand, that he controlled and manipulated the government to his advantage. What cannot be contested is that at each stage he had to fight to prove that government policies were wrong. It took decades for the government to realize that synthetic textiles were not a rich person's fabric and did not deserve to be punished with luxury taxes. It took years of lobbying to get the government to open petrochemicals to the private sector. It took months of negotiations to make the government realize that world-scale plants would be the most efficient. He had to move mountains to get the controller of capital issues to agree to his pioneering financial instruments, such as convertible debentures for his shareholders.

Dhirubhai's story is an Indian morality play. At one level, it is a classic rags-to-riches story. It is about the ascent of a simple village boy who created against all odds a globally competitive enterprise to become the most powerful businessman of modern India. At another level, it highlights the dilemma posed by a decaying and corrupt system. Does one give up one's dream of an outstanding, world-class enterprise defeated by retrograde laws or does one match wits against the system?

The inevitable conclusion from Dhirubhai's story is that a world-class enterprise—with global capacities, rapid response to customer needs, vertical integration—could never have been created under the laws that prevailed in India between 1965 and 1991. For one Dhirubhai who succeeded, there were hundreds who failed.

FOURTEEN

Licensing Blues

No system of regulation can safely be substituted for the operation of individual liberty as expressed in competition.

—LOUIS BRANDEIS

n the spring of 1981, I was thirty-eight years old and managing director of Richardson Hindustan. We had recently returned after five years in the Spanish-speaking world, in Mexico and Spain. I had gone to Mexico soon after the Emergency to run our food and nutritional business. Now, I was thrilled to be back, as head of the company where I had started at the bottom seventeen years ago. Our children were ten and eight and we thought it was time they began to learn to become young Indians.

My homecoming was spoiled, however, because our Indian business was in serious trouble. Profits had plunged because of rigid, poorly administered price controls. Labor relations had become adversarial. The quality of our products had suffered, partly because of an obsession with volumes in a price-controlled environment. The company had no cash, the morale was poor, labor was hostile, and one-third of the managers had left the company in the past year.

On a busy day in March, I got a call from Orville Freeman inviting me to participate in "a three-day industry and government roundtable." The former U.S. secretary of agriculture was now running a business that had the laudable objective of improving the relationship between business and government. I told him that my company was in trouble and I did not think I could spare the time. He persuaded me easily, saying that it was the opportunity of a lifetime to dialogue with ministers and civil servants in a unique atmosphere. The icing on the cake, he promised, was a breakfast with Indira Gandhi, who had returned to power in the 1980 general elections.

At the roundtable, I was surrounded by the "greats" from both the industry and the government. After the first day I said to myself that this is hardly a dialogue—the government speaks and industry listens. The captains of industry were a meek flock. Pranab Mukherjee, the finance minister, was totally closed to any new idea and embarrassingly arrogant when he answered questions. L. K. Jha, adviser to the Prime Minister, on the other hand, was remarkably open as he confessed that the government had made some mistakes in the past and it was time to change and open up.

The next day was a ringing spring morning—one of Delhi's best. We were ushered into the PM's garden. Mrs. Gandhi looked charming, surrounded by spring flowers. She wore a white Bengal cotton saree with a narrow red border and looked cultivated, aloof, and imperious. She was not a particularly good speaker, although she had the instinctive ability to come up with the right phrase. Looking at her, it was hard to believe that this unimposing woman was the astute politician who had single-handedly destroyed the old Congress bosses and emerged the new messiah of the poor in the 1971 elections. She had dismembered Pakistan after a victorious fourteen-day war and given birth to the new country of Bangladesh. She had stood up to President Nixon of the United States; she had been unimpressed by his diversion of the Seventh Fleet with its nuclear-powered aircraft carrier to the Bay of Bengal. Finally, she had declared an Emergency and become a dictator for twenty-two months.

After a brief speech, she opened the forum to questions. A few sycophants from the industry got up and eulogized her for her achievements. Then there was silence. Not a single person was willing to risk a hard question. This is embarrassing, I thought. Surely someone will get up. Just as she was about to close the forum, I got up and decided to take my chances. "Madam Prime Minister," I said. "May I have your views on

two subjects that have been troubling me? The first concerns a friend of
mine who cannot introduce a new product into the market because he
does not have a license. Meanwhile, his competitor has preempted all
the licensed capacity. What should he do?"

Mrs. Gandhi turned to one of her advisers and then artfully defended
licensing. "We are a poor country, you see; we have limited resources,
which we ration through the licensing system. If we let anyone produce
what he wants, we will have no foreign exchange left for the country's
necessities." All very plausible, I thought, but very bad economics all the
same.

"It is a brilliant new product, madam," I persisted. "What do you
think he should do?"

"Has he made a proposal?" she asked.

"Yes, it was rejected because of 'excess capacity in the industry.' "

"Send me the proposal," she said. Surely it was wrong for the Prime
Minister of the country, I thought, to get into such matters. "I was won-
dering, Madam Prime Minister, shouldn't the market decide what
should be produced?"

"Does the market always make the right decision?" she asked.

"Not always, madam, but always better than bureaucrats," I said.

"Ah, we have a market-wallah, do we?" She smiled and gave me a
look as though I belonged to the school for the mentally disabled that
she had opened the previous day. Others laughed as well and the tension
eased.

My second question related to the high cost of our products. I suggested that if we brought down our exorbitant excise taxes and import
duties, costs would come down, goods would become cheaper, markets
would begin to grow, and government revenues would boom. Mrs.
Gandhi shook her head and gave me the same indulgent look. Patiently
she explained, "I don't think industrialists will pass on lower taxes to
consumers; lower import duties will fritter away our foreign exchange
reserves and businessmen will again clamor for protection because they
won't be able to compete against imports. As for income taxes, if we
lower them, who will pay our salaries?" She smiled charmingly. The
audience laughed again. I was unconvinced. She had a static view of the
economy, which ignored the power of competition and growth. She
also had a poor opinion of businessmen.

My questions emboldened an American businessman to get up. He said, "My issue, Madam Prime Minister, is with the government's insistence on limiting foreign ownership in companies to 40 percent. Consequently, multinational companies have lost interest in India. And your country is neither getting investment nor technology."

Mrs. Gandhi sniffed the air. Her advisers began to get impatient. "We want to be self-reliant," she said. "Our foreign investment laws have parliamentary sanctity. We want multinationals to bring technology and we permit them 51 percent foreign equity. We don't want multinationals to sell Vicks VapoRub, like our young friend here." She looked at me and there was more laughter.

With great charm, on the spring morning, amidst shining marigolds, Mrs. Gandhi had attempted to preserve three myths of the ancien régime—the value of licensing, the importance of high taxes, and the need to limit foreign investment. As I was leaving the PM's house, an elder statesman of industry nudged me and whispered, "Watch it, young man!" I turned around, but he was gone. Since it was a nice morning, I decided to walk. I walked along the wide, tree-lined avenue towards Raisina Hill and past what André Malraux had called the "colossal vistas of red sandstone with Sikh guards presenting arms in the solitude." Malraux was right. It was only the departure of the British that had given this soulless architecture some sort of soul. It seemed to become great only when it became a tomb of the Raj in a city that had a surfeit of tombs. It seemed right that it was Mrs. Gandhi with her old myths who presided over these tombs like a grand priestess.

I asked myself why she could not see what I saw. The sheer number and diversity of enterprises in India backed by vast human energy and talent was so impressive. From the largest, Tata Steel, to the millions of artisans, wholesalers, and street vendors, I saw a deep source of strength not available to many other economies. We had the sophisticated underpinning of trained managers and professionals and a capital market, with ready availability of specialists in advertising, audit, and legal services. Linked to it was a formidable diaspora of nonresident Indians who could mobilize capital and knowledge of overseas customers and markets. Yet India failed to perform. Alas, it was precisely because of the attitudes I had observed that morning. We were shackled by the excessive regulation of a heavy-handed state which was suspicious of profit yet happy to seek rent; this, combined with protection and fear of foreigners, had left a weighty legacy of uncommercial habits. How long would we stand and watch our talents and our strengths consistently undermined?

The economic reforms came in 1991 and exploded Mrs. Gandhi's myths of the License Raj. With the scrapping of licensing our foreign exchange reserves did not decline. The Indian entrepreneur, freed from control, responded with new investment. Lower taxes did not destroy government revenues. Competition ensured that lower import and excise duties were passed on to consumers. Demand rose and markets grew. Lower income taxes brought greater compliance and more revenues for the treasury. Direct taxes in 1995–96 accounted for 29 percent of revenues, compared to 19 percent in 1990–91. Foreign investment rose thirtyfold, but we did not lose our sovereignty. A senior bureaucrat, looking back, admitted to me in a fit of candor, "How could I have administered such lunatic policies?"

After the interlude in Delhi, I plunged into the serious business of turning around my company. First, I dealt with the labor problem, which I concluded was a management problem. To begin with, I had to replace the personnel manager, who believed in "sticking it to the workers." And the workers, I am sure, would happily have reciprocated. I got a new personnel manager, Ginil Shirodkar, who felt that we needed to change attitudes on both sides. Both of us agreed that we ought to be transparent with the union and the workers, sharing our troubles and our triumphs. The workers were shocked that we were not making money; it took months before they believed us. A year of patient and constant dialogue succeeded in winning their trust, attitudes changed, and we signed a three-year productivity–linked contract.

I held the belief that every employee in the company could grow. To help people grow, we needed to invest in training and developing them. I was also convinced that a consultative and participative style was more effective than an authoritarian or paternalistic one. My premise was that achievement was the best form of motivation. Shirodkar shared these beliefs and helped me in creating an open, people-oriented workplace. As a result, motivation rose rapidly and executives stopped leaving us.

Meanwhile, the government relaxed the Drug Price Control Order in 1982. We were able to raise prices and we became profitable. As productivity improved in the factory and motivation improved among managers, profits rose. So did the price of our shares on the Bombay Stock Exchange. As our surplus grew, we got the opportunity to offer bonus shares. I wanted our employees to share in this prosperity. However, government rules did not permit it. We put up a fight with the government's controller of capital issues. I argued that our performance would improve if employees were to behave like "owners" of the company. The controller thought that this might be a fraud by the employees to steal money from the company. He could not believe that "participative" management might work. In the end, I made such a nuisance of myself that he got tired of saying no and after nine months reluctantly allowed us to offer 5 percent of the bonus shares to employees. Our investment bankers helped Shirodkar devise a formula to distribute the shares fairly, depending on performance and seniority. Everyone got shares. I had hoped that they would hold on to them for at least three years, but as the share price rose from $2 to $20, the majority sold out after three months. Many employees eventually built homes from their capital gains.

M y father worked hard all his life and retired with a meager pension. His only savings after a lifetime of work was our house in Chandigarh. All of us loved the house, especially my youngest brother and sister, who had spent their happiest years in it. It sprawled on a quarter of an acre, facing the lower Himalayas and Kasauli, which nestled seven thousand feet above. Chandigarh was an attractive town with wide boulevards, parks, and trees, with the bonus of Le Corbusier's brilliant sculpture-like buildings.

One morning my father was in a hurry. He was late for an important meeting when our young neighbor came around and asked him to sign an innocuous-looking paper. "It is a simple procedural matter," he said. My father signed the paper in a neighborly spirit. It turned out that my father had signed his house away. Our neighbor and his vivacious and statuesque wife had moved in the previous year. After working for a company in Bombay, they had decided to become entrepreneurs. They planned to set up a malt factory to supply the rapidly growing beer industry. They were young and energetic, and their excitement infected the neighborhood. My father's signature got them a small loan of Rs 200,000 from the local bank. Other loans followed.

When people realized that our neighbors had money, they began to make demands. The bank manager who had advanced the loan wanted his share. The factory inspector came as the equipment was being installed and he would not give them a clearance without being paid. The engineer of the State Electricity Board was unwilling to give their factory power if he was not compensated. The boiler inspector had to be paid. The labor inspector wanted his cut. The excise inspector told them they could not hope to start production without an excise number, for which they had to pay his fee. Meanwhile, the minister did not want to be left out. He threatened to change the rules, which would prevent them from supplying the breweries. Our neighbors were not deterred and they struck a deal with the politician. They agreed to give him a share in the company, and he rescinded his order.

Over the year, we noticed that our neighbors' standard of living rose visibly. He got a new car. She began to sport expensive jewelry and sarees. One day they borrowed the papers of our house "for a few hours," saying that the bank needed to verify them (in support of the letter that my father had given). That was the last that my father saw of his house papers. He did not know that the bank had called back the loan. We did not know that our neighbors had run out of money and were yet to produce a single kilo of malt. They were bankrupt, and our house was lost to the bank.

It is a harsh life for an entrepreneur. He has to bribe from twenty to forty functionaries if he is serious about doing business. The nationalized banks are encouraged to give loans to entrepreneurs, but the bank managers often want a cut. Our neighbors were also crooked for they spent the bank's money on themselves. In another place, they would have had to either return it or go to jail. This does not happen in India. Hence, hundreds of thousands of small enterprises have become officially "sick." The entrepreneurs are able to walk away as freely as our neighbors did. The bank auctioned their factory, it is true, and recovered part of its dues. But our neighbors did not do too badly in the end. The bank did move the courts to recover the remaining dues, but the Indian legal system is so slow that it is unable to catch any crooks. For this reason, we did not physically lose our house.

Soon after retiring, my father shifted to the ashram of his Radhasoami guru on the banks of the Beas and spent the rest of his life in quest of the spirit. My mother accompanied him and they set up a middle-class home with modern conveniences—hot and cold running water, a modern kitchen with a refrigerator and gadgets, and even air-conditioning. My father took charge of a vigorous building program initiated by the guru. He built roads, prayer halls, dormitories for the devotees, and a large hospital. For the next twenty-five years, he meditated two hours a day and lived an enormously busy and fruitful life.

I visited my parents often, and on each visit the quiet efficiency, the organization, and the easy use of technology struck me in their clean spiritual haven. Science seemed to combine well with the spirit. Everything worked. It was a dramatic contrast to the world outside—especially the soiled world of the public sector. The Radhasoami faith fused an ascetic form of spirituality that went back to ancient Vedanta with an international managerial style that reflected the modern, casteless outlook of its devotees. The community had expanded rapidly over the decades, across India and to many parts of the world, and numbered more than a million initiates.

Skeptical of religion and shy of certainties, I was impressed by the scientific temper of the guru. Our purpose in life, he said, was to connect with the spirit. We could do this by conducting a series of experiments with our consciousness through the practice of meditation. Religion was an uncertain, searching path and not an exclusive institution. There were no ready-made solutions—only hints, suggestions—and one had to seek out the answer for oneself.

In the evenings I used to walk along the river in silence. Along the banks grew giant reeds and bulrushes whose stems had been bleached by the sun. I breathed drafts of pure river air and gazed at the evening sky filled with silence. I looked down the river into the horizon and I thought of our ancestors who had lived on these lands and recorded their primordial experiences in man's first book, the Rig Veda. From these riverbanks, Vedic civilization had flowed into the valleys of the Ganges and spread across the rest of India. Occasionally I felt the pull of the old culture, but I was unable to resist the seductive charms of the other, more virile one of the West that had become the dominant culture of the world.

I n the autumn of 1982, I began a series of visits to New Delhi. Our
manager in Delhi, Virender Khaneja, would set up the meetings in
advance and together we would trudge the corridors of power to
kowtow before civil servants and politicians. We were supplicants—
seeking price increases, approvals to introduce new products or expand
our production capacity, defending our foreign ownership, and dozens
of things which needed government sanction. Often our finance director, Sumit Bhattacharya, would accompany us. He was a quiet man; he
listened well, and he commanded respect when he gently interjected his
point of view. In contrast, I was passionate and obsessed. It was difficult
to make me stop when I started in on the regime of controls. Khaneja
constantly worried that I did not give the officials sufficient respect. The
bureaucrats and politicians would usually brush us off but sometimes
they would surprise us and actually listen.

I flunked my biggest test when I failed to retain majority ownership
for my parent company. Since the late 1970s, the government had been
pressuring foreign companies to lower their foreign equity to 40 percent. Some foreign companies had left India rather than dilute ownership, including IBM and Coca-Cola, and new foreign investment had
come to a halt. Executives at our U.S. headquarters were afraid that the
company might lose control if it reduced its holding. The exception to
this 40 percent rule was foreign companies engaged in "high technology." My company put up a strong defense based on our technological
contributions in agriculture. I brought in agricultural experts to argue
that our R&D station in Uttar Pradesh had adapted the *Mentha arvensis*
plant to Indian soil conditions, raising its yields and making it disease-
resistant. I explained that we had pioneered a new crop in India, provided employment to sixty thousand farmers and farm labor, and made
the country self-sufficient in menthol. We made three major presenta-
tions. But it was to no avail and we were ordered to dilute our foreign
ownership in thirty days.

I flew to Wilton, Connecticut, where the international management
of Richardson Vicks was in an angry mood. I defended the importance
of sticking it out in India. I explained that there was no risk of losing
control because they still owned the trademarks. Without the trade-

marks, the company was worthless and a hostile takeover impossible. I said that our company was doing well and growing, and we should keep building the business and one day majority ownership would be restored. Reluctantly they agreed, but only after roundly cursing the Indian government.

Since there was nothing to lose now, I decided to go public. I wrote a series of articles in the *Times of India* and the *Economic Times* on the harmful effects of the Foreign Exchange and Regulation Act of 1974. I talked about India's desperate need for foreign investment and technology. I showed that countries open to foreign investment were outperforming the closed ones and none had lost their sovereignty. I called our xenophobia the symptom of an inferiority complex and ultimately suicidal. After the articles appeared, I got many congratulatory phone calls and letters, but I also became unwelcome in some government offices.

My visits to Delhi now became more painful. My lowest moment came when I was summoned to meet a joint secretary in connection with our application for a new product. He insisted that I rush to Delhi immediately. Indian Airlines, the government monopoly carrier, used to run only three flights a day to Delhi, and seats would get booked weeks in advance. So it was not surprising that I was 182 on the waiting list. (Ten years later, after the reforms, there are twenty-two flights daily run by three airlines on the same route.) We asked if the appointment could be postponed and the answer was negative.

Despite the hopeless situation, I decided to take a chance on the six o'clock flight the following morning. I arrived at the airport at 4:30 a.m. Our administration manager and travel agent came to assist me. We begged and pleaded with the duty manager for a seat. By extraordinary luck, a foreign travel group did not show up—their flight from Aurangabad was canceled the previous night—and I was able to get a coveted seat. The flight, however, was five hours late, which was not unusual for Indian Airlines. While I hung around the airport waiting listlessly, my office was able to shift my appointment to 2 p.m. On arriving in Delhi I went directly to the ministry from the airport, just in time for my appointment. I was told that the joint secretary was away on a long lunch but I should wait. He came back after an hour but got busy "on an urgent matter." I swallowed my pride and waited for another two hours outside his smelly office. I had been warned that the officer was hostile to multinational companies and enjoyed making executives wait. Finally, at five o'clock I was led into his paper-strewn office. He sat smugly in his chair reading the afternoon paper. After five minutes he put down the paper and looked up at me.

"What is it you wanted?" he asked.

"It is you who wanted to see me," I said politely, but without inserting "sir" in my reply. Having spent so much time in the United States, I could not get used to saying "sir" to people in authority. He rang for his secretary and asked for our file. Since the file took time to locate, he decided to lecture me on foreign "devils." "They are all CIA spies, you know." He asked me about the car I drove and the foreign trips I took. "Real perks, eh!" he said. I began to feel ridiculous. At last the file came. He glanced at it and said, "Can't do anything about it, I'm afraid."

"Can't do what?" I asked.

"What is it you want?" he said, impatience showing in his voice. I explained that we were seeking approval to introduce a new product. He replied that he needed time to study it. "It is not a straightforward thing." I asked why had he wanted me to rush to Delhi, especially when he knew that there were no seats available. "Why, so that we could get to know each other." He smiled malevolently. He started to talk about capitalism. He said that the market might work in other countries, but that in India it could not because Indian businessmen were dishonest. I tried to convince him that the market took no notice of the character of the player. Competition between two dishonest businessmen was better any day than the monopolies created by the alliance between politicians and businessmen. He was unmoved. I asked him when we could expect a decision on our file. "Can't say. It's complicated business." With that, he noisily pushed back his chair, which was the bureaucrat's signal that the interview was over.

It was the end of a long and tiring day, and a feeling of defeat and futility overtook me. I felt like Sisyphus, condemned to push a rock up the hill, only to see it come tumbling down just as it reached the top. I looked out at the evening sky and understood how Sisyphus must have felt. I also knew that I had no choice but to start afresh the following day. I wandered about aimlessly until it was dark. Soon I spotted a empty taxi and got in.

By the time we reached India Gate it was pitch-dark. Like animals possessed by a strange uneasiness, a few poor men were prowling along the pavements, sometimes in shadow, sometimes lit by the headlights of the passing cars. The streetlamps threw a pallid light in the compact darkness. I told the driver to go to the Yamuna near Nizamuddin. There I got out and walked over the stones onto the dry bed of the stream. It was not an easy walk over the stones between brambles and stagnant pools. Nearby a stream of dirty water was flowing quietly. I wandered about the rubbish dump of the slum colony. The air was black and smelled of smoke in patches. Scattered among the refuse were packing cases with plastic roofs that bore witness to the presence of human life. Amidst the poverty in the gutter, the feeling overcame me that it was the License Raj that frustrated the attempts of the poor to rise.

Sam Pitroda was one of our few bright spots in the 1980s. I met Sam on one of my visits to Delhi. I discovered that we were born in the same year. Unlike me, he came from a poor village in Orissa, where there was no electricity, no telephones, no running water. He was of lowly carpenter caste, and his early education took place in one-room schools where most of his classmates had no shoes or books. By the time I took over as head of Richardson Hindustan, he had become a self-made telecommunications millionaire in America. By then he had brought his parents and his eight brothers and sisters to the States, and they were living the middle-class suburban dream.

All his life Sam had dreamt of wealth and success, and when they came, he suddenly felt guilty. The huge gap between his luxurious life and the struggling poverty of his Indian village bothered him. Sam was a technology buff. He had done his best work at GTE in Chicago with analogue–digital conversion technology and had nearly thirty patents to his credit. Sam believed that technology had profound effects, and that a modern telephone system could revolutionize India. It could bring about "openness, accessibility, accountability, connectivity, democracy, decentralization—all the 'soft' qualities so essential to effective social economic and political development," he said. "It was not so much wealth that created telephone density as telephone density that created wealth." Here was a man who believed that telephones were as important to nation building as other necessities.

Filled with these thoughts, Sam Pitroda returned to India. Here he found the opposite mind-set. Indians, and Gandhians in particular, believed that telephones were a luxury and that it was wrong to supply state-of-the-art technology to villages; they needed "appropriate technology" (the buzzword of the 1980s). A poor farmer did not need a telephone but water, literacy, and basic health care. As a result, India had only 2.5 million telephones in 1980 and most of them were in the big cities. It had only 12,000 public telephones for 700 million people. Managing this system was a rigid bureaucracy of a quarter million employees. Millions of people were waiting in line to get a telephone. Those who had one needed to know someone in the telephone department to get any service. The telephones that existed were not dependable—it was rare to get a number on the first attempt. The employees of the telephone department were arrogant and corrupt. If the line went down, it could take months to fix unless one bribed the linesman. When an MP complained in Parliament of these breakdowns, C. M. Stephens, Mrs. Gandhi's communications minister, replied that telephones were a luxury, not a right, and that anyone who was dissatisfied could return the telephone, because there was an eight-year waiting list for this "broken-down product."

Sam was going to change all this. He decided to start at the top, with Mrs. Gandhi. After waiting five months to get an appointment, he met her and impressed her. He also met her son Rajiv Gandhi, with whom he struck a chord. He told them he could bring telephones to villages, improve customer service, change to digital switching, and that he could do all this for very little. To everyone's surprise, the government bought his dream. He began with a core group of young R&D engineers to develop the hardware and software which would set India on the path of universal telephone accessibility. It was a private nonprofit society funded by the government with a $36 million corpus to develop a digital switching system suited to the Indian network. "We found five rooms on rent in a government hotel and we went to work using beds as desks." Sam earned one rupee a year, inspired by Roosevelt's dollar-a-year men of the New Deal. It was an unusual arrangement for Indians and his motives were the subject of constant speculation in Delhi.

Soon Sam Pitroda had built an organization of 420 young scientists and technicians whose average age was twenty-six. They worked in an open American style, with optimism, teamwork, flexibility, and simplicity. In three years, they delivered a 128-line rural exchange; they created a private automatic branch exchange for businesses; they developed a small central exchange with the capacity of 512 lines. They licensed some forty public and private companies to manufacture and market their products. Based on his success and his personal equation with Rajiv Gandhi, who was by now Prime Minister, Sam was promoted to head the Telecom Commission and given the status of minister of state. As head of telecom, he began to implement his dream. He got the thirty-seven telecom unions to agree to quadruple the number of lines without adding to the workforce. He replaced existing electromechanical equipment with indigenous digital equipment. He set up two factories to manufacture fiber optics and he began to build a high-speed fiber-optic highway to connect the large cities. He connected the four hundred district headquarters with automatic dialing and introduced international direct dialing to more than 120 countries. By 1990, there were five million telephones and a million new ones being installed every year, which went up to two million in a few years. By the end of 1998, there were twenty million telephones and the waiting lists had practically disappeared.

However, Sam's idea had gone much further. He had realized that if more telephones could be put in the bazaars, millions could be brought within reach. The coin-operated public phone was not a good idea because it was expensive and it quickly deteriorated in the heat and dust of India. He and his team came up with a simple idea: equip ordinary telephones with small meters; put these into the hands of thousands of entrepreneurs, who would set them on a table in the bazaar. He himself would go back to America, but his scheme unleashed a revolution. By 1998, there were half a million Public Call Offices in bazaars across the nation, most of them offering long-distance phone calls, and they had created 1.5 million new jobs. By 1995, 100,000 villages had telephone service through the rural exchanges. By 2000, three-quarters of India's half a million villages had telephone service.

Sam Pitroda's story ended badly. Rajiv Gandhi was defeated in the elections at the end of 1989. Sam came under political attack from the minister in the new government, who accused him of corruption. Although many people came forward in Sam's support, the strain was great and he had a heart attack. His family moved back to the United

States and he was a broken man. Rajiv Gandhi was assassinated in May 1991, and with that Sam's connection with India virtually ended. Thanks to his revolution, however, I can now dial my mother in a village in Punjab from our farm in coastal Maharashtra. Apple farmers in the Himalayas take harvesting decisions based on a call to the wholesale market in Bombay. The improvement in our phone services has made it possible for India to participate in the information technology revolution. India is becoming a major exporter of software and information technology services. The improved connectivity is enabling dozens of Internet start-ups and e-commerce ventures. All of them owe a small debt to Sam Pitroda.

Sometimes I think that if Sam had not been sacked, he would have ushered India quickly into the new era of telecom privatization, technology convergence, and the Internet. Unfortunately, the government has made a mess of bringing competition in both basic and long-distance services, as is being done around the world. With all its improvements, India's telecom is still unresponsive and below par. Because of their monopoly, the employees of the Department of Telecommunications are still arrogant and corrupt. They remain the ugliest face of the License Raj.

The Rebirth of Dreams

(1991–99)

A nation has character only when it is free.
—MADAME DE STAËL

FIFTEEN

The Golden Summer of 1991

All reformers are bachelors.
—GEORGE MOORE

History is full of ironies. The economic revolution that Narasimha Rao launched in the middle of 1991 may well be more important than the political revolution that Jawaharlal Nehru initiated in 1947. It is the same in China, where the economic revolution that Deng Xiaoping introduced at the end of the seventies will prove to be more important than Mao's revolution of 1949. Yet Rao behaved as though he did not believe in his revolution. And the people responded with a verdict that booted his party out.

How does one begin to explain the defeat of the Congress in the 1996 general elections? The nineties had been among the best years in India's economic life. Apart from delivering outstanding macroeconomic results, the reforms created a sense of confidence and excitement. Many people felt the same sense of possibilities that existed in the early fifties. The *Economist* called India an "uncaged tiger" in a cover story. Yet no one in India celebrated the reforms. Rao did not stand tall and take credit for his historic achievement. The Congress Party did not bother to make its finest achievement an election issue. It is true that the average voter did not understand the details of the reforms, but he was not unaware of his improved economic circumstances. The Delhi-based

Center for the Study of Developing Societies, together with the Indian
Council of Social Science Research, conducted an extensive poll in late
1996, which found that 70 percent of the respondents were either "satisfied" or "somewhat satisfied" with their financial condition; the same
poll in 1971 had found only 40 percent "satisfied" or "somewhat satisfied." One explanation for the Congress defeat is that people perceived
Rao merely as a gatekeeper to history—he was there at the right time
when history broke. They did not credit him for their improved lot.
To understand these ironies, it is necessary to see how the reforms
unfolded, step by step, in the golden summer of 1991.

    A human bomb killed Rajiv Gandhi in May 1991. He was in the
midst of an election campaign, and he died at the hands of a young
woman armed with explosives strapped around her waist. His death sent
around a wave of sympathy that carried the Congress to victory. The
party chose Narasimha Rao as Prime Minister. It chose him because he
was seventy, quiet, dull, and he threatened no one. He had been in the
top political circles in a long career, and had managed the major ministries of the government with distinction—although he had never held
an economic portfolio. He was also an intellectual and knew nine Asian
and European languages. He was getting ready to retire from Parliament
when the party installed him as its "stopgap leader" to head a minority
government which no one thought would last very long. However, he
surprised everyone as he unleashed the biggest revolution in India since
1947.

    The financial crisis was long brewing. Its main cause was the profli-
gate and short-term commercial borrowing resorted to by Rajiv
Gandhi's government since 1985. When the Gulf crisis came and oil
prices went through the roof, India found that it had no money to buy
oil. The country's foreign exchange reserves had dwindled to a dangerous level and there began a flight of capital by nonresident Indians.
There are an estimated twenty million people of Indian origin living
abroad (compared to more than fifty million Chinese), and many had
invested in repatriable accounts in Indian banks because of attractive
interest rates. When Rao came on the scene, a dialogue had been going
on with the International Monetary Fund for a bailout package. But
Rao's predecessors, Chandrashekhar and V. P. Singh, had not been brave
enough to face the crisis. Rao understood that India was bankrupt, and

his first and most important decision was to get a good finance minister. He did not trust a politician to do the job; he wanted a professional, and he chose the reticent and soft-spoken economist Manmohan Singh. He had been governor of the Reserve Bank, and had recently headed the South-South Commission in Geneva, where he had made a serious effort to understand the East Asian miracle. That is when he had realized that India had to abandon many of its old and foolish policies.

The President swore in the new cabinet on 21 June 1991. The next day Rao announced to the nation that there was a crisis and his government intended to "sweep the cobwebs of the past and usher in change." The cautious Narasimha Rao realized that the crisis was an opportunity for making bigger changes. He called a closed-door meeting of important opposition leaders, where Manmohan Singh told them that foreign exchange reserves were down to two weeks of imports. Only a loan from the IMF could bail us out, he said. However, we had to first put our house in order. He spoke about the need for basic reforms. Short of telling them that he was going to devalue the currency, he sought their support for the tough actions that the government intended to take. The gravity of the crisis hit the leaders only when they realized that a part of the nation's gold reserves had been flown out to London to provide collateral against the $2.2 billion emergency loan from the IMF. Gold, as I have noted, is the ultimate symbol of trust and honor in India, and that we had pawned it to stay afloat must have been traumatic, amounting to national humiliation.

The government devalued the Indian rupee by 20 percent in two steps over the first three days in July. After the second devaluation, Manmohan Singh met P. Chidambaram, the new commerce minister, and Montek Singh Ahluwalia, the commerce secretary, and told them that he wanted to abolish the export subsidy. He argued that the devaluation had made the subsidy redundant by giving the exporter the same incentive through a cheaper rupee. Its abolition would help him reduce the fiscal deficit significantly—by 0.4 percent.

Chidambaram's first reaction was that it would be political suicide for a new commerce minister in the first days at a new job. The subsidy was his most important instrument for encouraging exports. How would he face exporters? "Let me think about it," he said. Manmohan Singh replied that he would have to think quickly because the PM wanted to announce it the following morning. Chidambaram sulked, but he had to agree in the end. He asked if he could also announce a comprehensive trade reform at the same time. The finance minister asked, "By tonight?" Chidambaram nodded. They agreed to meet in the evening to review the trade proposals.

Although it was his first assignment in an economic ministry, the new commerce minister had proved to be a fast learner. During his first week on the job he had put in long days and nights and understood the major issues. He had read reports voraciously and realized that the country desperately needed trade reform. A Harvard M.B.A., Chidambaram understood business, and he was instinctively for opening up. As a lawyer for industry, he had seen the damage caused by the old policies. He told a colleague that if it were up to him, he would burn every copy of the infamous Red Book—the commerce ministry's bible, which minutely spelled out the controls applicable to thousands of products. Dreaded by businessmen, it was a "rent seeker's guide" for the thousand-strong staff of controllers. The earnest colleague was not amused.

On returning to his office in Udyog Bhavan, Chidambaram called in Montek Singh and asked if he was up to dismantling the trade side of the License Raj. Although it had taken over forty years to build, they had only eight hours to demolish it. They knew that their main job was to kill import licensing. If they could replace licenses by a marketable incentive, there would be no need for them. Because of foreign exchange scarcity, exporters used to be given licenses to import materials that went into making products for export. Montek Singh knew of such an incentive; it had been kicking around the ministry for several years. Called Exim scrips, it would allow exporters to earn foreign exchange for part of the value of their export. They could sell these in the market or directly import goods. Nonexporters or domestic industries that needed to import raw materials, instead of applying for an import license, could buy the Exim scrips in the market.

Chidambaram loved this instrument because it would abolish the bureaucrat from the process. He grabbed it and within hours the two men eliminated miles of red tape, months of delays, and the hassles, anguish, and corruption that the Indian state had built up over decades. They worked like maniacs and by seven o'clock they had a dramatically liberalized trade policy. Manmohan Singh was pleased when he saw the proposals. They would send a clear signal to the world that India was opening up and moving to a market-determined exchange rate. The three then went to the Prime Minister's house.

Narasimha Rao came out of his bath looking fresh in a lungi. Chidambaram sat next to the PM and briefly explained the proposals. The PM turned to Manmohan Singh. "Do you agree with this?" he asked. Manmohan Singh nodded. "In that case, sign it." Manmohan Singh did so, and the PM penned his own signature at the bottom of the page. Thus began the most comprehensive structural reforms in India's history. The specifics of some of the proposals went over his head, but Narasimha Rao was satisfied with their general direction to deregulate. He also trusted his three visitors. To those who understood the tortuously slow pace of decision making in the government, this was a revolutionary event. Four men with commitment and courage had achieved what seemed impossible twelve hours ago.

To Chidambaram's credit, the following year he agreed to abolish Exim scrips for an even better arrangement—dual exchange rate—that cut red tape further and eliminated the bureaucrat from the process. It was courageous to sacrifice an instrument with which he had become identified. The country kept growing intellectually, and the following year the finance ministry introduced the unified exchange rate, an even better mechanism, which took India to currency convertibility on the trade account. However, Manmohan Singh was too cautious and unwilling to go the full distance, and the rupee is still not free on the capital account. Many argue that his conservatism has been a blessing for India as it was later spared the "Asian flu." Chidambaram's failure in 1991 was his inability to close the massive departments of the CCIE and the Directorate General of Foreign Trade, which continue to do mischief and are a major stumbling block for our exports.

Rao now wanted to dismantle the industry side of the License Raj. He had watched Rajiv Gandhi's modest attempts at reform in the 1980s. Even these small efforts had yielded significant benefits. He had traveled abroad and he knew what was happening in the world. The collapse of communism had pulled the rug from under the planning and controlling state. So he had deliberately decided to retain the industry portfolio. He brought in A. N. Varma to become his principal secretary to drive this process. He remembered that Varma had championed delicensing in a large number of industries during the earlier V. P. Singh government, when he had been industries secretary. He asked Varma to dig up the old proposal. Varma was delighted that the reform package might finally see the light. When he saw the proposal, Rao felt that it did not go far enough. He wanted to delicense more industries and give foreign investors majority share in their Indian subsidiaries. A small group of officials spent the next few days finalizing the policy. There was opposition from finance ministry officials, but Manmohan Singh stepped in and overrode their objections. The minister of state for industries, Ranga Kumaramangalam, was not a reformer and Manmohan Singh had to lobby hard to get him in the boat. The PM, thus, took a radically liberal industrial policy to the cabinet.

Cabinet meetings in India are quiet affairs and there is little open debate. They are also secret. When Rao, in his role as industries minister, presented the new industrial policy, he heard no complaints. Taking it as assent, he asked, as though thinking aloud, "If we are going to open up, why not go the whole hog? Why don't we delicense cars and a whole lot of other things as well?" Manmohan Singh concurred, "In that case, let's open everything except for a small negative list related to security and the environment." Varma and other senior officials sitting at the back could not believe their ears. In a matter of minutes, Narasimha Rao and Manmohan Singh seemed to be destroying the License Raj.

Suddenly, the Prime Minister turned cautious. He looked at the glum faces of the old Congress guard. They would neither argue against the new ideas nor support them. They had led an unexamined life. They had never really thought about the old policies—they had just accepted them as party policies. Although Chidambaram and Manmohan Singh defended the reform courageously, it was clear to everyone that the policy was in trouble. The Prime Minister, to save the policy, asked Chidambaram to work on the language to make it politically palatable. To show that there was continuity with the past, Chidambaram hit upon the expedient of inserting a paragraph from Nehru, another from Indira Gandhi, and a third about Rajiv Gandhi's reforms. Thus, the policy came out sounding furtive and apologetic. Instead of boldly announcing a change in direction and explaining why we had to change, the new policy tried to sound as though it was a continuation of Nehru's socialism. Although Manmohan Singh wanted to announce the new industrial policy by mid-July—he did not want it linked to the budget because it might risk both—opposition from the Congress Party delayed it. In the end, it was announced on the morning of 24 July. In the evening, Manmohan Singh presented the budget.

In the next morning's papers, the new industrial policy had completely upstaged the budget and all other news. No one in the government could have imagined the positive response. Over the next few days, the media and the public were euphoric. There was some criticism by the left and in the backward states of Bihar, Madhya Pradesh, and Orissa. Narasimha Rao realized that the people were indeed ahead of the politicians in wanting reform. Only the fertilizer price increase in the budget drew opposition, and that too from the powerful farm lobby in the Congress.

To capitalize on the euphoria, Manmohan Singh decided to move rapidly. He called a meeting of the important secretaries associated with economic policy, including the cabinet secretary, Naresh Chandra, and Varma, the PM's secretary. He spoke to them about the economic crisis and the need for change; he again talked about being worthy of the IMF's trust; then he spelled out what more had to be done; and it had to be done with speed. While the Prime Minister respected differences, he said, he would not tolerate anyone putting obstacles in the way. This was the time to speak up. No one would be penalized and they would be relocated in good jobs. It was an unusual meeting. Most secretaries reacted positively. They had rarely been given such clear directions.

"People have the wrong impression," says Montek Singh. "The top bureaucracy is highly disciplined, and it is not obstructive when there is clarity at the top." Rao then set up a steering committee of secretaries, headed by Varma, which began to meet every Thursday morning. The committee became the crucial instrument for carrying the reforms forward at an unprecedented pace over the next two years. Varma ran the committee tightly. No one was allowed to travel on Thursdays. The committee met for two hours during which the concerned secretary presented one or sometimes two reforms. They discussed the issues openly. Varma summarized and minuted the discussions, and the reform proposal was taken to the cabinet for approval and then on to Parliament. I recall my feelings of excitement in those days as the government announced a new reform almost every week.

Over the next two years, the reformers had major achievements to their credit. The central government's fiscal deficit came down from 8.4 percent of GDP in 1990–91 to 5.7 percent in 1992–93. Foreign exchange reserves shot up to $20 billion from $1 billion in July 1991. Inflation came down to 6 percent from 13 percent by mid-1993. The reformers virtually abolished industrial licensing. They freed large industrial houses from the control of the MRTP Act, which had hindered expansion and investment. They drastically cut the realm of public-sector monopoly and opened banking, airlines, electric power, petroleum, and cellular telephones, among other businesses, to the private sector. They opened the country to foreign investment, allowing "automatic entry" in thirty-four industries and majority foreign ownership; they set up the Foreign Investment Promotion Board, which established a record of speedy clearances under A. N. Varma's leadership. Foreign investment began to double each year, and it rose from $150 million to $3 billion by 1997 (and would have been much higher but for our failure to deregulate the power and telecom sectors properly).

They dismantled the complex import control regime. Raw materials, components, capital goods could now enter virtually free of restrictions. Customs duties gradually came down from a peak of 200 percent in 1991 to 40 percent by the mid-nineties—the average duty declining to 25 percent. The rupee went from a typical fixed overvalued exchange rate to a unified market-determined floating rate and current account convertibility in the same period. Tax rates came down from 56 percent in 1991 to 40 percent by 1993 (and further to 30 percent in Chidambaram's 1997 budget). They simplified the vast network of multiple excise duties, shifting to an ad valorem duty. In the financial sector, they reduced the high reserve requirements of banks (designed to give the government cheap funds) and let interest rates on government securities be determined by the market. They placed a cap on government borrowings with the Reserve Bank and opened capital markets to international portfolio investors, whose investments rose to $11 billion by the end of the decade. At the same time, they allowed Indian companies to borrow abroad through global depository receipts. They introduced screen-based trading on the stock markets and dematerialized the shares.

It was quite an achievement! But how did it happen? It seems astonishing that a minority government led by a lackluster seventy-year-old intellectual who was about to retire from active politics suddenly turned his party's forty-year socialist legacy on its head. Some think that it was because of Manmohan Singh, but I feel reasonably convinced that Narasimha Rao was the key factor behind the 1991–93 reforms. Although Manmohan Singh, the helmsman, got the credit, it was Rao who took the tough and aggressive decisions and provided the energy and political support. He was shrewd and knew how to deal with dissent. The manner in which he pushed through the industrial policy in the cabinet is an example. At the same time, the reforms would not have happened without Manmohan Singh. To the extent that there was one, he created the road map. In a brilliant move, he set up a set of committees—bank reform under Narsimhan, tax reform under Chelliah, and insurance reform under Malhotra—and they provided crucial intellectual sustenance and legitimacy for reform measures in these areas. It needed Manmohan Singh to come and change the nation's mind-set to growth. But Manmohan Singh is a reticent man and cautious by nature. On his own, without Rao's constant support, he would not have done it. The new trade policy would not have come about as speedily without Chidambaram. Varma was a terror as the head of the steering committee and he provided the momentum for the implementation of the reforms for two years. He knew the system well, and he played it in favor of the reforms. Varma's crucial contributions, I believe, have not been understood or appreciated. In the end, all three—Manmohan Singh, Chidambaram, and Varma—derived their strength from Narasimha Rao.

The economic reforms, however, would not have happened without a crisis. There was no grand design behind them. The pressure from the IMF and the World Bank was palpable. Once the crisis went away, the pressure diminished and the reforms stopped. They did not halt entirely, but henceforth they moved at a slow, incremental pace. Meanwhile, there was much left undone. The government had not begun to privatize the public sector, which was bleeding the economy. It had not introduced labor reforms—it is still impossible to lay off a single worker even if there is no production. It is still impossible to close a private company even when it is bankrupt. It had not opened agriculture or insurance. It had not dared tackle the vast subsidies that were slowly eating away the financial health of the country and were primarily responsible for the unacceptably high fiscal deficit. It had practically abolished the License

Raj, but it had not done anything about "Inspector Raj"—or the army of inspectors who make life hell for an Indian entrepreneur. Most of the inspectors were in the state governments, it is true; but the most vicious ones, by common consent, were in the central departments of excise and customs. It had not solved the problems of India's creaking infrastructure. It had not begun the reform of education and health, the two areas of the greatest opportunity. Nearly ten years after the golden summer of 1991, the reforms remained half complete.

The second half of the 1990s was a frustrating time for reform-minded Indians. We mistakenly thought that we had become a "tiger." But we have moved at such a painfully slow pace since 1994 that I have resigned myself to the fact that India is an "elephant," as I said earlier. It takes two steps forward and one step backwards. This is the pace of Indian democracy. Ironically, the economy in the nineties grew more like a tiger, at an average 6.5 percent a year, despite a recession in industry. The biggest failing is that no one has tried to sell the reforms to the people. As such, the perception has grown that reforms help the rich and hurt the poor. Nor is there a clear, holistic vision of the future. Admittedly, there are interests and obstacles—many of them the result of democracy. Trade unions prevent public-sector restructuring; the powerful farm lobby prevents the removal of subsidies; the left wants to stop everything. However, other democracies have succeeded in tackling these reforms. Why has India failed? What are the lessons from the summer of 1991, when everything seemed to be going right? Why did the reforms suddenly stop after the first two years?

To find the answers, I decided to meet the main players in the drama in the autumn of 1998—Narasimha Rao, Manmohan Singh, P. Chidambaram, Montek Singh, A. N. Varma, Ashok Desai, Rakesh Mohan, and Deepak Nayyar. This was not difficult, because some of them read my column in the *Times of India;* others I knew socially. I did not know the former Prime Minister. All of them were remarkably open, but they suffered from unusually poor memory. I find it odd that none kept a diary, considering the historic nature of their acts. But this is a common failing of Indians, and all our historic sources down the ages have been foreigners. A. N. Varma had to persist for months to get me an appointment with Mr. Rao. First, he wanted my questions in writing. Next, he wanted a preliminary meeting to size me up. Then he replied to my questions in writing. Finally, he wanted Varma to be present at our face-to-face meetings. When we met, he was circumspect and defensive. He appeared to be a man on the run. I did not find the reformer who had changed the course of history for one-sixth of the world's people.

As we sat down, the former Prime Minister confessed that he was a Congress man and not a revolutionary. "Congress has always stood for something. I merely continued its legacy and never wished to reverse the past." His chief concern, he said, was poverty, but he had realized that growth was needed to eliminate it. His reforms were designed to raise the growth rate. However, growth alone was not enough. We had to attack poverty directly through employment schemes, and his government had spent more on these schemes than on any other. He was against privatization of the public sector because of his deep faith in Nehru's mixed economy. "You don't strangulate a child to whom you have given birth," he said. However, he sought to improve the public sector's performance by introducing competition from the private sector. He disagreed that he had stopped the reforms after two years—"India has had the right pace of reform, and a faster pace might have led to chaos." As he talked, I felt that he was more interested in defending his policies; sadly, he seemed to be defending the status quo.

At the end of the interview I concluded that Narasimha Rao was a reluctant liberalizer. He was not a Deng. Neither was he a Thatcher, a Salinas, a Mahathir Mohamad—or even a Menem, a Keating, a Rawlings, or a Václav Havel—all of whom, in their own way, were able to translate their liberal measures into a language that the voter understood. Rao failed to do so because he himself lacked deep conviction. He kept talking about "reforms with a human face"; a reformer would have known that the reforms are the only hope for the poor. Thus, there was no political platform built up for the measures. "While Prime Minister Narasimha Rao speaks nine languages," said *Time* magazine's Rahul Jacob, "he has not made a loud enough case in any of them for the liberalization that is his government's most notable achievement." There was no pro-reform coalition created among the people. Ideally, Rajiv Gandhi, with his vast majority in Parliament, could have done it. But he had thrown the opportunity away, and we lost six years. In some ways, Rao had a tougher job than Deng, who achieved his market revolution in a homogeneous, autocratic society. Rao had to create his within the bounds of a heterogeneous, noisy democracy. His biggest failure is that he failed to create a reform coalition within his own party, and it was his party that finally let him down. Rao's most important legacy is that the succeeding coalition governments did not change his direction but continued with the reforms, albeit in a slow and incremental manner.

When the crisis receded and the reforms slowed, the truth came out, revealing the true character of India's policymakers. Barring a few exceptions, no one in the political class—bureaucrats or politicians—was truly enthusiastic about the changes. There had been no radical change in personnel. Without a change in people, the planners of yesterday became the liberalizers of tomorrow. The Prime Minister did not have the courage to close down redundant ministries. There was no national soul-searching about the causes of our disease. The nation did not internalize the drastic need for restructuring. Hence, the policymakers could not defend themselves against the cries for protection which rose after the reforms, cleverly dressed up as complaints about the inequities of liberalization. They had not publicly admitted that the Nehru–Indira Gandhi path had failed.

The lack of new people meant the old, vested interests which had flourished in the old dirigiste regime and had never admitted responsibility for their failure were still in important positions waiting to restore the status quo. Restructuring results in losers and winners, and the losers in India would have to be the interests that had benefited from the old regime. Business houses stood to lose high tariff walls and would have to compete; farmers stood to lose subsidies in water, electricity, and fertilizers; banks would lose the comfort of easy monopoly; public-sector employees would lose their guaranteed jobs which insulated them from performance and inflation. The old interests kept arguing that liberalization would lead to inequitable outcomes, but little evidence emerged to support this.

There are troubling questions about Manmohan Singh. He became the icon of reforms around the world. He spoke brilliantly in international and business forums and he single-handedly created the image of an investor-friendly India. He was a hero to millions of young Indians who felt that India had changed and now had a future. Then he too stopped reforming and even stopped the rhetoric of reform. He too did not make the patient effort to educate his own party. He lost opportunities to meet the younger Congress MPs to propagate the message that he had given to foreign investors. Politics, perhaps, slowed him down. He faced a brutal attack in Parliament and the press after the Harshad Mehta stock market fraud. Every stock market has its crooks, and every finance minister comes under pressure when a fraud is uncovered. But the intensity of the criticism this time meant that all the antireform lobbies ganged up against him. The Joint Parliamentary Committee on the fraud trained its sights on him. Twice he threatened to resign, and each time Rao had to come to his rescue.

After leaving office, Manmohan Singh's language became political and cautious. He too began to talk of "reforms with a human face." Was he the committed reformer that the world thought he was? For thirty years he had made and defended policies that were opposed to liberalization. He had become a convert after seeing the ruin that the policies had wrought, and how far India had been left behind by the East Asian nations. But was he a true convert? If so, then it has been a poor performance for a convert ever since 1994. In a number of conversations, I have noted his ambivalence, as though he needed to convince himself that the reforms would really deliver in the end, especially to the poor. This is not how visionary reformers talk and act. I have sadly concluded that he is not a passionate reformer, although he is a man of great integrity.

Talk of the poor, I am convinced, obfuscates the debate on reforms. In any society the top 15 percent of the people will do well and look after themselves. The bottom 15 percent will fail and will need to be looked after by the state. The focus of the reforms must be the 70 percent in between, the vast majority of the people, which in successful economies becomes the middle class. Given the right circumstances, the middle class invariably pulls itself up through hard work, self-reliance, and education in a competitive economy. This did not happen in India because our earlier policies suppressed growth. Our middle class was less than 10 percent of the population in 1980. Since the economy started seriously growing in the eighties and accelerated after the reforms, the middle class has tripled but is still less than 20 percent of the population, according to the National Council of Applied Economic Research. The reforms, I will later show, will succeed in making a majority of India's population middle class within a generation. It will also be easier to look after the poor if they are 15 percent of the population rather than 40 or 50 percent.

In the long term, the reforms will help the poor. Reforms lead to growth. With growth, there are more jobs, lower inflation, cheaper goods, more labor-intensive manufacturing, more opportunities in services and agriculture. Reforms mean fewer subsidies for rich farmers and the middle class, less bleeding from an inefficient public sector. With growth and fiscal health, there are more resources available for poverty programs. However, the most powerful and immediate reform for the poor is more and better primary schools and primary health centers. This is their ticket to prosperity. Unfortunately, this reform has not happened—although Narasimha Rao articulated on a number of occasions his desire to raise expenditure on education to 6 percent of GDP from 3.7 percent.

When the reforms first came, the Congress Party was just as shocked as the people of India. After all, this was the party that had given Indians the "License Raj," "End poverty," and the antimarket policies, and had placed the public sector at the "commanding heights." Narasimha Rao's historic role has been to shift the nation's center of gravity. Since then, all the parties have learned to value the efficiency of the market. There is now broad consensus for *incremental* reform across all political parties (except the extreme left and right). This explains why the reforms have not been undone. This is Narasimha Rao and Manmohan Singh's great legacy.

Since the Congress Party's ignominious defeat in the 1996 elections, India has faced unprecedented political instability. No single party has been able to win a majority, and we've had too many elections and too many prime ministers. First came the United Front, a coalition of leftist parties, which ruled with the parliamentary support of the Congress Party. It had the indefatigable reformer P. Chidambaram as its finance minister, who, to his credit, pushed hard to keep the reforms going, but he was hemmed in by the leftists in his own coalition. Next came the Bharatiya Janata Party (BJP), the rightist Hindu nationalist party, which has been a growing force in Indian politics since the eighties. It has played to upper-caste Hindu sentiment, and its campaign against Muslims culminated in the demolition of the Babri Masjid, a mosque in north India, in December 1992. The violence that accompanied this tragic event shook even the leaders of the BJP, who realized that they could not succeed in winning power unless they became moderate and centrist. The present BJP government, under the leadership of Prime Minister Atal Bihari Vajpayee, has followed a restrained path. Although it has kept up a strong rhetoric for economic reform, its achievements have been modest, except in information technology.

In the end, none of the political parties has tried to sell the economic reforms to the people. Most politicians believe, however, that the reforms are necessary. Hence, they have tried to do them through stealth. No member of the political class believes that such correctives can translate into votes. Congress politicians seem unable to rise above petty factionalism. The left or the "third force" in Indian politics is against the reforms because it identifies with the interests of the labor aristocracy and the bureaucracy. The BJP, who were the original owners of the reform package, behave as though wealth and poverty is a secondary issue.

If there is a widespread consensus on economic reforms, why are there such frustrating delays in implementing them? If we are agreed on what is to be done, why don't we just do it? One reason is that the agenda of our political class is not economic. Second, we haven't had reformers heading our economic ministries. Third, our discourse is dysfunctional. We continue to waste our energies in debating the "what" when we ought to focus on the "how." The issue is not private or public electricity, but how to create more power capacity when the customer—the State Electricity Board—is bankrupt and the politician insists on free power for the farmer. How to reform is a more difficult challenge and it is not for lazy minds. It needs the full application of the mind; it needs problem-solving ability; and it needs mental toughness.

SIXTEEN

A Million Reformers

Every man is a reformer until the reforms tramp on his door.

—EDGAR HOWE

We are all susceptible to easy abstractions about uneasy facts around us. We tend to simplify and try to fit into comfortable categories of the mind the dissonant things that we observe in our day-to-day lives. In our laziness, we settle for the easy rhetoric of the newspapers, and the treachery of words like "reforms" and "new middle class." It is even more difficult in India, where as we change and go forward, we cannot easily give up the past. As we take a few steps forward, we also take a step backwards, and the past is always with us. In this chapter I have tried to make some general observations about the changing India from stray street encounters over the past five years. This is always dangerous, for one tends to select facts that fit in with one's prejudices and predispositions. However, the weight of anecdotal evidence seems to point in a clear direction. My meetings with Raju, Sushila, Golam Mandal, and Madhu Verma were not exceptional. My skeptical wife has also come around. I could narrate a dozen more stories, but the weight of my evidence suggests that India has changed since 1991. It may have something to do with the reforms; it may also have to do with television. But I have found a new mind-set, and I believe it will increasingly determine India's identity and future.

On the last day of 1994, I took "early retirement" from the Procter & Gamble company. At the time I was based in Cincinnati as vice president and managing director of worldwide strategic planning, and I was attempting to "reinvent" the global Vicks business. It was a challenging and absorbing assignment, but I was finding the transition from the excitement and tension of running a day-to-day business to corporate strategy a difficult one. After virtually running my own company for a dozen years, I had found the headquarters bureaucracy oppressive. After almost thirty years, I was tired of the corporate world. For some time I had begun to feel confined. I also wanted to do a great deal more with my life. I thought Cincinnati provincial. I missed India and I wanted to be closer to the great changes taking place at home, and, if possible, influence them.

Possibly, it was also the tug of the old Hindu idea of the four stages of life pulling at me from the collective unconscious. The first stage, called *brahmacharya,* is the life of a student or a celibate. The second stage, *grihasta,* literally householder, is a life of worldly pleasure, when one marries, has a family, and discharges one's responsibilities to society. All manner of sensual pleasures are sanctioned at this stage, including courtesans, I once reminded my dismayed wife. At the third stage, called *vanaprastha,* when the children are settled and debts repaid, one is expected to start detaching oneself from the rough-and-tumble of worldly affairs and begin the quest for the meaning of life. The fourth stage is called *sanyas* or renunciation, when one abandons society and its comforts to single-mindedly seek unity with the Absolute.

My wife said, "Are you sure about what you are doing? I mean, we are earning a lot of money. Anyone else would have thought that this is the time to harvest all those years of hard work and to enjoy the fruits of power and money." Of course, she was right. It was not easy to give up the largesse of the corporate life. We went through a struggle.

"But I want to do other things," I protested. "I mean, don't we have enough money? At this point of my life, I don't want to jet around the world for fifteen days in a month. I want to write. The important thing is to agree that our wants are limited. After that it's straight arithmetic."

She understood. She reminded me, in fact, that many years ago I had told her that I wanted to quit the corporate world at fifty. We sat down and calculated how much we would need to live on for the rest of our

lives, including the cost of supporting our children, who fortunately
were grown up and were finishing college. Against our needs, we tried
to match the likely income we would earn from our savings and investments. It turned out that we might just be able to make it.

Having decided to quit, we wrote to a number of friends in India.
My own company was extremely gracious. It suggested a number of
alternative jobs where I might be happier, but when John Pepper, the
CEO, realized that my mind was made up, he offered me early retirement with its attendant benefits. The *Times of India* offered to let me
write a regular column. Since I had been writing for the paper off and
on for many years, this was not a complete surprise, and I immediately
accepted. Manmohan Singh, the finance minister, wrote back to say,
"Come back. Can't promise you anything, but we shall try." Several
Indian groups invited me to run their companies, but I declined. My tax
consultant at Deloitte advised me to return my green card; otherwise, I
would have to pay heavy and unnecessary taxes to the U.S. government
on my non-U.S. income. He added that I must remember to obtain
Form I-407 when I returned my green card.

A few days later I went to the immigration office in Cincinnati. As I
was returning my green card, the immigration officer asked, "Sir, what's
the problem? Don't you like our country?" I told him I liked his country, but not its tax laws. When I asked him for Form 407, he looked puz-
zled. "Never seen it," he said. He called Washington, and they faxed him
the form, which was titled "Wilful Abandonment of Lawful Permanent
Residence Status."

"Hold your horses, young man! I gotta ask you some questions," he
said. The questions had to do with making sure that I was leaving voluntarily—that I was not being forced out of the country for any reason. I
left the office, impressed with the U.S. government's concern for human
rights.

On returning to India we decided to settle in Delhi rather than Bombay. It made sense for me to settle there because, in my new career as a
writer, I needed to be near libraries, editors, intellectuals, and think
tanks. Delhi has plenty of these, unlike Bombay, which is primarily a
commercial city. If one is not making business deals, I felt, there is no
fun in living in Bombay. However, my wife hated Delhi. She said it had
no soul, and that its street life was aggressive.

They say that the measure of a civilization is how it treats its women. Since coming to Delhi I have met many women who long for Bombay. My wife explains that Bombay gives women dignity. If Bombay respects women, Delhi looks on them as sex objects. In Bombay, she can take a taxi at midnight; in Delhi, a girl cannot walk freely on the street in the evening. It seems that it takes more than education to bring civilization.

Bombay has this civilizing quality, I think, because of its origins as a city of commerce. Montesquieu wrote in his *Spirit of the Laws* that "it is almost a general rule that wherever manners are gentle, there is commerce; and wherever there is commerce, manners are gentle." He felt that commerce diverted people away from brutal wars and bloodshed. A few years later, Samuel Richard added that "commerce makes him who was so proud and haughty, suddenly turn supple, bending and serviceable. Through commerce, man learns to deliberate, to be honest, to acquire manners, to be prudent and reserved in talk and action." Commerce, they say, encourages the bourgeois virtues of thrift, hard work, self-reliance, and self-discipline. My experience of businessmen—Marwaris, Jains, and Gujarati banias—is that they possess these qualities in abundance, particularly the virtue of restraint.

The first rule of business is that unless both the buyer and seller are happy, the business transaction is not stable. If the buyer drives too hard a bargain or if the seller's goods are less than promised, the transaction fails. Thus, businesspeople learn interdependence. Both the buyer and the seller have to be satisfied, and this promotes a positive-sum game. People in business also understand the importance of "growth." They learn to believe that there is enough to go around, and this creates an "abundance mentality."

The origins of Delhi are feudal and monarchical. Because of the hierarchical nature of bureaucratic society, Delhi regards life as a zero-sum game. The pyramid gets smaller as you move up. There can be only one Prime Minister. Not everyone can be secretary. If you have to win, someone has to lose. Instead of becoming interdependent as buyers and sellers, you learn to put people down. Transactions in Delhi—as in Washington, D.C.—depend on influence and patronage, and it matters less what you know than whom you know. Person for person, Delhi people are better fed, better clothed, and better off. It is a middle-class city with a higher per capita income. However, it is not a very pleasant city. The Delhi resident wears his bad manners on his shirtsleeves. Fortunately, Delhi has changed a great deal in the last decade; it has increasingly become a commercial city. New business have come in. Multinational companies have established their headquarters here. A new middle class has emerged. This is the best hope of civilizing the manners of Delhi. My wife despairs that it will not happen in her life-time.

Soon after we returned to India in 1995 and people discovered that I had nothing better to do, they began to invite me to join their board of directors. At first, I was flattered by this attention, and I began to accept the invitations indiscriminately. Before I realized it, I was a member of fourteen boards and I was traveling twelve days in a month, hopping from one board meeting to the next. After three months of this, I dis-covered that this was a terrible way to live. Board governance is of vital importance, but given the way boards are structured there is little hope of penetrating a company as a nonexecutive board member. This means that there is little satisfaction in being a board member.

At the same time, I did want to stay in touch with developments in the business world. I also felt I could contribute something to the success of some of the companies. So one afternoon I picked up the phone and I spoke to fourteen board chairmen and I said, "Look, I am deeply hon-ored to be on your board. But I have decided that I must restrict myself to a few companies, and these I can get to know well and contribute to their success. If you think I can help your company, give me a challeng-ing assignment. I shall give you one day a month and charge you a very high fee to ensure that both you and I take the assignment seriously. In this way, I shall be able to penetrate your business and be a more useful board member."

To my surprise, six companies agreed to appoint me consultant. I stepped down from the other boards. I checked from a regulatory point of view whether a consultant could also be a board member. The answer was that if the company's lawyer or chartered accountant could be a board member, so could a consultant. My consultancy took off and soon I was having a lot of fun working six days a month helping six compa-nies to become competitive. I began to help one company build a global brand; another to regain market share in the domestic market; a third company to innovate and upgrade its product line; a fourth company to

expand the market since it already had the leadership position; a fifth to
transition from a family to a professionally run business; and a sixth to
get its managers to work cohesively against preagreed objectives. I had a
ringside view of Indian business.

My consultancy assignments took me to distant parts of the country.
Occasionally I was able to get away from the big cities, where I would
meet a different type of businessman. One such trip took me to
Pondicherry. We set out in the morning from Madras, and after an hour
stopped in a village cafe, where we were served the most wonderful
south Indian coffee by fourteen-year-old Raju, who wanted to become
another Bill Gates when he grew up (and whom we met in the introduction). Returning from Pondicherry, I came upon a stream of young
girls, brightly dressed in sarees of different colors, walking in a single file
along the two-lane highway. There were hundreds. My first reaction was
that they must be going to a temple. It must be a festival day. What else
could be happening, early in the morning, in the middle of nowhere?
We stopped the car and asked one of the girls what was going on.

"Nothing," she giggled. "We are walking to work at the leather factory." She made leather shoes. I asked her about her customers.

"Florsheim, Hogarth, Marks and Spencer." She said the names in a
clear and deliberate manner. She was very proud of her customers. "Yes,
we make very good shoes," she added.

She told us that her name was Sushila. She was twenty years old, and
she earned Rs 15,000 a month. She had been working in the factory
since it started three years ago. Ever since then things had changed
rapidly in her village, Guduvencheri. All the girls had jobs now. They
could make their own dowries, and they got respect. I seem to find
more job opportunities for women in the south then in the north. Probably it is because they are better educated. South India, for the most part,
treats its women better than the less-educated north. Suddenly, Sushila
dropped her bag and she became flustered. A small bottle of Oil of Olay
spilled out. Fortunately, it didn't break, and she was relieved.

"Isn't it expensive?" I asked. It used to be very expensive, she said, but
the price had come down. Her shopkeeper had told her that excise
duties had come down on all cosmetics. Looking at her watch, she
said abruptly, "I must go." She ran off to join the colorful line to the factory. I had liked the way she had confidently rattled off "Florsheim,

Hogarth." She had said the names as though she really cared for her customers. She clearly knew the secret of success in the global economy.

Meeting Sushila brought back uncomfortable memories. On the crowded road back to Madras I recalled my fruitless visits to Delhi's North Block. I had paced the corridors in the 1980s trying to persuade anyone who would listen in the finance ministry that a 120 percent excise duty on toiletries was counterproductive. I had felt frustrated that we could not introduce our shampoos—Pantene, Pert Plus, Head & Shoulders, and Vidal Sassoon—because the tax structure more than doubled their price. All the Asian subsidiaries of P&G had built successful hair care businesses except India. For the same reason, our Oil of Olay had also not grown. P&G China, in contrast, had built the second-largest Olay business in the world with half our consumer price.

My lowest point had come in a meeting with the finance minister. I had argued that lowering the excise duty would lower consumer prices of shampoos, skin creams, and other toiletries, which in turn would raise their demand. The tax revenues would thus rise, although the tax rate might be lower. Indian women did not need lipsticks and face creams, felt the minister. I replied that all women wanted to look pretty.

"A face cream won't do anything for an ugly face. These are luxuries of the rich," he said. I protested that even a village girl used a paste of haldi so that she could look pretty.

"No, it's best to leave a face to nature," he said impatiently.

"Sir," I pleaded, "how can you decide what she wants? After all, it is her hard-earned money."

"Yes, and I don't want her wasting it. Let her buy food. I don't want multinational companies getting rich selling face creams to poor Indians."

I patiently explained to him that many more Indian companies would benefit from lowering their prices. In any case, whether Indian or foreign, there would be many more jobs for Indians as volumes grew—not only more jobs in the companies but in their suppliers and in the suppliers of their suppliers. These were the spread effects of investment. He stopped me, saying that he did not need a self-serving lesson in economics, and he motioned me out of his office.

Sushila had opened a wound that I thought had healed. It had happened ten years ago, but I could still get angry at the stupidity of the command economy and the arrogance of its commanders. As we hit the traffic on Mount Road, I calmed down. Raju and Sushila, I realized, were already a part of the global economy—Raju in his dreams of Bill Gates and Sushila in the way she thought about her customers. Manmohan Singh had not only halved the excise duty on toiletries, he had let loose a bigger revolution. Liberalization in trade, besides information technology, tax reform, and free access to the airwaves, was beginning to change Sushila's and Raju's minds.

On the flight back to Delhi, I met a friend, Nalini Singh, and I told her about Raju and Sushila. She told me in turn about a young girl in Connaught Place from whom she bought flowers for her hair. Recently, she said, she had pulled over at the traffic light near Nirula's. As she was selecting a jasmine band, she had remarked to the girl that her *gajras* were remarkably cool and fresh. Their perfume had filled the evening air.

The girl pointed to a tiny refrigerator, which was partially visible in the corner grocery store. This was her secret. "Do you really keep your flowers in the fridge?!" Nalini exclaimed. Not in those words, but the girl explained that this is how she derived competitive advantage over the girl who stood at the Janpath traffic corner.

A few months later, my friend S. K. Singh invited me to his brother's farm in Uttar Pradesh. "Bartoli is a sleepy village. There are mostly low-caste families, some Muslims and a sprinkling of Rajputs. They only talk of corruption and influence, *rishwat* and *sifarish*." So said SK's brother as we turned off the Grand Trunk Road between Bulandshahr and Khurja, a hundred kilometers east of Delhi.

I looked around the village and I saw another story. Fields were laden with sugarcane, tractors were plowing the land; tractor-trailers had created a traffic jam on the narrow bridge connecting the village to the main road; diesel pump sets were pumping out gallons of water; well-fed uniformed schoolchildren walked home from a new Montessori school that was only six months old but had already enrolled eighty students.

The schoolmaster at the old government school wanted to know when the government planned to start the new "midday meals" scheme. He had read in the newspaper that it was coming soon. It was hot inside my host's simple village home, and we pulled out our charpai. My host explained to me that the only reason the schoolmaster expressed concern about the new "free lunch" program was that he expected to get a cut from the scheme.

Fateh Singh, a neighbor, came to greet us. He was a young fiery-eyed Dalit whose diffident manner hid an alert mind. He would not sit on the same charpai because my host was Rajput. Fateh Singh owned four acres and plowed another six on contract. The Dalits in the village had been "unclean" leather workers, but now they plowed the land with five tractors, which they rented to each other. "The problem is labor, sir. I can't get anyone to work the land." Krishan Pal Singh, a Rajput, who owned thirty acres between the two villages of Bartoli and Mamman Khurdua, joined the refrain. "Our biggest problem is getting someone to work in the fields. I pay Rs 45 a day plus three meals and free fodder for the cattle—and I still can't get anyone."

"It isn't easy working the land," said Fateh Singh. "We get power only at nights. So someone needs to stay awake to water the fields. In May and June it gets so hot that you are reminded of your grandmother." This drew a laugh, but it explained why the young were leaving the village.

"What are you complaining about?" said my host provocatively to Fateh Singh. "Mayawati is now the chief minister. You can have anything you want." Fateh Singh was hurt. He did not like to be reminded of his caste, even though the new chief minister was a Dalit too. "I am a liberal, and above these caste distinctions," said my host, turning to me, "but I cannot tolerate the sight of a low-caste girl sitting beside a Brahmin boy. I saw it with my own eyes on a bus in Delhi the other day. Mind you, the boy was the son of a Supreme Court judge."

"What is wrong with them sitting on the bus together?" I asked artlessly.

"What's wrong—she is unclean!" said my Rajput host, rising imperiously from the charpai and assuming the dignity of a retired transport commissioner. "They used to carry muck on their heads."

"That was probably two generations ago," I said, impatience showing in my voice.

After a few months, my consultancy with a garment company took me on a field trip to Calcutta, where I visited the prosperous Sumangal Clothing Store on Lindsay Street. There I met Golam Mondal, a mustachioed salesman in his forties from Babnam village in Hooghly district. Mondal had spread out his chikon embroidery on two counters and he was trying to sell it wholesale to Sumangal.

"It is exquisite!" I exclaimed at a blouse. The store owner reminded me not to get too enthusiastic since he was trying to beat down the price. Mondal explained that his cousin had spent three months to complete it along with a matching saree. Both were for Rs 5,000. I asked how much his cousin earned doing this work. He looked around to ensure that the store owner was not within hearing.

"Are you a customer, sir?"

"No," I said.

"Then I can tell you—she earns plenty, sir. Our people prefer to work on piece rate. Simple chikon workers can earn Rs 350 for shadow work or reverse stitching. For kantha, our traditional Bengali needlework, they earn as much as Rs 1,000 per piece. We are a village of two hundred families, and the average family earns Rs 8,000 per month, which is a lot. The women do the embroidery and the men go out and sell the work. I concentrate on the south, and my order book is bursting this year. The Punjab National Bank has already upgraded our Babnam branch. The manager says that deposits from the chikon workers are more than Rs 1.5 crore."

"Does the government help?" I asked.

"Help, sir? We don't want the government near our village. I am ashamed to take you to our village, sir. In the rains our road gets washed away. The trucks carrying raw materials get stuck in the slush. We get half the power that we need. I don't know how I am going to fulfill this order book, with the power situation being what it is."

"What accounts for your order book?"

"I don't know. Ten years ago, we were as poor as mice. Today nursing homes, schools, hotels—they all want our chikon work. Earlier, we depended on saree and handloom shops—" He stopped mid-sentence, seeing the store owner approach.

"Yes, you ungrateful wretch. I know, you are a big man now."

In the evening, I went to meet some old friends in Calcutta. They complained that there were no jobs for the young in Calcutta. I told them about Mondal. But they couldn't relate to his life. I felt sorry for middle-class Bengali mothers whose educated sons either were unemployed or had left for other parts of India to look for a job. "Despite the hype, no sensible industrialist will invest in a communist state," said Bandopadhyaya. "Ironical, isn't it, we finally have good infrastructure—power, telecom, the metro—but no jobs." It was different in the country-side, they said. People were more positive. Many had benefited from land reforms. "The green revolution has finally come to Bengal," said Bandopadhyaya.

The following month I happened to be in Rajasthan, in the pink city of Jaipur, in the company of an American visitor. While he went to see the tourist sights, I decided to visit Madhu Verma, whom I had first met in Bombay but had not seen for a dozen years. Her husband was the manager of a public-sector bank. They had lived in Jaipur for the past fifteen years. On the way to their home, I was caught in a traffic jam. I fretted that I would be late.

Jaipur seemed to have shed its sleepy, apologetic, small-town air. I felt a new aggressiveness on the streets. People who earlier walked were on bicycles; those who rode bicycles were now on scooters; those on scoot-ers were now riding shining new Maruti cars and causing this traffic jam. Jaipur was also filthier. Fifteen years ago, the same street had been a clean, wide boulevard. Today, garbage was piled on both sides of the road and vied belligerently with the fumes of the traffic. It was hot in the taxi, and the exhaust and the din of the traffic was relentless. The after-noon sun was burning hot and my shirt began to stick to my skin.

Finally, the traffic came unstuck, and we turned into a newly built colony of Jaipur's upwardly mobile middle class. We passed garishly painted houses, in bright pink and green, with satellite dishes on the roof, cars parked outside, and open garbage mounds at the back. Soon I arrived at Madhu Verma's house. I guessed that it must be hers—it was quiet, surrounded by bougainvillea flowers, a nicely cut lawn, and lots of greenery. Inside it was cool and I was surrounded by old-world charm.

"Jaipur has changed," Madhu said in a pleasant way—soothing like a dentist promising not to injure. "It is such a quiet change that no one notices it. Much of it I don't like, but there are good things too." She served me tea and asked me about my parents. I asked what had changed.

She looked out at the kachnar tree outside the window as though to help her think. "I have four children, and all of them are working. The two younger ones have got jobs on their own without any connections. And my older girl has recently changed her job for a better one. My fourth has started a business. He is not doing too well right now because there's too much competition in his line. He doesn't want to work for anyone."

"What is changed?" I asked again.

"That's the change. My kids have jobs, careers. There's excitement in the house. They bring news of the world. Do you think ten years ago they'd have got settled on their own? There would have been panic. I would have been phoning the whole world to find out if someone knew someone in the UPSC [Union Public Services Commission]. Mind you, they are not alone. Their friends from college have also landed good jobs or are thinking about starting businesses."

"What do you think is responsible for this?"

"I don't know. I am no expert. Maybe it's the economic reforms. I just know that my kids in Jaipur have got jobs, and my cousin's kids in the UK haven't. And they have been looking for two years."

Even the judiciary and the trade unions have been infected by the changing attitudes. "Justice Sawant of the Bombay High Court now delivers five out of ten judgments in favor of business; earlier, ten out of ten judgments were in labor's favor," Zia Mody, a young, high-powered lawyer, tells me in Bombay. T. A. Francis, the general secretary of the communist trade union, AITUC, confesses that unions had put off the middle class because "we blindly supported the public sector [even when] it had failed to provide efficient services." Labor attitudes have mellowed. There are fewer strikes and labor agreements now routinely include productivity clauses. Francis is a new kind of labor leader. He sits before a computer in his Delhi office, wears a fashionable striped shirt, tinted aviator spectacles, smart loafers, and smokes Wills. He studied at the Delhi School of Economics and became a communist during the student movement in 1972–73. Francis says that closing a public-sector company should not be viewed from the point of view of job losses alone. If it releases resources and makes fresh investments possible elsewhere, then it makes sense.

The debate in the country seems to be shifting from politics to economics. The circulation of the leading business daily, the *Economic Times,* was less than 100,000 copies in 1989. In March 1994, it touched

500,000 copies, making it 60 percent larger than the United Kingdom's *Financial Times*. It subsequently came down to 380,000 with the decline in the stock market. Similarly, the readership of the three leading business magazines has doubled over the past five years. During the summer of 1995, the entire country was mesmerized by the American energy company Enron's power plant in Maharashtra. In Parliament, in the newspapers, on glamorous TV chat shows, Indians discussed the intricacies of Enron's power purchase agreement with the same avidness as they discussed the cricket genius Tendulkar's batting average. Students in Maharashtrian colleges mentioned Enron's plant load factor with casual sophistication, as though they were talking about the latest affair of their favorite hero on the Bombay screen.

Even the politicians have changed. I visited a former cabinet minister at his home in Delhi. He lived in an old imperial bungalow with neoclassical columns on one of the wide avenues in Sir Edwin Lutyens's Delhi, surrounded by a magnificent lawn and guards at the gate. There were no suppliants, however. Then I remembered that the great man was no longer in power. In the old days, there were always dozens of people waiting outside his door. The dignity of a great man was judged in those days of the License Raj by the number of people waiting to see him.

The great man walked in punctually at five, fresh after a bath, in a starched kurta. Five minutes later an impeccably dressed attendant brought us tea.

"You don't come and visit us anymore," he said with a gentle smile which covered the mild rebuke. "But then no one comes to visit politicians these days."

I looked around the comfortably appointed room. I realized that this house would have to be soon given up. If he still had clout, he would find ways to keep it. But it must rankle to be illegally occupying a government house. He must have caught the drift of my thought. "Yes, everything in this house belongs to the government: every cup, every saucer, this tea tray, the attendant and even this uniform." His helpless look seemed to say, "How can a man give up all this and become a nothing?"

He offered me a cup of tea and said, "I am glad you have offered to help the government with the reforms. We need to globalize our econ-

omy and to make our businesses more competitive." He talked for half
an hour in this way, saying all the right things. As he warmed up, I could
see the politician in action. It was a well-rehearsed performance. I was
amused to see an amazing turnaround by this great advocate of socialism. Five years ago, he had lectured to me in the same way, but he had
said exactly the opposite.

As I was leaving, he lowered his voice. "Yes, by all means, go and help
the government in its liberalization program, but remember us as well.
Don't forget the old friendships. It is sad that businessmen don't come to
see us now." He looked to me for a response, and then he said to no one
in particular, "Can't we have reforms and still keep the old contacts
flowing?"

The veranda with the round old pillars was dulled by the evening
sunlight. The cane chairs, which had earlier looked restful, suddenly
seemed ugly and heavy in the bleached light. The rotted chick blinds
added to the dull, official feeling of the house. For a few minutes I had
almost believed that the great man had genuinely changed and that he
spoke sincerely for the reforms, so good had been his performance.
In the end, the dirty truth had come out, staining an otherwise fine
evening.

I wondered if corruption had come down or had it increased since
the reforms, as many said.

"Corruption may have grown in the areas where the reforms are half
complete, such as power, telecom, aviation, environment," says Swaminathan Aiyar, "But there is also more *talk* of corruption because of an
activist judiciary and a sensationalist press. It has certainly not increased
because of the reforms."

Of this I am clear—the minds of the people have begun to change. It
has happened more in the middle class; it is more apparent in the young;
it is more obvious in the business world. People have begun to look at
the world differently. There is a quiet confidence in the air. People genuinely believe that their children will be better off than they were.
Young managers and entrepreneurs exhibit a "can-do" attitude. Nor is it
only on account of the reforms. The middle class is growing rapidly.
Television is freeing the mind. However, the single biggest factor in
opening the floodgates seems to be the liberalization of 1991. Becoming
rich has also become acceptable. Whereas a government job was the

route to success in the previous generation, now the thing to do is to go into business. Money has replaced power and privilege. Older, traditional people are quick to condemn the changing attitudes. They call it "greed." They are upset and see it as a threat to Indian culture. But the younger people defend themselves, saying that it is not greed but a desire for achievement. They want to "get things done," to "produce results," and business offers to them a stage to do so.

Business people are the most prophetic when speaking of the reforms. "Narasimha Rao came out of Jurassic Park in 1991 to become the biggest revolutionary in India since Gautama Buddha," says Aveek Sarkar, the Calcutta publisher, with a mischievous smile. "But he doesn't realize it!" Anil Ambani of Reliance says, "It is not economic reform, it is a revolution!" Others have also expressed similar sentiments. Sharad Joshi, the leader of half a million farmers in Maharashtra, told me, "It is our second independence. In 1947 we only got our political independence; we struggled for another forty-four years before we finally won our economic independence in 1991." Arun Shourie, the author and commentator, says, "Today we have the same sense of possibilities that existed in the early fifties."

"How else do you explain the sight of eighty-two-year-old Jyoti Basu, the communist lord of Bengal, standing before an audience of Wall Street investors trying to drum up investment for his state?" says Aveek Sarkar. "How did you do it?" exclaims a German businessman on an Indian Airlines flight to Calcutta. "It is going to take us a whole generation to assimilate East and West Germany, yet in a few short years you have succeeded in changing attitudes."

India is no longer the stable land of certainties. There is new energy, a new sense of freedom. Listening to Golam Mandal of Babnam village, I realized that the state was no longer the protector "mother-father" to many people. Suspicion of the state was a part of the new mind-set. Instead of viewing the end of old reverences as a cynical condemnation of a corrupt government, I see it as the sign of a new maturity in our democratic journey. Had not the liberal philosophers always expressed a suspicion of state power? The American founding fathers had gone to a great deal of trouble to create a system of checks and balances on the different agencies of the state. Whether the change is due to an activist judiciary, or a powerful election commissioner, or the impact of television, or the Mandal social revolution, or economic liberalization, it is hard to be sure. When the former finance minister, Manmohan Singh, announced the economic reforms in July 1991, I thought it was about technical matters like "structural adjustment," "tariff levels," "industrial delicensing." I now realize that the reforms are creating a revolution in ideas and changing the attitudes of the people. Raju, Sushila, Kum Kum, define a new image of India. I encounter it frequently—in the hopes of the young, in the way people talk, in the way mothers think about their daughters. It is a new way of looking at the world. A revolution in ideas does not of course mean that jobs are immediately sprouting or that poverty is disappearing. Heartbreaking poverty is still the pervasive face of India. It is a terrible prison in which far too many Indians live in fearful anxiety. However, one day, and sooner than we perhaps expect, the mental revolution should lead to a physical one.

SEVENTEEN

New Money

The secret of business success is not who you know. It's what you know.

—*WALL STREET JOURNAL* ADVERTISEMENT

I read somewhere that China boasts a million millionaires and eighteen million entrepreneurs. This was twenty years after its reforms. I do not know how many we have in India, and our reforms are only ten years old, but we have always had our entrepreneurs. Despite its best efforts, our government could not wipe out the spirit of enterprise. A walk to the bazaar is all one needs to see that commerce is well and alive. The industrialists of the License Raj may have got into bad habits— born of protection—but their behavior even then was entrepreneurial in the way they won and lost market share in bureaucrats' offices. They merely played by the rules of that game. The entrepreneurs of the 1990s, however, are creatures of a competitive economy. And today's young are no longer embarrassed about wanting to be rich. Without the shackles of licensing, FERA, MRTP, closed borders, and high taxes, the country is filled with new confidence and I expect there will soon be a million millionaires in India.

My management consultancy gave me a box seat to observe the changing business scene. I met businesspeople of all kinds. I empathized with their problems, marveled at the opportunities before them, and discovered to my delight that I also began to grow again under the stimulus of new business problems. I jumped at every opportunity to talk to businesspeople—at airports, in trains, at seminars and conferences. It was not difficult because Indian managers are not shy to talk about their business. By far the most interesting people I met were in the new "knowledge" industries. Not since the industrial revolution has any group brought so many improvements and added so much value to their customers as information technology professionals. And the best is still to come. In the new century, these managers and their companies will shape the lives of billions from the boardrooms of New York to the bazaars of Kathmandu. It is here that "the passion and the excellence of our times," in the words of Oliver Wendell Holmes, is being enacted.

The new spirit is reflected in the vast number of rags-to-riches stories. This is not surprising. It has happened in many countries in periods of economic expansion. Money is replacing power and privilege. Many people think that business is about greed. It is, to an extent. But it is also about the pursuit of excellence. It is about young people with ideas reaching out to do the impossible, and creating jobs and wealth for society. Most of us are not tuned in. We are still listening to the background noise of democracy when we could be listening to the music of entrepreneurship.

Two south Indian temple priests sit peacefully beside me waiting to get on the Jet Airways flight from Madras to Bangalore. They are old cronies and they sit side by side, each with a steel tiffin carrier filled with idlis. Their foreheads are smeared with horizontal stripes of paste, their brown faces creased with gossip and laughter. Their jocose voices conjure up coconut groves and the sweet sounds of the veena and a Carnatic musical heaven. Both wear starched white dhotis and they have cell phones dangling from them, which seems just about right on the polished floor of the new Madras airport. Their voices are light and accented in the manner of their caste, and they look like a pair of characters from an R. K. Narayan novel. They are a comfortable sight as they create around themselves a rich aura of incense, temple gods, and Chola bronzes. Why is it, I ask myself, that middle-aged men in such disguise should look both kindly and wise?

The two cronies, it turns out, have started a software company. I had come to Madras to spend a day consulting with Vellayan's T. I. Cycles, trying to bring discontinuity into the mature Indian bicycle market. Sitting at the airport and observing the Brahmins, I feel confused. But isn't that a condition in which we exist in contemporary history, as distinct from the way we try to tidy it up afterwards? Can one expect this city to have peculiar virtues—springing from its old, spiritual way of life—that might help it survive the present pace of industrialization? If my journey to the airport is to be believed, the automobile will soon choke Madras. The rapid growth of the past few years seems to envelop it in a grasping nastiness, like a blight in which human beings are ground down to insects. The Brahmins say that the maddening traffic, the pollution, the noise, and the pace does not bother them. On the contrary, it is a nice change from their old suburban temple life.

My flight is soon called. I sit next to a young six-foot American on the plane. He is a customer of one of Bangalore's software companies. There are at least five cites in India, he thinks, which are ready to leap into the information age. I am going to Bangalore for several reasons. One of them is to visit Infosys, Bangalore's revered software company. Infosys is in a technology park on the Hosur road, but cows are grazing outside the offices. Once inside the campus-like office, I feel transported to Silicon Valley in California. Software professionals are hunched over screens in an atmosphere of quiet discussion, and training rooms are full of bright young engineers. Of the three thousand professionals working in Infosys, two to three hundred are in classes at any moment, updating their technical knowledge or learning about quality. In a spacious classroom filled with the latest equipment, twenty alert minds are in avid discussion of customer service. Infosys's secret is its ability to hire the best talent and keep them motivated in a "learning environment." It is able to do this because of an outstanding stock option plan, which is open to every professional who has worked there for three years. Thus, many of its junior and middle managers are rich by Indian standards and have visible assets to show for their hard work. Infosys spends 5 percent of its turnover on education, research, and on developing its people.

Started by six computer engineers with a capital of Rs 10,000 ($600), Infosys was worth $15 billion in February 2000. It develops software for the best global companies, who have kept its sales growing at an average of 40 percent a year, in the past five years. It also designs, erects, and maintains Internet infrastructure for leveraging the power of e-commerce. It sells Bancs 2000, a software system, to banks, and recently sold a warehouse management system to Reebok. With the steady appreciation of its stock, it has more than a hundred managers individually worth a million dollars.

"The secret of our success is teamwork," says suave Nandan Nilekani, the managing director. It is partly luck, partly chemistry, partly Narayana Murthy, who is the catalyst and the glue. "Infosys makes you subordinate your ego and you invariably put the job above your interest." The CEO is smallish, bespectacled, soft-featured Narayana Murthy, who is one of its six founders. "I got into IIT [Indian Institute of Technology] Kharagpur in 1962, but I didn't go because my father couldn't afford the Rs 120 per month for the hostel." His father was a government servant—an assistant education officer in the old Mysore government—earning Rs 500 per month, and with that he supported eight children. Murthy is in his early fifties and he speaks without shyness and to the point. He is a billionaire now and has cultivated the CEO manner, which means that he is conscious of his image.

So, how did he go from rags to riches? "Since I couldn't go to IIT, I had to settle for the local engineering college in Mysore. From there I went to IIM [Indian Institute of Management] Ahmedabad. After that, I hopped through several early jobs, including one with a defense contractor in France, until I landed at Patni Computer Systems in Bombay, where I worked for five years. They were good people—a business family from Agra. Being professionals themselves, they had succeeded in collecting some real talent. That is where six of us had the idea of starting our own software company. That dream has come true."

As a student, Murthy was a committed Marxist. Disillusionment and conversion came in 1974, when he was hitchhiking from Paris to Bangalore. He boarded the Sofia Express one night at Nishe, a small railway station near the border of Bulgaria and Yugoslavia. On board, he met an East German and an Austrian girl with whom he struck up a conversation in French. At the next station, the police stormed in, dragged him out of the train, and informed him that the East German had accused him of exchanging sensitive state secrets with the Austrian girl. They bundled him into jail, without food or water. "That was the turning point," he muses. "I thought, if this is communism, it isn't for me."

Infosys is a creature of the economic reforms. So are the other 325 software companies of Bangalore. Earlier Indian software engineers had to fly back and forth. With liberalization and the zeal of a visionary civil servant, N. Vittal, the companies got their own satellite link, which lets them do most of their work in Bangalore. Three-fourths of the software companies in Bangalore are Indian, but they account for only one-third of the investment. Foreign companies like IBM, Texas Instruments, Motorola, Group Bull, and Sun Microsystems are also developing software in Bangalore. It makes sense because an Indian engineer costs only 20 percent of an American. The difference between Bangalore and many East Asian cities is that it has prospered through cheap brains rather than cheap hands. Although India produces two million graduates, it trains fewer than fifty thousand computer science engineers. With demand growing so rapidly, wages have been climbing 20 percent a year and companies routinely lose a quarter of their workforce every year. The pressure is accelerated by the foreign companies, who transfer their best Indian engineers to the United States or to their other foreign operations. Many Indians are also lured to Silicon Valley, where one-third of the high-tech companies are today run by Chinese and Indian engineers, according to London's *Financial Times*. Hence, Narayana Murthy's stock option plan has become the model for all of India's entrepreneurial ventures in order to retain talent.

Because traditional universities and educational institutions cannot cope with the exploding demand, computer education has spilled into the marketplace. Two young entrepreneurs from IIT Delhi, Vijay Thadani and Rajendra Pawar, saw in the early 1980s what the government did not. They realized that the world was changing and no one would be employable without computer skills. India had a huge and growing appetite for IT professionals and our schools and colleges were only creating an army of unemployables. They stepped into the vacuum, set up the National Institute of Information Technology (NIIT), and began to offer computer lessons in the bazaar. They were so successful that they could not cope with the exploding demand. Since they did not have the resources to expand rapidly across the country, they hit upon the idea of franchising their schools. Soon NIIT centers were flourishing even in the smallest towns. In Bombay, another entrepreneur had the same idea and he started Aptech. Today, India has three thousand centers, training half a million students a year. Infotech training has been growing 30 percent a year. NIIT has 40 percent market share of the $225 million market—its alumni base is almost a million.

When NIIT and Aptech started expanding in the early nineties, there was a palpable sense of excitement among the youth. Young people everywhere began to flock into the new computer schools. These became the hip places to hang around. It was the second revolution in the Indian bazaar. The first had occurred a few years earlier, when Sam Pitroda's telephone counters came up in towns and villages across India. A third information revolution is around the corner, as Internet kiosks and cybercafes are becoming common, creating virtual villages.

NIIT dreams of becoming a world leader in computer education. It is present in thirty-one countries, and it recently opened in China, where six hundred Shanghai residents are on its rolls. Pawar proudly says that eleven professors from Chinese universities spent more than a year preparing NIIT's lessons in Mandarin and adapting them for the Chinese audience. To become a world leader, they will have to conquer the United States, and they are planning to acquire a company there to get a jump start. An American company would be expensive—it might cost as much as $100 million. How can an Indian company with sales of $150 million buy a $100 million American company? It can, on the shoulders of NIIT's market capitalization of more than two billion dollars.

The tall, bearded, forty-eight-year-old Pawar speaks avidly. Everything seems to come from the heart. Although his head may be in the clouds, his feet are on the ground. The breakthrough came when NIIT discovered that it could franchise education. It is the first time in the world, as far as he knows, that someone has franchised education. Their secret lay in finding the right franchisees, who turned out to be professionals (not local traders) and owned real estate in their hometown. NIIT trained them to become businessmen–educators. NIIT helps its franchisees to replicate standardized classrooms, gives them training material, helps them hire and train teachers, teaches them to advertise locally, audits them regularly, and administers exams with rigorous ethical standards. The attention to the detail and quality, backed by innovative advertising, has rapidly built the NIIT brand. Not having to invest in real estate, and spared the day-to-day problems of administering hundreds of centers in far-flung towns across the country, it devotes its energies to improving its courses and programs. It has thus ensured that all its thousands of students get jobs within days of graduating.

Its most daring innovation is a four-year program, equivalent to an undergraduate degree. The outstanding curriculum was created by a team of visionary educators. Ten thousand graduates have passed out of the "world university" (100 percent placed in jobs), and twenty thousand are currently enrolled. NIIT's edge over our formal colleges is that learning is interactive. Students spend the fourth year as paid interns in two thousand affiliated companies. Since society expects its young to have a formal degree, most students are also enrolled in formal colleges, although they spend most of their time at NIIT. "Success in education comes not from having the best teachers but attracting the best students," says Pawar. NIIT does that. The matrimonial ads in the Sunday papers routinely boast the four-year G-NIIT qualification, and a girl with G-NIIT after her name, they say, needs a smaller dowry. My young neighbor tells me that she is spending Rs 55,000 for the four-year course, which she confidently expects will put her on a par with engineering students on the job. The most important thing she has learned, she says, is self-confidence and teamwork.

NIIT has been reinventing itself over the past five years. Increasingly, it has turned to software solutions and educational multimedia and already has 269 titles. Almost half its revenues now come from noneducational services. Its software business has the advantage in being able to hire from the best graduates in its own "world university." Out of NIIT's 3,800 employees, 1,500 are G-NIITians. The software business returns the compliment by creating case material for the education business. Like Infosys, NIIT retains talent through stock options, which it has given to about 1,000 of its 3,800 employees. Since the stock has also zoomed, 900 of them were worth over Rs 1 million, 88 were worth Rs 1 crore, and 8 were dollar millionaires in July 1999. More important, it has created 1,750 entrepreneurs through franchising and given indirect employment to 15,000 people through its franchisees.

NIIT's most fascinating experiment is to take computer education to 371 schools in Tamil Nadu. "During the day schoolchildren are trained in computerized classrooms," says Pawar. "After school hours the facilities are thrown open to residents of the town to help our franchisees make up for the lost profits during the day." If there is profit to be made, competing education companies will scramble to replicate this across the country. If the Tamil Nadu experiment succeeds, the country might have found a model for taking computer education into government schools, and computer literacy could explode across the country. When

Prime Minister Vajpayee's IT Task Force offered us the dream of making all schoolchildren computer literate by 2010, we thought it was a pipe dream. If the NIIT model works, that dream might come true.

Infosys and NIIT are the best examples of the new type of entrepreneurial companies making a mark in the brave new India after the reforms. There are many more, and new ones are cropping up every day. One of them is Satyam Infoway, which was born in November 1998, when Vajpayee liberated the Internet from the clutches of the government. It is one of forty Internet service providers, and had a dream debut in October 1999 on the Nasdaq. Increasingly, information technology services ought to overtake software. Among these, "remote services" offer the greatest employment potential for India. A friend of mine has set up a business in Madras employing medical students to edit and proofread medical texts electronically for a British publisher for a fraction of what it would cost to do the job in the United Kingdom. Aditi Technologies in Bangalore offers a mentoring service for Microsoft products, where customers post their problems on the Net and Aditi resolves them via e-mail. More than a hundred people at Data Tree of Hyderabad convert mortgage documents from American cities into digitized CD-ROMs. British Airways and Cathay have shifted their back offices to India to reconcile worldwide accounts online. Citibank, American Express, and other international banks are doing the same.

Increasingly, American doctors dictate the diagnosis and prescriptions of their patients into a Dictaphone. These voice files are electronically transferred to Health Scribe, a company in Bangalore, where they are deciphered, entered into the computer, and transferred back. GE Capital employs more than two thousand people in a global facility near Delhi to process mortgage and loan applications from around the world, answer questions from its credit card holders in Europe and the Americas, and do payroll accounting for its plants and offices across the world. Since most employees do their work without ever seeing the customer, it should be possible to transfer lots of back-office jobs to India. I am on the board of Crest Communications in Bombay, which makes digital animated drawings for movies. It recently won a contract to make a 3D film for one of the Hollywood studios. Geographic Software Systems in Kerala has bagged an order for digitizing five thousand maps for Flensburg, a county in Germany.

There is no reason why many toll-free call centers cannot shift from the United States to India. What makes all this possible is India's universities, which produce two million degree holders every year. They have varying levels of proficiency in English; most Indians employed in the remote-service business would be overqualified in the West. A certified public accountant working on account reconciliation costs GE $15,000 to $20,000 a year. In America, a less qualified worker doing the same job would cost three times more, and GE Capital's Indian operation expects to save GE $10 million next year. McKinsey reckons this business could create one to two million jobs and be worth $50 billion to India by 2010. For this to happen, the wholesale price of international calls would have to become competitive. We will also need to reform our labor laws to allow the hiring and firing of workers depending on market demand.

When President Kennedy amended the U.S. immigration law, replacing quotas by skills as the basis for entry, he set in motion the steady drain of talent from India and the rest of the world to America. Indians moaned about the brain drain, but they couldn't stop their children from emigrating. I too feel uneasy that when the world is moving into the information age and knowledge increasingly separates the winning from the losing nations, we are losing our best and brightest. But I have a lurking faith that Indians abroad will one day return the favor to the land that nurtured and educated them.

Payback time has arrived for some. A tiny company in Bangalore called Armedia made its forty-three employees rich beyond their wildest dreams in 1999. It had been started two years earlier by Tushar Dave, a tall and soft-spoken chip designer who lives in Silicon Valley but retains his Indian passport and accent. America's Broadcom bought Armedia for $67 million in mid-1999 and gave every single Bangalore employee stock in the American company. Wall Street analysts think that Broadcom is one of America's smarter companies, and when it acquired its first overseas venture in India, it sent a powerful signal to the world's investment community. The impact of this acquisition will be profound. It will bring investment, high-paying jobs, and exports for India, and it will inspire tens of Tushar Daves to do the same.

Tushar Dave went to Silicon Valley, where he worked for sixteen years as an engineer with Intel, and he acquired a gold mine of knowledge about chip design. He realized that Intel had made a fortune by making more and more powerful chips which made computers run faster. However, the world no longer needed more computing power, it needed computers and TVs to transmit data at very high speeds. He left Intel and set up Armedia to design these new chips in Bangalore. He desperately needed experienced engineers. But no one wanted to leave a secure job to join a small, risky venture. Eventually, he got the right engineers because he offered all his employees shares in the company. In two years, Armedia developed chips that would go inside digital TVs and decode pictures and sound. However, it did not have the resources to make and market the chips. But Broadcom in America did, and it realized that Armedia had created a world-class product. They decided to marry.

Tushar Dave has paid back. So have Raj Vattikuti, Bharat Desai, Ashok Trivedi, Sunil Wadhwani, and Nandu Thondawadi. They are Indians who made good in America, came back, and created jobs and software development centers here—even before India's own IT boom began. They belong to the "billion-dollar club" of Indian software entrepreneurs who have had a meteoric rise in Silicon Valley. India matters to them because they can have the best of both worlds: a creative environment in America, which encourages enterprise, and the marvelous software development skills of India.

When Ramesh Chauhan sold Thums Up, the leading Indian soft drink, to Coke for $40 million a few years ago, Indian companies shivered. There were howls of protest. How could we let foreigners seize our jewels? There was an emotional reaction across the country, which was far worse than when the Japanese bought New York's Rockefeller Center. When Tushar Dave sold Armedia for $67 million, no one protested and many applauded. What has changed? For one thing, we have become more mature. We have begun to understand that ownership and national wealth are not the same. It does not matter who owns Thums Up or Armedia as long as jobs and economic activity are on Indian soil. We have also learned that buying and selling companies is part of the game. It makes for a stronger economy and gives Indian entrepreneurs a chance to be rewarded for their hard work. Today's entrepreneurs want to create a company, sell it after a few years, and reinvest their wealth in another venture. Thus, they need an exit route, and often the only one is acquisition by a foreign company.

The story of Ramesh Chauhan and Tushar Dave is a modern Indian parable. It took Ramesh Chauhan decades of sweat, toil, and brand building in a protected market to make a success of Thums Up. In between he got distracted and wasted his energy to keep Pepsi out of India. But he failed to do so. Had he focused his considerable skills on building his business, Thums Up would have been an even stronger brand, and Coke would have paid him an even higher price.

The parable teaches that in two years Armedia became a powerhouse of knowledge and 50 percent more valuable than decades-old Thums Up. All the employees shared the rewards at Armedia, while only Ramesh Chauhan and his family did at Thums Up. Armedia is a creature of the reformed, liberalized Indian economy; Thums Up belongs to the old, protected socialist economy. Armedia is our future; Thums Up is our past.

I do not live in Bombay anymore, but I am still very fond of it and visit it frequently, thanks to my consulting assignments. I have seen a creeping change. Earlier, this fine port city used to be liberal and cosmopolitan. For fifty years, it stood aloof, contemptuous of socialist India. Its heroes were its stylish cricketers, its flamboyant film stars, and its sedate merchant princes. Bombay was a miniature India which opened its arms to people from all over, and it contained an infinite number of social worlds, intricately interwoven yet separate, which moved back and forth over the long strip of island.

In 1996, Bombay became Mumbai. If this had been a change in name alone, everyone would have dismissed it with an amused smile, as they did when Madras changed to Chennai. They would have shrugged their shoulders and said, "What's in a name?" But the change from Bombay to Mumbai also signaled a new, intolerant spirit which rejected the mercantile, pluralistic ethos of a city built by traders and immigrants from all over India. At first I dismissed the alarmist talk of my Mumbai friends. I used to think that it was business as usual. I believed that once it licked its transport bottlenecks, Mumbai could still aspire to become the premier commercial capital of South Asia—a sort of Hong Kong. Ironically, as the city began to build overpasses and tackle its movement problems, I began to turn pessimistic.

The once liberal city began to turn into an ugly, disturbing shrine city called Mumbai with a malicious political identity. The change began on 6 December 1992, when the Babri Masjid was pulled down. After that tragic moment, the events unfolded that Mumbaikars, to their shame, know only too well: the December–January riots, the retaliatory bomb explosions a month later, the 1995 assembly elections in which the Shiv Sena captured the state government from the hopeless Congress Party. The issue is why the liberal-minded, articulate Mumbaikars did not lead a countercharge against the communalists. Why have they sat and watched the city bleed as the old traditions of tolerance and amity disappeared? There is no easy answer, except to say, as Christopher de Bellaigue has in the *New York Review of Books,* that "the elite of the city has decided that it pays to get on with the Shiv Sena." He quotes the poet Javed Akhtar's poignant metaphor: "If the water is boiling, the frog will naturally leap out. . . . Put the frog into cold water and turn on the stove, and you end up with a poached frog."

I met many businessmen in Bombay during my consulting days, but the most fascinating by far was Subhash Chandra, the founder of Zee Television. Subhash Chandra comes from a cotton and grain trading family in Hissar in Haryana, not too far from Delhi. He barely got through high school and never finished college, but his ambition was outrageous. When his family's business went bust in 1967, he left Hissar with Rs 17 in his pocket. In 1999, he controlled a global entertainment empire with his Indian company alone worth over $11 billion. Having acquired a stake in the ICO Global Satellite Communications business, he plans to create a seamless communication infrastructure in India that could overtake all his other businesses. People call him "the Murdoch of Asia."

Subhash Chandra's great-grandfather was a blind Marwari from Shekhawati district who left Rajasthan with his brothers to start a cotton trading business in the old, undivided Punjab. "Only the weak and the unsuccessful Marwaris leave home," Subhash Chandra reminds me. They were successful and eventually had a dozen branches in Punjab and one in Manchester in England. Subhash Chandra grew up in his grandfather's joint family home in Hissar, where he only heard talk of cotton and helped his grandfather to write hundreds of postcards daily to suppliers and customers. In 1967, when he was at the Government Polytechnic College in Sirsa, he got the bad news. His family had been wiped out in the speculative cotton ginning business and he would have to withdraw from college because they couldn't afford the fees. As he was leaving home, his grandfather said, "Do anything but don't touch cotton."

A bumper grain harvest in 1976 presented the first opportunity to rebuild capital. The state-owned Food Corporation of India was desperately seeking additional storage space for 14 million metric tons of grains, and Subhash Chandra stepped in with a plan to store the grain mountains in the open under plastic sheets. Thus, he found himself fabricating polyethylene covers and learning about plastics. He reinvested these profits in a venture exporting rice to Russia which generated a great deal of money—and some controversy. Now he had serious capital. He knew about plastics and he wanted to become an industrialist. He came to Bombay and set up a packaging plant to make plastic laminated tubes (for toothpaste) when everyone else made aluminum tubes. With 40 percent lower costs than aluminum tubes, he eventually succeeded in becoming a supplier to Colgate, Lever, and others. It took five years of losses and humiliation before "the grain trader" was accepted by the multinationals, but in a decade he became the second-largest and the lowest-cost producer of packaging tubes in the world, earning $23 million profit before tax.

Subhash Chandra had also invested part of his Russian profits in 730 acres of jungle in Borivili, in the distant suburbs of Bombay. He got it cheap because it was in a "nondevelopment zone" and builders were not interested. He was allowed to set up a Disney World type of family entertainment center in the jungle called Esselworld. Hoping for three million visitors, it only got a million and was not a commercial success. Nevertheless, Subhash Chandra was convinced that "Indians were hungry for entertainment." He persisted in seeking opportunities in entertainment, but all his harebrained schemes met a regulatory roadblock. His breakthrough came in 1991, when he heard that satellite TV was starting in Hong Kong. Private broadcasting was forbidden in India, but why couldn't he show Hindi films on TV from overseas?

It took him months before the Hong Kong executives of Star TV would even see him. When they finally met, they said India was poor and starving and Subhash Chandra must be crazy to think of cable television. Besides, they said, they didn't want a "grain trader" for a partner. It hurt. He swallowed his pride and he told them not to make him a partner but lease him the transponder for an India footprint for $1.5 million a year. They were tempted, but they didn't believe he had the money. To get rid of him, they mentioned the outrageous figure of $5 million. "Done," said Subhash Chandra, "but only if you sign today."

Everyone thought Subhash Chandra had gone mad. There was no certainty that the government would not try to stop him. How would he earn revenues when the Indian government forbade advertisers to pay money overseas? But he had a dream and nothing was going to stop him, and Indian TV broadcasting has never been the same. Eventually, Star TV signed with him for a joint venture (weighted in their favor). His great coup was to persuade the Reserve Bank of India to allow exporters to pay for advertising in foreign currency. Starting with a three-person shop, he went on to build a media empire spanning the globe. His Zee TV now reaches twenty-two million homes in India and its advertising revenues have crossed $140 million, ahead of the state-owned Doordarshan, which reaches sixty million homes. Indians abroad in the Middle East, the United Kingdom, Africa, the United States, and Canada watch the Zee channel on their cable, and his overseas earnings now equal those in India.

There have been obstacles. The most formidable one was Rupert Murdoch, who bought the ailing Star network in 1993. He wanted Subhash Chandra out. He understood the power of an Indian-languages network in India, and he wanted it for himself. Although Zee's contract with Star was weak, Subhash Chandra was able to bluff his way in the negotiations, convincing Murdoch that he needed him. They remained equal partners in the Indian broadcasting business until October 1999, when Chandra bought Murdoch's share for close to $300 million.

In ambition, Subhash Chandra is a match for Murdoch. He is also equally ruthless. Although he has made twenty of his executives millionaires (in dollars) through stock options, he dumps people when he doesn't need them. He can be tough with his cable operators and can lobby hard for government policies that suit him. However, he matters because Zee has created an estimated quarter of a million jobs directly and indirectly. This could become a million in the next five years with his ambitious new ventures—four regional channels, a sports channel, a news channel, an Internet portal and service provider based on its vast film library of three thousand films, a new TV magazine, Zeenet interactive Internet service through its SitiCable network, and direct-to-operator pay-TV service through its cable network. Every sixth person in the world is an Indian, he says, and his ambition is to eventually have two out of three Indian eyeballs (including the diaspora) tuned to Zee.

I have recounted the stories of Infosys, NIIT, Zee Television, and Armedia. Other new and successful companies have emerged after the reforms. Jet Airways has created arguably the best domestic airline in the world. Sun TV started as a Tamil channel from Madras, and it was so successful that it now controls the regional cable TV market in all four languages in the south. Ranbaxy, Dr. Reddy's Laboratories, Cipla, and Wockhardt are building successful global generic pharmaceuticals businesses. In September 1999, Ranbaxy sold the global marketing rights for a new dosage form of an anti-infective to Bayer for $67 million plus royalties. Dr. Reddy's similarly discovered a new molecule for diabetes and licensed it to Novo Nordisk, a Danish multinational, for clinical development.

All new ventures are not going to succeed. Some companies started brilliantly after liberalization but did not have the ability to sustain success. They crashed during the economic downturn of the late nineties, partly because their ambitions overtook their financial capabilities. They have brought a great deal of pain to their customers, shareholders, employees, suppliers, and bankers. Among the shooting stars that fizzled out were Rita Singh, founder of the much hyped Mesco group, and Nandan Gadgil of the Gadgil Western Group. Other high fliers who were grounded were Ved Prakash Agarwal, K. B. Kedia, and Ravi Khemka of NEPC Airlines. The saddest tale is that of R. Subramanium of Madras, who created Sterling Resorts and made it the largest holiday time-share company in the world with forty-nine thousand customers and ten resorts. From there he went on to build an exciting venture in commercial agriculture, Maxforth Orchards, to grow fruit trees on dry lands. He started it in 1993 and quickly built an excellent team of young professionals. By 1996, he had twenty thousand customers and 25,000 acres of dry lands. One day an impressive salesman from Maxforth came to sell me a mango orchard for Rs 120,000 in Jallipati, Tamil Nadu. He explained that I could hope to earn a 20 percent return after the fourth year and 100 percent from the twelfth year for the next forty years. He compared my investment to blue-chip stocks and gold. I did not invest but I was thrilled by the enterprising spirit.

Subramanium had the vision of creating Israeli-style orchards on vast amounts of Indian dry lands, which lie fallow and wasted across the country because the peasant doesn't have the capital to farm them. He felt that it needed the transfer of capital from urban to rural India to make them productive, and this is what he set out to do. He set up a training school for agricultural graduates near Madras in collaboration with Camtec of Israel. He planned to drip-irrigate the orchards with groundwater. His experts would manage the farms scientifically and even provide efficient postharvesting facilities via a cold chain. Sales of the fruit minus the cost of materials and management would become the returns to the investor. Since government rules did not permit a company to own farmland, he devised the ingenious solution of giving the land title to thousands of urban investors who would own one-acre plots within a Maxforth orchard. The investor could buy and sell his title much like a mutual fund. Thus, capital would be transferred from urban to rural areas, and he would one day green 240 million acres of India's fallow wastelands and create millions of jobs in the rural areas. It was a wonderful dream.

The dream soured because Subramanium's ambition was too big and he wanted to move too quickly. He was not satisfied with orchards. He wanted to start his own cold storage, packaging, and transport facilities, a chain of 640 supermarkets to sell his produce, an export company to export the fruit, his own schools, teak plantations, ecovillages. There is only so much a man can do. When the liquidity crisis came, everything collapsed. Today, he sits in Madras, a tragic figure hounded by his creditors. In the end, he has done incalculable damage because he has destroyed thousands of others' dreams.

All the stories of the entrepreneurs I have told are a testimonial to liberalization supported by globalization. They reflect a new social contract for postreform India, to which I will return in chapter 22. The critics of the reforms remind us ad nauseam that liberalization will only make the rich richer. This is not true. All the millionaire entrepreneurs in this chapter started modestly. By opening the economy, we seem to have opened the way for a new merit order, where talent, hard work, and managerial skills matter far more than inherited wealth. The old business houses no longer appear to have an advantage, because international fund managers are blind to the past and seek only the best ventures today, run by the most talented professionals. Over time, this ought to lead to a fairer society. The old industrial empires will sell out gradually to new, more able entrepreneurs. No one, it seems, has a head start. The Internet has also leveled the playing field. Any mad, passionate Indian entrepreneur can do it!

Literature is about passion. But so is business. How else does one explain the insane behavior of otherwise sensible Indians who have pulled out all their hard-earned savings after the reforms to start a business and chase a dream? Are they aware that nine out of ten businesses close after twelve months? The remarkable thing about a vibrant economy is the very high failure rate of its entrepreneurs. Success in business goes against the odds. In India, there is also the indignity of having to grovel before and bribe a dozen inspectors. Thus, an entrepreneur has to be a gambler or a lunatic with an impaired judgment about life. Some will call this courage, others stupidity. It is passion at the root which inspires it. These entrepreneurs are as mad as our medieval Rajputs who went to battle time and again when they knew in their hearts that defeat was their only prize.

EIGHTEEN

Old Money

The interval between the decay of the old and the formation and establishment of the new constitutes a period of transition, which must always necessarily be one of uncertainty, confusion, error, wild and fierce fanaticism.

— JOHN C. CALHOUN

Old money has always looked down on new money. Over the centuries, the newly rich have been objects of scorn and derision. Now, perhaps, for the first time in our history, the new millionaires are looked up to with pride and even reverence. For they are a new meritocracy—entrepreneur-professionals who are creating value by innovating in the global knowledge economy. In September 1999, the *Business Standard* published a list of one hundred Indian billionaires, in which eight out of the top ten were first-generation entrepreneurs. Six out of the top ten had made their fortunes in the knowledge industries. They did not inherit wealth, nor did they have a family name. They reflect a new social contract of postreform India where talent, hard work, and managerial skill have replaced inherited wealth. This is one of the most exciting developments of our time. The Internet has also made the marketplace more democratic, so that many more persons with ideas can now become rich. Business is changing so rapidly that those who can foresee the changing needs of the market will not only become rich but also create millions of jobs and transform our poor, hierarchical society.

In 1947, when India became free, the nation's wealth resided with the
landed gentry. Talukdars and zamindars lorded over impoverished peasants. There were a few trading and industrial families, to be sure. Some
of them had even avidly supported Mahatma Gandhi and the freedom
movement. But they were socially inferior to the large landlords. After
Independence, the new government took over the princely states, abolished zamindari, and decimated the "old money." The industrial families
thought that now their time had come. But their hopes were short-lived
because the socialist government shackled them with the most stifling
controls and raised tax rates to extortionate levels. Wealth did not shift
from zamindars to the business class. It went to finance the public-sector
enterprises.

The middle and small landlords, meanwhile, were not destroyed
(because we did not fully implement land reforms). When the green
revolution came in the 1960s, these farmers in Punjab, Haryana, and
western Uttar Pradesh seized the opportunity. They got tractors, put in
tube wells, imported Bihari labor, and no one grudged them their new
wealth because it was earned through hard work and not from rents
from peasants. The rent seekers were a new class of bureaucrats and
politicians who were getting rich from the License Raj. By the seventies,
Indians started leaving in large numbers for the Middle East and a new
monied class of nonresident Indians (NRIs) came up who invested their
gains in garish bungalows in Kerala and Punjab. NRIs, green revolution
farmers, and corrupt public officials became the "new money."

With the coming of the reforms in 1991, moneymaking again
became respectable, and the old business houses suddenly acquired the
esteem and power that had eluded them for fifty years. They finally
became "old money." However, socialist controls had so emasculated
them that they did not know how to respond to the new competitive
climate. Like hungry children, they began to set up ventures with foreigners promiscuously, without a thought to their own capabilities.
They expanded capacities unthinkingly. When the recession came in
1997, supply was hopelessly ahead of demand and they were in trouble.
The joint ventures began to come apart as foreigners realized that their
Indian partners were not up to scratch—they had neither the competence nor the capital. The Bombay Club began to clamor for protection.

Ten years after the reforms, "old money" is floundering. It has still not acquired the skills to succeed in the global economy. It continues with a factory mind-set when the industrial age is disappearing. If old businesses are in trouble, fortunately there are new businesses emerging. The 1991 reforms have enabled young Indians to attempt new challenges. The world has also changed to our advantage. Unlike the industrial age, the information age speaks to our strengths. Our bureaucrats and incompetent industrialists may have killed our industrial revolution at birth. "Old money" may have let us down. But "new money" will create millions of new jobs and prosperity in the twenty-first century.

It is becoming increasingly clear that a definite divide has emerged in Indian business. There seem to be two India Incs. One is the new, vibrant world of knowledge-based, globally competitive companies in software, Internet, IT-enabled industries, generic pharmaceuticals, and entertainment. We encountered some of these entrepreneurs in the previous chapter. The second is the world of the old family business houses, which is hopelessly diversified in a vast number of commodity businesses. Its venerable companies are dying, its joint ventures with foreigners are unraveling, and it cries for protection.

When I first started my consulting work, I met many skeptics who claimed that the economic reforms had been superficial and would not have lasting impact. However, one businessman, Abhijit Sen, catalogued eleven ways in which his telephone cable business had been transformed by liberalization, thereby demolishing the skeptics. Sen said that without the reforms, his business would not even have existed. Until 1991, the government imposed severe licensing obstacles in the manufacture of telephone cable by the private sector. The bureaucrat made the key decisions in the running of the business. These licensing restrictions went away in 1991, and the company rapidly increased its capacity (by five times). Second, he had to split his business before 1991 into three uneconomic units because he did not want his assets in any one unit to exceed Rs 100 crore, which would have made him a "monopoly" company under the MRTP Act and denied him the ability to expand. He merged the companies after 1991 with enormous savings in taxes.

Third, he used to have four full-time people in Delhi to do government liaison; now he had one part-time person because all his raw materials had been decontrolled. Before 1991 he had one person to kowtow to the steel controller, a second to kowtow to the aluminum controller, a

third to kowtow to the copper canalizing agency, a fourth to kowtow to
the State Trading Corporation for the import of special plastics. Fourth,
he no longer needed to get capital expansion approval from the Controller of Capital Issues. The merchant bankers got it done in less than
half the time through the Securities and Exchange Board of India. Fifth,
he did not need Joint Controller of Imports and Exports approval for
the import of raw materials. Sixth, he no longer needed Finance Ministry approval for loans above Rs 5 crore. Seventh, he did not need
Reserve Bank permission to travel abroad; earlier it took a month to get
foreign exchange. Eighth, Modvat had been extended to his line of products, which had provided significant tax savings. Ninth, West Bengal had
abolished octroi check posts and that speeded up movement of his goods.
Tenth, he could travel to most cities in India even at the last minute,
without having to rely solely on Indian Airlines. Eleventh, his productivity was up 35 percent because of changed work attitudes. His two thousand workers produced three times more cable than they did in 1991.

This is merely one example, but it illustrates the changed manner in
which Indian managers run their businesses. Industrial liberalization has
allowed them to expand existing businesses or start new ones without
government approval. Hence, they have invested heavily in new capacity,
in some cases in world-scale plants (because there is no bureaucrat to
decide whether such scale is appropriate). In other cases, they have used
the opportunity to leapfrog in technology without the Directorate General of Technical Development telling them which technology is appropriate. Trade reform has made it possible to import raw materials and key
components without a license. Tariff reductions have reduced their costs
and helped them become more cost-competitive. The freedom to choose
between an Indian or foreign supplier has forced Indian suppliers either to
improve their products to the standards of the imported ones or to lower
their costs in order to compete against cheaper imports. The weaker suppliers have lost significant market shares to imports.

Indian markets have become progressively competitive after the
reforms. Even where new competition has not yet emerged, managers
are worried that their businesses are under threat from potential rivals.
The awareness of competition has finally come to occupy the central
place in the mind of the Indian manager. For the first time, companies
are having to face tough choices about what products to make, for

which markets, and aimed at which customers. They are having to become strategic rather than opportunistic.

Forty years of socialism, I discovered, was not able to destroy India's legendary entrepreneurship, although it had distorted its behavior. Indian companies had real strengths. They had been set up largely by our trading castes with enormous financial acumen, an austere lifestyle, a propensity to take calculated risks, and an ability to accumulate and manage capital. For the past fifty years, the Birla companies had monitored performance of their numerous enterprises across the globe on a daily basis. The Ambanis had single-handedly created the "equity cult" in India by building a base of more than two million shareholders—one of the largest for any company in the world. Because many Indian industries had been under severe price controls in the socialist raj, companies had been forced to become low-cost producers in order to survive. These constituted significant strengths and provided a basis for competitive advantage as India joined the global economy.

Indian companies also had clear and numerous weaknesses. The most important ones were the inability to separate ownership from management; a lack of focus and business strategy; a short-term approach to business, leading to an absence of investment in employees and in product development; insensitivity to the customer, largely because of uncompetitive markets, but resulting in weak marketing skills; an indifference to technology; and, lastly, poor teamwork. Many of these weaknesses were the result of a closed economy.

A striking characteristic of Indian business is that it is family-owned and family-managed. However, family firms, I discovered, are nervous. They are worried that their family-run business will not be able to cope with the competitive demands of the postreform world. I have tried to reassure them by pointing out the persistence of family businesses in advanced societies. I told them that they had acquired a distorted view of economic history, in which the family firm is regarded as the beginning of corporate evolution. As the firm grows and needs more capital, it employs professionals, goes public, and becomes a giant corporation owned by faceless shareholders.

The reality is that family firms still dominate business life around the globe, and they are especially important in the emerging markets of Asia and Latin America. France, Italy, and capitalist Chinese societies like

Hong Kong and Taiwan are dominated by small family-owned and -managed businesses. The success of the Italian, French, and Chinese small enterprises suggests that being a family firm per se is not necessarily a disadvantage. However, a successful family firm must be able to professionalize. It must be capable of recruiting and retaining outside professional talent. In a competitive world, it must be able to get the best person to run the company. If the family member is not the best person, then it must be willing to hand over the management to an outsider. Thus, to professionalize means that the family must make the mental leap and separate ownership and management, and distinguish between the family's interest and the company's interest.

Most Indian companies are in transition today. They are coping painfully with the problem of incompetent or unprepared family members at the top. Rahul Bajaj says, "It is easy to get rid of an outside manager, but how do you get rid of a family member? You must either do what is right for the business or the family. Either way, you will end up with an unhappy family or a weak company." Because of competitive pressures, it is beginning to dawn on Indian businessmen that superior companies are built by superior people; that the success of their company depends on their attitude towards men and women of high ability and advanced training. A businessman of a $450 million company confessed to me: "In the past, I was extravagantly wasteful of talent or myopic in believing that I could do it all by myself." Almost every industrialist I come across says that his biggest challenge is to find men and women of ability to manage crucial positions in his company. This is a profound change in the Indian business world after the reforms.

The inability of Indian business to create large-scale nonfamily organizations, I believe, may not necessarily constitute a constraint on the rate of economic growth, at least at our stage of industrialization. What small companies give up in terms of financial clout, technological resources, and staying power, they gain in flexibility, lack of bureaucracy, and speed of decision making. Throughout the 1980s, the economies of Italy and other family-oriented Latin Catholic societies in the European Union grew faster than Germany's. Max Weber, who argued that the family orientation of China would impede economic modernization, was simply wrong. Indeed, it is likely that small Chinese and Italian family businesses will prosper more than large Japanese or German corporations in sectors serving fast-changing, highly segmented consumer markets. If our objective in India is to maximize aggregate wealth, then we have no particular need to move beyond relatively small-scale family businesses.

However, some sectors of the economy cannot be managed by family enterprises. It is hard to imagine how manufacturers of aircraft, automobiles, semiconductors, or pharmaceuticals, which require huge R&D commitments over long periods, can be managed as family companies. Since some Indian companies have ambitions to become multidivision, multinational enterprises, Japan's example may be instructive. Japan's large corporations also started out as family businesses, but professional managers called *banto* quickly replaced family managers relatively early in the nation's economic development. Public policy specialist Francis Fukuyama tells us that the merchants of Osaka in the eighteenth century made a pact not to turn their businesses over to their children, who they were afraid were too easygoing and would fritter away the family fortune. More recently, Soichiro Honda, founder of Honda Motor Company, was determined not to let his sons enter the business lest it become a dynasty. Many large Japanese firms today forbid their employees from marrying each other, and entry into the firm is strictly governed through entrance exams or university credentials. After 1945, General Douglas MacArthur broke the large family firms (zaibatsu) during the American occupation and purged their top managements. As a result, a new group of young Japanese managers took their place, and Japanese enterprises began to resemble their American counterparts. They became large, multidivision corporations. Without their newfound large scale, it is hard to believe they could have challenged the American auto, electronics, or semiconductor industries. The lesson for Indian companies is that if they want to gain significant global market shares, scale matters, and it can be achieved only by going beyond the family and turning the business over to professionals. Ranbaxy, the leading Indian pharmaceutical company, with operations in more than thirty countries, has learned this lesson. Before its founder died, he turned over the business to professional managers rather than his own sons.

Whether businesses here can create managerial capitalism depends partly on Indian society's ability to build "social capital." Where strangers spontaneously trust each other and cooperate with each other, there is high social capital. Indeed, Tocqueville regarded this "art of association" as an essential virtue of American society because it moderated the American tendency towards individualism. Trust and cooperation are necessary in all market activity. Social capital can help companies make the transition from small family units to large, professionally run enterprises. High trust can dramatically lower transaction costs, corruption, and bureaucracy. While family capitalism may be successful in Italy, Taiwan, Hong Kong, and France, it seems also to be accompanied by education and a strong work ethic. Otherwise, it leads to nepotism and stagnation. Many large and successful Indian companies have begun to realize that educated, hardworking professionals usually outperform lazy, uneducated nephews. But thousands of small and medium enterprises, which form the core of the private economy, are still struggling with this issue.

A more unique characteristic of Indian business, at least until recently, was that it was managed as a joint family, where brothers and nephews worked and often lived together. An example is the Palanpuri Jains of western India, who have established commercial colonies in the diamond centers of Tel Aviv, Antwerp, Bombay, London, and New York, and who today account for roughly 50 percent of all purchases of rough diamonds in the world. Because of the inherent trust in a joint family, Jain diamond merchants rely on brothers and cousins to keep this highly scattered, specialized, and intrinsically high-risk business together, according to Joel Kotkin in *The Tribes,* a provocative account of tribal behavior in the global economy. It is the family and ethnic ties that give them competitive advantage and partially explain their recent gains in market share at the expense of the Orthodox Jews. Does a joint family business provide a competitive advantage in business? I put this question to Rahul Bajaj, whose family is one of the few surviving joint families in Indian business. His answer was an emphatic no. "Business has to be efficiently managed," he said. "Efficient managers are more likely to be outside the family rather than within. You have no choice but to bring them in to run the family businesses. Otherwise you won't be competitive."

"Does the joint business family have any advantages?" I asked.

"Prima facie, there might be two, but I doubt if they are, in fact, sustainable," he said. "One is commitment, which in a simpleminded way is translated into hard work. The other is continuity. I am not sure about either because I have seen just as much commitment and hard work among professional managers. And I have seen just as many lazy family managers. As to continuity, it seems to be often a liability rather than an advantage when you can't replace a family member who does not perform."

Twenty years ago the majority of large business in India was run by joint families. Today the joint business family is almost dead. The question is, why did the families separate and what is the fallout of the splits to corporate performance and strategy? Pulin Garg, the thoughtful professor at the Indian Institute of Management, Ahmedabad, believed that it was a law of nature that families should break up. He used to say, "Haveli ki umar saath saal [The life of a family is sixty years]." Thomas Mann expressed the same sentiments in *Buddenbrooks*, arguably the finest book ever written about family business. It describes the saga of three generations: in the first generation the scruffy and astute patriarch works hard and makes money. Born into money, the second generation does not want more money. It wants power; and it goes after it with the single-mindedness of a Joseph Kennedy. Buddenbrook's son becomes a senator. Born into money and power, the third generation dedicates itself to art. So the aesthetic but physically weak grandson plays music. There is no one to look after the business and it is the end of the Buddenbrook family.

If there are advantages to life and work in a joint family, why indeed have most of them fallen apart? In unusual cases, where a joint family manages to survive, it is because of the practice of strict equality within the family. Neeraj, Rahul Bajaj's cousin, who runs Mukund Iron & Steel jointly with the sons of Viren Shah, finds many financial advantages to a joint business family, and attributes Bajaj's success in remaining together to the strict equality with which they divide the pie. "We may run businesses of different sizes, but we have the same standard of living. Rahul runs the $850 million Bajaj Auto and Shekhar runs the $80 million Bajaj Electricals, but they get equal salaries and equal pocket money. We travel in the same types of cars, in the same class on airlines; we usually vacation together; thus we minimize differences and comparisons."

A Birla scion says, "In a sense, life in joint families is a bit like life under socialism. They do not work in the long run in the same way that socialism does not work. Joint families require strict equality. Because human beings are unequal and need material incentives to perform, joint families break down." A member of the Murugappa family says that "young Vellayan, who runs the TI group of companies, was refused an air-conditioned car some years ago; if the old patriarch, M. M. Arunachalam, did not have an air-conditioned car, how could Vellayan?"

The family splits have reduced the advantage of the combined group to borrow money or to negotiate common purchases. In a few cases, they have had a positive fallout in making the businesses smaller and more manageable, especially where the families split businesses logically along industry lines. This has helped make the businesses more focused and strategic. In most cases, however, the families ignored business synergies and split the assets in a manner that only served the family interest. In the latter case, the next generation is grappling with the issue of divesting unrelated businesses which lack critical mass.

In the new environment, mediocre children will not survive on the basis of inherited wealth. Since gifted entrepreneurs are a tiny part of the population in any society, most heirs are bound to fail. Their companies will eventually die, destroying in the process the careers of hundreds of managers and workers. So the best course open to them—and this is the advice I have given to several companies—is to sell out and enjoy a life of ease and luxury. Both their family and their company will be happier. This is what the industrial families have done in the United States for a hundred years. However, this is precisely what they do not wish to hear, and in all the cases my advice was ignored. In fact, the families compounded the sin by dividing the companies among their children in a democratic manner, and this weakened the entire business group. What they ought to have done is to have given their children equal shares in the entire business, and had the most talented family member or an outside manager run it.

Swaminathan Aiyar, the consulting editor of the *Economic Times,* suggests a reason why they chose not to do so. According to him, it is because of bad habits acquired during Indira Gandhi's rule, when income tax rates were 97 percent and industrialists could either pay taxes and go broke or operate in the black economy. They chose the latter. This meant that each family member needed a company to generate black money in order to survive. High tax rates also hastened family quarrels and splits because most of the profits were off the books. As no one knew who was making how much, each heir wanted his own company.

The bigger failing of Indian companies, I find, is that they want to do everything. Whether it is the Tatas, the Birlas, Singhanias, Modis, or Thapars—the vast majority of big business in India lacks focus. The average business house is engaged in eighteen different businesses. Reliance, in refreshing contrast, makes only a few products (all from petrochemicals) and does it well. Ranbaxy makes only generic pharmaceuticals; Infosys only creates software.

Whereas companies overseas have been shedding unrelated activities, Indian companies seem to have gone the other way. Among the fifty leading Indian companies studied by Dr. Freddie Mehta in 1993–94, there was a specific mention of starting a finance company in the majority of the chairmen's statements. The 1994–95 chairmen's speeches proclaimed their interest in the power sector. The 1995–96 reports showed a strong desire to enter telecommunications. It takes decades to master the fundamentals of an industry through painstaking attention to detail— building suppliers, creating distribution networks, understanding customer needs. Yet Indian business treats the serious decision of entering a new and unrelated industry as though it were a "flavor of the year." It is difficult to have sympathy with the Bombay Club when some of its members behave in this amateurish, drawing-room manner. Particularly in infrastructure, the stakes are very high, and Indian companies do not have the business fundamentals or the funding capability.

Having said that, there are many responsible businessmen who are questioning their basic strategy and have asked themselves, "What is our core competence?" and "Where can we create competitive advantage?" They have brought in consultants like McKinsey to help them restructure their businesses. The laws governing buying and selling companies have also made mergers and acquisitions easier. Thus, the diversified house of Tatas has divested itself of Tata Oil Mills and Lakmé toiletries. The Thapars are getting rid of all businesses other than chemicals and paper. And so on.

The disease of diversification goes back to the origins of Indian business, to the managing agency system that prevailed during the British days, when a single management oversaw varied business activities—tea, jute, textiles, cement, shipping, etc. The typical British company in India was a managing agency which raised capital in England and invested it in half a dozen business activities in India. Since managerial talent was scarce, a small group of managers oversaw diverse activities. When the British left, Indian businessmen took over these managing agencies. Meanwhile, the managing agency had become the model for Tatas, Birlas, and other Indian houses. After Independence, the licensing system and inefficient capital markets reinforced diversification. Since a businessman did not decide what he should produce and depended on what licenses were available, there was a mad scramble for these, and business houses ended up producing all manner of unrelated products. Although licensing was unique to India, diversification is not. The Japanese zaibatsu and Korean chaebols were similarly diversified. However, the Japanese have realized that the success of Toyota, Honda, Sony, Panasonic, and Toshiba depends on focus. Indian firms are now learning this lesson painfully. Soon after 1991, they went on a spree, forming ventures with foreign companies. These joint ventures had no relationship with one another, ranging as they did from automotive components to fast food and fashion garments. Many of them unraveled after a few years.

Another flaw in most postreform joint ventures was that they were hopelessly unequal. The Indian partner was far weaker than his ownership share in the joint venture. It did not take long for the foreign partner to realize that he was "carrying" the venture, and he resented the Indian partner taking a free ride. This led to trouble. In a typical venture, the foreigner brought technology or the product and the Indian brought market access—that is, a distribution network and skills in managing labor and the government. This seemed to be a reasonable basis for collaboration. The trouble began when the Indian partner insisted on (and got) majority equity without realizing the inherent inequality of the situation—namely, that the venture could not exist without the foreigner's product or brand name. The Indian government's bias also encouraged the inappropriate equity structure. After some time, the foreigner discovered the Indian partner's weaknesses—the distribution network was weak or nonexistent, government contacts mattered less after the reforms, and shockingly, the quality of the Indian partner's managers was second-rate. To be fair, some joint ventures have been successful and many Indian partners overdeliver. However, these are exceptions, and my guess is that a large number will come apart.

Under the circumstances, the best that Indian industrialists can do is to concentrate on learning whatever they can from the foreign partner. These joint ventures represent a window of opportunity to absorb technology and management practices and to upgrade their skills. Historically, India is at the stage where Korea and Taiwan were twenty years ago. These two East Asian nations concentrated on absorbing technology with a passion. "The joint venture is one of the most efficient ways to learn," said Anand Mahindra, managing director of the automotive major Mahindra and Mahindra, recently. "It is a membrane for technology to pass between a developed and a developing country, and it is the responsibility of the joint venture to ensure that the membrane is truly porous." Samsung did not learn as much about making aircraft from Boeing as it did about Boeing's legendary project management skills, which it later applied to its electronic assembly operations. Ownership matters less to Indian society. What matters is that knowledge and skills are transferred to Indians.

Competitive markets are forcing other changes on companies. An important failing of Indian business has been its short-term focus. Companies have invested too little in employees. The lack of attention to human capital begins with lack of attention to recruiting new employees. I recall that when Procter & Gamble used to recruit its trainees at the campuses of the Indian institutes of management, we competed mainly with foreign companies like Citibank, Lever, and Nestlé for the best graduates. There were few Indian companies—Asian Paints was one of them. Exactly the opposite situation prevailed in Japan at the time, where foreign firms found it difficult to get the best graduates from top institutions, such as the University of Tokyo, because of fierce competition from Japanese companies and the prestige and rewards attached to working for a home firm.

If the success of a firm rests on the quality of its managers, why do Indian companies not recruit from the best at the IIMs and IITs? Indian industrialists say that IIM and IIT graduates are not culturally suited for their businesses. If the products of the premier schools are culturally unsuited, the industrialists should have put in place recruitment programs from other colleges. Their solution to hiring is to "place a wanted

ad." Mukesh Ambani of Reliance expressed his allergy to the Westernized, "tie-wallah golf-playing" executive. The issue he should have
addressed is why the best products of Indian colleges are reluctant to
join Indian companies and prefer foreign ones. The main reason is that
the Indian business world is still largely feudal with the owner centraliz-
ing decisions. Some owners treat their employees no better than they
treat domestics. In fact, I once heard an industrialist refer to his finance
manager as a "servant" within the earshot of his foreign collaborator.
Employees feel more respected in the professional environment of a foreign company. Therefore, even when Indian companies are able to hire a
good manager, they are often not able to retain him.

The weakness in recruiting is compounded by the lack of attention to
training. Companies hire a young person and just throw him or her into
the job. Multinational companies, on the other hand, prepare detailed
training plans for their young managers and closely guide them for the
first two years. They reward senior managers not only for the results they
produce but also for the on-the-job training they impart to their subordinates. Amiya Kumar Bagchi, director of the Centre for Studies in
Social Science, Calcutta, attributes the lack of attention to human capital to our feudal social structure. "As a result, the owners are arrogant
and the managers are servile," he says. "In East Asia, the owner will happily sit down with an employee for a meal. It is this attitude which has
helped them succeed, create universal education, and wipe out poverty.
India, in contrast, is like the Philippines, which is a relative failure in
East Asia because it shares our social structure."

Indian companies are in a state of transition after the economic
reforms. One of the potent effects of the new competitive environment
is a mad scramble for talent. Dozens of companies have created outstanding recruiting and training programs. Some companies are seriously
attempting to globalize. A number of examples are available, but I shall
illustrate with two. Sundaram Fasteners of Madras quickly responded to
the reforms by bidding and winning a contract to supply radiator caps to
all General Motors plants in the United States in competition against
twelve global suppliers. Within six months, it installed a used GM facility from the United Kingdom—it would have taken years to do so
before the reforms. Now it is electronically linked to all GM plants via
its warehouse in Detroit, and it has not missed a delivery in five years.
Within forty-eight hours, it can turn around a new shape for a cap.

Against a standard reject rate of 150 parts per million, it has achieved 6 parts per million.

After building the largest pharmaceutical company in India, Ranbaxy made a big push into the international market. It now sells its products in forty-five countries, manufactures in eight countries, including the United States and China, and half its total revenues come from outside India. In 1998, its turnover was $450 million and it expects to cross a billion dollars by 2003. It is vigorously engaged in R&D to bring low-priced generic drugs to the global market under the Ranbaxy brand name—thus tapping into the worldwide trend of containing health-care costs through generics. It spends 5 percent of sales on research, making it the second-highest spender among all industries in India. Its research recently paid off when Bayer, the German drug company, agreed to pay $67 million plus royalties for the rights to a new dosage form of the drug ciprofloxacin; Ranbaxy scientists had discovered a way to deliver the drug in a more consumer-friendly way. Its strategy is based on three advantages enjoyed by Indian pharmaceutical producers: (1) low-cost but excellent R&D scientists; (2) extremely low manufacturing costs achieved by Indian producers due to tough price controls, which pushed them to continuously lower costs for twenty years; (3) the experience of reverse engineering of drugs because of low patent protection in India; thus, Indian scientists became experts at cracking new drug molecules.

These two examples illustrate that Indian companies are capable of acquiring a global mind-set. To do so, they have to focus on a single area of competence—Sundaram in auto components, Ranbaxy in generic drugs—and not be hopelessly diversified. Second, they have to initially win in the domestic market and then leverage their economies of scale overseas. Third, they have to be able to capitalize on global trends. Sundaram tapped into the desire of Detroit's automakers to outsource their components rather than produce them in-house. Ranbaxy is taking advantage of the global shift to generic drugs as a way for all societies to contain health-care costs. Fourth, they cannot ignore quality even when they are pursuing a low-cost strategy. For this reason, Sundaram was one of the first in India to obtain ISO 9000 quality rating. Fifth, they must be able to overcome our historical phobia about investing in product development.

There are only three ways that a company can create competitive advantage. It can compete on the basis of superior cost or a superior product or superior service. India's best companies have largely adopted the superior cost strategy. Pursuing a clear-cut strategy is in itself an advance over the past, when Indian companies were ad hoc and opportunistic and exported undifferentiated products based on factor advantage. Firms are realizing, however, that to compete as a cost leader does not mean that they can ignore quality. On the contrary, world-class quality is a given for any company that aspires to compete in the world market. It means, however, that on an ongoing basis one does not differentiate oneself on the basis of quality but on the basis of cost.

It is unrealistic to expect Indian companies to become technology leaders. This is not because Indian scientists are not capable, but because Indian companies will take time to mobilize the power of science and become a technology-driven culture. The companies of Korea and Taiwan still do not have a technology edge.

The essential question is whether Indian companies can realistically adopt another strategy besides cost leadership. A cost strategy is vulnerable to exchange rates of competitors and rising labor costs of domestic employees. I find it surprising that Indian companies have not directed their energies to a strategy based on superior service. Not only because it is more enduring but also because it builds on the proven capability of Indian traders in the competitive bazaar economy. Anyone who has shopped in a saree store or eaten in a Udipi restaurant knows the Indian traders' ability to deliver superior service.

A strategy based on superior service can be especially powerful where the value added is high. Superior service delivered by highly trained "knowledge" workers—scientists, engineers, market researchers, lawyers—provides a powerful insulation against competition. Not only can knowledge workers harness the power of information technology, they can also be trained to benchmark their deliverables against competition and against customers' needs. Commitment to this strategy implies that one hires new employees on the basis of their attitude and trains them in business skills. Most companies do the opposite. It is an attractive strategy because it is practically "free" compared to the other two. Yet I am not aware of a single Indian company with global ambitions which is seriously and strategically pursuing it.

The competitive advantage of a firm arises from its distinctive capabilities. These capabilities are generally based on the stability and continuity of relationships which the firm builds with its suppliers, customers, and employees. Its competitive advantage is thus the product of history and is not easy to duplicate. It emerges from within the company, from a recognition of its strengths, and is never imposed from the outside by consultants or created by corporate communication programs. These relationships are uniquely different and the search for generic strategies or recipes for corporate success is doomed to failure.

Creating competitive advantage takes years of painstaking effort and few Indian companies have had the patience or the inclination to do so. It requires the ability of the top management to penetrate into the messy details of the business, without losing sight of the big picture. Most Indian businesses have found themselves hopelessly unequal to this task. Until 1991, their talents and their attention were misdirected by the socialist raj. While they were busy negotiating the shoals of our byzantine bureaucracies, their competitors in other countries were carefully crafting relationships with suppliers, distributors, and customers. Honda, in the 1960s, captured a third of the U.S. motorcycle market in less than five years. It had no great vision; it simply did what it did best—making a simple, inexpensive motorcycle. However, the crucial ingredient in its success lay in its unglamorous attention to building long-term ties with its distributors.

The lesson for Indian companies with global ambitions is that success will come not from merely imitating the successful but from identifying and nurturing their own distinctive capabilities.

Can the old Indian companies deliver the goods? The Indian stock markets in 1999 and 2000 did not think so. The market capitalization of the old family companies on the Bombay Stock Exchange had plummeted to 15 percent of the total in February 1999. Although the old family houses still accounted for two-thirds of *Business India's* top hundred companies as measured by sales, in terms of market capitalization forty-five companies had been forced out of the list of the top hundred, according to *Business World* on 22 August 1998. Although the old houses have begun to change, they continue to resist the shift from "family wealth" to "shareholder value." Only a few are comfortable with the idea that today wealth, status, and power do not derive from controlling the management of the companies that their ancestors promoted. It

comes from the rising value of their equity from competitive and professionally run companies. Parvinder Singh of Ranbaxy sent the most
powerful signal to "old money" in March 1999 when he announced that
his company would pass into the hands of a professional manager rather
than to his sons. He was suffering from cancer, and he jolted a number
of old houses into realizing that shareholder value is a better way to create wealth.

Most of the debate on the Indian economic reforms has centered on
what the government needs to do. Little attention has been paid to what
Indian industry and business need to do to respond successfully to the
reforms. Clearly the future of the Indian economy after the reforms
increasingly depends on the success of Indian industry and business. The
historical performance of Indian business is weak. Certainly it has not
succeeded in bringing about an industrial revolution in the country.
Before 1947, it could blame the British Raj; after 1947, it could blame
the overregulated License Raj. Now, after the 1991 economic reforms, it
has no one but itself to blame.

NINETEEN

The Rise and Rise
of a Middle Class

*The most perfect political community is one in which the middle class
is in control, and outnumbers both of the other classes.*

—ARISTOTLE

It was a rare Sunday afternoon in Delhi's March. The sky was blue,
the sun was shining, and the quiet breeze sent me on a walk to the
Lodhi Gardens on the way to a haircut at Khan Market. Once in
the gardens, I thought I'd take a nap in the park—actually lie down on a
patch of green grass and go to sleep.

I was leaning against a lamp pole by the Bara Gumbad on the Lodhi
Road side watching overgrown boys argue over a controversial decision
that turned into a heavy debate on the politics of cricket. I'm not a big
fan of the game so my interest flagged. My attention turned to a game of
catch played by a middle-class father with his two small sons. Just then
the little fellow missed; he ran after the ball and heroically dove in the
grass to save it from going in the ditch.

It has been years since I ran deep near the boundary to save a four, but
I used to, and the smell of grass recalls it. They say that smell is the key to
memory, and in my school days I would end up smelling a fair amount
of grass. I disengaged myself from the lamp pole and headed for a spot in

between but yet sufficiently far from two groups of picnickers. Here I thought I might close my eyes and snooze.

Sleeping in the park in a city is a form of civilization. First, you need a city with enough bustle and clatter to make a person yearn for a calm, green spot. Then you need a first-class park, as the Lodhi Gardens certainly is. And finally, you need the right sort of person, one who is capable of dropping his guard and flopping down on the ground and falling asleep with his mouth open and snoring like a yodeling walrus.

The grass behind the Bara Gumbad that day didn't quite work out. I lay down but couldn't sleep. Perhaps the mass of the Bara Gumbad was too great, or the impending humiliation at the barber's was on my mind. I lay for about fifteen minutes, eyes closed, listening to the passing scene, and then sat up.

I watched the first picnicking family and it was immediately clear that they belonged to the new middle class. They spoke roughly and aggressively. From their talk I gathered that the family had a flourishing export business in garments. All the adults, including the women, worked hard in the business. I admired the ease with which they talked about their customers in Sydney, Toronto, and Brussels. They insisted on sprinkling their conversation with English words that they did not understand too well. They were newly prosperous. Yet they were less than a generation away from the village well, dust-raising cattle, and the green revolution in Haryana.

I turned to look at the other, quieter family. Three generations were enjoying the afternoon sun after a tidy lunch. The grandmother watched her young grandson roll in the grass; her stern-looking husband, from his self-important manner, had probably just retired as a senior civil servant. Their son, an IIT-IIM-trained manager, was on his way up. They were the old middle class.

The most striking feature of contemporary India is the rise of a confident new middle class. It is full of energy and drive and it is making things happen. That it goes about it in an uninhibited, pragmatic, and amoral fashion is true. It is different from the older bourgeoisie, which was tolerant, secular, and ambiguous. The new class is street-smart. It has had to fight to rise from the bottom, and it has learnt to maneuver the system. It is easy to despair over its vulgarity, its new-rich mentality. But whether India can deliver the goods depends a great deal on it.

This new middle class is displacing the older bourgeoisie—people like my grandfather and father—which first emerged in the nineteenth century with the spread of English education. It had produced the professionals who had stepped into the shoes of the departing English in 1947, and had since monopolized the rewards of the society. The chief virtue of the old middle class was that it was based on education and merit with relatively free entry, but it was also a class alienated from the mass of people and unsure of its identity. The new middle class, on the other hand, is based on money, drive, and an ability to get things done. Whereas the old class was liberal, idealistic, and inhibited, the new order is refreshingly free from colonial hang-ups.

We may regret the eclipse of the old bourgeoisie, especially because it possessed the unique characteristic of being a class based on free entry, education, and capability. We may feel equally uneasy that a new class based on money alone—without social responsibility, let alone spiritual values—is replacing it. However, this is not a new phenomenon. This has happened repeatedly in all societies, particularly after the advent of the industrial revolution. Whether old or new, the middle class is growing very rapidly in India. If one draws a line from Kanpur to Madras, I reckon that by 2020 half the population west of the line will be middle class. It will take another twenty years for half the people east of the line to get there. When half of India is middle class, this will have a major impact on politics, markets, and society.

When India became independent, the middle class was tiny—around 5 percent of the population—but we had a clear idea of what our parents wanted us to grow up to be. They wanted us to be nice young men, well bred, handsome, intelligent, and good at games. We were groomed to be brown sahibs, the rightful rulers of free India. They educated us at private schools. Those who could afford it sent theirs to Doon and Mayo (even when it pinched their pockets). We became good at cricket and tennis and adequate at studies. "He is a good all-rounder," was the model held up before us. After school, we went on to Delhi's St. Stephen's College or Presidency College in Calcutta and Madras. A few lucky ones even managed to go to Oxford and Cambridge. We were expected to acquire the basic intellectual equipment at the university, but not to become scholars.

From the 1960s, the path became more competitive and those who could get in chose technical and managerial institutions—the Indian Institutes of Technology (IITs) and Indian Institutes of Management (IIMs). After college, we were ready to join the civil service or industry or the professions—all the pleasant niches for which the older Indian bourgeoisie groomed its young. With secure jobs in our pockets, we were married off to good middle- or upper-middle-class girls whom we courted in the gymkhana clubs and in hill stations during our summer holidays. We were ready to become pillars of the establishment and repeat the process with our young. As we prospered in our jobs, we built houses in south Delhi and went to lots of stylish parties where we met our friends, rubbed shoulders with diplomats, and enjoyed the wit of the intellectual elite of our land. Could one have a better recipe for the enviably happy life? We had fulfilled the dreams of our fathers. Why then, with all our advantages, do we feel a gnawing pain in the gut? What has gone wrong?

As civil servants we face humiliation daily at the hands of our political masters, whose background and values are alien to ours. We are even willing to bend with the breeze, but it gets intolerable when we have to lie, cheat, and be unjust on their behalf because we are afraid that otherwise they will transfer us to an unmentionable provincial job. As managers in the private sector, we meet the same ministers and bureaucrats to get licenses and permits. But when we are treated in Delhi as though we are merely a cow to be milked, our self-respect is wounded. When our own school friends in the IAS treat us with suspicion, we feel hurt. Nonetheless, either as civil servants or as company managers, we tolerate the politician because he is an inevitable growth of democracy with which we largely identify. However, it is harder to accept the new monied class. The contractors, the intermediaries, and the potbellied sycophants of the ruling party are abhorrent.

Our children are leaving or have left to go abroad and this is another source of discontent. We did not create enough jobs at home because of mistaken economic policies. Our children are forced to look abroad for opportunities—many of them never to return. When friends and children leave, life begins to feel insipid.

The old middle class complains constantly of the decline in our national character. In the abstract, it sounds like a cliché, but when you discover that your friend in the civil service is corrupt or that your

roommate in boarding school, who joined the police, is now under suspicion for murder in an "encounter" in Andhra, or that your clerk's wife
committed "suicide" because of a dispute on dowry with her in-laws,
then the pain in the gut returns to stay.

Our inner lives are a parody. We have one foot in India, the other in
the West, and we belong to neither. We speak a hodgepodge of English
and our regional language, the combination varying with the status of
the listener. When speaking to a servant or shopkeeper, our verbal brew
leans towards the local language; with a peer, we are capable of invoking
the purest English. We are alienated from the mass of our people. We
mouth platitudes about Indian culture without having read the classics
in Sanskrit. Instead, we read *Time* magazine to "keep up." We are touchy
about India and look to the West for inspiration and recognition.

We are Macaulay's children, not Manu's. Our ambivalence goes back
to that day when Macaulay persuaded the British government to teach
English to Indians. Our position is similar to Rammohun Roy's, who
had two houses in Calcutta. One was his "Bengali house" and the other
his "European house." In the Bengali house he lived with his wife and
children in the traditional Indian way. The "European house," on the
other hand, was tastefully done up with English furniture and was used
to entertain his European friends. Someone teased him by saying that
everything in the Bengali house was Bengali except Rammohun Roy;
and everything in the European house was European except Rammohun Roy. The dilemma of today's "brown sahib" is similar. We can live
our hypocritical lives only for so long; ultimately we must question our
recipe for the enviably happy life.

The bureaucracy is quintessentially old middle class, and no single
institution has disappointed us more. We bought the cruel myth that our
civil service was our "steel frame." Today, our bureaucracy has become
the single biggest obstacle to the country's development. Indians think
of their bureaucrats as "self-servers, rent seekers, obstructive, and corrupt," says Madhav Godbole, the former Union home secretary. Instead
of shepherding the economic reforms, the bureaucracy is responsible for
their faltering pace. The way it is going, it looks as though it is the
bureaucracy versus the rest of the people.

Compare this to the situation in China. Mr. Sahgal, managing director of Phillips Carbon Black, visited China last year to set up a plant. A

senior Chinese official met him at the Shanghai airport. It was Sunday but bureaucrats came to see him at his hotel. The land officials promised him a plot within thirty days. The tax officers in their uniforms and epaulettes patiently explained their seven-page income tax code and three-page excise code. The head of the electricity board committed to laying a two-kilometer transmission line in thirty days. The mayor came by in the afternoon to take him in his car to Wuxi, two hundred kilometers away, a distance they covered in two hours on the new superhighway. On follow-up visits, the mayor again came to Shanghai to escort his operating managers to Wuxi. In contrast, Phillips Carbon Black took nine months and a half dozen bribes to acquire land in Durgapur and six months to get an electricity connection, with a full-time person chasing after the officials.

It is widely accepted that East Asian bureaucrats played an important role in engineering their economic miracle. Why did they succeed and Indian bureaucrats fail? A Korean businessman told me that "man for man, your bureaucrats are smarter." But that may be part of the problem. "Whereas your bureaucrat is a know-it-all, who prejudges people's needs and dictates to them, ours listens to us and forms a collaborative relationship with businessmen." Second, East Asian bureaucrats are specialists, who are not shifted from job to job. Thus, they acquire expertise and commitment. Even in the United Kingdom, you join the Treasury, not an amorphous civil service. Third, East Asian bureaucracies are smaller, with shorter lines of authority, and this makes for quicker decisions. Fourth, when you bribe, your work gets done; in India, even after a bribe you are never sure.

What is the answer? Certainly, it is not to abolish the permanent civil service. Every country needs and has one. The real solution is to change work processes and procedures and reward bureaucrats for results and not for adherence to process. To achieve result orientation, we should downsize the bureaucracy, decentralize decisions, give more autonomy to officers, and delegate authority to those lower down. Second, we should relentlessly invest in training civil servants. We should empower them with managerial skills and educate them in the economics and values of a liberal economy.

Proud laughter from the garment exporters diverts my mind from uncomfortable thoughts about the bureaucracy and old middle class.

Certainly this new, innocent middle-class family is only half educated; they proudly show off their new riches and they laugh too loudly, but let's face it, they are our future. The old middle class is not going to deliver the goods. The new bourgeoisie, represented by these garment exporters, do not have our false sense of national grandeur; they are not worried about phantom external interferences with our national sovereignty; they don't need to engage in Pepsi-bashing in order to feel Indian; they want politicians and bureaucrats out of economic life; they want India to open up and join the world; they want the latest technology and our rupee to be convertible; in short, they want India to become and behave like other successful nations.

The new bourgeoisie is highly visible. You can recognize the man a mile away in an expensive suit with a briefcase in one hand and glossy magazines in the other. The woman in her Ruby Queen polyester saree alights from her new red Maruti to shop for the latest gadgets. Their children in Arrow shirts and Colour Plus pants are found in Nirula's sipping Pepsi with a pizza, or at night dancing awkwardly at the disco to Indiapop. They go on holidays to the new resorts springing up across the country, carrying a matched set of Skybags. But when they reach Goa, instead of going for a long walk on Bogmalo Beach, you find them packing the video room.

The new middle class is free from the inhibitions that shackled the older bourgeoisie. It doesn't seek endorsement from the West: what works is good. It is nonideological, pragmatic, result-oriented. It is here to stay. The old bourgeoisie had a liberal humanistic outlook which was tolerant of ambiguities and shy of certainties. Self-government and economic freedom were clearly its political objectives. Since the English language and education was the only hurdle for entry into the old bourgeoisie, people came from various backgrounds. By and large, opportunities were open to all, although the upper castes were the first to seize them. Once the new elite was formed, it tended to close ranks. Slowly after 1947, however, it lost vigor and started to decline. Manners became more important than content. How you spoke mattered more than what you said; your calligraphy was valued more than your thoughts. After Independence, a determined effort was made by the business class to acquire respectability as an extension of its financial power. However, the old bourgeoisie in the bureaucracy and in politics checked these ambitions with controls, a crippling system of taxation, and legislation like the MRTP Act.

When I was growing up, the middle class was tiny. It began to expand in the 1950s. Those who were newly admitted had a triumphal feeling, but they also suffered constant anxiety that they might slip down into the laboring poor. The early entrants came up through government jobs—they were clerks and peons in offices, carrying messages and files, bringing tea and coffee, keeping citizens away from officers. As the government began to produce steel and other goods, they got new jobs as factory labor and supervisors in the public sector. In the seventies with the green revolution, the children of farmers in Punjab, western Uttar Pradesh, and other pockets of prosperity, such as the sugar belt in Maharashtra, seamlessly entered the middle class. The children of laborers who went to the Middle East during the oil boom were similarly integrated.

A person had arrived in the middle class when he did not have to do physical labor. Another conspicuous sign of arrival, according to Ashok Desai, the economist, was that you wore something on your feet, either sandals or shoes. The laboring classes had usually gone barefoot. Today, this is no longer true. The lower classes now wear PVC sandals and clothes of synthetic fiber. Today's distinctive class marker is housing, says Desai. The middle class live in houses of brick and cement (while the lower classes live in urban slums in the cities or in mud homes in villages). They send their children to the new English-speaking schools and second-rate colleges, read film magazines, and go on holidays in video coaches. They ride on scooters and buy blenders to grind chilies. India is now the world's largest market for blenders and the second-largest for scooters (after China).

In the 1980s the middle class doubled as the economic growth rate rose to 5.6 percent. Marketing professionals were amazed by the extent of rural prosperity. As the rural family's expenditure on food dropped from roughly 68 percent to 55 percent of its income, rural demand for consumer products multiplied. Soaps and detergents in villages grew 20 percent a year through the eighties while the urban market grew only 5 percent. By 1990, the rural market for washing products, for example, had become 55 percent of the total, compared to 30 percent in 1980. With rural prosperity, India became the world's largest consumer and producer of tractors. The spread of TV was a cause as well as an effect. In the end, millions of rural families joined up with the national middle class.

In the nineties, the economic growth rate rose beyond 7 percent and this gave another boost to the middle class. The National Council of Applied Economic Research (NCAER) systematically tracks the middle class based on periodic national-sample surveys. Its focus is ownership of consumer products, and it prefers the term "consuming class" to the fuzzier "middle class." It estimated that in the mid-nineties the consuming class was 32.5 million households. Since there are roughly five persons in a household, this means that the middle class was 169 million, or 18 percent of the population. NCAER's consuming class has an annual income between Rs 45,000 and Rs 215,000, and typically owns a TV, cassette recorder, pressure cooker, ceiling fan, bicycle, and wristwatch. Two-thirds of the "consuming class" own a scooter, color TV, electric iron, blender, and sewing machine, but less than half own a refrigerator. (Of course, the penetration of TVs, bicycles, radios, and fans goes far beyond the middle class—TVs are in over 62 million homes, bicycles in 80 million, wristwatches in 125 million, and fans in 50 million homes.) Most strikingly, the consuming class appears to have tripled in ten years. NCAER has projected the consuming class to reach 91 million households by 2007, or 450 million people. That may be too optimistic, but it is easier to imagine that the middle class could become 50 percent of the population west of the imaginary line linking Kanpur and Madras by 2020, and east of the line by 2040.

Thus, we start off the twenty-first century with a dynamic and rapidly growing middle class which is pushing the politicians to liberalize and globalize. Its primary preoccupation is with a rising standard of living, with social mobility, and it is enthusiastically embracing consumerist values and lifestyles. Many in the new middle class also embrace ethnicity and religious revival, a few even fundamentalism. It has been the main support of the Bharatiya Janata Party and has helped make it the largest political party in India. The majority, however, are too busy thinking of money and are not unduly exercised by politics or Hindu nationalism. Their young are aggressively taking to the world of knowledge. They instinctively understand that technology is working in our favor. Computers are daily reducing the cost of words, numbers, sights, and sounds. They are taking to software, media, and entertainment as fish to water. Daler Mehndi and A. R. Rahman are their new music heroes, who have helped create a global fusion music which resonates with middle-class Indians on all the continents.

Cinema, however, continues to be their great passion. Indian movies are the largest cinema industry in the world, and they affirm the middle-class world. They create its values, nourish its soul, and are the source of its dreams and role models. The markets ring to the sound of the latest hits, and it is a common sight in provincial towns to see young men (and women) dressed in the latest "film fashions," strutting about the street, imitating their heroes while humming their latest songs. Films are just as popular today as they were in the 1950s, although one sees them more often on television. They still provide the defining image. But there is a difference. The hopes and the dreams of the fifties and sixties are gone. Films today are faster-paced. They have bigger budgets. The dancers have more pelvic thrusts. The villains are more violent.

When I was young, the actors Guru Dutt and Raj Kapoor had touched a sympathetic chord with people. With heavily charged sensuality, their films summoned up all our romantic dreams. They were the dreams of the new nation. The middle class was filled with hope and it thirsted for romance. It had put up with the independence struggle; it had suffered the tragedy, the bloodshed, and the dislocation of Partition; now, it wanted the romance of freedom. It identified with Guru Dutt's search for the pure and the innocent, unscathed by the compromises of society. It was drawn to his theme of unrequited love, which led to self-inflicted suffering. It put a bit of itself in each of his films. It contrasted the innocence of its new government with the cynicism of the old global order. It literally believed in the Mughal gardens of the celluloid world, complete with bumblebees, jasmine flowers, and torpid breezes. It believed in them as it believed in Nehru's dreams. Today, the dreams of Guru Dutt are gone, just as its post-Independence hopes have died.

Today's middle class has no illusions. It accepts both affirmative action for the lower castes and Hindu nationalism (with the ascent of the BJP). It has no clear ethos beyond money and the here and now. It has no heroes other than cricketers and Bollywood stars. The soul has gone out of the old merit-based middle class, and an aggressive capitalism has replaced the socialist idealism of the youth. The ones who are setting the pace today are the PR boys, the new media elite from Zee and Star TV and the whiz kids from Morgan Stanley.

On a recent visit to Bombay, I met two boys in their early twenties. I had known their father many years ago. We stopped to look at a tall building at Nariman Point. "So this is it!" said one of them to the other, filled with awe. "This is it," replied the other, looking up with reverence at the office of Dhirubhai Ambani. "He came from nowhere and went up and up. They expected him to fall, but he refused and he built instead the largest company in India."

The two young men did not have business backgrounds. They came from an old Brahmin family from Pune and they were paying homage to their hero, who had created the magical Reliance Industries. Eighty years ago, their heroes would have been the nationalists Gopal Krishna Gokhale and Bal Gangadhar Tilak. Fifty years ago, they would have been Gandhi and Nehru. Today they are business tycoons like Ambani and Azim Premji. It is a sign of our changing times.

The young men took me to their home in Bandra. They also had a teenaged brother, who had just finished high school. Over dinner that evening, he gave me his recipe for the ideal life. "First, I shall go to IIT, then to IIM, and then get a job in consulting or financial services. Eventually, I want to own and run my own company."

"Have you thought of doing arts in college?" I asked. He looked at me as if I needed to have my head examined. "Arts is for duffers," he said. "It's for those who can't get into science. Besides, what is the use of poetry?"

I suggested that business leaders of tomorrow needed to have vision, had to build high-performing organizations. In order to achieve global competitive advantage they had to recognize change and innovation, and promote sustained investment in human skills. The lessons of history and literature might better prepare a young person for those challenges.

"Arts subjects aren't high-scoring," he said dismissively. "And I don't want to spoil my CV." I suggested that he would have to do a lot of science at IIT. Did he like science?

"You just have to memorize a bunch of facts. I have a good memory, fortunately." He was obviously confident and good at studies, but I was distressed by his approach to his education. The fault lay partly with his parents and his teachers. No one had told him that science was not about "a bunch of facts" but rather about learning to think more exactly. Scientific education meant the implanting of a rational, experimental habit of mind. As I was leaving their house that night, I felt ambivalent. All three youngsters were self-assured and optimistic. They were confident about the future. Yet they looked at education as slogging work.

It is a popular pastime with the old middle class to grumble about the new rich and the decline in values. They complain incessantly, especially after the reforms, that the young are self-centered and motivated only by greed. They speak of a "crippling ideological barrenness which threatens to convert India into a vastly unethical and insensitive aggregation of wants." They believe that the naked self-interest of the new middle class has subverted the idealistic goal of an egalitarian society, which was part of the Gandhi–Nehru consensus of their own younger days. I feel differently. I believe that the young are no less virtuous today. Nor is the new middle class any greedier. (It is less well educated, certainly, but then its children will be better educated.) The chief difference is that there is less hypocrisy and more self-confidence. Self-interest has always been the basic motivator of individuals and classes. In denying this basic truth about humanity, we embraced treacherous ideologies and failed economic policies. We certainly do not want to repeat those experiments.

TWENTY

Modern vs. Western

It is only the modern that ever becomes old-fashioned.
—OSCAR WILDE

Our continuing inability to distinguish between the "modern"
and the "Western" is surely the cause of some of our grief. If
we could only accept that a great deal of modern Western culture is no longer the property of the West but a universal, critical way of
thinking which belongs to all rational, civilized human beings, we
would not suffer quite as much. We would conserve our energy for better things rather than waste it on swadeshi, Hindutva, national language
debates, U.S.-bashing, multinational-baiting, and other futile activities.
The debate between modernization and Westernization, begun in the
early nineteenth century by Rammohun Roy, continues to rage in India
today, especially with the ascent of the Bharatiya Janata Party (BJP). The
verbal confusion makes us ambivalent about foreign trade and investment. It makes us clamor for protection in a globalizing world. It slows
our responses to the economic reforms and delays our ability to create a
competitive economy. At the root of the issue is a legitimate fear of the
loss of Indian tradition, culture, and way of life. But the fear is often a
symptom of an inferiority complex apropos the West, especially with
the older generation that is in power.

Ironically, some of our nineteenth-century intellectuals understood this distinction well and used it to critically examine our tradition and shake off the institutions and practices which had deformed its spirit through centuries of stagnation and superstition. Equally, the younger generation today seems self-confident and pragmatic, and does not suffer from colonial hang-ups. My neighbor's daughter, for example, is an exporter and a daily participant in the global economy. No matter what her customers' nationality or where they are located, she receives and answers queries in English, quoting her prices in dollars, while employing Windows software. She does not feel diminished because "English" is also the national language of England, "dollars" is the national currency of the United States, or that "Windows" originated in Seattle. In her functional world, English is the universal language of commerce, dollars the currency of global trade, and Windows is an enabler of communication.

When I was twelve, my aunts used to talk endlessly about our attractive neighbor in middle-class Delhi. "You mean you don't know her? She is such a modern lady—she smokes, she drinks, she even dances with men." After a year we moved and left our neighbor behind, but I grew up with a wrong conception of the "modern." To my aunts, "modern" was a derogatory word, meaning someone "Westernized," with false and superficial values compared to our traditional, God-fearing ways. My aunts' usage was not unusual. I came across an advertisement in the *New York Review of Books* in 1965 about an "ardent novel, available only by mail." It went on to describe the book as "the story of a *modern* American marriage." By "modern," the advertisement suggested something not particularly agreeable—as having to do with "the ambition, aggression and infidelity of women."

In college, I discovered that "modern" was not necessarily something negative or Western. The word as we use it today originated in nineteenth-century Europe when dazzling changes occurred in Western society. Economies became industrialized, nation-states came into being, social democracy arose, national bureaucracies emerged, and the world saw the beginnings of mass society. In trying to make sense of all these revolutionary changes, historians concluded that they were interconnected. For lack of a better word, they called it "modernity." Moreover, they linked these changes to the broad acceptance of a set of values and institutions which they termed "modern." The values had flowered in the eighteenth-century

Enlightenment and the French had fought their revolution for "liberty, equality, and fraternity." Among the values were also individualism, rationality, a secular (nonreligious) temperament, the rule of law (rather than loyalty to individual rulers), representative government, and faith in the market economy. Underlying these beliefs was an optimistic feeling that man's condition could be improved.

At the time of our independence—despite Gandhi's hesitations—there was a consensus among educated Indians that we had to become a modern society in order to succeed. We had to build a strong nation-state and have a competent bureaucracy to administer it; we had to be secular in order to preserve communal peace; we had to raise the lower castes in order to promote social democracy. We had to be socialist in order to have equality; we had to be democratic with universal franchise so that there could be true liberty. To make all this happen, the values of modernity were enshrined in our Constitution in 1950.

The fifties were special in our history because the educated middle class actually believed in these modernist values. It amazes me that many in the middle class genuinely thought that we could better human society. Prior to the nineteenth century, our intelligentsia concerned itself primarily with its own individual nirvana and spiritual enlightenment. Beginning with Rammohun Roy in the early nineteenth century and climaxing with Mahatma Gandhi's nationalist struggle and Independence, we gradually came to believe that to be genuinely modern we had to be concerned with improving society. After Independence, our ruling class attempted sincerely to practice these ideals, at least for a short while.

My uncle in Delhi took up my aunts' refrain. My mother's brother-in-law used to remind my parents that we were growing up too Westernized. The problem, he said, was with our schooling. We were losing touch with our culture. My parents didn't know quite what to do until our neighbor, my father's boss, offered to teach me Sanskrit one day. My mother jumped at the idea. Thus began my Sunday morning lessons at Handa Saheb's home. For the first half hour, I used to try to memorize a sloka from the Bhagavad Gita; during the second half hour, he instructed me on the meaning of the sloka. I hated having to memorize the verses, but I enjoyed listening to his stories, especially about the battles of the Mahabharata.

The success of Western man, Handa Saheb used to tell me, was due to his devotion to human reason. Science and engineering—he was an engineer, like my father—were the result of subjecting the problems of the physical world to the test of reason. As a result, the West had made enormous progress and gained material prosperity. However, material progress wasn't everything, he said. Excessive devotion to reason had turned Western man agnostic and made him lose touch with his spirit. Eastern man, on the other hand, retained the "spiritual" in his everyday life. Even highly educated and successful Indians in Western professions continued to be drawn to the spiritual life. He referred to my father, and many of our neighbors and friends. A man's life was not complete unless it combined reason with the spirit. The Gita, he said, offered the right combination for living the ideal life.

Handa Saheb used to talk about three kinds of knowledge: knowledge of the world, of the self, and of God. Knowledge of the world came through reason and the physical sciences. Knowledge of the self came partially from psychology and the social sciences, and the West could teach us something about this as well. But for the knowledge of God one had to turn to the Gita, he said. The Gita taught that knowledge from books was not enough—it had to be combined with action and it had to be experienced. Right action was desireless and selfless, that is, it was an act performed with detachment, without thinking of the reward or the benefits of the action. One acted from a sense of duty and not because it suited one. The knowledge of God came also through the experience of meditation. The ideal life for the modern Indian, he said, combined the spirituality and wisdom of the East with the rationality and technology of the West. "What we now need in India," said Handa Saheb, "is to create the industries based on the science of the West while retaining our spiritual tradition." This was our national project. "So back you go to memorizing those slokas!"

Many years later, I thought about my lessons with Handa Saheb. The idea that my father's boss should give me his Sunday mornings meant something. It seemed the most natural thing at the time. My father and Handa Saheb were typical of educated Indians of the time: they had a spiritual dimension. I found that even the most agnostic Indians, who had contempt for India's superstitions, were drawn to religious and philosophical issues. The notion of Indian spirituality is, thus, not a myth. Even I, who went to college initially to study engineering, then shifted to economics, ended up with a degree in philosophy, because that is where I thought I might find answers to the great spiritual questions.

Nehru was our chief modernizer. His elegant autobiography and his unique interpretation of India's past testified to his faith. For the first seventeen years of free India, he got the chance of a lifetime to practice these ideas and to transform India. He called his approach "a third way, which takes the best from all existing systems—the Russian, the American, and others—and seeks to create something suited to one's history and philosophy." The third way tried to combine the growth of capitalism with the equity of socialism without the violence of communism. In the end, the third way failed. Even before Nehru died in 1964, we had begun to despair. We were getting neither the dynamic growth of capitalism nor the equity of socialism. We were not making significant impact on mass poverty. We began to wonder whether India could modernize without a violent communist revolution. A modest growth in income was being virtually neutralized by a demographic explosion as population growth began to rise from 1 percent in the first half century to 2.5 percent. Corruption had begun to grow and was becoming ubiquitous, and discipline in public life was plummeting. Reality had begun to catch up and facts began to diverge from our modernist ideals.

Nehru may have been a great modernizer, but he was a poor manager. He had no patience for organization, implementation, and detail. More than policies, it was their administration that failed us. It was all very well to proclaim the ideas of the French Revolution, but it was apparent to everyone that "liberty" was deteriorating into indiscipline, an all-powerful bureaucrat-political class was rising in the name of "equality" for the poor, and "fraternity" existed mainly between the giver and taker of bribes. The unions, especially in the public sector, were becoming invincible, and it was increasingly difficult to administer the country. The symbol of this decline was the Congress Party. Socialist ideals need not have degenerated into the License Raj. If care had been taken to monitor performance, periodically assess the impact of policies, remove roadblocks to effectiveness—all the things that a good manager does in the course of a working day—things might have been different. Policies could have been corrected early. Unfortunately, Indira Gandhi compounded the problem.

Nehru had counted on the "steel frame" of the Indian Civil Service to ensure efficient implementation, and it let him down badly. Created by the British Empire to keep law and order and collect land revenue, it was not up to the task of developing and modernizing a backward society. Economically, it was illiterate. It piled up control upon control and created an economic monster. In the end, it is difficult to tell whether it was the policies or their bad implementation that failed us. I believe it was more of the latter. Nehru's main preoccupation was foreign affairs and his place in the world and in history. It was not development. He insisted on being his own foreign minister, which trapped him in the minutiae of running the foreign department. He did not delegate well but felt compelled to do everything himself. Michael Brecher, who observed him closely for many years, wrote, "His attention to trivia is startling for a man in his position." If Nehru had got his priorities right—if he'd been hungry for development—and had been a better manager, he might have been able to modernize our attitudes and institutions in the best sense of the word.

It was at Harvard that I had my first brush with modernization theory. Although I was not a student of sociology, Professor Talcott Parsons of the sociology department was a pervasive intellectual presence, and no one could escape from his ideas. Parsons and the modernization gang struck me as the late children of the Enlightenment with their ample faith in progress. In typical American fashion, they were filled with a naïve belief that only a modern society could be a good society. They felt that as a society modernized, it brought rationality to day-to-day decision making; gradually, it undermined feudal ties and restored dignity to the individual; as it industrialized, it became more prosperous and more equal; finally, it became freer with democracy and the rule of law. Like development economists, sociologists were an optimistic lot in the 1950s and early 1960s. They were excited by the prospect of poor traditional societies becoming modern. Today, scholars are much less certain that they understand how modernization affects traditional societies, or whether its consequences are necessarily benign. They hesitate in saying that the United States, the first "modern society," represents the direction in which other societies should be moving.

Although Mahatma Gandhi took modernity to the masses, he suffered deeply from the dilemma that continues to afflict many educated Indians. He used the railways and the telegraph vigorously, but he hated them. He linked Western technology to colonialism and regarded it as a tool of enslavement. He could not reconcile himself to the idea that Western technology was a rational approach to solving universal problems, and its products, once created, were the universal property of all human beings. He felt that modern urban man had become dehumanized and a victim of machines, and he yearned for the self-sufficient village. Nehru thought his scheme hopelessly utopian. In October 1945, as freedom and self-rule came nearer, Gandhi wrote to Nehru: "The first thing I want to write about is the difference of outlook between us . . . I am convinced that . . . sooner or later the fact must be recognized that people will live in villages, not in towns; in huts, not in palaces. Crores of people will never be able to live at peace with each other in towns and palaces. . . . While I admire modern science, it should be reclothed and refashioned aright. . . ."

Nehru, on his part, decided that it was the time to be honest and not fudge the issue as he had done all his life. He replied from Anand Bhawan: "I do not understand why a village should necessarily embody truth and non-violence. A village, normally speaking, is backward culturally and no progress can be made from a backward environment. Narrow-minded people are much more likely to be untruthful and violent. . . ."

After this last effort to re-create the India of his dreams around idyllic villages employing "appropriate technology," Gandhi did not take the issue further. Nehru was now free to pursue his plans to build a modern India of socialist planning and heavy industries, based on Western science and technology. I believe that Gandhi was wrong in rejecting modern civilization, for it was a rejection of the tools of self-defense. Gandhi's legacy and our ambivalence towards "modernity" continue to afflict significant sections of our society.

Many Indians wonder if Japan is a possible model for us. The Japanese seem to have been able to adopt the modern institutions of the market, and to transform their ancient and feudal society into a competitive, performance- and education-based meritocracy. They also seem to have done it without giving up some of their traditional family duties or their ancestral moral emotion of "losing face" and "public shame."

No one reads Arthur Koestler anymore. But in the 1940s and 1950s Koestler was a powerful intellectual presence. He visited India and Japan and punctured the myth of Eastern spirituality in *The Lotus and the*

Robot. The Indian government was so put off that it banned the book—but only after everyone who was going to read it had read it. Koestler wrote much nonsense in the book, but there were great moments of insight as well. In it, he compared India and Japan—"the most traditional and the most 'modern' among the great countries of Asia." Koestler found that India and Japan had similar social structures, based on the family with its clan extensions and a caste hierarchy. In both societies, the old sought respect from the young; the male dominated the female; pupils were meant to venerate their teachers; conformity was valued more than individuality. Both approached reality intuitively rather than rationally and empirically.

Koestler also noted important differences. We have already seen that Japan's caste system was fluid; India's was rigid. In Japan, caste was a matter of social hierarchy, to be dealt with pragmatically. In India, it had a religious character. The Indian was careless in dealing with society but careful in dealing with the deity. In Japan, it was the reverse. The Japanese nonchalantly clapped his hands at the Shinto shrine to attract the attention of the gods, but in matters of social etiquette he was punctilious. He knew thirty-five ways to wrap a gift parcel, and his worst tragedy was to lose face in society. The Indian was full of religious anxiety; the Japanese worried about prestige. The Indian thought that sex is only for procreation; the Japanese knew that sex is also for recreation. The Indian was consumed by guilt over masturbation; the Japanese thought it a casual pleasure, almost like smoking. The Indian woman was a temptress who sapped a man's strength; the Japanese woman was a provider of manifold pleasures. The Indian child was deluged with affection and his education started late and remained lax. The Japanese child was subjected to strict social conditioning from a very young age.

Koestler's insights, generic as they might seem, have implications for national competitiveness. Japan's secular spirit may explain, for example, its greater interest in technology. Indians, in contrast, are less curious about how the world works. Indian social hierarchy was more rigid than Japan's, and this may explain why Indians are poorer team players. Japan's fluid caste system made it easier for the ascent of the merchant class during the Meiji times and helped create a social revolution earlier. India is experiencing this social revolution only now, after the economic reforms and after fifty years of practicing democracy.

Japan, despite its present economic troubles—with pervasive layoffs and suicides among out-of-work businessmen—is regarded as a great nation capable of defining the future of the world. Yet many contemporary scholars who share Gandhi's skepticism about modernization increasingly ask about the price that Japan has paid for its success. They wonder whether the Japanese salaryman, who has enjoyed a dramatic rise in his standard of living since the war, is not losing touch with his traditional strength, and whether his prosperity is not eroding the very conditions of his success.

Robert Bellah, a student of Talcott Parsons at Harvard in the 1950s, attempted for Japan what Max Weber had done for the West. He examined the cultural roots of modern Japan and the relation between religion and the rise of industrial society. Weber had suggested that the industrial revolution came first to northern Europe and North America because they were Protestant and had an ethic of individualism, austerity, and hard work, particularly among their entrepreneurs. The countries of southern Europe and Latin America, in contrast, did not have these virtues to the same extent because they were Catholic, and they remained laggards. In a similar fashion, Bellah hypothesized that Japan would succeed because of its culture, which instilled loyalty to the family, the company, and the state. It made the Japanese hardworking, socially disciplined achievers. Subsequent events proved Bellah right, for between 1960 and 1990 Japan achieved miraculous and sustained growth, making it an economic superpower.

Thirty years later, in the mid–eighties, Bellah brought out a new edition of his book. Instead of gloating, Bellah questioned, in a new introduction, if Japan had not paid too high a price for its success. Certainly he found that Japan was the most effectively administered society in the world; Japanese bureaucrats were dedicated and efficient—nowhere more true than in the Ministry of Trade and Industry, the darling of India's BJP ideologues—who had successfully used credit and information to make the Japanese entrepreneurs respond to changing international markets. But Japan had not become "modern" in the way that the sociologists had hoped. It had not developed a universalistic ethic that respected the dignity of each individual. The Japanese were still closely tied into groups that demanded their loyalty and did not exhibit sympathy for outsiders. Neither had Japanese women made much progress in their quest for equality.

Bellah believed that rapid growth threatened traditional Japanese life.

The family home used to contain a garden, no matter how small, that conveyed a sense of the seasons and of nature. Now the Japanese lived in apartments and TV dominated the living room; the children were cut off in their own rooms, where they studied day and night. Fathers were strangers who traveled vast distances between home and work. Ties to the "home village" and its shrine were broken, and so was the harmony, the central tenet of Japanese religion. Although the surface of life was pleasanter in Japan than in most societies, the landscape was being ravaged. The biggest weakness of his book, Bellah confessed, was with modernization theory itself. He had failed to foresee that wealth accumulation might not necessarily lead to the good life, and might, in fact, undermine the very conditions of a stable society. Parsons had assumed that individualism was inevitably linked to modernity. The Japanese experience made this link less self-evident.

The "pathology of modernization" has many takers in India, ranging from academics to the doomsayers of the BJP. They never tire of reminding us about the evils of modernity. The academic climate has changed since my undergraduate days, and our modernity project is one of its biggest victims. It is under heavy attack by Western and Eastern academics. In the 1950s and 1960s everyone was agreed that the Third World had to develop and transform its societies from traditional to modern. Today we are less sure, partly because no one is quite certain what constitutes modernity. The historical experience of the twentieth century, moreover, has raised uncomfortable questions. The Soviet Union and fascist Germany industrialized without democracy. The Far East became industrial and prosperous without individualism. The bureaucracy in India, far from promoting development, became its greatest obstacle. With modernity, reason was supposed to displace religion, but, in fact, America witnessed a great religious revival in the twentieth century. (Europe had witnessed a similar revival in the nineteenth century.)

David Washbrook, a historian at Oxford, has recently posed other problems. Modernity was supposed to have arisen first in the West, become a universal ideal, and then spread around the world. However, Washbrook points out that the historical roots underlying the West's road to modernity existed previously in the Asian societies of China, India, and Islam. Formal rationality, which gave birth to modern science, was a part of the Sanskrit and Arabic cultural universe long before it came to the Anglo-Saxons. Commerce and the money economy, which led to the rise of modern capitalism, existed in the Asian societies before medieval Europe. Property and class relations, similarly, were prevalent in them. Washbrook shows that precolonial Indian society demonstrated a fair amount of individualism in the Brahminic ethic and the Bhakti movements. There is also evidence of equality in the kinship systems and temple sects. He concludes, like Edward Said, that modernity at its root is an ideology of Western dominance and not a scientific phenomenon.

For several years now the post-Confucian hypothesis has challenged the standard concepts of modernity and has enjoyed a certain vogue. Despite the recent problems in the Far East, the hypothesis has won much popularity. It argues that the economic miracles in Japan and in East and Southeast Asia are best explained by Confucian values. A positive attitude to the world and its affairs, a sustained lifestyle of discipline and self-cultivation, respect for authority and order, frugality, and an overriding concern for stable family life—these are the major Confucian values, which have spread through education in the Far East and account for its economic success.

There is also an intriguing corollary to this hypothesis. It argues that "as Buddhism crossed the Tibetan plateau and the great Himalayan passes, it underwent a profound transformation, changing from what was perhaps the most world-denying religion in human history to an emphatically world-affirming one." Although there was already some degree of world affirmation in Mahayana Buddhism in India, it was really in China and in the Mahayana Buddhist countries of East Asia that nirvana was consistently located in this world. Hence, we often hear in the Far East that nirvana and samsara are one and the same, or that the "true body of Buddha, the dharmakaya, is in this world as we know it empirically." If the Confucian hypothesis and the Chinese Buddhist corollary are correct, then it certainly spells bad news for the prospect of rapid economic growth and modernization of India. It means that we cannot easily transfer their lessons to India and the great Himalayan passes remain an insurmountable barrier.

In the early part of the twentieth century, ironically, Confucianism had a bad odor. Chinese intellectuals thought that the root of China's backwardness lay in her cultural traditions, especially in Confucian values. Not surprisingly, they vigorously attacked all aspects of Confucianism. Max Weber wrote in *The Religion of China* that China's culture and religious tradition was deeply uncongenial to modernization. He explained that its ethic hampered economic growth because Confucianism placed the scholar at the top of the social hierarchy and alongside him the government bureaucrat. It emphasized a chain of loyalties beginning with filial piety and extending upwards to subservience to government. Weber did not think that such a rigid, feudal order would promote capitalism, which was innovative, individualistic, and destructive of past traditions. I think we can say today, based on recent experience, that Weber was simply wrong. Equally, the post-Confucians have overstated their case and they have bit the dust in the recent Asian economic crisis.

Whatever name we give to the ethic—Protestant, Confucian, Marwari—the fact is that certain values seem to promote economic development. We sometimes think of them as "middle-class values." They are hard work, education, savings and investment for the future, and the ability to cooperate towards a common objective. Professor Rod MacFarquhar of Harvard recently rebuked the proponents of Confucianism, (especially of the Singapore variety) for trying to create an exclusive club. "There is no difference between the entrepreneurial dynamics of certain Indian merchants and the Chinese merchants in Southeast Asia," he said. "I am not sure that a religion which preaches rejection of the world necessarily implies one cannot have entrepreneurial spirit. In fact, Hinduism is essentially about individuals. The individual has to decide whether or not in this life he performs acts which force him to a worse rebirth in the next life."

I agree with Professor MacFarquhar. I also believe that cultural factors are of limited use in explaining economic performance. The success of modern capitalism in the Far East is on account of good economic policies and practices, and these can be transferred. The Far East countries achieved and sustained high growth rates because they efficiently employed their resources—they emphasized labor-intensive manufacturing for export; they vigorously educated their population; their governments intervened to build competitiveness and to correct distortions. In India, by contrast, government policy created distortions. It made scarce capital cheap, labor expensive, overvalued our exchange rates, and reduced competitive pressures. Our economic reforms have begun to eliminate some of these distortions, and we have begun, in effect, to transfer some elements of the Far East's success. However, we have not yet begun a serious reform of our educational system, which more than anything is capable of delivering equity with growth. Hence, we ought to focus more on economic and educational reforms and worry less about culture.

As to the "pathology of modernization," I believe that the BJP and the academic critics of modernity fail to realize that modernization offers the only opportunity for the majority of our people to raise themselves to a decent standard of living. To eschew modernization is to condemn the masses to degrading poverty and the injustices of caste in our traditional society. It is easy for the top 20 percent in society to decry the evils of modernization from the comfort of their upper- and middle-class lives. But ask the people. They will any day put up with Coca-Cola and KFC if it means two square meals, a decent home, and a job. Given a chance to exchange the Japanese standard of living for their own, they will always vote to give up their traditional life in the village for a better standard of living. The daily migration into our cities is adequate testimony. Thus, Bellah's concerns or Ashish Nandy's critique will not find resonance among the people involved.

This is the dilemma of modernization for a poor country like India. It is difficult to disagree with the BJP's desire to retain the good things in our traditional culture. This will, however, not be achieved through xenophobia or excessive tariff protection. It will come by having a vigorously competitive economy and improving the quality and quantity of education, which will ultimately give Indians confidence in their lives and their culture. There is no question that modern life will erode many features of traditional society, but a better understanding of the past through education will give a person perspective and make him or her better able to retain that which is good and reject what is bad in tradition.

The ascent of the BJP in the last decade has made us rethink the place of nationalism in our lives. Nationalism has two fatal charms: it presupposes self-sufficiency, which is a pleasant prospect, and it suggests, very subtly, that we are superior just because we belong to a certain time and place. Unfortunately, both these assumptions are wrong and even dangerous—especially now, when we live in an interdependent, globalized world.

There is nothing wrong in being self-confident and proud as a nation, but protection will bring the opposite result. There has been a powerful sentiment in India that the way to national success is to be self-reliant, keep out foreign companies, and try to make as many things in India as possible (even when it did not make economic sense). This thinking goes by the name of swadeshi and in recent years it has had a popular revival, especially among sections of the BJP. I can think of ten reasons why swadeshi-type protection is bad policy. First, it reflects an inferiority complex. Those who seek protection assume that Indians are inferior and cannot compete. They forget that Palanpuri Jains have captured half the world's market share for uncut diamonds; Aditya Birla group is the world's largest producer of rayon; Laxmi Mittal's global steel empire has made him richer than the Queen of England; Reliance is among the ten most admired companies in Asia; Taj and Oberoi have created world-class hotel chains. India's software companies have the best computer engineers in the world and Indian entrepreneurs in Silicon Valley are at the heart of the Internet revolution. The proponents of swadeshi need to have more confidence in Indian abilities.

Second, it seeks to protect the interests of a few thousand industrialists at the expense of millions of Indians. A swadeshi policy will restrict entry of foreign companies, foreign products, and raise import duties. It will deny our people the cheapest and best-quality products in the world. Good governments first protect the interests of their consumers and only then its producers. Third, swadeshi does not further the interests of our companies either. Robust competition is the best school in which industry learns to succeed. Rivalry pushes companies to lower costs and improve quality and makes consumers demanding. By reducing competition, swadeshi will keep our companies weak. Thus, swadeshi is bad not only for consumers but also for producers.

Fourth, we need $200 billion to build up our infrastructure. No one in India has that kind of money. We have to depend on global capital. It was British capital which financed America's infrastructure in the nineteenth century and launched its industrial revolution. America did not lose its sovereignty in the process. Even the BJP concedes that it needs foreign capital for infrastructure. But if it is willing to turn over strategic assets like power plants, roads, ports, and bridges to foreigners, it should not worry about potato chips and aerated water.

Fifth, the protectionist is wrong in believing that we can open our doors to foreigners in infrastructure and close them for consumer products. Global capital is integrated and operates with a herd mentality, on the basis of images and "market sentiment." We cannot be selective or half pregnant. Sixth, there is nothing new about swadeshi. We have practiced it since Independence. It has only delivered us shoddy, high-priced goods and weak, uncompetitive companies. The BJP ideologues want swadeshi only for ten years in order to create a level playing field. But ten years from now Indian companies will still want protection because businessmen basically dislike competition. Seventh, every country has its swadeshi movement, but smart governments ignore their swadeshi lobbies. For twenty years, American Presidents have ignored the pleas of their automakers that sought to limit the import of Japanese cars. When the Japanese captured a third of the American market, their swadeshi lobby predicted the death of the American automobile. But what happened? Japanese competition forced Detroit to improve its cars and recapture market share. Americans drive excellent cars, and if the Presidents had opted for protection, they would still be driving Pintos.

Eighth, swadeshi will bring back the License Raj. The BJP wants high-tech products but not consumer products. However, the personal computer is also a consumer product. Inevitably, political or bureaucratic discretion will decide who gets in. This is another name for corruption. Ninth, swadeshi presumes that someone should tell me what is good for me. Lurking deep in the swadeshi mind is a "command mentality" which wants to build an autocratic society. Tenth, swadeshi is irrelevant. In a country where a third of the people live in poverty and half are illiterate, does it matter if a few people eat Kellogg's corn flakes? If foreign investment is less than 2 percent of total investment, we ought not to waste our time on debating insignificant issues. We should focus our energies on improving the delivery of our programs.

Although I had read his books, I did not meet Amartya Sen until 1992, when I was on sabbatical from P&G and attended his seminar, "Equality and Inequality," at Harvard. He had not yet won the Nobel Prize, but he was one of the greats on the campus. Yet he was quite wonderful in the way he had time for everyone. One day I showed him a column I had written for the *Wall Street Journal* in which I suggested that the BJP become a true conservative party. It would suit the BJP's temperament, I thought, because it wanted to conserve tradition, and the country might end up with a two-party system. Sen thought I was hopelessly idealistic in thinking the BJP would accept this personality and agenda. To him it was a fascist party. This, however, led us to a discussion of tradition and modernity. He felt that BJP's nationalist phobia about foreign products and ideas arose from mental confusion. He asked if the use of penicillin amounted to Westernization. What about the enjoyment of Shakespeare? Was Goethe somehow betraying the European team because he was moved by Kalidas? Indian cooking was not less Indian because it used chilies, which were brought by the Portuguese into India.

Sen developed these thoughts into a talk that he gave some years later at the India International Centre in Delhi. He said that it is very difficult to pinpoint the origin of scientific ideas. Some of the basic ideas of trigonometry were developed in India, although they came back to India through Western textbooks. He gave the example of "sine," which was used by Aryabhatta, the Indian mathematician, in the early sixth century A.D. He mentioned the decimal system, which was well developed in India by the sixth century, and was taken from here by Arab mathematicians and reached Europe mainly in the last quarter of the tenth century. Related to it was the migration of the "zero" at about the same time from India to Europe via Arab mathematicians.

Indian civilization is so diverse and plural, and has been shaped by so many influences—Dravidian, Aryan, Hindu, Greek, Buddhist, Scythian, Islamic, European—that it should be able to withstand the influence of the globalized culture. Unlike the alarmists, I feel that Indian culture is robust and should be able to maintain its richness and identity. Those who fear the loss of Indian culture ought to read Rabindranath Tagore. As usual, he got it right when he wrote, "Whatever we understand and enjoy in human products instantly becomes ours, wherever they might have their origin. I am proud of my humanity when I can acknowledge the poets and artists of other countries as my own. Let me feel with unalloyed gladness that all the great glories of man are mine."

It is no good hoping that Indian values and the Indian "way of life" will survive intact. All the triumphant talk of "Asian values" has grown quiet. Critics have said that Asian values are indistinguishable from Victorian values (strong family, strong state, strong nationalism). It simply underlines the fact that in everything from industrialization to democratization we are following the well-trodden historical path of development. It has its positive and negative consequences, and we have to live with them. There appear to be two global tendencies which are going to define India's future. The first is the relentless push of the global economy and communications, supported avidly by the rapidly growing middle class. Domestically, we will see the irresistible spread of competitive markets and social democracy. The preoccupations of the people will be with a rising standard of living, with social mobility, with the peaceful pursuit of middle-class values and culture, influenced increasingly by the homogeneous global culture.

The second is the growing consciousness of religious identity in the world, which is leading to fundamentalist and separatist attitudes. In India, it manifests itself in the apparent desecularization of our society. This tendency encourages conflict, instability, divisiveness, rigidity, and irrationality. It is in sharp contrast to the former tendency, which promotes peace, stability, integration, flexibility, and rationality.

East Asia has followed the first trend; West Asia has followed the second trend. Which of these two trends is likely to prevail in India? Or will Indian society evolve uneasily from a constant clash of both these forces? The two impulses find parallels in the world outside. The first vision was provocatively enunciated a few years ago by the public policy specialist Francis Fukuyama, who prophesied that with the collapse of communism, and in the absence of a competing ideology, liberal democracy based on free markets would sweep the globe. As a result, the world would increasingly become a homogeneous middle-class culture in which there would be no place for global conflict.

Opposed to this utopia was the vision of Harvard professor Samuel Huntington, who argued that instead of tending to a universal, homogeneous culture, the world was becoming increasingly fundamentalist and separate. He divided the post–Cold War world into eight distinct civilizations—the West, Islam, Confucian, Hindu, Japanese, Latin American, Slavic Orthodox, and possibly African. He argued that civilization-consciousness was increasing, and conflict between civilizations would supplant ideological conflict and become the dominant form of global conflict.

There is some truth in both these accounts. The world is becoming more democratic and capitalist. Most of the former communist countries have become capitalist democracies. Sixty-two countries are in the midst of "market-friendly" economic reforms, including the fourteen largest developing countries. The world is enthusiastically embracing middle-class values and the lifestyle of the Coke-MTV popular culture. Global defense expenditure is also down. Of the two biggest spenders, the USSR has disappeared. Thus, from one perspective the world is turning more peaceful, more homogeneous, more middle class, more capitalist, and more democratic.

At the same time, there is abundant evidence of the second tendency. Tribalism, ethnicity, and fundamentalism have grown over the past decade. Yugoslavia is the most dramatic example, but there were, by the last UN count, thirty-seven hot spots of ethnic strife in the world. The growth of Islamic fundamentalism is the most widely reported. The crescent-shaped Islamic bloc from the bulge of Africa to Central Asia has inflamed borders—against the Serbs in Bosnia, the Jews in Israel, the Hindus in India, the Buddhists in Burma, the Catholics in the Philippines. Fundamentalist movements are also growing in Christianity, Judaism, Buddhism, and Hinduism. The Chinese countries are avidly embracing Confucian values; the BJP has become the largest political party in India. Everywhere, it is the young college-educated professionals who are most active in fundamentalist movements around the world. Like the rest of the world, India too is headed in the direction of some form of a democratic capitalist society whose peace will be occasionally punctured by religious extremism.

For all its positive features, there is also a bleak side to Fukuyama's generally sunny vision. It is that bourgeois life tends to become consumerist, lonely, banal, and unheroic. The irony of liberalism is that it gives the individual free space in order to fashion his life, but he is unable to cope with the free space and fills it with trivial objects. Without a God or ideology, bourgeois life is reduced to the endless pursuit of cars, VCRs, cell phones, and channel surfing. The reference point is the self, and the individual becomes self-absorbed in a world of physical security and rational consumption. Even when it comes to sport and exercise, one prefers to jog rather than play team sports. Without a higher moral purpose, there are no heroic acts to perform. Is this the life that India has to look forward to in this century?

This is the experience of democratic capitalism in the West. The recent lessons from the Far East suggest that these nations too are likely to repeat the Western experience. My guess is that life in India will also change, but it will resist more than others in becoming "dull and bleak" because of the powerful hold of religion. Although India may compress the economic timetable and become prosperous in the next twenty-five to thirty years, I believe it will not lose out on religiosity quite as rapidly. Religion has a powerful place in Indian life, and the persistence of God will be its strongest defense. However, the challenge will be to keep religion a private matter.

TWENTY-ONE

Democracy First, Capitalism Afterwards

Reformers have the idea that change can be achieved by brute sanity.
——GEORGE BERNARD SHAW

erhaps because I am one of "midnight's children," I have always
felt a certain amount of pressure to join politics and *do* something. In recent years this has grown because I have found it frustrating to live in Delhi and sit on the sidelines, watching the painfully
slow progress of liberalization. It has been distressing to get up each
morning, open the newspaper, and read about the appalling state of our
governance. The Election Commission estimates that forty members of
the Parliament and seven hundred members of state legislative assem-
blies across India face criminal cases, many for assault and murder. A few
individuals have also goaded me on, including John Pepper, the CEO of
Procter & Gamble, who in his idealistic way always thought that I was
meant to enter politics in India. Elections, too, have come around with
surprising frequency, thanks to coalition politics and fractured electoral
mandates; so there have been plenty of opportunities.

  With some misgiving I decided to do something about it. I had several meetings with leaders of the Congress Party and very quickly discovered that they had no use for me. I also found that the Congress
culture was feudal, reeking of sycophancy. It was all too distasteful and
alien, and I fled. The only other viable alternative was the BJP. But I

have been "genetically programmed," as it were, against identity politics. Still, I overcame my inhibitions and went to meet several BJP leaders. Initially they welcomed me, thinking perhaps that I might help them in raising funds from industry. I spoke to them of the urgency of pushing the reform agenda, and invariably they seemed to agree—they were politicians after all—but I could tell from their eyes that they were humoring me, and reforms were not their priority. I persisted, against my better judgment, with both parties over several months. Eventually, I think I became such a nuisance that they were happy to promise me anything as long as I would go away. I concluded that neither party had any use for a reform-minded manager in politics. Today, a lingering sense of defeat gnaws at me. My conscience tells me that politics is abrasive everywhere and has always entailed sacrifice, and I wonder if I have chosen the safer, but less courageous, route in opting out.

Many would agree that 1991 was a great milestone in India's history. Another observer of the past decade, however, might easily conclude the opposite—that 1991 was only a small kink. He would argue that the economic reforms of 1991 were due entirely to pressure from the International Monetary Fund. When the economy bounced back, the pressure went away and India returned to its old ways. This would explain why the reforms slowed after 1994. There were no reformers, only pressures. The year 1991 was not a permanent break with the past, just one of those oscillations of democracy. Democracies, in any case, are known to swing between wanting to contract government activity and seeking to expand it, between deregulating and regulating the market.

This is a plausible reading of history and many in the Indian political class might be tempted to buy it, especially the old Congress guard. It is easier to see the world in continuous rather than in discontinuous terms; Indians also tend to be conservative by nature, and conservatives find continuity reassuring; moreover, it is difficult to see a revolution when one is in its midst; a contemporary observer in early eighteenth-century England would not have seen the industrial revolution—he would have seen only vigorous textile exports. Nevertheless, I believe that this is a misreading of history, one that does not give due credit to the historic nature of the acts of 1991. The IMF pressure was certainly real, but the reformers went much further than what was needed to satisfy the Fund. The macroeconomic stability that the IMF wanted could have been bought by tried and tested formulas that our finance ministry knew only too well: brutally cut imports and expenditure, raise taxes, cause deflation, and the economy might stop growing for a few years, but the exchange crisis would come under control; so would the fiscal deficit and the balance of payments. But the reformers did the opposite—they opened the economy to imports, lowered tariffs and tax rates, and decontrolled industry; they gambled for investment and growth, and they got it. This was a new approach for India.

Communism also collapsed in the world around the same time, and this too had an impact. Indians began to realize that political and economic freedoms were linked, and our dirigiste policymakers were put on the defensive. We could not escape the liberal revolution sweeping the world. The worldview of young Indians and the business class was the first to change after 1991. Slowly it infected the political class as well. This explains why every party that has come to power in the last decade—and every single major party did—followed a reform agenda. Each one, as it changed from the opposition to a ruling party, maintained a strong rhetoric of reform while in power, even though it managed to achieve only slow incremental change.

More difficult to understand is why there has been almost no appetite for education reform when there is universal consensus that education is not only good in itself but also helps a nation become competitive. India followed a socialist path before 1991 but has progressed slowly in education over the past fifty years. This is almost incomprehensible: education is, after all, one of the few things that socialists around the world generally have done fairly well. The answer may well lie in the liberal fallacy—that is, the naïve assumption that reasoning will prevail over interests. For the opposite happens too often in the real world, whether in democracies or in autocracies. The road to power is through satisfying interests. It is not enough to point out what the wrong policies are, as liberals tend to do: one has to go beyond the irrational policies and trace them to the interests—both economic and political. The agenda of the state is set by interest equations, and the discourse of knowledge is effective only to the extent that it is congruent with the discourse of power. Reasoning about right and wrong policies, while not entirely irrelevant, is of limited use if one's agenda is to shape a new reality. For this one has to come to grips with the interface of democracy and capitalism.

There are only two nations, as far as I know, where democracy pre-ceded capitalism—the United States and India. The United States is the oldest modern nation, and India is one of the oldest civilizations. The United States got democracy in 1776 but did not embrace full-blooded capitalism until the early nineteenth century with the industrial revolu-tion. India gave itself democracy in 1950, but capitalism only came in 1991 with the reforms. For the rest of the world it has been the other way around. This historic inversion has made all the difference, and it goes a long way towards explaining these two noisy democracies.

India's democracy, however, has an overwhelming majority of poor voters. This too makes a difference to the way things work. The journal-ist T. C. A. Srinivasa-Raghavan points out that in the long run the forces that drive markets and democracy will converge; in the short run, these forces often tend to pull in opposite directions. Since politics is a short-run game and growth is a long-run one, there will never be a situation that is completely optimal, with the result that at every point in time most of the people will be disappointed. No one bothers about education because results take a long time to come. When a politician promises rice for two rupees a kilo when it costs five rupees in the market, he wins the election. N. T. Rama Rao did precisely that in the 1994 state elections. He won the election, became the chief minister, and nearly bankrupted the state treasury. He also sent a sobering message to Prime Minister Narasimha Rao in Delhi, who, according to some observers, slowed India's reforms because he realized that votes resided in populist measures and not in doing what is right for the long term. Since the 1980s politicians have vigorously competed in giving away free goods and services to voters. When politicians do that, where is the money to come from for creating new schools or improving old ones?

I became thoroughly depressed the day the Punjab chief minister, Prakash Singh Badal, gave away free electricity and water to farmers in February 1997. He had lived up to his electoral promises, but twelve months later the state's fragile finances were destroyed and there was no money to pay salaries to civil servants. It was a poignant moment, because the state had everything going for it. Peace had returned after more than a decade of Hindu-Sikh troubles and terrorist violence. Investors were ready and waiting to come in. When this largesse was announced, they turned shy. I felt that competitive politics had again failed us. It taught me that the demand for publicly provided goods and services is insatiable in a democracy. Mancur Olson, the social scientist, makes the same point. He says that the behavior of individuals and interests in stable democracies inevitably leads to collusive lobbies that make their economies less dynamic and efficient and their politics less governable. Democratic societies tend to foster special-interest groups, which subvert the dynamism of capitalism. Writing in 1982, Olson compared the experiences of postwar Britain with those of Germany and Japan. Narrow-interest groups were destroyed by the war in Germany and Japan and they had to begin from scratch; in Britain, however, a powerful and dense network of trade unions and professional associations created "institutional sclerosis" that dragged down the economy. Germany and Japan created miracles of economic growth in the postwar decade, while the British economy remained slow, even sick in some years. Olson hoped that a public educated to the harmful effects of special interests might begin to resist such behavior. This is what eventually happened in Britain: tired of its unions, high taxes, and overregulation, the British voter brought in Margaret Thatcher to right the balance. Does this mean that we have to wait for a Thatcher or a Reagan to come to power in India?

Most Indian intellectuals would probably say no. Conditioned by years of socialism, they are wary of capitalism and afraid that it may, in fact, subvert democracy rather than the other way around. Like John Stuart Mill, they think that existing property systems are unjust and that the free market is destructively competitive—aesthetically and morally repugnant—and its excesses have to be controlled. They worry that the large corporation creates a new upper class with an excessively loud voice. In their eyes, executives of large multinational corporations are the contemporary counterpart of our zamindars of the feudal era, except that their voice is amplified by the technology of mass communication. In short, modern global capitalism, powered by multinational corporations, threatens democracy.

Indian intellectuals, I think, need to remember that modern democratic institutions have existed only in countries with privately owned market economies. Socialist countries always had command economies with centrally directed economic orders and were ruled by authoritarian dictatorships. The market economy seems to be a necessary condition for democracy, although it is not, of course, a sufficient condition. Empirical research also suggests that there is a positive relationship between capitalist and democratic institutions. In a major investigation of the social psychology of industrialization and modernization, a research team led by the sociologist Alex Inkeles interviewed several thousand workers in the modern industrial and the traditional economic sectors of six countries of differing cultures. Inkeles found a far greater propensity to participate among modern capitalist workers than among workers in the traditional sector in each one of these countries regardless of cultural differences.

Historically, as I have mentioned, modern democracy came after capitalism in most countries. Suffrage was extended in the last century, and as mass political parties developed, democracy began to impinge on capitalist institutions and practices. The democratic propensity for redistribution and regulation plus trade unions and leftist parties started to constrain the productivity and risk-taking spirits of entrepreneurs. This process culminated after World War II in the welfare state in the Western world and Japan, with social insurance and health care and extensive regulatory frameworks designed to address the shortfalls of capitalism. It can be argued that had capitalism not been so modified by democracy, it might not have survived.

In India, on the other hand, democratic institutions were set up before we had the chance to create an industrial revolution. Two-thirds of the people still live in rural areas, organized labor constitutes less than 10 percent of total labor, and until 1980 the middle class was less than 10 percent of the population. In a sense, we tried to redistribute the pie before it was baked. We set up intricate regulatory networks before the private economy had transformed a rural society into an industrial one. We began to think in terms of "welfare" before there were welfare-generating jobs. The result, as we have seen, was a throttling of enterprise, slow growth, missed opportunities. It is the price we have paid for having democracy before capitalism—or rather too much democracy and not enough capitalism.

Democracy and capitalism are thus both positively and negatively related. I believe, with all its flaws of special interests, populism, and indecisiveness, democratic capitalism is worth fighting for because it

offers the promise of preserving and enlarging human freedoms, fostering prosperity, diminishing poverty, and upholding the dignity of a
human being, and it does it better than any other system tried so far.

We are used to thinking in terms of dualisms in India—rich versus
poor, urban versus rural, upper versus lower castes, and so on. The most
striking dualism of today's India is, however, the contrast between the
vibrant private space and the impoverished public space. What could
stop our future is the latter—our weakness is governance. This is ironic,
for we have had much greater experience with the institutions of
democracy than with those of capitalism. Yet governance is what is letting us down today. With states bankrupt and pervasive corruption, our
confidence in government institutions is at its lowest. Although we may
rely more on markets now, we still need clean and efficient civil servants
to regulate them. Some economists, I know, secretly hope that the states
become bankrupt because this will force the pace of market-oriented
reform. However, I wish that Indians would begin to trust the market a
little bit more. It will, I think, take time. Over the centuries, the economist Robert Heilbroner tells us, human beings dealt with the problem
of survival through tradition or command. They organized society
around custom and usage, the son following the occupation of his father
from generation to generation. Adam Smith tells us that in ancient
Egypt "every man was bound by a principle of religion to follow the
occupation of his father." In India, our caste system assigned us occupations in the same way.

The whip of authority was the other method of organizing the jobs
of society. The pyramids of Egypt and the temples of India were built by
the command of pharaohs or maharajas. More recently, the Five Year
Plans of the Soviet Union were carried out by the command of the
Politburo. It is only in very recent times that human beings invented a
third solution to the problem of making a living, the market system, that
is, capitalism, which gives individuals the freedom to follow their inclination to do what is in their best interest, and in which lure of gain (not
tradition or authority) steers a person to his task or occupation.

Banias and bazaars have been around for thousands of years, ever
since there was an agricultural surplus. This began between 10,000 and
8000 B.C., when the first towns emerged as centers of exchange. But
markets are not the same thing as the market system. For one thing, it

requires that moneymaking be regarded as respectable, and we know that historically, commerce has had a bad odor in all societies, including India. Although we see today the wondrous spectacle of thousands of young Indians starting new business ventures all around us, the idea that their struggle for personal gain might actually promote the good of the whole society is too bizarre for most people. Even the most sophisticated Indians distrust the market—perhaps because no one is in charge. No wonder Samuel Johnson said, "There is nothing which requires more to be illustrated by philosophy than trade does."

Democracy, in contrast, is easier to understand, but it is more difficult to achieve. Because exchange is natural to human beings, capitalism is easier to achieve, but it is more difficult to understand. The irony is that in India we established the more difficult political institutions of democracy over fifty years ago, but it is the younger institutions of capitalism that are currently more successful. The lesson in all this is that we cannot take democracy or capitalism for granted. Institutions have to be renewed, and it is time we did that with our political institutions. We must also remember that democracy and capitalism do not necessarily go together, even though they have human freedom in common.

We tend to forget that liberal democracy based on free markets is a relatively new idea in human history. In 1776 there was one liberal democracy—the United States; in 1790 there were 3, including France; in 1848 there were only 5; in 1975 there were still only 31. Today 120 of the world's 200 or so states claim to be democracies, with more than 50 percent of the world's population residing in them (although Freedom House, an American think tank, counts only 86 countries as truly free). Clearly there has been a liberal revolution around the globe, accelerated in part by communism's collapse. More than 50 countries are engaged in the transition to open, market-driven economies. India is one of these, and is among the most likely to make a quick and successful transition to capitalism. Unlike Russia, it has had a highly developed national market going back (as we saw in chapter 5) to the days before the British came in the seventeenth century, which was integrated further when the railways came in the nineteenth century. Unlike China, it has had a robust, indigenous financial system, which was upgraded into a modern banking system in the early twentieth century. Despite Nehruvian socialism, three-fourths of the economy has been in private hands, including all of agriculture. Roads, ports, irrigation, power, banking, insurance, airlines, railways were in government hands, but the public sector accounted for less than a quarter of the domestic product. Unlike Russia and China, India also has clearly defined property rights, well-developed commercial law, and an English-speaking entrepreneurial class. With all these advantages, why does India remain half reformed? Why doesn't it quickly become an attractive place to do business?

The answer partly is that we underestimate the difficulty of transforming a closed, centrally planned economy into an open, market-oriented one. The state cannot merely withdraw from market activities by privatizing them. This is what some liberals think, and their belief is based on what Adam Smith called "man's prosperity to barter, truck and exchange one thing for another." They think markets are natural and spring up on their own. However, markets do not work in a vacuum. To function smoothly they need a largish network of regulations and institutions; they need umpires to settle disputes. These institutions do not just happen; they take time to develop. For example, with the decision to allow private investment in telecommunications, electricity, and insurance we have set up regulatory agencies, but we are still learning how to make them work. Worldwide experience over the last two decades teaches us that markets generate perverse results in the absence of good institutions.

Another reason for our slow pace is that the reform agenda is constantly being derailed by vested interests. Politicians lack the courage to privatize the huge, loss-making public sector because they are afraid to lose the vote of organized labor. They resist dismantling subsidies for power, fertilizers, and water because they fear the crucial farm vote. They won't touch food subsidies because of the massive poor vote. They will not remove thousands of inspectors in the state governments, who continuously harass private businesses, because they don't want to alienate government servants' vote bank. Meanwhile, these giveaways play havoc with state finances and add to our disgraceful fiscal deficit. Unless the deficit comes under control, the nation will not be more competitive; nor will the growth rate rise further to 8 and 9 percent, which is what is needed to create jobs and improve the chances of the majority of our people to actualize their capabilities in a reasonably short time.

"Collective action" is a problem in all democracies. To some extent, we have to be resigned to a slower pace of reform. But India's problems of governance go far beyond the need to appease interests. The weakening of our democratic institutions since the 1970s has caused widespread corruption, political violence, populist giveaways, and a paralysis of problem solving. Conspicuously absent are disciplined party organizations, which help leaders in other democracies to mobilize support for specific programs. Hence, there is an excessive reliance on the personal appeal of individual leaders to win elections. When in power, leaders find it difficult to push through programs, for when opposition mounts, they find few supporters and tend to take the easy way out, which is not to act at all. For this reason, the Indian state is sometimes called a "soft state."

This diagnosis applies particularly to the Congress Party, which has ruled India for most of the past fifty years. Enormous power has always been concentrated in the hands of the Nehru-Gandhi family, and it became actually negative under Indira Gandhi, who did great harm to institutions; she tried to snuff out democracy itself. The leftish amalgam of Janata parties has not done much better at institution building. Neither have the regional parties. While the BJP seems to have a more coherent organization, it has not been in power long enough to assess its long-term capabilities.

In a perceptive analysis, the political scientist Atul Kohli explains that political institutions are weak because India's democracy came from above and not from below. It was a "gift from the elite to the masses," and the masses are comfortable adoring an all-powerful leader. He shows, however, that even a powerful leader like Rajiv Gandhi, with a vast electoral support in the mid-eighties, could not implement major economic reforms. After a good start in 1985, when he introduced modest fiscal and industrial liberalization, Rajiv Gandhi got scared by vested interests and abandoned these initiatives after two years. Professor James Manor of the University of Sussex does not agree. He thinks that Rajiv Gandhi was not a political leader and that the problem lay "in the former Prime Minister's confusion and his chronic, indeed radical inconstancy." I believe the truth lies somewhere in between. Opposition from public-sector workers and middle peasants did partly force him to back down.

But how was Narasimha Rao able to produce such spectacular results between 1991 and 1993? Why didn't vested interests stop him? There are several reasons. First, all his reforms were "soft reforms": they did not really mean job losses for organized labor or an attack on subsidies. In fact, after opposition from the farmers' lobby to a reduction in the fertilizer subsidy in the July 1991 budget, he backed down. Second, he was able to reform by stealth, as it were, because the nation's attention was diverted by communal passions generated by the 1992 demolition of the Babri Masjid. Ashutosh Varshney, the political scientist, says that this "gave the reformers room to push the reforms." Third, of course, there was the fiscal crisis, and there's nothing like a crisis to focus the mind— even a politician's mind. Narasimha Rao deserves credit for his deft handling of the reform process, especially in sequencing the acts in a politically shrewd manner. India thereby avoided the political damage— or even collapse, as in Russia's case—that many countries suffer after economic reforms. The succeeding governments after Rao's have followed the same strategy—they have continued to reform the "softer areas" and have not confronted the five main interest groups: prosperous farmers, the industrial bourgeoisie, middle-class professionals (including government employees), unionized workers, and the poor (both urban and rural). They have trodden gingerly, either skirting them or giving them pain in a slow incremental manner. This, of course, does not bode well for the future of reform in India. Who is going to bell the cat? The present BJP-led government appears to be serious—it has announced an ambitious privatization program and made a beginning in the reduction of subsidies. But most Indians remain cynical about its ability to deliver results.

Will capitalism and its cousin, globalization, succeed in establishing a comfortable place for themselves in India? The answer depends on their ability to deliver prosperity broadly. It also depends on leaders in the government and in business to champion the classic liberal premises of free trade and competition. It needs leaders to come out and say that (1) some people will not fare as well in the competitive marketplace; (2) the winners will far outnumber the losers; (3) capitalist democracy is the best arrangement we have found; (4) globalization is not only a good thing, it is a great leap forward in history. My fear is that capitalism's success in India is threatened not so much by the leftists or protectionists as by the timidity of its defenders.

The triumph of market economics and the continued spread of democratic governance through village self-government are reasons for optimism. But twentieth-century history teaches us not to be too enthusiastic about any ideology. Instead of celebrating, our energies should go into figuring out how to make these arrangements more sustainable and stable propositions. How to change the thinking of politicians from territory to trade? Economic integration between India and Pakistan will do more to diffuse political conflict. It is economic integration of the European Union that has ruled out war between Germany and France. South Asian economic integration can do the same for India and Pakistan. India's politicians can learn a great deal from President Clinton's battles over NAFTA—it required huge political skills to win that victory.

Who then will save our capitalist democracy from its enemies? The job usually falls on politicians and businesspeople. But neither seems an ideal steward. Businesspeople are too busy making money and politicians are too busy serving vested interests. Meanwhile, capitalism is socially disruptive. Marx understood this and he made his famous remark in the *Communist Manifesto*—"All that is solid melts into air." Democracy, on the other hand, is messy. But capitalism can succeed if it has the consent of the governed. It requires taking into account the needs and fears of ordinary Indian citizens. Economic growth is the easy part of the equation. Gaining consent from voters is more difficult because there will be stark disparities in wealth. Many Indian politicians recognize that democracy and capitalism are inseparable, but binding them will be crucial if the nation is to succeed.

The great hope of Indian democracy lies in decentralization. This is beginning to happen as governments at the center in Delhi have weakened during the past decade. Since no party has been able to gain a majority in Parliament, leaders have depended more and more on regional parties to survive; neither have there been charismatic and overbearing leaders like Nehru and Indira Gandhi. Hence, the states have grown stronger by default. With liberalization, competition for private investment has also grown among the states. The competition in turn forces them to reform. This is a good thing as the behavior of the state government has a bigger impact on the average citizen's day-to-day life than the center.

The best news for Indian democracy, however, is the revolution at the local level—in the village and in the town. For forty years we did not have local self-government. But during the nineties, local elections have been held in most villages and municipalities across the country and we have around three million legislators—a world record of sorts—of which one million are women. Local self-government (the panchayat raj) will not immediately transform people's lives, but it has to make a difference in the end. By law, one-third of our local representatives have to be women, and this too will make a difference.

Basrabhai is one such woman. She lives in Mohadi, an impoverished village on the Gujarat coast, where the villagers' straw huts were blown away in a cyclone. Basrabhai is the first woman to be elected chair of her village's local council, or panchayat. She conducts regular village meetings and, with the support of SEWA, a women's nongovernmental organization, has succeeded in getting about a dozen concrete homes out of the state government from its cyclone relief budget. One such permanent structure is the school, but the schoolteacher rarely shows up from the neighboring town. He is accountable only to the state bureaucracy at the capital and does pretty much what he pleases; contemptuous of the fisherfolk in the village, he calls their children "junglee"—animals from the jungle. SEWA is the acronym of the Self Employed Women's Association, and it supports the craftwork of the women in the village, providing microcredit, and marketing support for their embroidered and tie-dyed products, which have become increasingly popular in Bombay and in Western cities.

Govind Nihalani's new film, *Sanshodhan,* describes the arrival of the panchayat raj in a Rajasthani village. In it, a woman member of the local panchayat mobilizes the village to build a primary school and successfully foils the local landlord who is bent on stealing the school funds. It is a simple political film, which explains the magic of civic engagement and the rewards of local self-government. The local elites will almost certainly try to subvert the democratic process when it goes against their interest. They will try to pack the panchayats with their relatives and friends, as they do in Nihalani's popular film, but eventually they will have to reconcile themselves to sharing power.

Both Basrabhai's tale and *Sanshodhan* tell us that Indian democracy is changing. Despite vested interests and the lack of accountability of teachers and state officials, an explicit affirmative action policy has allowed Basrabhai to become the head of her village and to fight for change. It shows what can be done through state action; SEWA's example demonstrates not only the virtues of civic engagement but also how the poor can make a difference if they organize themselves to defend their rights and take advantage of market opportunities. Basrabhai's story also teaches the crying need for education reform—we have to make schoolteachers accountable to parents and communities rather than to the state bureaucracy. Teachers' unions are fighting this in state after state, but politicians will soon realize that there are votes in enacting this measure.

India Today, a widely read national magazine, recently recounted a similar story of community action in Gujarat's drought-prone region of Saurashtra. During four months, between May and August 2000, villagers in six districts of Saurashtra have built ten thousand check dams in response to the state government's "Build Your Own Check Dam" scheme. Mobilized by voluntary organizations like SEWA, villagers provided free labor and the government matched it with 60 percent of the cost of the dam. A few sporadic rains filled the check dams, and as water percolated into the ground, it raised the water table of the region. This simple water-harvesting effort is greening the driest region in the country. An even more dramatic story is that of the activist Rajendra Singh, who has mobilized people in six hundred villages in the dry Alwar area of Rajasthan. His check dams have made a river flow that had gone dry many years ago, and it has greened the desert.

During the past two decades the voluntary movement has helped to connect the people to their rulers. Literally hundreds of voluntary organizations have become embedded in local communities across the country, and have reinforced the message of self-help, cooperation, and civic solidarity to the villagers; women's and environmental groups have especially made a strong mark in some communities. An urban example is that of "citizen's cards" in Bangalore, which asks citizens to rate the services by governmental agencies. Administered by the Public Affairs Center, a voluntary organization, the report cards assess the quality and cost of citizens' transactions with government departments. The Bangalore Development Authority, responsible for housing and other services, scored the lowest in one of the early report cards, with only 1 percent of respondents "satisfied." As a result, the authority director launched a citizen-government initiative to correct the problems.

A successful nation has three attributes: politically, it is free and democratic; economically, it is prosperous and equitable; and socially, it is peaceful and cohesive. The Indian nation enters the twenty-first century with considerable strengths in all three areas. Despite our frustrations over governance and interests, politically India is unquestionably free and democratic. During the past fifty years, Indians have learned to change their governments peacefully; thanks to a revived Election Commission, all parties have affirmed that elections during the last decade have been fair. Indians jealously value their vigorous free press and television. They have given free rein to their litigious nature in the courts, and justice, while slow, provides an opportunity to right many wrongs. Recently, power has begun to devolve to villages and municipalities, and women especially have shown an eagerness to embrace the fruits of local self-government. A civil society still has to grow to save democracy from electoral populism.

Economically, the reforms are creating the conditions for widespread prosperity as the nation has attained a sustainable 6 to 7 percent growth rate. This could climb to 8 or even 9 with more reform, and once prosperity spreads across all classes, Indians will also gradually lose some of their distrust of capitalism. Socially backward castes have come forward, a more pluralistic middle class is developing, and there is a greater balance of opportunity. No longer does the Indian peasant have to grovel before autocratic zamindars and feudal lords. To be sure, in backward Bihar, bonded labor is not totally erased and the Ranvir Sena terrorizes the Dalits; there is pervasive corruption in the lower bureaucracy and some policemen are venal; and gender inequalities are huge, especially in the north. But all in all, the average Indian has never been as free and can look forward to a better future. Education expansion holds the key, for with it will come better governance, less inequality, and a better quality of life.

TWENTY-TWO

Knowledge Is Wealth

The raft of knowledge ferries the worst sinner to safety.
—BHAGAVAD GITA

The Vedic adage "Knowledge is wealth" sums up the Indian opportunity in the new century. For the world has changed from an industrial to a knowledge economy. We have witnessed epochal and transforming innovations in electronics and information technology. For the first time in history we are able to see a technological revolution that offers the opportunity for bridging the gap between the haves and the have-nots. As the technology converges between television, computer, and telephone, the Internet could touch everyone's life and break the barriers that have divided us up to now. Although it is not a panacea for all our developmental problems, used imaginatively, it can be a powerful vehicle to transform the lives of ordinary people, both socially and economically.

The transformation of the world from an industrial to a knowledge economy means that jobs, exports, and economic activity with the highest value added will come from the knowledge sectors of the economy, and countries that participate vigorously in these sectors will be rewarded with a growing and higher standard of living. The history of how country after country went from poverty to prosperity over the past two hundred years teaches us that the transformation was generally powered by one sector, which became the engine of its economic growth. In Britain, it was textiles; in the United States, the industrial revolution was led by the railways. Timber and timber products were responsible for Sweden's takeoff; milk and dairy products did the same for Denmark. In business terms, the nation's leading sector reflects its competitive advantage. Over the last fifty years India has struggled to find its leading sector, and this explains, in part, its inability to create an industrial revolution. Now, it may have found it in the knowledge sectors of the economy.

India's emerging success in information technology is the first evidence of competitive advantage. Its electronics industry has been the fastest-growing sector of the economy between 1994 and 1999, rising 25 percent a year, with turnover of $8.5 billion in 1999. Software exports have been growing 60 percent a year over the past five years; they crossed $5 billion in 2000 and are expected to rise to $50 billion by 2008. On 1 August 2000, the market capitalization of listed IT companies was more than $78 billion. Out of 19 top global software companies that had achieved the highest certification for quality, as many as 12 were Indian. More than 400 portals were being launched every month during the first two quarters of 2000, backed by 28 venture capital funds with close to $1.5 billion investment, which is expected to rise to $7 billion by 2005. Supporting this effort is over 123,000 kilometers of fiber-optic network over 24 million lines. Even the government has established an Internet site—http://itformasses.nic.in—on which it invites suggestions from citizens on how to bring information technology to the masses as part of a national campaign called "Operation Knowledge."

Yet this is only a beginning, for India still has a vast distance to travel before it can call itself an IT power. Its $5 billion software exports are a fraction of global exports of more than $200 billion. It has only three computers per thousand persons (which is expected to rise to twenty per thousand by 2008). And even for people with computers, getting connected is slow. The root of the problem is the government telecom monopoly, which insists on protecting its turf rather than allow private competition. Prime Minister Vajpayee has opened the Internet to private providers and recently broke the government monopoly on long-distance telephone calls, and this should ease the situation. The National Association of Software and Service Companies has launched a campaign to boost Internet bandwidth eightyfold by 2003 with the backing of at least three large companies—Enron, Hughes Telecom, and Reliance, each of whom plans to invest $500 million to $1 billion.

Although information technology is becoming a mantra inside the government, many Indians remain skeptical of bureaucratic intentions. When the government started a new Ministry of Information Technology in 1999, entrepreneurs and the media were not amused. They believed that the IT industry had grown because of official neglect. When the new ministry announced a new $20 million venture capital fund, the media dubbed it the "Nephews and Nieces Fund," and people expect that it will be used to fund companies owned by the relatives of politicians and bureaucrats. The government should realize that even in Israel, a tech-savvy country with better governance, government funding of technology has failed. The head of its $100 million program admits that "not even one profitable project has come out of the incubators." Bureaucracies move slowly and technologies move rapidly, and this reassures entrepreneurs. The Indian bureaucracy is still trying to tax and regulate the physical movement of goods in the old economy of the pre-1991 era, and fortunately has failed to fasten its claws onto knowledge-based products and services.

The short-term answer to wiring India lies in cable television. Right now, in mid-2000, around 3.5 million Indians have Internet access through personal connections, Internet kiosks, and cybercafes. However, investment bankers like Goldman Sachs and Crédit Lyonnais Securities project that the number of Internet users could rise to 30 million by 2004. And cable television will pave the way. Of the 68 million TV homes in India, more than 32 million have cable connections and they are growing 8 percent a year. This is more than the number of telephones in India—22 million—and more than all cable homes in South America. Cable TV is cheap (Rs 150 per month for up to seventy channels) and it is largely unregulated. "The land of the license raj somehow forgot to regulate cable," says the *Economist*. An enterprising person can run wires along trees to a few hundred homes, beam programs from a room, collect money, and he or she is in business. The result has been a boom: 60,000 to 70,000 cable operators have come up, according to the Cable Operators Federation. It is a cut-throat business with low margins, but it is fast consolidating. Hindujas' INCableNet is investing up to $500 million in upgrading its cable networks. It has already laid 150 kilometers of fiber-optic cable in Bombay and is now offering speedy Internet access to some of its 1.9 million customers in the city. Intel, the world's largest chip maker, is so impressed that it has valued INCableNet at $1.5 billion and invested $49 million in it. Its big rival, Siticable, run by Zee Television, claims to be worth $3.5 billion, and has even more ambitious plans to offer Internet access over cable lines by the end of 2000.

Not since the heady days of the green revolution more than thirty years ago have we felt the same excitement and fever. This time around, it is the educated young in our largest cities who are leading the charge. I visit and speak often at college campuses, and there I have found new energy and fire, once again coming from the thrill of a new technology. In the early 1990s, it was software. This time it is the Internet and IT services. Although the subject of my lectures varies, the students want to talk only about how to become Internet entrepreneurs. They have amazing ideas, which they call their "inner dreams." I encourage them to pin their dreams to a business model and seek venture funding. "The moment is yours," I tell them. "Seize it."

Some brave ones have taken the plunge, and are beginning to burn the midnight oil. And venture companies are falling over each other to grab the best early players. Established companies are setting aside funds to incubate hundreds of entrepreneurial ventures. One has only to read the *Economic Times* and *Business World* to follow this revolution from week to week. *Business World* reported in February 2000 that a dozen venture capital companies are evaluating five hundred business plans a month. Hundreds of young managers in the industrial companies and banks have also been bitten by the Internet bug and are beginning to leave their secure jobs and become partners in the new start-ups. Indian subsidiaries of multinationals like Lever, Citibank, GE, and Motorola lost dozens of managers in the first two quarters of 2000.

There are three kinds of companies, according to Professor David Birch, formerly of MIT. He calls them elephants, mice, and gazelles. The elephants, of course, are the large Fortune 500 companies like General Motors. The vast number of tiny enterprises in the bazaar—retail shops, restaurants, and services—are mice. The third are gazelles, which start small and grow extremely rapidly through innovation.

Microsoft, Intel, Oracle, Netscape, and America Online started as gazelles. Sometimes gazelles create entirely new industries, as did FedEx and UPS.

Professor Birch says that a vast majority of the new jobs in the United States have been created by gazelles. It is well known that the United States has been extremely successful at generating employment, having created tens of millions of new jobs in the last two decades. The elephants have not added much to employment; in fact, they have downsized. Neither have the mice: for every new one that comes up, another usually closes. The gazelles eventually become elephants, but on the way (as they ride the "S-curve") they create an enormous number of productive, high-quality jobs. Successful economies create conditions for the gazelles to come up and to succeed.

In India, we too have had gazelles—Reliance, NIIT, Jet Airways, Infosys, Zee TV, to name a few. Our challenge as a nation is to find entrepreneurs who have a vision and a dream, and who will be the gazelles of tomorrow. This is not easy, for the scarcest resource in any society is entrepreneurship, and four out of five entrepreneurs fail. So it is a real art to find out who will succeed. The question is, how do we identify and nurture gazelles? And who should do it? Clearly the government should not—it does not understand business and will only succeed in killing them.

The answer is venture capitalism. Many of America's gazelles came up this way. A venture capitalist doesn't go into business himself but looks for a young person with an idea and offers him or her capital (and management help) in exchange for a share of future profits. Since banks are risk averse and will not lend to a young person with an idea, every entrepreneur is always short of capital and welcomes a backer. When the business has built a record of profits, the sensible thing is to take the company public and raise the capital for expansion through the stock market. This is also the opportunity for the venture capitalist to book his profit, sell his shares, and exit from the venture. And look for another gazelle to nourish.

A number of successful Indian industrialists have asked me over the years for advice on philanthropy. Typically they say, "I have made my money and I am not getting any younger. What should I do? Where should I donate my money?" When Indian businessmen think of philanthropy, they usually think of temples, hospitals, and schools. These are good things, but I generally turn them in the direction of a good nongovernmental organization (NGO), because I find they are doing a better job of social uplift than private charities. However, after reading Professor Birch, I think that spotting and nourishing gazelles can also be a kind of philanthropy. What could be better than to provide seed capital to a young person with a dream and thereby create thousands of productive new jobs in the economy and build national competitiveness at the same time?

This is not an entirely new idea in India. Some business communities—notably the Jains in Gujarat—provide risk capital to young entrepreneurs with the understanding that they will repay it later in life. In the nineteenth century, there existed a similar support system for Marwari youngsters who went off to Calcutta from the villages of Rajasthan. My son argues that venture capitalism is not philanthropy, it is business. But if one retains the capital and reinvests the profits in new ventures, then I think it is philanthropic. To further my own venture capital ambitions, I met a number of experts and discovered that venture capital funds had not done well in India. To do the job properly, I realized, it should be a biggish fund, and it should be run by professionals.

As luck would have it, one spring morning in 1999, quite out of the blue, two young Harvard Business School graduates, Ashish Dhawan of Goldman Sachs and Raj Kondur of Morgan Stanley, phoned me from New York. They were thinking, they said, of quitting their jobs and starting a venture capital fund in India. They thought they could raise $50 million from Wall Street, and would I be the chairman and adviser of their Chrysalis Capital Fund? It was like a dream come true, and I jumped at the idea. They flew to Delhi and we finalized our agreement. I also agreed to invest a modest sum in the fund. The following month I went to New York, where I met one of their lead investors, Jeffrey Kiel, the former president of Republic National Bank, who, like me, had quit at age fifty; he had joined Edward Stern, senior partner at Lazard, to start a private equity company called International Real Returns LLC. I asked him why he was planning to invest a large sum in Indian ventures. He said he had done well by investing in Israeli high-tech ventures, and India offered the same opportunity, only in a bigger way. By now my young associates had also quit their jobs. They told me that they had cre-

ated a data bank of one hundred Indians in America who were report-
edly worth over $50 million each, many of them in Silicon Valley. We
agreed that they would be promising candidates for funding our venture
capital project. As it turned out, we were able to raise over $100 million
and we had to cap the fund at $65 million. We were able to raise part of
the capital from a dozen Indian CEOs in Silicon Valley.

By July 2000, seven months later, Chrysalis had invested in thirteen
information technology companies and was recognized in India as a leading venture capital fund. Its team had grown from three to twenty-three;
it was in the process of closing two more deals in July, and with that it
would have committed the entire fund. Based on its early success, it was
planning a second, larger fund. We defined our mission early and with
vast ambition: "To build a new India by inspiring and nurturing passionate entrepreneurs." With that motto as a guide, Dhawan and Kondur
moved at a feverish pace to seek out IT service providers and fill the
Indian Internet spaces based on models that had worked in the United
States. Hence, Chrysalis quickly invested in firms that designed Web sites,
or provided software solutions or remote services. It also bought into an
auction site called Baazee.com, started by two young Harvard Business
School graduates, who hoped to make it the eBay of India. It funded
Fabmart.com, the leading e-tailing site, which aims to become the Ama-
zon.com of India and which has expanded from selling books and music
to offering jewelry and groceries online. It invested in JobsAhead.com,
the leading jobs site in India, which wants to duplicate the success of
America's Monster.com. Started in March 2000, by 1 June it had
acquired 700 corporate customers, 8,000 job listings, 90,000 resumes,
and 150,000 registered users with 70 employees. Our most interesting
investment is egurucool.com, a distance-learning portal for students
preparing for high school finals and college entrance examinations. It has
a homework helpline in the evening where teachers help students with
their homework. Aside from such business-to-consumer sites, Chrysalis
has also invested in Spectramind, started by the former head of GE Capital's outsourcing center, and it aims to become India's leading call center
and remote services provider. Similarly, we have invested in TransWorks,
a Web-based customer service center providing e-mail management support for customers like Citibank. Other investments include ITNation, a
vertical business-to-business portal for IT products and services, Avigna

Technologies, a Web-design firm based in Madras, and Ivega, a software development and consulting company in Bangalore that targets financial services.

It is too early to say how many of these companies will succeed, but Chrysalis's ability to source good deals is the result of its coming at the right time to India and moving rapidly to close the deals. It devotes a great deal of time to holding the hands of entrepreneurs—helping them to find technology partners and locate high-quality employees, introducing them to customers in the United States and Europe. I personally have been devoting three to five days a month to helping some of our portfolio companies build their brand name and develop their strategy and marketing plan. I am on the boards of four of our portfolio companies and it is one of the most interesting things that I have done in my life.

Dhawan and Kondur are beginning to inspire other Indian youngsters in America. One of them is my nephew, Yuvraj Singh, who is twenty-nine years old and worked as a bond trader with Lehman Brothers on Wall Street after he graduated from Princeton. He quit his job in July 2000 to become a venture capitalist and plans to fund software entrepreneurs in financial services. By mid-2000 more than two dozen venture funds were operating in India. Though it is difficult to say how many Internet companies have started in India—estimates range from 220 to 500—60,000 domain names were registered out of India, and between the airport and South Bombay 160 billboards, 85 percent of the total, belonged to dot-com start-ups in the summer of 2000.

Technology stocks in India, as in the United States, had defied gravity in 1998 and 1999, scaling one peak after another. Then, on 14 April 2000, came the Nasdaq crash, which brought carnage in new economy stocks in India as well. India's dot-com fever had begun in 1999, four years behind the U.S. cycle; nevertheless, the tremors of the U.S. crash affected venture capital sentiment in India. Fund flow has not declined—on the contrary, it is projected to double in 2001—but investors are more cautious and now focus on business-to-business sites, software services, and technology applications. Business-to-consumer sites have fallen out of favor—especially e-commerce models, which have also failed in the United States. At Chrysalis we believe that services which people pay for in the real world will migrate to the Web.

This is why we consider some of our better bets to be distance learning (because students pay college and prep fees) and job sites (because companies pay a headhunter's commission). Edelweiss Capital, a venture firm, looks for businesses which use the Internet as an enabler. Gary Wendt, another venture capitalist, believes that the Internet will not change business itself, but the way it is done—by reaching customers faster and reducing costs in the supply chain; thus, he would prefer to invest in a brick-and-mortar company which moves to the Web.

The dot-coms are also changing. They are attempting to marry the online with the offline world in what is now called the "click and brick" strategy. India Infoline has acquired a thirty-two-branch company in the south that distributes financial products; Net2Travel has bought two travel agencies to improve delivery; the entertainment site Hungama has cultivated a network of 560 cybercafes for promotions in order to drive traffic to its site; Jobsahead.com holds fairs in large cities where recruits meet potential employers; shaadis.com, an Indian weddings site, not only helps find grooms and brides on the Net but has tied up with an event management company that specializes in arranging theme weddings—Rajasthani-style weddings and rural temple marriages are especially popular.

Despite the cool stock market, the gold rush is real. There is a frenzy with which new ventures are starting. Mantra Online's CEO, N. Arjun, believes that there will be one thousand portals by mid-2001. Even though 80 percent of the people connected to Internet in India use it mainly for e-mail, everyone is looking two to three years in the future when thirty million Indians will be connected. These ventures will soon face tough competition from established companies and from Internet companies in America. This is happening in Japan, where Sony and Fujitsu are linking with American dot-coms; NEC has recently acquired a 30 percent stake in eBay, and Yahoo Japan's share price was quoting at two thousand times projected earnings for fiscal 1999. Indians know that foreign portals are coming, but they point out that in China the top three portals are Chinese. They believe their advantage over foreigners will be creative local content that ultimately brings traffic to a site. But I believe success will depend on execution. Ideas can be copied, but it is the ability to execute ideas which will define the winners.

The inspiration for our new economy is the 250,000 Indian warriors now living in Silicon Valley. *Business Week* reported on 6 December 1999 that an extraordinarily large number of new enterprises in Silicon Valley—more than 30 percent according to the article—were started by Asians, with the overwhelming number being Indian. Many Indians have also had a huge success on the Nasdaq; K. B. Chandershekhar's $200 million Exodus Communications carries 30 percent of all Internet content, hosting popular Web sites like Yahoo, Hotmail, and Amazon; Suhas Patil's $628 million Cirrus Logic makes chips; Ajay Shah's $750 million Smart Modular Technologies makes memory chips and modules in four countries; Prakash Aggarwal's $240 million Neomagic integrates memory and logic in a single chip—this makes the chips more powerful and gives him a 50 percent share of the laptop graphics market; Vinod Gupta's 120 million Integrated Systems makes software for home appliances, while his wife Vinita's $66 million Digital Link makes network equipment.

The legendary heroes and mentors to the young are the visionary masters of the World Wide Web, "serial entrepreneurs" and venture capitalists. Vinod Dham, father of the Pentium chip, now wants to revolutionize telecommunications. Founder of Silicon Spice, he will, he says, "do for telecom what Intel did for PCs." He envisions a world where telecom, like water, is available on tap. There is thirty-year-old Sabeer Bhatia, who created Hotmail and sold it to Microsoft for $400 million in 1998. He has started a new company that will "do to e-commerce what Hotmail did to e-mail." The portly Kanwal Rekhi, who founded one of the first Indian companies in the valley, Excelan, and sold it to Novell for $250 million, is now a venture capitalist and claims to have made $100 million from investing mainly in Indian ventures. Vinod Khosla originally founded Sun Microsystems, and he has a net worth over $100 billion, placing him forty-four on *Forbes'* list of the wealthiest Americans in 1999. Among the richest Indians in the United States, however, is Ravi Deshpande, who sold his company Cascade Communications to Ascend for $3.7 billion and promptly started a new multibillion venture called Sycamore Networks to make network routers. Other "serial entrepreneurs" include Prabhu Goel, who has started three high-tech companies and is an investor in five others, and Purna Pareek, who sold his Java-based server, Apptivity, for $30 million in 1998. A hardware success is Hemant Kanakia, who sold his Torrent

Network Technologies to telecom giant Ericsson for $450 million. Prakesh Bhalerao, a Ph.D. from MIT, has investments in thirty companies and is CEO of four others, all of which he has housed in a single rented 15,000-square-foot space. Finally, Bipin Shah, CEO of Invox Technologies, is selling an innovative new chip to Motorola, Hyundai, and others that could transform digital voice recording; he is also an angel investor in five other companies.

Almost all of these Silicon Valley entrepreneurs have followed the same script. They came to the United States in the seventies and eighties as young engineering graduates—usually with a degree from one of the prestigious Indian institutes of technology. They got a Ph.D. from an American university and worked in a high-tech company for a few years before setting out on their own. Although "their brains are in Silicon Valley, their hearts are in India," says *Business World,* and they are now beginning to finance Indian students at U.S. universities and fund new start-ups in India and by Indians in the United States. They formally came together in 1992 to form a network called The Indus Entrepreneurs (TiE), which has one thousand members today, divided into four chapters for the purpose of fostering entrepreneurship. The members meet regularly and examine business plans proposed by young Indians. TiE has pledged $7 million to the Center for Civil Society in India. Individually members have contributed to their alma maters, mainly Indian institutes of technology. Venkatesh Shukla, CEO of WebBy-Phone, runs the "Foundation for Excellence" and has funded nine hundred students in the past three years. Prabhu Goel and Kanwal Rekhi have committed to finance fifteen thousand students. Prabhu Goel had his chips designed at Noida, near Delhi. Vinod Dham sources his software from Bangalore for Silicon Chips; Murali Chirali does the same from Bangalore. K. B. Chandershekhar has funded two high-profile start-ups in Bangalore—Aztec Software and Gray Cell—and wants to "create six world-class entrepreneurs out of India." Dilip Sontakey of E-Z Data in California is establishing a $5 million IT township near his hometown, Nagpur, in Maharashtra, to create five hundred high-tech jobs. This is how Indians abroad are beginning to give back.

Every age has its Left Bank, says the author Dennis Cass. It is "the place where hot, restless souls test their capacity for adventure, the place like Silicon Valley today, where people are more alive than you or I." It is

the spirit of our age that twenty-five-year-old tech-born hipster pro-
grammers in their hundred-thousand-dollar cars and wearing khakis and
polo shirts working fifteen-hour days in lusty start-ups define the
romance of our Left Bank. It is not surprising that Silicon Valley, where
"cool people work," should inspire Indians—after all, high-tech is the
mantra of our times. But why Indians should succeed in Silicon Valley is
a more difficult question.

Many Indians are skeptical about India's ability to succeed in the
knowledge economy when it failed in the industrial economy. They
insistently ask how will a few hundred thousand "knowledge workers"
transform the lot of a billion people, particularly when 40 percent are
illiterate and our infrastructure is so poor? One answer is that knowledge
industries operate in the service economy and are typically employment-
intensive compared to manufacturing. Indian knowledge workers also
have a clear cost advantage. Companies like NIIT, Zee Television, and
Bharti Telecom are creating masses of new jobs in services. Subhash
Chandra, whom we met earlier, claims that Zee TV alone has directly
and indirectly created 250,000 jobs by outsourcing production and content creation. Remote or IT-enabled services over the telephone or the
Internet are beginning to create large numbers of new jobs in call centers. Increasingly international companies are outsourcing back-office
work, answering customer queries by telephone or e-mail to India, as we
saw in chapter 17. As noted, McKinsey projects that remote services
could become a $50 billion business employing one to two million Indi-
ans. These alone could employ all of the two million graduates coming
out of Indian colleges.

The power of remote services worries unions in the West. I read one
morning in the online edition of the *Times of India* that customers of the
venerable London store Harrods would now have their telephone calls
answered from a small town near Delhi, and that this had set alarm bells
ringing across Britain. A regional radio station in Yorkshire reported in a
rather blunt manner that the local community which had earlier operated the Harrods call center was deeply concerned; trade union officials
in London quickly issued a statement expressing reservations about
British companies shifting their "back offices" to India. Another newspaper raised questions about whether the distinguished customers of
Harrods would be able to understand the English spoken by Indian boys

and girls. And how might these Indian lads know about caviar, Stilton cheese, or Churchill shoes? To their credit, Harrods jumped to the young Indians' defense, saying that Indians spoke English just as intelligibly as the citizens of Yorkshire.

The Leeds chamber of commerce said that if more British companies followed suit this might set a "strange" precedent. It quoted the example of British Airways' remote-processing center, which employs a thousand people in India (and this number is growing). Some insurance companies have also shifted their data processing to India, which is encouraging other insurance companies to do the same. British Airways said that not only is this shift to India saving it millions of pounds, but the accuracy and timeliness of the work is of a very high order—everything is done and delivered back to them as they open for work in the morning in London.

But one trade unionist, deeply skeptical of the telecommunications revolution, asked, what happens when the link goes down? The *Times* report said that India must not be complacent, and may have to open its call centers to inspection by NGOs or visiting British ministers to prove that they were not employing eight-year-olds or providing one bed for five to sleep in during the off-duty hours. It added that a British Labour MP had recently suggested that British patients waiting for months for surgery be sent to Indian hospitals. The British Medical Council had found that suggestion "strange" and raised questions of hygiene and care. The report went on to talk about a similar backlash in Germany after the German Chancellor had publicly invited Indian information technology experts to come to Germany to help out with its technology problems. Finally, the *Times* suggested that India might have to employ a public relations company in the West to reassure local citizens and neutralize the criticism.

As I read the story, I realized that these fears were the manifestation of perhaps even deeper anxieties about globalization. The prospect of job losses in local communities is real, and statesmen in the West need to reassure their citizens that in the long run free trade is good for everyone, even though it causes pain to some in the short run. It is part of the rules of the capitalist game. The same fears were expressed in America some years ago when the North American Free Trade Association (NAFTA) agreement was being debated. Bill Clinton had to reassure American workers incessantly that although some American jobs would be exported to Mexico and Canada, more higher-paying jobs would in the end be created in America. And he was right, for all kinds of studies have since proven that everyone has gained with NAFTA—in Mexico, Canada, and the United States. The very real concern about job losses in the West in remote services supports my point that the "death of distance" and the communications revolution will create masses of job opportunities in India. India's advantage over other countries is that English is pervasive and call center operators have found that it takes only six weeks to get Indians talking with an American accent.

The Internet may not change everything we do, but it has already revolutionized business and will continue to do so. In 1999, 15 percent of stocks and 5 percent of books in America were sold on the Web and 40 percent of car buyers consulted the Net. While many services like travel are beginning to migrate to the Internet, most Web businesses have still not made any profit. E-commerce in America recorded only 1 percent of retail sales in 1999. Products still have to be produced and delivered in the brick-and-mortar economy. The mania for infotech stocks has proven to be a technology bubble—three out of four Internet stocks in America now trade below their issue prices. Many Internet businesses will not survive. Nothing unusual about that, surely. After all, businesses fail all the time. Dozens will merge into larger entities with a better chance of survival. It is obvious that the Internet will create new jobs as dot-coms become successful. But it is, in fact, already creating thousands of new jobs in Indian bazaars. It is almost as thrilling as the last time around a dozen years ago when manned public telephone centers arrived, and they created 1.5 million new jobs. Many of us remember in India the excitement when mothers could talk for the first time to their sons working thousands of miles away. Now the same thing is beginning to happen with the Internet, as many of the call centers are turning into Internet kiosks, and cybercafes are opening up on street corners across the country. For some phone centers it is a matter of necessity—as long-distance rates have fallen so have their revenues. The way out, some of them are discovering, is to either acquire computer skills or hire someone with skills. The Telecom Industry Service Association is offering training programs to telephone center operators to handle e-mail, chat rooms, browsing, and e-commerce.

Sustained success in the knowledge economy will obviously require greater attention to education—both the expansion of primary education and improving the quality of higher education. More and better primary education will help wipe out illiteracy and ensure equity—that is, the rewards of economic growth will penetrate down and more people will share in the prosperity. But critics wonder how we will create computer literates when we still lack blackboards. The answer may lie, in part, with the success of experiments like the one in the Tamil Nadu that I alluded to in chapter 17. The Tamil Nadu government and private companies like NIIT are collaborating to bring computer education to government schools. NIIT provides computers and teachers and the school provides the real estate, the most important cost in private IT education. During the day children get practically free education, and after school hours it becomes a regular NIIT commercial center open to the town's residents. Whatever profits NIIT loses during the day are made up between 4 p.m. and 11 p.m. If there is profit to be made in teaching computers to young Indians, then we may have found a model for self-generating, broad-scale computer literacy in the country. If there is profit to be made, competing education companies like Aptech and Tulec will scramble to replicate this across the country. Two other states, Karnataka and Punjab, have already begun a bidding process to invite private computer academies to come and train schoolchildren under similar terms.

In another experiment, Sugata Mitra, NIIT's head of research, placed a computer in a Delhi slum. He fixed it into a boundary wall along with a touch pad (but without a keyboard). He also hung a hidden camera on a tree to monitor what happened. Within a week he found that illiterate slum children without any formal training had begun surfing the Net and in three months had created a thousand folders among them. The most avid users were six-to-twelve-year-olds, who had taught themselves to draw on the computer and browse the Web. Disney.com was the most popular site because of its games; they also liked Microsoft's Paint site—being poor, they had never had access to paper and paint; now they could paint without paper. And once they discovered MP3 digital music files, they began to download Hindi film music and play it all day long.

This experiment suggests that curious children in groups can train

themselves to operate a computer at a basic level without formal instruction. It means that you can multiply the effectiveness of teachers many-
fold by giving children access to the Internet. In another experiment,
Dr. Mitra found that some ninth graders were able to teach themselves
physics concepts (such as viscosity) directly from the Internet without
the aid of a teacher. The teacher's job, thus, could be to help the children ask the right questions. The slum experiment also teaches that up
to a point the English language is not a bar. Dr. Mitra's slum computer
had a Hindi interface which gave the kids links to hook up with Web
sites in their own language. But the children quickly shut it down and
went back to Internet Explorer. Dr. Bose says that they may not know
the dictionary meaning of English words, but they quickly achieve
operational understanding—they don't know how to pronounce *File,*
but they know that within it are options for saving and opening files. He
likens this sort of functional literacy to learning to ride a bicycle. "No
one asks you how you learned," he says, "You just did it." His hope is
that one day the computer will become as ubiquitous in India as the
bicycle. "You don't have to worry about content either," he adds. "Once
Indians start surfing, the content will quickly appear in Indian languages, which is what happened with cable TV."

I have two sons. Both are in their twenties and both left to live abroad
because our socialist raj didn't create jobs for them during our dark
decades. Like most Indian parents, my wife and I would like them to
return and make a life at home. Now that India is changing, they have
begun to talk of returning. While our older boy, Kim Kanishka, is happy
doing advertising in China, the younger one, Puru, has quit his job in
New York and is planning to start a "click and brick" company to sell
lifestyle furniture to the Indian middle class. Just two years ago, I could
not have imagined Puru becoming an entrepreneur, but he's caught up
in the spirit of our times, when every young person is willing to risk the
security of a job to pursue his passion. He talks like many of his friends
about the power of democratic India that has unleashed the market to
make more of its human capabilities than ever before possible. Freeing
the individual has indeed released vast amounts of energy and creativity.
This is now channeled into software, entertainment, remote services,
Internet start-ups, as well as Indipop, fashion, cricket mania, and Indian
novels in English. These have become "global industries" and they pas-

sionately engage Indians everywhere in the world. The hand of family, caste, and the state, which had blocked human possibilities until now, is letting go and Indians are discovering new forms of social and economic organization that make more of their potential.

The twenty-million Indian diaspora consists of Indians spread all over the world and has an enormous appetite for things Indian. Thanks to the global economy and the communications revolution, Indians abroad feel closer to India than ever before. Subhash Chandra of Zee Television realizes this, as we have already seen, and he offers the popular Zee cable channel in many parts of the world. So do a number of spiritual gurus, whose discourses are available to the Indian global community through cable TV and the Internet. Indipop is the fusion of Indian pop music with Western rhythms which first emerged among Indian youth in England and successfully traveled back to India. It has created millionaire pop stars like Daler Mehndi and A. R. Rehman, who routinely travel around the globe entertaining the diaspora. Indipop has also given birth to successful TV channels like VTV, and changed the style and offerings on MTV in India. Many in the diaspora have discovered classical Indian music, which went global a generation ago at the time of the Beatles, with Ravi Shankar and Ali Akbar Khan, but now has become big business; many classical musicians devote a third of their time to concerts overseas.

Indian cinema has always had a market abroad in the Middle East, Russia, and East Asia. Now it is becoming big business in many parts of the world. Cinemas have sprung up which show only Indian films in many cities, and foreign revenue has become important to the film producers of Bombay and Madras. Salman Rushdie and V. S. Naipaul, both products of the diaspora, have made a great impact in literature, and because they write in English, their popularity extends far beyond the diaspora. After the critical and commercial success of Arundhati Roy's *The God of Small Things,* both my editor and literary agent tell me that Indian fiction in English is a "hot property" among publishers in New York and London. Pankaj Mishra, Rohinton Mistry, Jhumpa Lahiri, and others have recently ridden this wave. The last World Cup of cricket in England in 1999 demonstrated to the cricketing world that the center of gravity of this British gentlemanly game had shifted to the subcontinent. The most popular and noisiest matches involved the teams of

India, Pakistan, and Sri Lanka, who were supported feverishly by fans from the diaspora. An English newspaper called it "the invasion of curry." All of these—Indipop, television channels, Indian films, cricket, food, fashion, and even fiction—are, in a sense, the products of the new information economy of India. And the importance of this new economy was a major theme of President Clinton's visit to India in 1999.

One of the consistent themes of the information revolution is that the Internet will diminish the importance of hierarchy of all kinds—political, economic, and social. Since information is power, goes the argument, those at the top of traditional hierarchies—for example, government officials—will not be able to maintain their dominance by controlling access to information. As a result, power will devolve down to the people and liberate millions who either work in or deal with large organizations.

The first signs of this liberation that I have heard come from a friend in Hyderabad, who claims to have bought a plot of land in a nearby village practically through the Internet. Hyderabad is the capital of Andhra Pradesh, whose Net-savvy chief minister has pushed through the computerization of land records in many districts of his state, much against the opposition of his bureaucracy. My friend says that he found the land records, including maps of the plots, on the Net. He downloaded the forms at a cybercafe near his house and within a few months the transaction was completed. To anyone who has ever tried to buy land in India, this is nothing short of revolutionary. Under normal circumstances, the process could take years and entail endless corruption. For the keeper of information is the village revenue official, who controls and manipulates information. Now, the Internet has come and broken this information monopoly of these lower officials; it threatens their incomes and they are not happy.

Most nations think that their bureaucrats are some form of low life. Nowhere do citizens enjoy dealing with their governments; they do it because they have to. But that doesn't mean that the experience has to be dismal. Now there is a new wind beginning to blow through government departments around the world which could take some of this pain away. Within the next five years it may transform not only the way public services are delivered but also the fundamental relationship between governments and citizens. After e-commerce and e-business, the next revolution may be e-government.

Examples abound from around the world. The *Economist* recently reported that the municipality of Phoenix, Arizona, allows its citizens to renew their car registrations, pay traffic fines, replace lost identity cards, and handle many other such transactions online without having to stand in endless queues in a grubby municipal office. The municipality is also happy because it saves $5.00 a transaction—it costs only $1.60 to process an online transaction, versus $6.60 across the counter. In Chile people routinely submit their income tax returns over the Internet, which has increased transparency and drastically reduced the time taken, the number of errors, and litigation with the tax department. Both taxpayers and the revenue department are happier.

The furthest ahead, not surprisingly, is the small, rich, and entrepreneurial civil service of Singapore, which allows citizens to do more transactions online with its government than any other. The purchasing and buying of Singapore's government departments is now on the Web, and cost benefits come through more competitive bidding, easy access to suppliers, time saved by online processing of orders, and lower stocks. Suppliers find tenders and purchase orders on-site, and they can post their catalogues, bid for contracts, submit invoices, and check their payment status over the Net.

The most useful idea for Indian municipalities is GovWorks, a private-sector site that collects local taxes, fines, and utility bills for 3,600 municipalities across America. It is a citizens' site which also provides information on government jobs, tenders, and so on. The city of Valencia in Spain combines government and private-sector activities, where citizens can not only pay local taxes but also pay utility bills, do their banking, check school activities—a sort of interactive version of the yellow pages, and citizens can access it not only through their PCs but also via public kiosks spread around the town.

The ultimate in e-government is, of course, being able to vote online, and the Arizona Democratic primary showed the way as forty thousand people voted via the Web—a 600 percent increase in turnout over the last election. But the election was marred by protesters arguing that the election was stacked against the poor, who did not have computers and who had to stand in line.

Cynics in India say, "Oh, e-government will never work in India. We are too poor and we don't have computers." But they are wrong! There are many experiments afoot in India as well. Chandrababu Naidu, the chief minister of Andhra Pradesh, is clearly the pioneer. A project has also started in seventy villages in Kolhapur and Sangli districts in Maharashtra, where Internet booths have been set up in villages and farmers can check daily market rates of agricultural commodities in Marathi along with data on agricultural schemes, crop technology, and when to spray and plant their crops. It also provides bus and railway timetables, vocational guidance on jobs, applications for ration cards, kerosene and gas burners, and land record extracts with details of land ownership. Sam Pitroda's WorldTel, Reliance, and the Tamil Nadu government are laying 3,000 kilometers of fiber-optic cables to create a Tamil network which will offer school, college, and hospital admission forms, land records, and pension records. If this project is successful, WorldTel will expand it to Gujarat, Karnataka, and West Bengal. In Kerala, all the villages are getting linked online to the district headquarters, allowing citizens to compare the development priorities of their village with those of other villages in the state. E-governance may also not be far behind in India.

TWENTY-THREE

A New Country

When old words die out on the tongue, new melodies break forth from the heart; and where the old tracks are lost, a new country is revealed with its wonders.

—RABINDRANATH TAGORE

A t the beginning of the twenty-first century, I feel as I believe my parents did on 14 August 1947. On that day, Nehru gave voice to their sentiments, saying, "We end today a period of ill fortune and India discovers herself again. The achievement we celebrate today is but a step, an opening of opportunity to the greater triumphs and achievements that await us. Are we brave enough and wise enough to grasp this opportunity and accept the challenge of the future?"

The brutal fact is that India's economic failure has hidden so many of the triumphs and achievements that Nehru dreamed of, and it is further behind, relative to the rest of the world, than it was at Independence. Fortune, however, works in mysterious ways. Just when we were resigned to our fate and had begun to believe that we were a hopeless case, our situation changed. The *Economist,* which has an uncanny way of penetrating these mysteries, agrees. It wrote in August 1997 that India "today stands at a new threshold, with greater triumphs and achievements once more in sight."

Based on modest reforms in the eighties, our growth rate picked up from the historic 3.5 percent "Hindu rate of growth" to 5.6 percent a year for the 1980s decade, and the middle class began to grow vigorously. But this growth rate was unsustainable because it was based on excessive borrowing, which plunged us into an unprecedented financial crisis in 1991. One could argue that we needed the crisis: it forced us to undertake the most comprehensive reforms in our history. The reforms have released entrepreneurial energies the like of which we have never seen before. They have also changed the mind-set of the Indian people.

Meanwhile, the world has also changed to our advantage. The communications revolution has brought the world into our homes and we have come to realize how far we have been left behind. The rapid flows of global capital have made us aware that lack of capital need not be an obstacle and we need not be capital-starved for all time to come—we can supplement our needs with imported capital. The information technology revolution and the Internet have come along and leveled the playing field, bringing with them the promise of solving some of our most intractable problems of development and doing so much quicker than we could ever have imagined.

India, thus, enters the twenty-first century on the brink of the biggest transformation in its history. The changes are more fundamental than anything that the country has seen, and they hold the potential to transform it into an innovative, energetic economy of the twenty-first century. We have realized that our great strength is our people. Our great weakness is our government. Our great hope is the Internet. Perhaps at last we have found the right policies, and there is a growing will to implement them. It is not going to be easy, for the old statist policies have enriched the vested interests, especially the state personnel—elected, appointed, or their hangers-on. But change will take place because too many know too much—through television, cable, and increasingly the Internet. Millions talk to their relatives overseas. They may not be able to articulate economic policies, but they see clearly enough who has power and who does not, and whose is legitimate and whose is not. While the impulse to control will diminish slowly in a country with a vast bureaucracy, the flood of information that will wash every village will force transparency in the government and lead eventually to prosperity.

The memory of the two temple priests who started a software company and were waiting peacefully beside me at the Madras airport with cell phones dangling from their dhotis jostles with that of fourteen-year-old Raju, who hustles between tables during the day and learns computers at night, and has visions of becoming "Bilgay." These are images of the brave new India. They compete with other memories: of Vikas, the proud Dalit in feudal Uttar Pradesh, who would prefer to make steel trunks rather than bribe someone to become a bus conductor; of Ashish Dhawan and Raj Kondur, who used to dream together when they were companions at Harvard Business School and who today run a $65 million venture capital fund with a mission to build a new India by empowering entrepreneurs; of Sushila, who makes shoes for Florsheim and Hogarth and a dowry for herself (she makes them with care because she knows that the secret of success in the global economy is to "exist for your customer"); of austere Narayana Murthy, who not only created India's most successful software company but has become the role model of ethical corporate behavior; of Parvinder Singh, who built India's largest pharmaceutical company, Ranbaxy, based on research, and who, before he died of cancer in 1999, passed on the reins of his company to a professional manager rather than his sons; of Kum Kum, the "flower girl" at the traffic light in Delhi, who stores her flowers in a refrigerator because it gives her competitive advantage. There are, I am sure, a million more such inspirations—they are the "million reformers" of India.

The new India's future depends on them far more than it does on the old politicians of the License Raj. It is ironic that the Congress Party, which liberated us in 1991 with the economic reforms, is now trying to stall them in the name of the poor. The insolent technocrats at the Department of Telecom are so bent on preserving their monopoly—the consumer be damned—that they sabotage every initiative to bring us competition and world-class communications. The unions in the public-sector banks go on strike every time there is talk of reform and privatization. The right wing of the BJP wants to close the economy to foreigners in the name of nationalism. The left-wing intellectuals in the universities continue to fill the minds of our young with postmodern, postcolonial theories of multinational conspiracies and other variants of impotence. The old protectionist businessmen still rely too much on natural resources, cheap labor, and government favors; they do not invest in capabilities to produce differentiated goods and services that create value for demanding global consumers; they continue to be trapped in their old ways and want to compete solely on the basis of price. In the end this tends to suppress wages, and to keep wages low is to compete to see which country can stay poor the longest. These are the many forces of reaction that could stop the million reformers. They fight the reforms at every step but they fight a losing battle.

The theme of this book is how a rich country became poor and will be rich again. We have seen that India had more than a fifth of the world's wealth and a quarter of the world's trade in textiles in 1700. It has seen its share decline to less than 5 percent of world income and less than half a percent of world trade by 1995. It may not have become poorer in absolute terms, but relative to the rest of the world it did get left behind. We have gotten so used to the inequality between the rich and the poor countries that we forget the astonishing truth that living standards around the world were roughly equal in 1750—everyone was poor. Even in 1850 things were not very different. Today the average person in the developed world is ten to twenty times richer. This happened, as we have seen, because of the capitalist breakthrough which began in England between 1760 and 1820, with the invention of the cotton gin and the steam engine, followed by a wave of technological innovations in Europe and North America, with the railroad, the steamship, and steel. Soon after came the advent of electricity and the beginning of the explosion in the middle class and of mass consumption in the West. In the first half of the twentieth century, the automobile became the driving force of growth. The invention of the chip and computers after the Second World War increasingly electronified life, and led to today's information society. With the emergence of Japan and the Far East in the last quarter of the twentieth century, the world became a global economy, abetted by the incredible expansion in world trade, communications, and cross-border capital flows.

This creative dynamic of technology and capitalism has dramatically shortened the time it takes for a nation to develop. It took Britain fifty-eight years to double per capita output (after 1780); the United States took forty-seven years (after 1840); Japan took thirty-three years (after 1880); Indonesia took seventeen years (after 1965); South Korea took thirteen years (after 1970); and China ten years (after 1978). Poor countries should grow faster and eventually catch up if there is political stability. The eight high-performing countries of East and Southeast Asia not only grew rapidly but also showed that they could eliminate poverty. In Indonesia the percentage of people below the poverty line dropped from 58 in 1972 to 17 in 1982; in Malaysia it declined from 37 in 1973 to 14 in 1987; in Thailand from 49 in 1962 to 26 in 1986; in Singapore it dropped from 34 in 1972 to 10 in 1982; in China an estimated 160 million people have emerged from poverty since 1979, when its reforms began. Life expectancy has grown from an average of fifty-six to seventy-one years across the Far East. Although many Far East countries did get into trouble in the late 1990s, they have shown that it can be done. And they have begun to recover.

India did not participate in this great adventure. We grew up believing that our "mixed economy"—the mixture of socialism and the free market that grew out of Jawaharlal Nehru's idealist vision—though not as efficient as capitalism, was better because it cared for the poor. It was better than communism because it preserved political freedoms. But its problem was of performance, not of faith. If it had worked, most of the Third World would be more prosperous today. Indians have learned from painful experience that the state does not work on behalf of the people. More often than not, it works on behalf of itself.

It is no use getting depressed at the thought that we might never have an industrial revolution. It is in the past, and there is no point in trying to re-create the past. We would do better to skip the industrial revolution and leap right into the information age. Our economy is increasingly powered by the knowledge sectors of the economy. Indian newspapers use the shorthand "ICE" to refer to these sectors—"I" for information, "C" for communication, and "E" for entertainment and media. As in America, these employment-intensive sectors have been at the forefront in recent years in creating exports, jobs, and wealth in India. Capital markets have understood this well. From 2 percent of market capitalization three years ago India's ICE companies have grown to account for 34 percent of the National Stock Exchange and are projected to cross 50 percent in 2001.

Many Indians are frightened by the idea of bypassing the industrial revolution. They ask, "But won't we still need clothes to wear, and cement and steel to build our homes?" The answer to such fears is that the value added in the new ICE economy is far higher than in the old economy. Put another way, a little bit of Indian software will be able to

buy a great deal of a generic commodity like steel. In the globalized
open economy governed by the WTO, we will make only what we are
good at—where we have a comparative and competitive advantage—
and we will import the rest. Fortunately, we are competitive in many
areas: we will, for example, make aluminum, cement, and pharmaceuticals, but we will import steel and fertilizers. We are also low-cost producers of at least twelve agricultural commodities. Once we reform our
agriculture and the world opens its agricultural markets, we should be
able to rapidly gain significant world market share. It is also worth
remembering that the new economy is largely a service economy and
creates many more jobs. The old economy is increasingly cutting jobs,
downsizing, mechanizing, and becoming even more capital-intensive.
India, with its vast intellectual capital—two million low-cost English-
speaking graduates—is in an excellent position to provide "knowledge
workers" to the global economy and benefit from the knowledge revolution. With competitive advantages in agriculture and the new knowledge economy, it may in the end be all right to skip the industrial
revolution.

If our bureaucrats and politicians killed our industrial revolution,
won't they do the same with the knowledge revolution? I believe they
will not prevail this time around, for several reasons. One, because our
economic reforms are curtailing their ability to inflict damage. Two,
because high-technology business is virtual and it is difficult to control
what you cannot see. Three, because the Internet creates transparency
and brings transactions into the public domain. It undercuts the bureaucrat's power, which is based on the bartering of knowledge.

Many are rightly skeptical about the new economy's ability to spread
to the masses. They can only see the "digital divide." It is true that
people will benefit only if they have education. It is also true that four
out of ten children in India are illiterate. It is worse for girls and in the
backward northern states, where teachers are often absent, schools lack
the basic facilities, children are not motivated and they drop out. But
there is a hopeful sign: there is a newfound thirst and enormous pressure
from below for education. In the past six years, literacy has risen from 52
to 62 percent. This is a huge improvement, and if this trend continues,
universal literacy is not far behind—despite the politicians. The happiest
news is from the most backward states, where growth has been the high-

est; and among girls, literacy has grown faster than among boys. These figures come from a smaller sample and will hopefully be confirmed in 2001. In some states responsibility for education is beginning to shift to the elected village panchayat councils, and this has brought more accountability. Madhya Pradesh and Andhra Pradesh are leading the charge, and their citizens have returned the favor by reelecting their leaders. So perhaps there is hope. If there is one thing that could secure our future, it is vigorous attention to building human capabilities.

Nature gave India the gift of immense human potential. In today's global economy a country's status is determined by the share of brains that it uses and the share of brands that it commands. When the government liberated the Internet from the monopoly of the state-owned VSNL, it harnessed millions of young Indians' minds. If it opened the trade in agriculture, it would harness millions of farmhands. The most effective way to unleash the power of human capital is through education. The ten most important Indians are the education ministers of the ten largest states; the next ten are the secretaries to these ministers. Alas, they do not realize their historic mission. The United States, the European Union, and East Asia are all embarked on massive plans to accelerate the development of their human capital, and we are in a race. We may, in fact, have some advantages over our competitors. For every student China sends to the university, India sends six. But these advantages will be quickly dissipated unless we act.

A truer measure of India's failure is not its poverty but its inability to create a middle class. India's middle class was less than 10 percent of the population in 1984–85, according to the National Council of Applied Economic Research (NCAER). Since then it has more than tripled but is still less than 20 percent. If the economy grows 7 percent over the foreseeable future and the population 1.5 percent, if the literacy rate keeps rising, and if we assume the NCAER's historical middle-class growth rate of the past fifteen years, then half of India will turn middle class between 2020 and 2040. To be sure, there will be huge disparities. Much of west and south India will turn middle class by 2020, but the backward states like Bihar, Uttar Pradesh, and Orissa won't get there before 2040. Disparities are obviously bad, but vigorous migration helps to ameliorate them and creates pressure on the backward states to catch up. At these milestones, based on the same growth assumptions, India's individual purchasing power will climb to $5,653 in 2020 (from $2,149 in 1999) and $16,500 in 2040. (These projections are based on current purchase power parity [PPP] with the U.S. dollar—whereas, of course, PPP index changes as income rises; the projections are indicative for our purposes of what is to come.) When half the population in society is middle class, its politics will change, its worldview will be different, its poor will be fewer, and society will have greater means to look after them. Thus, to focus on the middle class is to focus on prosperity, unlike in the past, when our focus has been on redistributing poverty. This does not mean that one is callous. On the contrary, the whole purpose of the enterprise is to lift the poor—and lift them into the middle class.

There are pessimists, however. Like Malthus, they moan about India's rising population. Like Ricardo, they worry about the ability of our land to feed the people. The fact is that Malthus and Ricardo have been proven wrong. India's situation illustrates this. In the spring of 2000, its population crossed a billion when the nation's warehouses were bulging with grain and the main concern of the agriculture ministry was how to dispose of this mountain of grain without incurring a loss. Admittedly nutrition levels are still low, but people no longer worry about India's food problem; as we observed, the last famine occurred during the last days of the British Raj in 1942–43. Marx understood far better than Malthus, Ricardo, or our current pessimists that growth is natural in a market economy and there is a positive link between technological advance and wealth. Although the old Malthusian perspective is no longer relevant, it is important to remember that there are wide diversities in India's population growth rate, which is falling very rapidly in some regions and very slowly in others. Studies show that the difference between the two trends is explained largely by female literacy and female job opportunities. Thus, gender equity and women's empowerment seem to be at the heart of the matter.

Critics also ask if it is actually wise for countries like India and China, possessing half a billion peasants each, to attempt to mimic the high-tech revolution emerging from the very different socioeconomic structures of California. One says, "Even a hundred Bangalores would not solve India's poverty." Another asks, "Given their social structures, can India or China take the strain of creating world-competitive high-tech enclaves (presumably enjoying the material benefits that would flow from their global success) in the midst of hundreds of millions of their impoverished countrymen? Enhanced technology is supposed to have a 'trickle-down' effect, but does that work when the ratio of highly skilled to unskilled in the population is so disproportionately low? Might not the resources allocated to catching up with the developed world's computer, aerospace, and communications technology and the rest be more usefully diverted into appropriate technologies to expand productivity in the village?"

These were the same doubts that people had in the 1960s when they wondered if it was appropriate for India and China to mimic the industrial path of the West. To ask such a question implies that India and China should not even attempt to catch up. That is a politically unacceptable choice. Even if it were feasible, the simple answer to these doubts is that we must push forward at all levels—advanced, intermediate, elementary, on the farm, in the factory, and on the Internet.

Words can be treacherous, and there is no expression in the English language more deceiving than "trickle down." It suggests that as an economy grows, the rich get richer, and then as a few crumbs fall off the table, the poor also become better off. The expression originated in the fifties, in the work of the influential Harvard economist Simon Kuznets, who concluded that inequality tends to increase during the early stages of development and then decrease later on. Serious economists no longer accept this hypothesis, but the power of popular expressions is such that we continue to remain victims of dead ideas. The latest evidence, which thoroughly demolishes the Kuznets hypothesis, comes from the World Bank's Development Research Group. An empirical study of eighty countries over forty years, entitled "Growth Is Good for the Poor," shows that the income of the poor rises one-for-one with overall growth—that is, the income of the poorest fifth of the population rises at the same time and at the same rate as everyone else's. Thus, simple economic growth does more to alleviate poverty than all the subsidies and poverty programs.

At the beginning of the twenty-first century, political and economic institutions have converged around the world in a most remarkable way. Deep ideological cleavages divided the world in the last century; monarchy, communism, fascism, and liberal democracy bitterly competed for political supremacy. Centralized planning, corporatism, free markets, and protectionism competed for economic supremacy. Today, virtually all countries have embraced or are trying to adopt liberal institutions of democracy and market-oriented institutions of capitalism as they integrate themselves into the global economy and the global division of labor. For fifty years India has been a political democracy, which has given voice to the lower castes through the ballot box and shown the world how political democracy can translate into social democracy. It has now become one of the fastest-growing economies in the world, and it wants to disseminate information technology tools to the common people. The government's goal of "IT for All by 2008" reflects an understanding that the spread of information technology is an opportunity to overcome historical disabilities and compress the time needed to reach comprehensive development goals. If India succeeds in its path of liberal market-based democracy—as it has every right to expect—it will shed new light on the future of liberalism in the world.

One of the great achievements of modern times is a liberal conception of humanity: the view that there are universal and inalienable human rights, and that powers of reason can honor these rights and eradicate poverty and social distress. The problem with liberalism, however, is that in search of freedom and social justice, liberals either get impatient or have to exert power through vast bureaucracies. This leads to experiments of political and social engineering. Nehruvian socialism was one such experiment, carried out in a relatively benign manner. Stalinism was the ruthless extreme, at the other end of the scale. Lionel Trilling, the American literary critic, feared that liberals in power always ran the risk of becoming illiberal. Nehru, the liberal, did not realize that socialism would lead to statism and seriously compromise the very freedom that he had fought so hard to win, suppressing the innovative energies of his people. Fortunately, we seem to have learned from our mistakes and there is again a liberal consensus in the world.

The consensus on capitalism and democracy does not mean, of course, that we have solved our material or social problems. Far from it. It merely means that in this postindustrial age we have given up the path of social engineering or total solutions. We have given up the hope that the government can solve our problems. It is still too early to say whether this consensus will deliver human progress for all. That is why India's is such an important test of liberalism.

Even a superficial reading of twentieth-century history teaches that it is dangerous to be too enthusiastic about any political, social, or economic system. Communism, fascism, and socialism have all done incalculable harm. So has nationalism of various enthusiastic varieties. Too much passion about one's ideals also encourages a moral self-righteousness, which is not pleasing to behold. For this reason E. M. Forster gave only "two cheers to democracy," reserving the full three for "love, the beloved republic," as he called it. Forster wisely believed that the satisfactions of private life are inherently superior to those provided by any political order.

There is a powerful consolation that India affords to the world at all times, which is even more precious today. The relentless onslaught of globalization makes people everywhere deeply uneasy. The prospect of living in a homogenized and faceless world is not a pleasant one. No one particularly likes the idea of the global culture. The global media ensures that we increasingly watch the same banal shows, hear the same capsuled news, listen to the same silly advertising slogans, and are moved by the same collective emotions. Regimentation under a mass consumer society of worldwide dimensions is a stifling prospect. And for what—so that we may have more and more consumer goods and material possessions? We are lost in a maze of large and anonymous organizations. We are filled with a profound sense of being alone in this unheroic world, with little control over our destinies. At other times we react to our alienated existence with tedium and boredom. These feelings of loneliness and alienation are the most acute in the most successful and competitive economies—the United States, Japan, Germany, and South Korea.

To this lonely and banal world India offers a spiritual guide to the art of living. Despite the spread of the industrial society in the past fifty years, spiritual practice and family bonds continue to be nurtured in Indian life. This is not confined to the uneducated masses. Some of the most successful and rational people in all professions continue to turn to the spiritual. They do so for a number of reasons—as a solace against the madness and emptiness of contemporary life, as a true search for the meaning of life, as a matter of observing tradition, as a turning away from failure in the material world. Whatever the reason, religion and spirituality continue to have a powerful hold on the Indian psyche in all walks of life.

In the past fifty years more and more spiritual movements from India have been exported to the West—a few of them were by charlatan gurus, but the vast majority of them provided attractive and established spiritual solutions to the art of living. This explains the persistent hold of India as a destination for young people in the West (and increasingly the East) seeking an alternative way to live their lives. Neither is this a new fad. The tendency goes back two thousand years. Fa Hien and Huen Tsang, two Chinese travelers, came looking for Buddhist wisdom. Alberuni, an Islamic scholar who was more interested in the rational achievements of the Hindus in mathematics and astronomy, was attracted by Vedanta. Later, after the West discovered India, great nineteenth-century intellectuals like Goethe, Schopenhauer, and Nietzsche were influenced by Indian philosophy. In more recent times, Theosophists, Ramakrishna Missions, Transcendental Meditation, and numerous spiritual and yoga organizations have introduced the world to the "Indian way of life."

This "Indian way of life" presents an appealing alternative to a developed postindustrial liberal society that has solved its material problems. It may also be attractive to those individuals who cannot cope with the "anxiety of liberalism." Indians, who have been economically slower, are in a better position to defend themselves against the challenges of globalization. Having said that, this "Indian way of life" is no substitute or excuse for a hardheaded, rational approach to solving our problems of poverty, illiteracy, and disease.

The history of the twentieth century has left the West deeply pessimistic. This is in contrast to its optimism in the nineteenth century, which was based on two beliefs: one, modern science would improve human life and conquer disease and poverty; two, democracy would rapidly spread across the world and vanquish tyranny. The futile 1914–18 war, followed by the genocides in Hitler's Germany, Stalin's Russia, Mao's China, and Cambodia, totally undermined its confidence. India's experience of the twentieth century was different. We won our freedom from colonial rule and followed it up by building a healthy, vibrant democracy and improving the situation of the lower castes. Economically, we may not have performed as well as the Far East nations, but we did conquer famines and end economic stagnation, and we have now begun to grow rapidly. The old Congress-dominated centralized Raj is as completely in the past as the British Raj. The new India is increasingly one of competition and decentralization. And now, thanks to our intellectual capital and the opportunities opened by technology and globalization, we face the very real prospect of conquering the pervasive poverty that has characterized the lives of the majority of the people. We have good reasons to expect that the lives of the majority of Indians in the twenty-first century will be freer and more prosperous than their parents' and grandparents' lives. Never before in recorded history have so many people been in a position to rise so quickly.

AFTERWORD

There's a tide in the affairs of men
which taken at the flood, leads on
to fortune; omitted, all the voyage of
their life is bound in shallows and in miseries.

—WILLIAM SHAKESPEARE,
JULIUS CAESAR

Ever since *India Unbound* appeared in 2000, some kind reader or another has unfailingly sent me an email asking me to write a sequel or an update. Each time I have resisted the idea because I think that the basic thesis of the book remains robust. If anything, India has surpassed my expectations. I did not think that India's democracy would allow its economy to grow much beyond 7 percent a year. But over the last four years—from 2002–2006—it has been growing at 8 percent plus, and it is now one of the world's strongest.

It is becoming increasingly possible to believe that India's economic problem will be solved during the first half of the twenty-first century. The problem, an age-old worry, is that there is not enough to go around. Some parts of Asia are already affluent and others are on the same path to prosperity. China is well on its way. India too, based on current trends, should reach a level of prosperity where, for the first time in history, Indians will emerge from a struggle against want into an age when the large majority will be at ease. More recently, population growth has begun to slow, and by 1998 it was down to 1.7 percent compared to its historic 2.2 percent growth rate. More than 200 million Indians have risen out of destitution in the past twenty-five years. Prosperity will, of course, not spread simultaneously across the map.

Some regions will get there before others—for example, Gujarat will be twenty years ahead of Bihar, but Bihar too will catch up (incredible as it may seem).

If our economy continues to grow at this rate for the next two to three decades—and there is no reason why it should not—then large parts of India should turn middle class in the first quarter of the century. At that point poverty will not vanish, but the poor will come down to a manageable level, and the politics of the country will also change. By 2025, India will see its share of world product rise from 6 to 13 percent, making it the third-largest economy in the world. By then, China will be the largest, and together India and China will account for 39 percent share of global output, which is about equal to the present share of United States and Europe combined. It is also almost what India and China's output was in 1750. One of the reasons behind this momentous shift in economic power is that countries like India have a large number of the world's children under fifteen. Europe, Japan and USSR will be left behind because of their sharp decline in fertility. The United States will hold on to its present 22 percent share of world output, because immigration will mitigate the declining population trend. All of this goes against the old wisdom that poor developing countries with ever-expanding populations are doomed to perpetual poverty.

The notable thing about India's rise is not that it is new—it has been among the best performing economies for a quarter century—but that its path is unique. Rather than adopting the classic Asian strategy—exporting labour-intensive, low-priced manufactured goods to the West—India has relied on its domestic market more than exports, consumption more than investment, services more than industry, and high-tech rather than low-skill manufacturing. This approach has meant that the Indian economy has been mostly insulated from global downturns, showing a lack of volatility that is as impressive as the rate of its expansion. The consumption-driven model—consumption accounts for 64 percent of India's GDP, compared to 44 percent of China's—is also more people-friendly than other development strategies. As a result, inequality has increased much less in India than in other developing nations. (Its Gini coefficient, a measure of income inequality, is 33, compared to 41 for the United States, 45 for China, and 59 for Brazil.) Moreover, 30–40 percent of its GDP growth is due to rising total factor productivity—a true sign of an economy's health and progress—rather than to increases in capital or labour.

What is even more remarkable is that rather than rising with the help of the state, India is in many ways rising despite the state. The entrepreneur is clearly at the centre of India's success story. India now boasts highly competitive private companies, a booming stock market, and a modern, well-disciplined financial sector. And since 1991 especially, the Indian state has been gradually moving out of the way—not graciously, but kicked and dragged into implementing economic reforms. It has started to lower trade barriers and tax rates, break state monopolies, unshackle industry, encourage competition, and open up to the rest of the world. The pace has been slow, but the reforms are starting to add up.

India is now poised at a great moment in its history. Rapid growth should continue—and even accelerate. But India cannot take this for granted. Public debt is high, which discourages investment in needed infrastructure. Overly strict labour laws, though they cover only 10 percent of the workforce, have the perverse effect of discouraging employers from hiring new workers. The public sector, although much smaller than China's, is still too large and inefficient, a major drag on growth and employment and a burden for consumers. And although India is successfully generating high-end, capital- and knowledge-intensive manufacturing, it has failed to create a broad-based, labour-intensive industrial revolution—meaning that gains in employment have not been commensurate with overall economic growth. Its rural population, meanwhile, suffers from state-induced production and distribution distortions that result in farmers getting only 20–30 percent of the retail price of fruits and vegetables (versus 40–50 percent in developed countries).

India can take advantage of this moment and remove the remaining obstacles that have prevented it from realizing its full potential. Or it can continue smugly along, confident that it will get there eventually—but twenty years late. Already there are signs of complacency, and the most difficult reforms are not yet done.

India has improved its competitiveness considerably since I wrote this book. There has been a telecommunications revolution, interest rates have come down, capital is plentiful (although risk-averse managers of state-owned banks still refuse to lend to small entrepreneurs), highways and ports have improved, and real-estate markets are becoming transparent. More than a hundred Indian companies have a market capitalization of over a billion dollars, and some of these are likely to become competitive global brands soon. Foreigners have invested in over a thousand Indian companies via the stock market. Three hundred and ninety out of 500 Fortune companies have outsourced to India and 125 out of the 500 Fortune companies now have Research and Development bases in India—a testament to its human capital. And high technology manufacturing has taken off. All these changes have disciplined the banking sector. Bad loans are now less than 2 percent of all loans (compared to 20 percent in China).

For now, growth is being driven by services and domestic consumption. Consumption accounts for 64 percent of India's GDP, compared to 58 percent for Europe, 55 percent for Japan, and 44 percent for China. That consumption might be a virtue embarrasses many Indians, with their streak of asceticism, but, as the economist Stephen Roach of Morgan Stanley puts it, "India's consumption-led approach to growth may be better balanced than the resource-mobilization model of China."

The contrast between India's entrepreneur-driven growth and China's state-cantered model is stark. China's success is largely based on exports by state enterprises or foreign companies. Beijing remains highly suspicious of entrepreneurs. Only 10 percent of credit goes to the private sector in China, even though it employs 40 percent of the Chinese workforce; in India, entrepreneurs get more than 80 percent of all loans. Whereas Jet Airways has become the undisputed leader of India's skies, China's first private airline, Okay, started flying only in February 2005.

What has been peculiar about India's development so far is that high growth has not been accompanied by a labour-intensive industrial revolution that could transform the lives of the tens of millions of Indians still trapped in rural poverty. We, in India, watch mesmerized as China seems to create an endless flow of low-end manufacturing jobs by exporting goods such as toys and clothes and as their better-educated compatriots succeed in exporting knowledge services to the rest of the world. Observing these two phenomena, some Indians ask insistently if India is going to skip the industrial revolution altogether, jumping straight from an agricultural economy to a service economy. Not surprisingly, the question frightens us. The rest of the world evolved from agriculture to industry to services. India appears to have a weak middle step. Services now account for more than half of India's GDP, 22 percent is from agriculture, and industry's share is only 27 percent (versus 46 percent in China). And within industry, India's strength is high-tech, high-skilled manufacturing.

Even the most fervent advocates of service-based growth do not question the desirability of creating more manufacturing jobs. That includes me. The failure to achieve a broad industrial transformation stems, in part, from bad policies. Perhaps the most egregious one was to "reserve" around 800 industries for small companies (SSI) who eventually were unable to compete against the large firms of competitor nations. Organized large firms were barred from making products like pencils, boot polish, candles, shoes, garments, and toys—all the products that helped East Asia create millions of jobs. Even since 1991, the government in power has been afraid to touch this "SSI holy cow" out of fear of a powerful SSI lobby. But this lobby has turned out to be mostly a phantom—little more than the bureaucrats who kept scaring politicians by warning of a backlash. The government has been pruning the list of protected industries incrementally in the past five years with no adverse reaction.

In the short term, the best way for India to improve the lot of the rural poor might lie in a second green revolution. Unlike manufacturing, India has a competitive advantage in agriculture, with plenty of arable land, sunshine, water and very low productivity. In order to achieve such a change, however, India will need to shift its mindset from peasant farming to agribusiness and encourage private capital to move from urban to rural areas. It will need to lift onerous distribution controls, permit "contract farming", allow large retailers to contract directly with farmers, invest in irrigation and slowly permit consolidation of hugely fragmented holdings.

Indian entrepreneurs still face a range of obstacles, many of them the result of lingering bad policies. Electric power is less reliable and more expensive than in competitor nations. Checkpoints keep trucks waiting for hours. Taxes and import duties have come down, but the cascading effect of indirect taxes will burden Indian manufacturers until a uniform Goods and Services tax is a reality. Stringent labour laws continue to deter entrepreneurs from hiring workers. The "License Raj" may be gone, but an "Inspector Raj" is alive and well; the "midnight knock" from an excise, customs, labour, or factory inspector still haunts the smaller entrepreneur. Some of these problems will hopefully diminish with the coming of new economic zones, which promise a reduced regulatory burden. Meanwhile, manufacturing too has begun to finally take off. Perhaps, after a decade, the distinction between China as the "world's workshop" and India as the world's "back office" will slowly fade as India's manufacturing and China's services catch up.

It is an amazing spectacle to see prosperity beginning to spread alongside the most appalling governance in today's India. In the midst of a booming private economy, Indians despair over the simplest public goods. It used to be the other way around. During India's socialist days

Indians worried about economic growth but they were proud of their world-class judiciary, bureaucracy and police force. Now, the old centralized bureaucratic Indian state is in steady decline. Where it is desperately needed—in providing basic education, health and drinking water—it has performed appallingly. Where it is not needed, it was long hyperactive in over-regulating private enterprise, stifling India's prosperity for four decades after Independence.

Labour laws, for example, still make it almost impossible to lay-off a worker—as the infamous case of Uttam Nakate illustrates. In early 1984, Nakate was found at 11.40 AM, sleeping soundly on the floor of the factory in Pune where he worked. That time, his employer let him off with a warning. But it happened again and again. On the fourth occasion, the factory began disciplinary proceedings against him, and after five months of hearings, he was found guilty and sacked. But then Nakate went to a labour court in Maharashtra and pleaded that he was a victim of an unfair trade practice. The court agreed, and forced the factory to take him back and pay him 50 percent of back wages. Only 17 years later, after appeals to the Bombay High Court and the Supreme Court, did the factory finally win the right to fire an employee who had repeatedly been caught sleeping on the job.

Aside from the problem of the speed of justice, Nakate's case dramatized to Indians that such labour laws actually reduce employment by making employers afraid to hire workers in the first place. These rules thus protect existing unionized workers—sometimes referred to as the "labour aristocracy"—at the expense of everyone else. At this point, the "labour aristocracy" comprises only 10 percent of the Indian workforce.

No single institution has disappointed Indians more than their bureaucracy. In the 1950s, Indians bought the cruel myth of Nehru's "steel frame", supposedly a means of guaranteeing stability and continuity after the British Raj. Indians also accepted that a powerful civil service was needed to keep a diverse country together and administer the vast regulatory framework of Nehru's "mixed economy". But in the holy name of socialism, the Indian bureaucracy created thousands of controls and stifled enterprise for forty years. India may have had some excellent civil servants, but none really understood business—even though they had the power to ruin it.

Today, Indians believe that their bureaucracy has become a prime obstacle to development, blocking instead of shepherding economic reforms. They think of bureaucrats as self-serving, obstructive and corrupt, protected by labour laws and lifetime contracts that render them completely unaccountable. To be sure, there are examples of good performance—the building of the Delhi Metro or the quickly expanding national highway system—but these only underscore how much most of the bureaucracy fails. To make matters worse, the term of the civil servant in a particular job before he or she is transferred at the whim of the political boss has been getting shorter. Prime Minister Manmohan Singh has instituted a new appraisal system for the top bureaucracy, but it has not done much.

The Indian bureaucracy is a haven of mental power. It still attracts many of the brightest students in the country, admitted on the basis of a difficult exam. But even with very high IQs, they fail as managers. One of the reasons is the perverse incentive system; another is poor training in implementation. The Delhi Metro is making great strides not because of its brilliant conception but because its head sets clear, measurable goals, monitors day-to-day progress, and persistently removes obstacles. Most Indian politicians and civil servants, in contrast, fail to plan well, monitor, or follow through on projects. India's performance failures have more to do with poor execution than with ideology or strategy.

The government's most damaging failure is in public education. Consider one particularly telling statistic. According to a study by Harvard University's Michael Kremer and others, one out of four teachers in a government elementary school is absent, and one out of two present is not teaching. Even as the famed Indian Institutes of Technology become a global brand name, less than half the children in fourth-level classes in Mumbai and Vadodra can do first-level math. It's got so bad that even the poor have begun to pull their kids out of government schools and enrol them in private schools, which charge $1 to $3 a month in fees and which are spreading rapidly in slums and villages across India. (Private schools in India range from expensive boarding schools for the elite to low-end teaching shops in markets.) Although teacher salaries are on average considerably lower in private schools, their students perform much better. A national study led by Pratham, a non-governmental organization, found in 2006 that even in small villages, 16 percent of children are now in private primary schools and scored 10 percent higher on verbal and math exams than their peers in government schools.

India's education establishment, horrified by this exodus out of the public education system, trashes these "private schools" and wants to close them down. NIIT, a private company with 4000 "learning centres" has trained 4 million students and helped fuel India's IT revolution in the 1990s, but it has not been accredited by the government. Ironically, legislators finally acknowledged the state's failure to deliver education a few months ago when they pushed through parliament a law making it mandatory for private schools to reserve seats for backward castes. As with so much about India's success story, Indians are finding solutions to their problems without waiting for the government.

The same dismal story is being repeated in health and water services, which are also de facto privatized. India's share of private spending in health is double that of the United States. Private tube wells account for nearly all new irrigation capacity in the country. In a city like Delhi, with greater endowment of water than most cities of the world, citizens cope with irregular supply by privately investing more than half the total cost of water supply. At government health centres, meanwhile, 40 percent of doctors and a third of nurses are absent at any given time. According to a study by J. Das and J. Hammer, there is a 50 percent chance of a doctor at such a centre recommending a positively harmful therapy.

How does one explain the discrepancy between the government's supposed commitment to universal elementary education, health and drinking water and the fact that more and more people are embracing private solutions? One answer is that the Indian establishment is caught in a time warp, clinging to the belief that the state and the civil service are the only way to meet peoples' needs. What they did not anticipate was that politicians in India's democracy would "capture" the bureaucracy and use the system to create jobs and revenue for friends and supporters. The Indian state no longer generates public goods but private benefits for those who control it. Consequently, the Indian state has become so "riddled with perverse incentives...that accountability is almost impossible", says the political scientist Pratap Bhanu Mehta. In a recent study of India's public services, S. Paul, the activist, concludes that "the quality of governance is appalling".

There are many sensible steps for improving governance. Focusing on outcomes rather than internal procedures would help, as would delegating responsibility to service providers. But more important is for the Indian establishment to jettison its faith in, as the political scientist James Scott puts it, "bureaucratic high modernism" and recognize that the government's job is to govern rather than to run everything. Government may have to finance primary services such as health and education, but the provider must be accountable to the citizen as though to a customer (and not to his or her boss in the bureaucratic hierarchy). None of the solutions being debated in India will bring accountability without this change in mindset.

~~~~

S hashi Kumar is twenty-nine years old and comes from a tiny village in Bihar, India's most backward and feudal state. His grandfather was a low-caste sharecropper in good times and a day labourer in bad ones. His family was so poor that they did not eat some nights. But Shashi's father somehow managed to get a job in a transport company in Darbhanga, and his mother began to teach in a private school, where Shashi was educated at no cost under her watchful eye. Determined that her son should escape the indignities of Bihar, she tutored him at night, got him into a college, and when he finished, gave him a railway ticket for Delhi.

Shashi is now a junior executive in an outsourced back office in Gurgaon with customers in America. He lives in a nice flat, which he bought last year with a mortgage, drives an Indica car, and sends his daughter to a good school. He is an average, affable young Indian, and like so many of his kind he has a sense of life's possibilities. Prior to 1991, possibilities only existed for those with a government job. If you got an education and did not get into the government, you faced a nightmare that was called "educated unemployment". But now, Shashi says, anyone with education, computer skills and some English can make it.

But in the long run, the state cannot merely withdraw. Markets do not work in a vacuum. They need a network of regulations and institutions; they need umpires to settle disputes. These institutions do not just spring up; they take time to develop. The Indian state's greatest achievements lie in the non-economic sphere. It has held the world's most diverse country together in relative peace for fifty-seven years. It has put a modern institutional framework in place. It has held free and fair elections without interruption. Of 3.5 million village legislators, 1.2 million are women. These are proud achievements for an often bungling state with disastrous implementation skills and a terrible record at day-to-day governance.

Moreover, some of the most important post-1991 reforms have been successful because of the regulatory institutions established by the state. Even though the reforms have been slow, imperfect and incomplete, they have been consistent and in one direction. And it takes courage, frankly, to give up power, as the Indian state has done for the past fifteen years. The stubborn persistence of democracy is itself one of the Indian state's proudest achievements. Time and again, Indian democracy has shown itself resilient and enduring—giving lie to the old prejudice that if people live in poverty they are incapable of the kind of self-discipline and sobriety that makes for effective self-government. To be sure, it is an infuriating democracy, plagued by poor governance and fragile institutions that have failed to deliver basic public goods. But India's economic success has been all the more remarkable for coming under such a democracy.

Still, the poor state of governance reminds Indians of how far they are from being a truly great nation. That will happen only when every Indian has access to a good school, a working health clinic and clean drinking water. Fortunately, half of India's population is below twenty-five. Based on the current economic growth trends, the economy should be able to absorb an increasing number into the labour force. Nor does India have to worry about the problems of an ageing population; this translates into what economists call a "demographic dividend", which will help India to reach a level of prosperity at which, for the first time in its history, a majority of its citizens will not have to worry about basic needs. Yet India cannot afford to take its "golden age of growth" for granted. To India's entire political class, Brutus's famous warning in *Julius Caesar* at the top of this afterword should be a timely warning: that we stand at a crucial moment in our history when the stars appear to be on our side. If we do not seize the moment and improve our governance and accelerate the reforms, then history will not forgive us.

Two reports appeared in my newspaper in March 2005 and they left me bewildered. The first said that the Karnataka government has still not decided to rescind its ban on English in primary schools despite huge popular pressure from parents. In the second report, a Karnataka minister, after a busy visit to China, announced, "Members of the Standing Committee of the Jiangsu Provincial People's Congress wanted the help of the Karnataka government in teaching English in its primary schools." This was in pursuit of its objective to make every Chinese literate in English by the 2008 Olympics. The contrast between the ambivalence of India and the certainty of China is always instructive.

It does seem bizarre that the state whose capital is Bangalore, the symbol of India's success in the global economy, and derives its competitive advantage from its mastery of the English language should remain hostage to the deep insecurities of its vernacular chauvinists. This is after more than fifteen years when it first banned English from its primary schools in the late 1980s. Meanwhile, Bengal and Gujarat have realized their mistake and have gone back to teaching English after they discovered they had created an unemployable generation.

I thought this debate was over, and English had won. But now I realize that many states, including Kerala and Karnataka, are still in a state of paralytic inaction, interminably discussing the language of school instruction. In a world where a quarter of the people already know the world language and where experts predict another half will be English literates within a generation, it is painful to see Indians, who are the envy of many countries for their English skills, being stopped in their tracks by vernacular Stalinists with their bogus arguments, telling parents, "You don't know what's good for your children. We do."

As for the Chinese, I try not to feel envious or fearful. While I am confident they will win plenty of medals at the next Olympics, I don't think learning English will be quite as easy. I cannot help but admire their ambition, but I console myself with the thought that India has been spared their earlier ambitions at social engineering, the most prominent being the Cultural Revolution. A Chinese engineer, who is in India to improve his software and English skills, tells me coincidentally that China's ambitions with regard to English are not only connected with their superpower ambitions but are also driven by envy over India's facility with English.

I sometimes wonder what language we Indians will be speaking fifty years from now.

If we look beyond the horizon of current events we will see, I think, two trends that are likely to determine our linguistic future. One is the rapid spread of English across India, including the aspiring lower middle classes; the second is the unprecedented popularity of Hindi, even in the South, thanks to Hindi movies.

At the intersection of these two trends is the fashionable collision of the two languages. It is called Hinglish, but should in fact be called Inglish because it is increasingly pan-India's street language. Mixing English with our mother tongues has been going on for generations, but what is different this time around is that Inglish has become both the aspirational language of the lower and middle classes and the fashionable language of drawing rooms of the upper and upper-middle classes. Similar attempts in the past were downmarket and contemptuously put down by snobbish brown sahibs. But this time Inglish is the stylish language of Bollywood, of FM radio and of national advertising. Advertisers, in particular, have been surprised by the terrific resonance of slogans such as, "Life ho to aisi", "Josh machine" and "Dil mange more".

Unlike my generation, today's young are more relaxed about English and think it a skill, like learning Windows. No longer does it fly the British or American flags, except in the insecure minds of the Left or the RSS. Bollywood, television, advertising, cricket—indeed, all our mass culture is conspiring to take English to the bazaar. Gone too is the ranting against English by swadeshi intellectuals. Every Indian mother knows that English is the passport to her child's future—to a job, to entry into the middle class—and this is why English-medium schools are mushrooming in city slums and villages across the country, and English has quietly become an Indian language fifty years after the British left our shores. David Dalby, who measures these things in *Linguasphere*, predicts that by 2010 India will have the largest number of English speakers in the world. The date may be optimistic, but it will happen soon, and one of the cheerful things happening in India is the quiet democratizing of English.

In Inglish, perhaps for the first time in our history, we may have found a language common to the masses and the classes, acceptable to the South and North. We are used to thinking of India in dualisms— upper vs. lower caste, urban vs. rural, India vs. Bharat—but the saddest divide, I think, is between those who know English and those "who are shut out" (in the phrase of my deaf friend Ursula Mistry in Mumbai, who deeply feels the tragedy of those who can't participate). The exciting thing about Inglish is that it may be able to unite the people of India in the same way as cricket. We may thus be at a historic moment. One day, I expect, we will also find Inglish's Mark Twain, the American writer who liberated Americans to write as they thought. Salman Rushdie gave Indians permission to write in English, but *Midnight's Children* is not written in Inglish, alas! And this is not surprising, for the young Indian mind was not decolonized until the reforms in the 1990s.

What exactly is Inglish is not easy to define, and needs empirical research. Is its base English or our vernacular bhashas? If its foundation is bhasha, then it is similar to Franglais, the fashionable concoction of mostly French with English words thrown in that drives purists mad. Or is its support English, with an overlay of bhasha? I think it is both. For the upwardly mobile lower-middle class, it is bhasha mixed with some English words, such as what my newsboy speaks: "Main aaj busy hoon, kal bill doonga definitely." For the classes, on the other hand, the base is definitely English, as in: "Hungry kya?"

In contrast to this vibrant new language, the old "Indian English" of our headlines is an anachronism: "sleuth nabs man", "miscreants abscond", and "eve-teasers get away". In the ultimate put down, Professor Harish Trivedi of Delhi University contemptuously says, "Indian English? It is merely incorrect English." Inglish has parallels with Urdu, which became a naturalized subcontinental language and flourished mainly after the decline of Muslim rule. Originally the camp argot of the country's Muslim conquerors, Urdu was forged from a combination of the conqueror's imported Farsi and local bhashas. As Urdu was transported to the Deccan, so is Inglish riding on the coat tails of Bollywood across India.

So, is Inglish our "conquest of English", to use Salman Rushdie's famous words? Or is it our journey to "conquer the world", in the words of Professor David Crystal, the author of the *Cambridge Encyclopaedia of the English Language*, who predicts that Indian English will become the most widely spoken variant of English based on India's likely economic success in the twenty-first century and the sheer size of its population. "If 100 million Indians pronounce an English word in a certain way," he says, "this is more than Britain's population—so, it's the only way to pronounce it." If British English was the world language at the end of the nineteenth century, after a century of British imperialism, and American English is the world language today after the American twentieth century, then the language of the twenty-first century might well be Inglish or at least an English that is heavily influenced by India (and China).

What will happen to our mother tongues? This is the insecurity behind the ancient, paralysing debate over teaching English in primary schools. The vernacular chauvinists believe that our languages and cultures will die under the mesmerizing dominance of the power language, English. They point to Gaelic and Welsh, which were eradicated by English. Vernacularists think we have made a pact with the devil: while fluency in English gives us a competitive advantage, losing our mother tongue impoverishes our personality. We have to teach English early, for unless you acquire the nuances before the age of ten, you are disadvantaged. But then I have more confidence in our own languages. When Indians embrace English in order to win in the global market place, they don't turn their back on their mother tongue. While English empowers us, our mother tongue continues to give us identity. I agree with Ananthamurthy that in our big cities, we retain our "home tongues", while using a "street tongue" and working in the "power tongue".

In a wonderful essay, "Cosmopolitan and Vernacular in History", Sheldon Pollock, a professor of Sanskrit at Columbia University, says that our vernaculars were also "created" and are not primordial, as vernacular nationalists would like to believe. The vernacularization of Sanskrit began in the ninth century as Kannada and Telugu became the languages of literary and political expression in the courts of the Rashtrakutas and Chalukyas. Hindi was fashioned by Sufi poets in principalities like Orchha and Gwalior in the fifteenth century. Bearers of these languages were the elite and not the people, as Gramschi and Bakhtin made us believe. Our consciousness of a "mother tongue" did not even appear until the Europeans arrived. Languages are evolving things and we ought not to do too much social engineering. Vernacular nationalism is bad because it goes against people's wishes for learning English. Instead of encouraging them by creating more English teachers, nationalists thwart their democratic aspirations. Meanwhile, instead of worrying about our phantom losses, let us celebrate our potential gains. Let's celebrate cool Inglish!

In the first chapter of this book I told a story about how I got my name. But it was an incomplete tale. I used to be called Ashok Kumar until the age of three. Like all Indian names, it had a meaning—the "prince of happiness" in this case. My grandmother, however, suspected my mother had given me this name because she was secretly in love with a famous film actor from Bombay of that name. Thinking this an inappropriate state of affairs, she persuaded my father to take me to his Guru and get me a new name. And as I have described, he renamed me Guru Charan Das. So, overnight, I was transformed from the "prince of happiness" to the humble "servant of the feet of the Guru".

I think the Guru knew about the perils of hubris in human life and that I, in particular, needed to be reminded constantly about the virtues of humility. I have been privileged to meet many leaders, and I have concluded that the best ones shared two virtues. One is determination or will power and the other is humility. Oh, they were ambitious, but their ambition was for their organization. When asked about themselves, they invariably turned the question around to talk about their work or their organization (and you couldn't get them to stop). So, I think my father's Guru was on to something. These days the word "guru" is increasingly associated with my name, but in another sense—as a "management guru". I must confess that I have always believed that this latter guru stood for "good at understanding but relatively useless".

Nations too need to be reminded about humility. Now that India has begun to rise economically, there are many who have begun to dream of "great power" status. For a country that was widely regarded as twentieth century's great disappointment, it must feel good that the twenty-first has begun rather nicely. But I must confess that this nationalistic talk leaves me cold. I ask myself what is "great" about a "great power". I learn more about India's greatness when an old friend in New Jersey tells me that she has decided to return home to Tanjore because she cannot live without Carnatic music.

India's greatness lies in its self-reliant and resilient people. They are able to pull themselves up and survive, even flourish, when the state fails to deliver. When teachers and doctors do not show up at government primary schools and health centres, they just open up cheap private schools and clinics in the slums and get on with it. Indian entrepreneurs claim that they are hardier because they have had to fight, not only their competitors, but also state inspectors. In short, India's society has triumphed over the state.

Larry Summers, the former President of Harvard University, is right when he says that the Americans have got it all wrong. The first quarter of the twenty-first century will be remembered in human history not for 9/11 but for the rise of China and India, an event that is as momentous as the coming of the Renaissance or the Industrial Revolution in the West. The simple lesson that I take from this event is that open societies, free trade and multiplying connections to the global economy are the pathways to lasting prosperity and comity among nations.

New Delhi
January 2007

NOTES

This is not a scholarly work. It is a personal account of the events and ideas that have pervaded our times in India. Hence, I have tried to avoid littering the text with footnote numbers. I have, however, quoted others and made liberal use of their ideas, and I acknowledge them below.

INTRODUCTION: THE WISE ELEPHANT

ix   ". . . the causes of wealth . . .": Quoted in J. M. Keynes, *Collected Works*, vol. 10, pp. 97–98. Cited in David Landes, *The Wealth and Poverty of Nations* (W. W. Norton, New York, 1998), p. vii.

xii   When I was in college . . . : The term "takeoff" originated in 1960 with Walt W. Rostow's *The Stages of Economic Growth* (Cambridge University Press, Cambridge, 1960). It was Rostow who had suggested that an industrial revolution would be marked by the rise of capital formation from under 5 percent to over 10 percent of income. Thirty years later, Rostow lamented the misunderstanding: "My colleagues insisted on regarding the rise in the investment rate in the takeoff as a primal cause in the manner, say, of a Harrod-Domar growth model. . . . A part of the fault was mine. If I had it to do over again, I would state emphatically, right at the beginning, . . . [that the] emergence of a rate of net investment sufficient to outstrip the rate of increase of population and to yield a positive net rate of growth is at least as much the result of prior sectoral growth as a cause of the growth." Walt W. Rostow, *Theorists of Economic Growth: from David Hume to the Present* (Oxford University Press, New York, 1990), p. 434.

xii   India's per capita income . . . : World Bank, *World Development Report, 2000–2001* (Oxford University Press, New York, 2000).

xviii   Between 1970 and 1990 . . . : Jeffrey D. Sachs and Andrew Warner, "Economic Reform and the Process of Global Integration," *Brookings Papers on Economic Activity*, no. 1 (1995): pp. 1–118.

PART ONE:

OUR SPRING OF HOPE (1942–65)

I "Some try to represent . . .": James Wilson, founder and editor of the
   Economist, in November 1843, in its tenth issue, in an article titled
   "Widow Biddle and the Poor Needle-Women of the Metropolis," from
   The Pursuit of Reason: The Economist, 1843 1993, by Ruth Dudley Edwards
   (Hamish Hamilton, London, 1993).

ONE

RANTING IN ENGLISH, CHANTING IN SANSKRIT

The family conversations in this chapter have been reconstructed from
interviews with members of my family, mostly in the early 1980s, except
in the case of my grandfather, with whom I spent long hours in the early
1960s.

4 three million people perished: The official Famine Inquiry Commission
   (1945) reported a death toll of "about 1.5 million." W. R. Ackroyd, a
   member of the commission, later wrote, "I now think it was an underestimate, especially in that it took little account of roadside deaths."
   Quoted in Amartya Sen, *Poverty and Famines: An Essay on Entitlement and
   Deprivation* (Clarendon Press, Oxford, 1981), p. 52. Sen has estimated the
   death toll to be around 3 million (Appendix D, pp. 195–216).

5 "liberator with clean hands . . .": The phrase belongs to André Malraux,
   Antimemoirs, trans. Terence Kilmartin (Hamish Hamilton, London, 1968),
   p. 133.

5 caused not by a decline in the food . . . : "The [food] supply for 1943 was
   only about 5 per cent lower than the average of the preceding five years.
   It was in fact 13 per cent higher than in 1941, and there was, of course, no
   famine in 1941" (Sen, *Poverty and Famines,* p. 58).

5 "Rangoon falls to Japan . . .": The excerpts from the reports of the district officers and commissioners are from the Famine Inquiry Commission (ibid., Appendix VI, p. 55). The newspaper reports are from the
   Statesman and quoted in K. C. Ghosh, *Famines in Bengal, 1770 1943* (Indian
   Associated Publishing Co., Calcutta, 1944).

6 "The Bengal Famine . . .": Patrick French, *Liberty or Death: India's Journey
   to Independence and Division* (HarperCollins India, Delhi, 1997), p. 181.

6 "I hate Indians . . .": John Barnes and David Nicholson, eds., *The Empire
   at Bay: The Leo Amery Diaries, 1929 1945* (Hutchinson, London, 1988),
   p. 832.

6 "the very different attitude . . .": Penderel Moon, *Wavell: The Viceroy's
   Journal* (Oxford University Press, London, 1977), p. 89.

6 "figment of the Bengali imagination": French, *Liberty or Death*, p. 181.
6 Amartya Sen reminds us: See his book with Jean Dreze, *India: Economic Development and Social Opportunity* (Oxford University Press, Delhi, 1995), chap. 4.
8 "To have FDR's . . .": Christopher Ogden, *Life of the Party: The Biography of Pamela Digby Churchill Hayward Harriman* (Little, Brown, Boston, 1994), pp. 122–23.
8 the truth was that . . . : Warren Kimball, ed., *Churchill and Roosevelt: The Complete Correspondence* (Princeton University Press, Princeton, N.J., 1984), vol. 1, p. 374. Quoted in French, *Liberty or Death*, p. 139.
8 "I feel absolutely satisfied . . ." and the remaining quotes in this paragraph are also from ibid., p. 145.
11 There were two competing visions . . . : I owe the inspiration for this paragraph to Tony Joseph's column, "Two Utopias, Three Preferences," in *Business Standard*, August 1997.

TWO

SMELLS OF THE BAZAAR

16 "The principle of . . .": Irving Babbitt (1865–1933), "Democracy and Leadership," address at Harvard University.
18 "possessed great influence . . .": Quoted in David Landes, *The Wealth and Poverty of Nations* (W. W. Norton, New York, 1998), p. 166.
18 "No Englishman who started . . .": Ibid., p. 162.
18 "not merely a crime . . .": Ibid., p. 167.
21 In the inner and outer . . . : Alan Ross, *The Emissary* (Collins Harvill, London, 1986), p. 8.
23 GD became the largest supporter of the Congress . . . : The historian Bipan Chandra says that he has found no evidence of GD financing the Congress. However, GD did generously support Gandhi's charities—Charkha Sangh and Harijan Sangh. Nevertheless, everyone believed that Birlas supported the Congress with money, including the British.
23 "every possible step . . .": Margaret Herdeck and Gita Piramal, *India's Industrialists* (Three Continents Press, Washington, D.C., 1985), vol. 1, p. 71.
24 "I think Queen Mary . . .": Lord Wavell, *The Transfer of Power*, vol. 4, cited in Minhaz Merchant, *Aditya Vikram Birla: A Biography* (Viking, New Delhi, 1997), p. 26.
24 "English rule without Englishmen . . .": M. K. Gandhi, *Socialism of My Conception* (Bhartiya Vidya Bhawan, Bombay, 1966), p. 225.

THREE
THE TRAIN TO NOWHERE

27 "They saw a Dream . . .": Charles Leland (1824–1903), "The Masher," *Brand New Ballads.*

27 "Long years ago we made a tryst . . .": *Jawaharlal Nehru, Independence and After: A Collection of Speeches* (Publications Division, Government of India, New Delhi, 1949), p. 3.

29 It had no such effect . . . : Daniel Thorner, *The Shaping of Modern India* (Allied, Bombay, 1980), p. 120.

30 They put together a powerful . . . : One of the promoters wrote, "This is a matter of extreme importance in India, where the energy of individual thought has long been cramped by submission to despotic governments, to irresponsible and venal subordinates, to the ceremonies and priesthood of a highly irrational religion, and to a public opinion founded not on investigation, but on traditional usages and observances." This was in a letter to the Right Honourable Lord John Russell, MP, on the subject of Indian Railways (London, 1848), cited in Daniel Thorner, *Investment in Empire: British Railway and Steam Shipping Enterprise in India, 1825 1849* (University of Pennsylvania Press, Philadelphia, 1950), pp. 151–52.

31 In comparison, the United States had . . . : Thorner, *Modern India*, p. 120.

32 She worked hard to get . . . : Macaulay summed up the aim of English education in India as being the raising of an English-educated Indian middle class "who may be interpreters between us and the millions whom we govern; a class of persons, Indians in blood and colour, but English in taste, in opinions, in morals, and in intellect." Macaulay had contempt for Oriental culture. He wrote in a famous and arrogant statement: "I have no knowledge of either Sanskrit or Arabic. . . . But I have done what I could to form a correct estimate of their value. . . . Who could deny that a single shelf of a good European library was worth the whole native literature of India and Arabia . . . all the historical information which has been collected from all the books written in the Sanskrit language is less valuable than what may be found in the most paltry abridgements used at preparatory schools in England." (The text of Macaulay's Minute is in M. Edwardes, *British India, 1772 1947* (Sidgwick and Jackson, London, 1967).

37 On a fine spring day . . . : The firsthand account of Alexander's battle comes from letters and accounts written by fifteen contemporaries of Alexander who fought under his command. Alexander knew that he was making history and he made sure that he had plenty of historians at hand. On the basis of these sources Arrian wrote his famous *Campaigns of Alexander*, from which I have largely drawn my narrative. Arrian, *Cam-*

paigns of Alexander, trans. Aubrey de Selincourt (Penguin Books, London, 1971). I have supplemented it with J. W. McCrindle, *The Invasion of India by Alexander the Great* (Constable, Westminster, 1896), and chapter 15 of *The Cambridge History of India* (Cambridge University Press, Cambridge, 1922), vol. 1.

41 On the soggy banks . . . : Arrian, *Campaigns of Alexander*, p. 274.

41 "the Indian cavalry . . . did not . . .": Stephen P. Rosen, *Societies and Military Power: India and Its Armies* (Cornell University Press, Ithaca, N.Y., 1996), pp. 80–83.

41 "checked the advance of his . . .": Arrian, *Campaigns of Alexander*, pp. 288–89. See also ibid., p. 83; Jadunath Sarkar, *Military History of India* (Sarkar, Calcutta, 1960), pp. 8–10, 20–23. The same views are echoed by Radhakumud Mookerji in *Chandragupta Maurya and His Times* (Rajkamal Publications, Bombay, 1953), p. 26, and by Bimal Kanti Mazumdar in *Military Systems of Ancient India* (Firma K. L. Mukhopadhyay, Calcutta, n.d.), p. 46.

41 "the Indian defenders of the Punjab were . . .": Sarkar, *Military History*, p. 21.

42 "private animosities, personal . . .": Major General Niranjan Prasad, *The Fall of Towang, 1962* (Palit and Palit, New Delhi, 1981), pp. 13, 20. See also D. K. Palit, *War in High Himalaya*, p. 106, cited in Rosen, *Societies*, p. 242.

42 Even in the victorious wars . . . : Harbakhsh Singh, *War Despatches: The Indo-Pak Conflict, 1965* (Lancer, New Delhi, 1991); Sukhwant Singh, *India's Wars since Independence,* 2 vols. (Vikas, New Delhi, 1981). Professor Stephen Rosen concludes from these two works that "in 1965 the Indian Army displayed low levels of cohesion within infantry units, which led to their early collapse in battle; low levels of cohesion among infantry units, which affected their ability to cooperate on the battlefield; and perhaps even lower levels of cohesion between tank and infantry units" (Rosen, *Societies,* p. 48).

42 The end result is that . . . : Dhirendra Narain, *Hindu Character* (University of Bombay Publications, Sociology Series no. 8, Bombay University Press, Bombay, 1957).

42 The adult Indian male personality . . . : P. Spratt, *Hindu Culture and Personality: A Psycho-analytic Study* (Manaktalas, Bombay, 1966), pp. 1, 9; Sudhir Kakar, *The Inner World: A Psycho-analytic Study of Childhood and Society in India* (Oxford University Press, Delhi, 1978), pp. 104, 134.

43 Although we normally . . . : The economic historians Douglass North and Robert P. Thomas write: "Efficient economic organization is the key to growth; the development of an efficient economic organization in Western Europe accounts for the rise of the West." *The Rise of the Western World* (Cambridge University Press, Cambridge, 1973), p. 1.

FOUR

BLIND THEN, BLIND NOW

44 "Good intentions . . .": Jami, "The Camel and the Rat," *Baharistan* (fifteenth century).

45 "the deceased king's jewellers": Dwijendra Tripathi, *The Dynamics of a Tradition: Kasturbhai Lalbhai and His Entrepreneurship* (Manohar, New Delhi, 1981), p. 24.

45 "without dispute, one . . .": Ibid., p. 26.

45 "light in weight and heavy in price . . .": Ibid., p. 28.

46 "If the price of textiles is low . . .": Niranjan Bhagat and others, eds., *Tribute to Ethics: Remembering Kasturbhai Lalbhai* (Gujarat Chamber of Commerce and Industry, Ahmedabad, 1983), p. 9.

47 "Sheth Kasturbhai has set up . . .": Tripathi, *Dynamics of a Tradition*, p. 99.

49 "Probably nowhere else . . .": Jawaharlal Nehru, *Jawaharlal Nehru's Speeches*, vol. 3, 1953–57 (New Delhi, 1958), p. 3.

FIVE

IF WE WERE ONCE RICH, WHY ARE WE NOW POOR?

52 "The greatest thing since . . .": Francisco López de Gómara, *History of the Indies.* Cited in David Landes, *The Wealth and Poverty of Nations* (W. W. Norton, New York, 1998), p. 60.

54 "From the most ancient times . . .": G. W. F. Hegel, *The Philosophy of History*, trans. J. Sebree (Dover, New York, 1956). Quoted in Sugata Bose and Ayesha Jalal, *Modern South Asia* (Oxford University Press, Delhi, 1998), p. 1.

54 When they arrived near Calicut . . . : M. N. Pearson, *The Portuguese in India*, The New Cambridge History of India, vol. 1.1 (Cambridge University Press, Cambridge, 1987), p. 5.

55 He spoke about spices . . . : The Portuguese discovered that a hundredweight of pepper could be bought in Calicut for three ducats and sold in Europe for eighty ducats. Landes, *Wealth and Poverty*, p. 89.

55 In the words of Adam Smith . . . : D. K. Fieldhouse, *The Colonial Empires* (London, 1982), p. 3. On the other hand, Dr. Samuel Johnson was dismissive: "I do not much wish well to discoveries, for I am always afraid they will end in conquest and robbery." John Wain, *Samuel Johnson* (London, 1974), p. 278.

55 The English got to this wealth . . . : The East India Company was founded on the last day of 1600 by a royal charter granted by Queen Elizabeth I to the "Governor and Company of Merchants of London trading

into the East Indies," vesting them exclusive trading rights. In 1613 the company was granted a *jarman* for trading rights at Surat by the Mughal emperor.

55 "unbeatable for quality . . .": Ibid., p. 225. According to N. Steensgaard, "The Growth and Composition of the Long-Distance Trade of England and the Dutch Republic Before 1750," in James Tracy, ed., *The Rise of Merchant Empires: Long-Distance Trade in the Early Modern World, 1350 1750* (Cambridge University Press, Cambridge, 1990), pp. 102–52. The East India Company's export of cotton fabrics rose from 221,500 pieces to 707,000 pieces in the 1680s.

55 "Indian cottons transformed . . .": Landes, *Wealth and Poverty*, p. 154.

56 During the Mughal Empire . . . : According to Irfan Habib, it was closer to 150 million. "Potentialities of Capitalist Development in the Economy of Mughal India," *Journal of Economic History*, vol. 29, no. 1, pp. 32–37.

56 "not in any way backward . . .": Ibid., p. 34.

56 "The annual revenues of the Mogul emperor . . .": John Kautsky, *The Politics of Aristocratic Empires* (University of North Carolina Press, Chapel Hill, 1982), p. 188. Cited in Landes, *Wealth and Poverty*, p. 156. Landes says that these estimates are based on pre–World War I dollars, and one must multiply them by twenty to twenty-four in order to match the 1990s dollar value.

56 India had a 22.6 percent share . . . : Angus Maddison, *Chinese Economic Performance in the Long Run* (OECD, Paris, 1998). China had 23.1 percent of world GDP in 1700 and the whole of Europe had 23.3 percent. By 1952, India's share declined to 3.8 percent and China's to 5.2 percent; Europe climbed to 29.7 percent and the United States had 28.4 percent by 1952. By 1995, India grew modestly to 4.6 percent, China doubled to 10.9 percent, while Europe and the United States declined somewhat to 23.8 percent and 20.9 percent, respectively. See also Paul Bairoch and Maurice Levy-Leboyer, *Disparities in Economic Development Since the Industrial Revolution* (Macmillan, London, 1981).

56 "More important, there was a . . .": Tapan Raychaudhuri, "The Mid-Eighteenth-Century Background," in *The Cambridge Economic History of India*, edited by Dharma Kumar and Meghnad Desai (Cambridge University Press, Cambridge, 1983), vol. 2, pp. 3–35. He goes on to say, "It drew upon a wide range of manufactures and commercial crops to supply an extensive domestic as well as overseas market. India's textile exports met the basic requirements of cloth in several part of South-East Asia and the Middle East. The competitive power of this line of trade—based on very low costs of production—is evident in the need felt by the British textile industry for protective tariffs despite the high cost of intercontinental trade."

56 It is not surprising . . . : The descriptions of eighteenth-century India by F. Buchanan, J. L. Holwell, Hove, F. Pelsaert, J. Ovington, M. Wilks, J. Forbes, and W. Bolts can be found in ibid.

57 "The competitive strength of Indian manufacturers . . .": Ibid., p. 32: "India had not witnessed any agricultural revolution. Her technology— in agriculture as well as manufactures—had by and large been stagnant for centuries. For a country so advanced in civilization, the technology was also rather primitive. The use of inanimate power in any form was virtually unknown."

57 . . . the peasant was extremely poor: The standard of living of the Indian masses when the Europeans first came to India is a controversial issue. Whereas European travelers and visitors reported general misery, a number of scholars think that these travelers did not really understand the true picture. Some have even calculated the food intake of peasants and concluded that the Indian ryot lived as well if not better than the English farm laborer. These income estimates seem to me hard to believe, although they have been calculated by respected scholars. It is risky business to project incomes backwards from the twentieth to the eighteenth century. Even a small mistake, when it is expanded over two hundred years, contains a huge multiplier and can be misleading. I find it hard to accept their conclusions because European agricultural productivity had begun to improve at this time with better techniques, labor-saving devices, and stronger property rights. Some historians claimed that India would have become an industrial economy had British colonialism not intervened and tragically cut it from its inevitable destiny. A Japanese scholar has reinforced this view. Writing on the economy of central India in *The Cambridge Economic History of India*, he cited the royal karkhanas of the seventeenth century, saying, "[O]ne is tempted to speculate if [these royal workshops] might not have moved in the direction of mechanisation and become the state model factories for the model industrialisation of India, had they not been terminated by the British conquest of the country." This is idle speculation particularly when after fifty years of trying as an independent nation, the broad industrialization of India still eludes us.

57 "In India it is seldom . . .": F. Buchanan, *A Journey from Madras . . . (1807)*, cited in Raychaudhuri, "Mid-Eighteenth-Century Background," p. 29.

57 According to Paul Bairoch . . . : Paul Bairoch, "Ecarts internationaux des niveaux de vie avant la Révolution industrielle," *Annales: économies, sociétés, civilisations*, vol. 34, no. 1 (January–February 1979).

57–8 India remained slow . . . : Was the Indian merchant somehow to blame? When the huge European market opened in the seventeenth century and there was huge escalation in demand, it created enormous supply problems in India. There were many reports of irregular supplies and delivery failures. This would have been the ideal incentive, one would think, to infuse innovation in the supply chain.

The Indian merchant also occupied a central place in the supply chain. He bought cotton pieces from the spinners and weavers, and sold them to the European traders and chartered companies; they in turn delivered them to their European customers. He normally advanced capital to the weaver against the promise of delivery. The weavers usually operated from their homes, employing their whole family as a small-scale family-based unit. The weavers were very poor, and they depended on merchants for their raw material. The merchants kept them "on a short leash," paying them by the day so that they would not run off with the goods or the advance.

This was different from the European "putting out" method, where the merchant took part in the production process. Because the European merchant was much more deeply involved in the process, he presumably had a greater incentive to innovate. Because of this leisurely system and slow transport, it often took years to deliver the product. Irfan Habib, a scholar of Mughal India, describes huge trains of bullock-carts, numbering tens of thousands, carrying raw cotton from the ports of the spinning and weaving villages. These bullock-trains moved a few miles a day and took six months to deliver the material.

Why couldn't the Indian merchant have taken charge of the whole process, especially when there were massive rewards to be had? Rather than merely advancing money to the weaver, he could have found, assembled, and bought the raw materials; he could have assembled a large number of workers in one place and supervised their manufacture. Certainly he would have had to face the challenges of organizing large-scale activity, but that is what entrepreneurship is all about. This process of organizational innovation would thus have led to opportunities for technological innovation.

58 England had achieved . . . : Simon Kuznets, "Underdeveloped Countries—Present Characteristics in the Light of Past Growth Patterns," mimeographed paper, 21 April 1958. Quoted in Gunnar Myrdal, *Asian Drama: An Inquiry into the Poverty of Nations* (Pantheon, New York, 1968), vol. 1, p. 454.

58 "the bones of the cotton weavers . . .": Quoted in Deepak Lall, *The Hindu Equilibrium,* vol. 1, *Cultural Stability and Economic Stagnation: India, c. 1500 BC–AD 1980* (Clarendon Press, Oxford, 1984), p. 184.

59 Since India consistently exported . . . : My uncle must have been quoting Paul Baran, *The Political Economy of Growth* (Monthly Review Press, New York, 1957), p. 148. Later a calculation by Irfan Habib put the drain in 1882 as 4 percent of national income versus 10 percent of Baran's. Irfan

Habib, "Studying a Colonial Economy—Without Perceiving Colonialism," *Modern Asian Studies*, 19 March 1985, pp. 375–76.

59 My uncle had put forth . . . : Indian nationalists had talked of the "drain" as early as the beginning of the twentieth century. Dadabhai Naoroji, *Poverty and Un-British Rule* (London, 1901); R. C. Dutt, *The Economic History of India in the Victorian Age* (London, 1906).

60 Also, the overhead cost . . . : It was around 20 million pounds or less than 2 percent of exports at the end of the nineteenth century and less than 1 percent of exports in 1913. K. N. Chaudhuri, "India's International Economy in the Nineteenth Century: An Historical Survey," *Modern Asian Studies*, 19 March 1985, pp. 375–76.

60 If India had maintained . . . : Vera Anstey, *Economic Development of India* (London, 1929), p. 511.

60 Only a part of that precious . . . : In world trade circles India was always the world's "sink" for gold and silver. Pliny was aware of India's appetite for precious metal in ancient times, and J. M. Keynes used it to argue for a gold exchange standard for India in *Indian Currency and Finance* (London, 1913). Nationalist historians had admitted that capital did increase partly because of bullion imports, but they argued that it went into the hands of landlords and aristocrats rather than helping to finance economic activity. Inequality may have increased with bullion imports, but this was not Britain's fault. In any case, it is not relevant to the drain theory. B. R. Tomlinson, *The New Cambridge History of India*, vol. 3, *The Economy of Modern India, 1870 1970* (Cambridge University Press, Cambridge, 1996), p. 15.

61 By 1900, India's share had declined . . . : Maurice and Taya Zinkin, *Britain and India* (Chatto and Windus, London, 1964), p. 67.

61 In 1896, Indian mills supplied . . . : Angus Maddison, "The Colonial Burden: A Comparative Perspective," in M. Scott and D. Lall, eds., *Public Policy and Economic Development: Essays in Honour of Ian Little* (Clarendon Press, Oxford, 1990), p. 57. The "drain" quite simply was equal to the current account surplus.

61 Manufacturing output grew . . . : Rajat Ray, *Industrialisation in India: Growth and Conflict in the Private Corporate Sector* (Oxford University Press, Delhi, 1982), p. 341.

62 The British government finally . . . : The general tariff was raised to 7.5 percent in 1917, to 15 percent in 1922, reaching 31 percent in October 1931. A special rate of 20 percent (15 percent for British goods) was fixed for low-quality cotton textile imports in 1930, and this rose to 50 percent for non-British goods in 1932 and 75 percent in 1933. Dharma Kumar, "The Fiscal System," *The Cambridge Economic History of India*, vol. 2, pp. 921–24.

62 Hirachand, the construction magnate . . . : Tomlinson, *Modern India*, p. 143; Ray, *Industrialisation*, p. 276ff.

62   "The Empire is a bread . . .": Quoted in John Strachey, "The Great Awakening," *Encounter*, no. 5 (1961): p. 9.

62   "If the British Empire fell . . .": Quoted in Michael Brown, *After Imperialism* (Heinemann, London, 1963), p. 294.

63   So did France, Holland . . . : John Strachey's *End of Empire* provides a wealth of evidence disproving the old idea.

63   By 1914, India had the . . . : Morris D. Morris, "The Growth of Large Scale Industry to 1947," in *The Cambridge Economic History of India*, vol. 2, p. 553.

63   Gunnar Myrdal found that . . . : Myrdal, *Asian Drama*, vol. 2, Appendix 2, p. 1843ff.

63   According to Myrdal, poor work . . . : Ibid., p. 1862.

63   These were compounded by . . . : Ibid.

64   "After all, China's level of technology . . .": Joseph Needham, *Science and Civilization in China* (Cambridge University Press, Cambridge, 1958), vol. 1.

64   Capitalism developed in the East . . . : Ernest Gellner, *Plough, Sword, and Book: The Structure of Human History* (University of Chicago Press, 1988), pp. 39–69. See also Robert Merton, "Science, Religion, and Technology in Seventeenth Century England," *Osiris*, vol. 4 (1938): pp. 360–632.

64   Deepak Lall, another economist . . . : Lall, *The Hindu Equilibrium*, vol. 1, pp. 2–3, 341. Also Morris, "Growth of Large Scale Industry."

65   "nature like life is unfair . . .": David Landes, *The Wealth and Poverty of Nations* (W. W. Norton, New York, 1998), p. 45.

65   But they do behave in that way . . . : There is now extensive empirical evidence from different cultures and climates that uneducated peasants are rational economic actors. See J. Nugent and P. Yotopoulos, *Economics of Development: Empirical Investigations* (Harper & Row, New York, 1976) for details of such studies.

65   Economic historians no longer . . . : Ray, *Industrialisation*, p. 339.

65–6 Amiya Kumar Bagchi suggests . . . : Amiya Kumar Bagchi, *Private Investment in India, 1900 1939* (Cambridge University Press, Cambridge, 1972).

66   An Indian entrepreneur, he feels . . . : Morris, "Growth of Large Scale Industry," pp. 553–676.

66   According to the Calcutta historian Rajat Ray . . . : Ray, *Industrialisation*, p. 2.

66   in the eighteenth century . . . : Anstey, *Economic Development of India*, p. 282.

67   It did not try to educate . . . : There were only nine agricultural colleges in the whole of India in 1946, with a total enrollment of 3,110 students. G. Blyn, *Agricultural Trends in India, 1891 1947* (University of Pennsylvania Press, Philadelphia, 1966).

67   "no colonial power helped . . .": Arthur W. Lewis, *Growth and Fluctuations, 1870 1913* (George Allen and Unwin, London, 1978), p. 225. It

would have needed massive investments in education and human development. A hugely motivated government could only have created this social infrastructure as in Japan and the USSR. But a colonial government did not have the same motivation. Of course, the building of such infrastructure would also have created jobs, put money in people's pockets, and promoted the growth in demand for the products of Britain's industrial economy. But the colonial government did not think in that way. For that matter, neither has independent India's government paid enough attention to human development and literacy, and this dramatically distinguishes India from the successful nations of the Far East. The question is why Japan (also an Asian country which did not experience a scientific revolution) took off industrially so rapidly after the Meiji reforms in the nineteenth century while India (and China) did not. The key reason seems to be that Tokugawa society had a higher level of literacy and this contributed to technological progress, first in agriculture, then in industry. The Japanese, even in the seventeenth century, showed a greater curiosity about Western science and technology than the Indians (or the Chinese). Whereas India was ahead because of its large export trade, Japan became more advanced technologically.

SIX

THE PAPER ROUTE

69   "In democracies . . .": Alexis de Tocqueville, *Democracy in America* (1835–39), bk. 2, chap. 2, p. 19.

72   they helped reform society: As C. A. Bayly and others have pointed out, the reforms began much earlier with the bhakti and sufi sects. There has been radical rethinking of Raj history, which thought of the eighteenth century as a time of troubles and chaos. The new history speaks about the vivid commercial activity that thrived once the Mughal monopoly disappeared. See C. A. Bayly, *Indian Society and the Making of the British Empire* (Cambridge University Press, Cambridge, 1988), and his later *Rulers, Townsmen and Bazaars* (Cambridge University Press, Cambridge, 1992).

76   Like most of my classmates . . . : The word "liberal" has been usurped by those left of center to describe a person who stands for change in the social order in favor of the poor and the weak. In the process, they have totally confused the word and the old verbal precision had been lost. The old meaning of liberal, what is now called "classical liberal," meant a person committed to maximizing liberty—via free markets, free trade, and small government. Many of these beliefs, in fact, attach to the conservatives of our time.

78   "dirigiste dogma . . .": Deepak Lall, a professor of economics at the University of California, Los Angeles, has used this expression in *The Poverty*

of Development Economics (Oxford University Press, New Delhi, 2000),
p. 57. He includes the work of the following non-neoclassicals, whose
writings have been influential in providing various elements of the
"dirigiste dogma": R. Nurkse, *Problems of Capital Formation in Underdeveloped Countries* (Oxford University Press, New York, 1953); G. Myrdal,
Economic Theory and Underdeveloped Regions (Vora & Co., Bombay, 1958);
A. O. Hirschman, *The Strategy of Economic Development* (Yale University
Press, New Haven, Conn., 1958); P. N. Rosenstein-Rodan, "Problems of
Industrialization of Eastern and South-Eastern Europe, *Economic Journal*,
June–Sept. 1943; T. Balogh, *Unequal Partners*, 2 vols. (Blackwells, Oxford,
1963); R. Prebisch, *The Economic Development of Latin America and Its Prin-
cipal Problems* (United Nations, 1950); H. Chenery, "The Interdepen-
dence of Investment Decisions," in A. Abromowitz (ed.), *The Allocation of
Investment Resources* (Stanford University Press, Stanford, Calif., 1959); P.
Streeten, *The Frontiers of Development Studies* (Macmillan, New York,
1972).

There has always been some opposition to these dirigiste views. See G.
Haberler, "A Survey of International Trade Theory," *Princeton Special
Papers in International Economics*, 1961; J. Viver, *International Trade and Eco-
nomic Development* (Oxford University Press, New York, 1953); P. T. Bauer
and B. S. Yamey, *The Economics of Underdeveloped Countries* (Cambridge
University Press, Cambridge, 1957); T. Shultz, *Transforming Traditional
Agriculture* (Yale University Press, New Haven, Conn., 1964).

80 "One of the best books . . .": According to Tocqueville, "Americans of
all ages, all conditions, and all dispositions constantly form associations.
They have not only commercial and manufacturing companies, in which
all take part, but associations of a thousand other kinds, religious, moral,
serious, futile, general or restricted, enormous or diminutive. The Americans make associations to give entertainments, to found seminaries, to
build inns, to construct churches, to diffuse books, to send missionaries
to the antipodes; in this manner they found hospitals, prisons, and
schools. If it is proposed to inculcate some truth or to foster some feeling
by the encouragement of a great example, they form a society. Wherever
at the head of a great undertaking you see the government in France, or a
man of rank in England, in the United States you will be sure to find an
association." Alexis de Tocqueville, *Democracy in America* (Vintage Books,
New York, 1945), vol. 2, p. 114.

81 Social scientists refer to this as "social capital . . .": The sociologist Max
Weber also remarked on this aspect of American life at the end of the
nineteenth century: "In the past and up to the very present, it has been a
characteristic precisely of American democracy that it did *not* constitute a
formless sand heap of individuals, but rather a buzzing complex of
strictly exclusive, yet voluntary, associations." Max Weber, "The Protes-

tant Sects and the Spirit of Capitalism," in *From Max Weber: Essays in Sociology,* trans. and ed. C. Wright Mills and Hans Gerth (Oxford University Press, New York, 1946), p. 310.

85   "Those who have given . . .": Anatole France, *The Crime of Sylvestre Bonnard* (1881), trans. Lafcadio Hearn, pt. 2.

87   In 1944, India's leading . . . : The industrialists came together as a part of a committee set up by Jawaharlal Nehru and the Congress in 1938. The Bombay Plan was the popular title given to *A Plan of Economic Development of India* (Penguin, London, 1945).

87   They preferred foreign debt . . . : Ibid., pp. 53–54.

87   "rights attached to private . . .": Ibid., pp. 94–95.

88   Not only was he a close associate of . . . : Sunil Khilnani, *The Idea of India* (Hamish Hamilton, London, 1997), p. 83. E. J. Thompson, who was a translator and friend of Tagore, apparently depended highly on Mahalanobis's literary judgment, and according to Khilnani, "he enlisted him in the preparation of a never-published Oxford Book of Bengali Verse."

88   It was Mahalanobis's deep commitment to rationality . . . : Nehru was attracted to other scientists as well. Meghnath Saha, an astrophysicist famous for the "Saha equation," was also at the Planning Commission; others who influenced Nehru were Homi Bhabha, Shanti Swaroop Bhatnagar, and K. S. Krishnan.

88   "subjects natural phenomena . . .": Quoted in Ved Mehta, *Portrait of India* (Yale University Press, New Haven, Conn., 1993), p. 286.

88   We used to have a great . . . : P. C. Mahalanobis, "The Asian Drama: An Indian View" *Sankhya,* series B, vol. 31 (1969), p. 446. Quoted in Khilnani, *Idea of India,* p. 87.

89   "possibly one of the most . . .": J. B. S. Haldane to P. C. Mahalanobis, 16 May 1955. Quoted in S. Gopal, *Jawaharlal Nehru* (Oxford University Press, Delhi, 1979), vol. 2, p. 305.

89   "a two-pronged attack on the . . .": Michael Brecher, *Nehru: A Political Biography* (Oxford University Press, London, 1959), p. 533.

89   The finance minister, C. D. Deshmukh . . . : C. D. Deshmukh, *The Course of My Life* (Orient Longman, Bombay, 1974), p. 209.

89   "Even if one is pessimistic . . .": Haldane is quoted by Gopal, *Nehru,* vol. 2, pp. 305–6.

90   a socialist revolution by consent . . . : Taya Zinkin, "Nehruism: India's Revolution Without Fear," *Pacific Affairs,* September 1955. Quoted in Gopal, *Nehru,* p. 307.

90   "the establishment of a socialist . . .": Indian National Congress, *Congress Bulletin*, January 1955.

90   intellectual joint venture . . . : Sanjaya Baru, "Paradigm Shift: The Indian Experience," *India Today*, 15 August 1997, p. 70.

90   ". . . in the spirit of high adventure": L. K. Jha, *Economic Strategy for the '80s* (Allied Publishers, Bombay, 1980), p. 7.

90   "The production of steel . . .": Ved Mehta, *Portrait*, p. 287.

91   In the 1950s, there was an . . . : C. N. Vakil and P. R. Brahmanand, *Planning for an Expanding Economy* (Vora and Co., Bombay, 1956). I am grateful to Meghnad Desai for reminding us about this alternative vision. See Meghnad Desai, "Development Perspectives: Was There an Alternative to Mahalanobis," in Isher J. Ahluwalia and I. M. D. Little, *India's Economic Reforms and Development* (Oxford University Press, Delhi, 1988); pp. 40–47.

94   "the bigger houses realized . . .": J. Bhagwati and P. Desai, *Planning for Industrialization* (Oxford University Press, London, 1970), p. 270. The data is from the Monopolies Inquiry Commission Report (1965), and R. K. Hazari's trenchant critique, *Industrial Planning Policy* (Planning Commission, Government of India, 1967), presents plenty of data to support this behavior.

95   "acceptance of controls came . . .": I. G. Patel, "Free Enterprise in the Nehru Era," in D. Tripathi, ed., *State and Business in India: A Historical Perspective* (Manohar Publications, New Delhi, 1987), p. 351.

95   "with the benefit of hindsight . . .": B. K. Nehru, *Nice Guys Finish Second* (Viking, New Delhi, 1997), pp. 270–71.

96   "greater emphasis on State enterprises . . .": R. Tirumalai, *TTK, the Dynamic Innovator* (TT. Maps & Publications, Madras, 1998), pp. 38–39.

96   "The one enterprise . . .": Ibid., p. 57.

99   "a rather weak and hollow reed . . .": I. G. Patel, "The Socialist Legacy," *Economic and Political Weekly*, vol. 16, special number, July 1964, pp. 1219–25.

PART TWO:

THE LOST GENERATION (1966–91)

EIGHT

BAZAAR POWER

103   "Commerce is . . .": Edmond and Jules de Goncourt, *Journal*, July 1864.

106   Years later, I realized . . . : Some of the ideas in this chapter were originally published in my article "Local Memoirs of a Global Manager," *Harvard Business Review*, March–April 1993, and reprinted in several anthologies, including Christopher Bartlett and Sumantra Ghoshal, eds., *Transnational Management* (Irwin, Boston, 1995), pp. 768–76.

NINE

LERMA ROJO AND TAICHUNG NATIVE NO. 1

123 "There is life . . .": Charles Dudley Warner, "Preliminary," *My Summer in a Garden* (1871).

125 Marx too, curiously enough . . . : The idea of an Indian villager as an independent unit was taken by Marx from Sir Charles Metcalfe, who expressed it in a famous and oft-quoted Minute in 1832 when Marx was still a boy. The idea was turned into a myth and appropriated by the nationalist movement. The myth continues. B. R. Ambedkar condemned this myth in the Constituent Assembly when he asked, "What is a village? It is a sink of localism, a den of ignorance, narrow-mindedness and communalism."

126 "These idyllic village communities . . .": Quoted in Daniel Thorner, *The Shaping of Modern India* (Allied, Bombay, 1980), p. 238.

126 "modern industry, resulting . . .": Ibid., p. 358.

126 "We must gradually return . . .": Quoted from M. K. Gandhi, "Hind Swaraj," in Penderel Moon, *Gandhi and Modern India* (W. W. Norton, New York, 1969), pp. 286–89.

127 We were proud that . . . : For a fine account of the drama that followed Nehru's death and Shastri's ascent, see Michael Brecher's fascinating *Succession in India: A Study in Decision Making* (Oxford University Press, London, 1966). See especially chapter 3 (pp. 32–69).

127 In the late 1950s . . . : Selig S. Harrison, *India: The Most Dangerous Decades* (Princeton University Press, Princeton, N.J., 1960).

128 "It is a painful thought that . . .": Unpublished Nehru letters, August 1957. Quoted in Brecher, *Succession*, p. 145.

129 "The representatives of the people . . .": B. K. Nehru, *Nice Guys Finish Second* (Viking, New Delhi, 1997), p. 431.

129 As usual, Indians were . . . : Brecher, *Succession*, pp. 139–50.

130 "What are you doing, Daddy? . . .": B. K. Nehru, *Nice Guys*, p. 467.

130 "reminding us of the . . .": Ibid.

131 "That Subber Maniyam of yours . . .": Ibid., p. 470.

131 He understood that if technology . . . : B. M. Bhatia, "India's Agricultural Performance Growth Amidst Neglect," R. A. Choudhary and others, eds., *The Indian Economy and Its Performance Since Independence* (Oxford University Press, Delhi, 1990), p. 209.

132 Some people worry that one region . . . : Ibid., p. 208.

132 There is new evidence that . . . : C. H. Hanumantha Rao, "Agriculture Policy and Performance," in Bimal Jalan, ed., *The Indian Economy: Problems and Prospects* (Viking, New Delhi, 1992), p. 121.

132 Hence, regional disparities . . . : Ibid.

132 The poor have gained . . . : A. V. Jose, "Agricultural Wages in India," *Economic and Political Weekly*, vol. 23, no. 6 (25 June 1988). See also G. S.

Bhalla and D. S. Tyagi, *Patterns in Indian Agricultural Development: A District Level Study* (Institute for Studies in Industrial Development, Delhi, 1989).

132   They had hoped for the . . . : Hanumantha Rao, "Agriculture Policy," p. 128.

133   "The task of developing agriculture . . .": Quoted in Deepak Lall, *The Hindu Equilibrium*, vol. 1, *Cultural Stability and Economic Stagnation: India, c. 1500 BC–1980 AD* (Clarendon Press, Oxford, 1984), p. 282. The emphasis is Lall's.

134   "For the life of me . . .": Thorner, *Modern India*, p. 225.

134   "It was rare to come across . . .": Ibid., p. 238.

135   "decade after 1947 witnessed . . .": Ibid., p. 245.

135   The land reforms, such as . . . : Ibid., p. 246.

136   "For many months of the year in Punjab . . .": Ibid., p. 233.

136   He has demonstrated . . . : Ashok Gulati and others, *Export Competitiveness of Selected Agricultural Commodities* (National Council of Applied Economic Research, New Delhi, 1994), pp. 286–300.

137   He has vividly demonstrated that . . . : Amartya Sen and Jean Dreze, *India: Economic Development and Social Opportunity* (Oxford University Press, Delhi, 1995).

TEN

CASTE

139   "Distribute the world . . .": John Ruskin, *Sesame and Lilies* (1869), vol. 2, p. 150.

141   For example, oil-pressers in Bengal . . . : M. N. Srinivas, "Varna and Caste," in *Caste in Modern India and Other Essays* (Asia Publishing House, London, 1962), pp. 63–69.

141   In the villages, Muslims and Christians . . . : David G. Mandelbaum, *Society in India* (University of California Press, Berkeley, 1970), vol. 2, pp. 545–52.

141   An anthropologist described . . . : J. M. Hutton, *Caste in India*, 4th edition (Oxford University Press, London, 1963), p. 1.

141   "a group's acknowledged . . .": Louis Dumont, *Homo Hierarchus: The Caste System and Its Implications* (University of Chicago Press, Chicago, 1980), p. 191.

141   Some academics have argued . . . : See, for example, Ronald Inden, *Imagining India* (Basil Blackwell, Cambridge, 1990), pp. 31–32, 69.

142   In recent years, sociologists have . . . : G. S. Ghurye, *Caste, Class and Occupation* (Popular Depot, Bombay, 1961).

142   André Béteille proved . . . : André Béteille, *Caste, Class and Power: Changing Patterns of Social Stratification in a Tanjore Village* (University of California Press, Berkeley, 1965).

142 Other sociologists have confirmed . . . : J. Lerche, "The Modernisation of Relations of Dominance Between Farmers and Artisans of Urban Families," *Sociological Bulletin,* vol. 42, nos. 1 and 2 (March–September 1993): pp. 85–112.

142 Adrian Mayer studied . . . : Adrian Mayer, "Caste in an Indian Village," in C. J. Fuller, ed., *Caste Today* (Oxford University Press, Delhi, 1997), pp. 48–49.

142 There are at least two cultures . . . : Myron Weiner, "India: Two Political Cultures," in *Political Culture and Political Development,* edited by Lucian W. Pye and Sidney Verba (Princeton University Press, Princeton, N.J., 1965), pp. 199–244.

143 "The man coming from . . .": Narendra Panjwani, "Living with Capitalism: Class, Caste, and Paternalism Among Industrial Workers in Bombay," *Contributions to Indian Sociology,* n.s., vol. 18, no. 2 (1984): pp. 267–92.

144 The artisan castes seem to . . . : Ibid., p. 35. Panini provides evidence from a number of studies by Navlakha (1989), Jayaram (1997), Sagar Jain (1971), Subramanian (1971), Lambert (1963), Panini (1993), Holmstrom (1976), and Panjwani (1984). Open entry does not ensure equality—that is an unfortunate truth—at least not for a long time. Competitive exams favor those who are already advantaged.

144 Caste is especially important . . . : Mark Holmstrom, *Industry and Inequality: The Social Anthropology of Indian Labour* (Allied, Bombay, 1985), p. 247.

145 They are now in competition . . . : E. R. Leach, ed., *Aspects of Caste in South India, Ceylon, and North-West Pakistan* (Cambridge University Press, Cambridge, 1960), pp. 6–7. See also F. G. Bailey, *Caste and the Economic Frontier: A Village in Highland Orissa* (Manchester University Press, Manchester, 1957), p. 224.

147 In the words of V. S. Naipaul . . . : *India Today,* 18 August 1997, p. 37.

148 "modern industry, resulting . . .": *New York Daily Tribune,* 8 August 1853.

148 "India's caste order formed . . .": Max Weber, *The Religion of India: The Sociology of Hinduism and Buddhism,* trans. and ed. Hans H. Gerth and Don Martindale (Free Press, Glencoe, Ill., 1958), p. 38.

149 He found that the village was . . . : Oscar Lewis, *Village Life in North India* (University of Illinois Press, Urbana, 1958), chap. 4.

154 One day . . . caste will be . . . : I owe this idea to the late M. N. Srinivas, the doyen of Indian sociology, in a lecture at the India International Centre, 21 September 1999.

ELEVEN

MULTIPLYING BY ZERO

155 "Though those that . . .": Shakespeare, *Cymbeline* (1609–10), act 3, sc. 4, l. 87.

156 To stop Morarji, the Syndicate . . . : I owe this account of Indira Gandhi's succession to Michael Brecher's fine book, *Succession in India: A Study in Decision Making* (Oxford University Press, London, 1966), pp. 190–225.

157 Many years later, L. K. Jha confirmed . . . : L. K. Jha confirmed this to Ashok Nehru, son of B. K. Nehru, at a gathering in Lala Bharat Ram's house in Delhi ten days before he died in Pune.

158 "1966–1980 is effectively . . .": Ibid., p. 102.

159 Economist Isher Ahluwalia estimates . . . : Isher J. Ahluwalia, *Industrial Growth in India: Stagnation Since the Mid-Sixties* (Oxford University Press, Delhi, 1985).

160 To pay for these losses . . . : V. M. Dandekar, "Forty Years After Independence," in Bimal Jalan, ed., *The Indian Economy* (Viking, New Delhi, 1992), p. 59, table 9.

162 Actual duties collected went up . . . : Rakesh Mohan, "Industrial Policy and Controls," in Jalan, *Indian Economy*, p. 109; see especially table 8.

162 yet we were in balance-of-payment difficulties . . . : Ibid., p. 108.

162 Despite these enormous defects . . . : Central Statistical Organisation, Government of India, at constant prices. Ibid., p. 101, table 2.

162 "India was amongst the worst . . .": Ibid., p. 108, although he neglects to mention the name of the report.

163 After Mrs. Gandhi returned to power . . . : I owe this account of I. G. Patel's career to Ashok Desai's column, "The Future of the Government," in *Business World*, 7–21 December 1998.

164 Bank deposits soared . . . : C. Rangarajan and Narendra Jadav, "Issues in Financial Sector Reform," in Jalan, *Indian Economy*, p. 147.

164 By 1990, the banks' gross profits . . . : Dandekar, "Forty Years," p. 149.

170 "She's not interested . . .": R. M. Lala, *Beyond the Last Blue Mountain: A Life of J.R.D. Tata* (Penguin Books, New Delhi, 1993), p. 274.

170 "I am convinced that a prime cause . . .": J. R. D. Tata, *Keynote* (Tata Press, Bombay, 1986), p. 39.

171 "it should have given way to managerial autonomy . . .": There was a growing recognition of this problem in the 1980s. Mrs. Gandhi's adviser L. K. Jha wrote in 1980 that the public-sector enterprises would be effective only "if they enjoy the requisite measure of autonomy" (L. K. Jha, *Economic Strategy for the '80s* [Allied Publishers, Bombay, 1980], p. 38). The majority inside remained unapologetically dirigiste, however. One of the most powerful former bureaucrats, P. N. Haksar, who had been Mrs. Gandhi's adviser in the late 1960s and early 1970s, wrote in 1986: "What-

ever may be the abstract charms of efficiency of the marketplace, Indian economic development cannot take place without the powerful intervention of the State. Public Sector, therefore, is an inescapable necessity and must be safe-guarded against the virus of the newly imported disease of 'privatization' as advocated by the World Bank" (in preface to R. K. Nigam [ed.], *Towards a Viable and Vibrant Public Sector* [Documentation Center, New Delhi, 1986]). The official Arjun Sen Gupta Committee on Policy for Public Enterprises claimed in 1984 that the problem of bureaucratic interference was the result of accountability to Parliament, but it did not have the courage to suggest genuine autonomy. Instead it wrote, "In general Parliament's intervention to the overall performance of public enterprises had a very beneficial impact," and went on to suggest the creation of holding companies as intermediaries between the enterprises and the government. Managers of state enterprises rightly saw the holding companies as an additional layer of bureaucratic control. (The committee's report is included in *Towards a Viable and Vibrant Public Sector.*)

TWELVE
MERCHANTS OF MARWAR

176 "No matter who . . .": Henry Ward Beecher, *Proverbs from a Plymouth Pulpit* (1887).

176 Gradually they turned to industry . . . : Government of India, Monopolies Inquiry Commission Report, New Delhi, 1965, pp. 119–21.

176 Eight were Marwaris . . . : "India's Fifty Business Families," *Business Today*, 22 August 1997, p. 218.

176 Similarly, in contemporary Pakistan . . . : Hanna Papanek, "Pakistan's New Industrialists and Businessmen," in Milton Singer, ed., *Entrepreneurship and Modernization of Occupational Cultures in South Asia* (Duke University, Program in Comparative Studies on Southern Asia, Durham, N.C., 1973).

177 In the latter half of the nineteenth century . . . : The great textile magnates of Bombay in the nineteenth century were the Petits, Wadias, and Tatas (Parsees); the Currimbhoys (Khojas); the Sassoons (Baghdadi Jews); and the Khaitans, Gokuldases, and Thakarseys (Bhatias from Kutch). In Ahmedabad the leaders were Jain banias—the Sarabhais and Lalbhais—who had been prominent shroffs (although Nagar Brahmins had set up the first mills). Rajat Ray, ed., *Entrepreneurship and Industry in India, 1800 1947* (Oxford University Press, New Delhi, 1992), pp. 42–44. Other prominent commercial communities were Guptas and Aggarwals in the north and the Chettiars in the south.

177 "nine-tenths of the bankers . . .": James Tod, *Annals and Antiquities of Rajasthan, 1829 32,* vol. 2, p. 166.

178 For example, Bhagoti Ram Poddar . . . : Tom Timberg, *The Marwaris* (Vikas, New Delhi, 1978), p. 128.

178 The arrival of the Delhi–Calcutta railway . . . : Ibid., p. 57.

178 During the First World War . . . : Ibid., p. 66.

178 G. D. Birla's grandfather, Shiv Narain . . . : Ibid., p. 5.

178 When the Marwari needed money . . . : Ibid., p. 6.

179 At the same time . . . : Omkar Goswami, "Sahibs, Babus, and Banias," in Ray, *Entrepreneurship and Industry,* p. 233. See also Ray's introduction, p. 52.

180 "create something really . . .": Minhaz Merchant, *Aditya Vikram Birla: A Biography* (Viking, New Delhi, 1997), p. 105.

180 "This permission is just a piece . . .": Ibid., p. 116.

183 When he died suddenly in 1995 . . . : Ibid., p. 257.

183 "human factory-making factory . . .": Gita Piramal, *Business Maharajas* (Viking, New Delhi, 1996), p. 153.

184 Finally, after hard lobbying . . . : Merchant, *Birla,* p. 220.

185 "Eat only vegetarian food . . .": Piramal, *Business Maharajas,* p. 208.

THIRTEEN
DREAMS IN KABUTARKHANA

This chapter is based partially on a longish interview with Anil Ambani in 1996 in Bombay.

187 "Boldness in business . . .": Thomas Fuller, M.D., *Gnomologia* (1732), p. 1006.

188 Like other traders . . . : Interview with Anil Ambani, 1996.

189 Dhirubhai is proud to belong to the "zero club". . . : This expression is attributed to Udayan Bose, the managing director of Credit Capital. Quoted in Gita Piramal, *Business Maharajas* (Viking, New Delhi, 1996), p. 17.

192 "In our country it would . . .": Ibid., p. 41.

192 As a result of such efficiencies . . . : Sumantra Ghoshal, professor at London Business School, who prepared a case study on Reliance. Cited in Piramal, *Business Maharajas,* p. 46.

FOURTEEN
LICENSING BLUES

196 "No system of regulation . . .": Louis Brandeis (1856–1941), U.S. Supreme Court justice.

199 "colossal vistas of red sandstone . . .": André Malraux, *Antimemoirs,* trans. Terence Kilmartin (Hamish Hamilton, London, 1968), p. 132.

THE REBIRTH OF DREAMS (1991–99)

211 "A nation has character . . .": Madame de Staël, from *De la literature* (1800).

FIFTEEN
THE GOLDEN SUMMER OF 1991

This chapter is based on a series of lengthy interviews that the author had with the actors in the reform drama throughout 1999: P. V. Narasimha Rao, Manmohan Singh, P. Chidambaram, Montek Singh Ahluwalia, A. N. Varma, Ashok Desai, Rakesh Mohan, and Deepak Nayyar. It was supplemented by discussions with the economist Arjun Sengupta, the editor T. N. Ninan, and Janaki Kathpalia, who was at the finance ministry at the time.

213 "All reformers are . . .": George Moore, *The Bending of the Bough* (1900), p. 1.

213 "The Delhi-based Center . . .": The results of this widely quoted opinion poll first appeared in the influential *India Today* magazine in November 1996 and were later quoted in the *Times of India, Indian Express,* and *The Hindu.*

223 "While Prime Minister Narasimha Rao . . .": Quoted in Shashi Tharoor, *India: From Midnight to the Millennium* (Arcade Publishing, New York, 1997), p. 194.

SIXTEEN
A MILLION REFORMERS

228 "Every man is a reformer . . .": Edgar Howe, *Country Town Sayings,* 1911. Cited in Rhoda Thomas Tripp, *International Thesaurus of Quotations* (Thomas Y. Crowell, New York, 1970), p. 780.

SEVENTEEN
NEW MONEY

The source material for this chapter is based on personal meetings and interactions of the author with the businessmen cited in the text between 1995 and 1999.

255   There is no easy answer . . . : Christopher de Bellaigue, "Bombay at War," *New York Review of Books*, 22 April 1999.

EIGHTEEN

OLD MONEY

The source material for this chapter is based on personal meetings and interactions of the author with the businessmen cited in the text between 1995 and 1999.

261   "The interval between the decay . . .": John C. Calhoun, *A Disquisition on Government* (1850).

267   depends partly on Indian society's ability . . . : I owe a great debt to Francis Fukuyama in this discussion of familial versus managerial capitalism. In his *Trust: Social Virtues and the Creation of Prosperity,* he points out the difference between the American, Japanese, and German managerial capitalism and the Chinese, Italian, and French familial capitalism. According to Fukuyama, social capital gets eroded during periods of strong political centralization. He illustrates this by the weakening of French guilds during French absolutism. This is an important lesson for India, which is coming out of fifty years of centralization preceded by a hundred years of a powerful colonial state. It will take time for Indians to rebuild their civil society and release the "arts of association." Our chambers of commerce, for example, will have to get over the habit of servility in their dealings with the government. As Fukuyama points out, "The left is wrong to think that the state can embody or promote meaningful social solidarity. Libertarian conservatives, for their part, are wrong to think that strong social structures will spontaneously regenerate once the state is subtracted from the equation. The character of civil society and its intermediate associations, rooted as it is in non-rational factors like culture, religion, tradition, and other pre-modern sources, will be key to the success of modern societies in a global economy. . . ." Francis Fukuyama, *Trust: Social Virtues and the Creation of Prosperity* (Free Press, New York, 1995), p. 31.

268   An example is the Palanpuri Jains . . . : Joel Kotkin, *Tribes: How Race, Religion, and Identity Determine Success in the New Global Economy* (Random House, New York, 1993), p. 206.

NINETEEN

THE RISE AND RISE OF A MIDDLE CLASS

279   "The most perfect . . .": Aristotle, *Politics* (c. 322 B.C.), bk. 4.

TWENTY

MODERN VS. WESTERN

291 "It is only the modern . . .": Oscar Wilde, "The Decay of Lying," *Intentions* (1891).
295 His elegant autobiography . . . : Jawaharlal Nehru, *An Autobiography* (Oxford University Press, New Delhi, 1980).
295 "a third way, which . . .": R. K. Karanjia, *The Mind of Mr Nehru: An Interview* (London, 1960), pp. 100–101, cited in Francine Frankel, *India's Political Economy, 1947 1977* (Princeton University Press, Princeton, N.J., 1978), p. 3.
296 "His attention to trivia . . .": Michael Brecher, *Nehru: A Political Biography* (Oxford University Press, London, 1959), p. 18.
297 "The first thing I want to write about . . .": Gandhi's letter to Nehru dated 5 October 1945 is in the appendix of D. G. Tendulkar's eight-volume biography, *Mahatma: The Life of Mohandas Karamchand Gandhi* (Government of India, Publications Division, Delhi, 1951).
298 "the most traditional and the most 'modern' . . .": Arthur Koestler, *The Lotus and the Robot* (Macmillan, New York, 1961), p. 280.
299 Robert Bellah, a student . . . : Robert Bellah, *Tokugawa Religion* (Free Press, Glencoe, Ill., 1957).
299 Weber had suggested . . . : Max Weber, *The Protestant Ethic and the Spirit of Capitalism,* trans. Talcott Parsons (Charles Scribner's Sons, New York, 1958).
300 David Washbrook, a historian . . . : David Washbrook, "From Comparative Sociology to Global History: Britain and India in the Prehistory of Modernity," *Journal of East and South East Asian History,* vol. 40, no. 4 (1997): pp. 401ff.
301 "as Buddhism crossed . . .": This corollary was put forth by Peter Berger, the professor of religion and sociology at Boston University, ten years ago. At that time Professor Berger also suggested that the roots of East Asian success might lie in the folk religions of the Far East rather than in the great religious traditions.
301 "true body of Buddha . . .": Ambrose Y. C. King, "The Transformation of Confucianism in the Post-Confucian Era: The Emergence of Rationalistic Traditionalism in Hong Kong," in Tu Wei-Ming, ed., *The Triadic Chord: Confucian Ethics, Industrial East Asia, and Max Weber* (Institute of Asian Philosophies, 1991). See also Tu Wei-Ming, ed., *Confucian Traditions in East Asian Modernity: Moral Education and Economic Culture in Japan and the Four Dragons* (Harvard University Press, Cambridge, Mass., 1996).
302 China's culture and religious . . . : Max Weber, *The Religion of China,* trans. and ed. Hans H. Gerth (Free Press, Glencoe, Ill., 1951), p. 151.

302 "There is no difference . . .": Rod MacFarquhar is quoted by Nathan
     Glazer, "Diffusion of Values and the Pacific Rim," in John D. Mont-
     gomery, ed., *Values in Education: Social Capital Formation in Asia and the*
     Pacific (Hollis Publishing Co., Hollis, N.H., 1997), p. 58.

307 The first vision was . . . : Francis Fukuyama presented his thesis in *The*
     End of History and the Last Man (Free Press, New York, 1992).

307 "Opposed to this utopia . . .": Samuel Huntington, *The Clash of Civiliza-*
     tions and the Remaking of the World Order (Simon & Schuster, New York,
     1996).

TWENTY-ONE

DEMOCRACY FIRST, CAPITALISM AFTERWARDS

310 "Reformers have the idea . . .": *Economist,* 24 June 2000. This quote
     from George Bernard Shaw appeared in a special survey in this issue,
     entitled "Government and the Internet," on page 10 of the survey.

313 The journalist T. C. A. Srinivasa-Raghavan . . . : T. C. A. Srinivasa-
     Raghavan, "Growth versus Politics in Democracies," *Business Standard,* 13
     May 2000. This was in a book review of the first edition of *India*
     Unbound. Although I initially reacted petulantly to this review (by shoot-
     ing off a letter the next day), I am grateful to him for pointing out the
     divergence between growth and politics, which has partially led to my
     writing this new chapter for this edition.

314 Mancur Olson, the social scientist . . . : Mancur Olson, *The Rise and*
     Decline of Nations: Economic Growth, Stagflation, and Social Rigidities (Yale
     University Press, New Haven, Conn., 1982).

315 In a major investigation . . . : Alex Inkeles and David H. Smith, *Becoming*
     Modern: Individual Change in Six Developing Countries (Harvard University
     Press, Cambridge, Mass., 1974).

315 This process culminated after World War II . . . : In the United States,
     manhood suffrage came quite early, and later the bargaining process
     emphasized free land and free education to the secondary level, an
     equality-of-opportunity version of the welfare state. With Disraeli,
     Britain had relatively early manhood suffrage and full parliamentary gov-
     ernment, while Lloyd George on the eve of World War I brought the
     beginnings of a welfare system to Britain. Bismarck in Germany pro-
     duced an early welfare state but postponed electoral equality and parlia-
     mentary government. While there were differences in the historical
     encounters with democratization and "welfarization," a century after the
     process began all the advanced capitalist democracies had similar versions
     of the welfare state—smaller in the case of United States and Japan, more
     substantial in Europe. Democracy has been supportive of capitalism in

this sense. Without this welfare adaptation it is doubtful that capitalism would have survived.

315 Democracy and capitalism are thus both positively . . . : I have benefited from Gabriel Almond's "Capitalism and Democracy," in the American Political Science Association's *PS: Political Science and Politics*, September 1991, pp. 467–74.

316 Over the centuries . . . : Robert L. Heilbroner, *The Worldly Philosophers: The Lives, Times, and Ideas of the Great Economic Thinkers* (Simon & Schuster, New York, 1953), pp. 19–27. The subsequent quote from Adam Smith is in the same chapter.

317 No wonder Samuel Johnson said . . . : This quote of Dr. Johnson can also be located in the same chapter in Heilbroner cited above.

317 Today 120 of the world's 200 or so states . . . : *Economist*, 24 June 2000, p. 21.

318 Worldwide experience . . . : See Justin Lin and Jeffrey Nugent, "Institutions and Economic Development," in J. Behrman and T. N. Srinivasan, eds., *Handbook of Economic Development* (North-Holland, Amsterdam, 1995), vol. 3A. It provides an excellent review of the huge literature on institutions and economic development. Robert Hall and Charles Jones offer insights into "social infrastructure" in "Why Do Some Countries Produce So Much More Output per Worker Than Others?," *Quarterly Journal of Economics*, February 1999, pp. 83–116. On bureaucratic quality and social capital, see Stephen Knack and Philip Keefer, "Institutions and Economic Performance," *Economics and Politics*, November 1995, pp. 207–28.

319 It was a "gift from the elite . . .": Atul Kohli, *Democracy and Discontent: India's Growing Crisis of Governability* (Cambridge University Press, Cambridge, 1991), p. 390.

319 He thinks that Rajiv Gandhi . . . : James Manor, "The Political Sustainability of Economic Liberalization in India," in Robert Cassen and Vijay Joshi, eds., *India: The Future of Economic Reform* (Oxford University Press, New Delhi, 1995), p. 354.

320 Second, he was able to reform by stealth . . . : Ashutosh Varshney, "Mass Politics or Elite Politics? India's Economic Reforms in Comparative Perspective," in Jeffrey D. Sachs and others, *India in the Era of Economic Reforms* (Oxford University Press, New Delhi, 1999), p. 225.

320 the five main interest groups . . . : To Pranab Bardhan's three "dominant proprietary classes" I have added James Manor's latter two groups. Pranab K. Bardhan, *The Political Economy of Development in India* (Oxford University Press, New Delhi, 1984). For James Manor, see above.

322 Basrabhai is one such woman . . . : Basrabhai's story provides the backdrop to the World Development Report, 2001–2, entitled *Attacking Poverty* (Oxford University Press, New York, 2001), p. 2.

323   *India Today,* the widely read national magazine . . . : *India Today,* 11 September 2000, p. 58. *India Today* has provided interesting coverage of volunteer activities in India over the past decade with many inspiring stories.

TWENTY-TWO
KNOWLEDGE IS WEALTH

325   "The raft of knowledge . . .": Bhagavad Gita, translation P. Lal, chap. 4.

326   India's emerging success . . . : The data quoted in this paragraph is courtesy of Mr. Dewang Mehta, head of the trade body, the National Association of Software and Service Companies (NASSCOM), New Delhi, March 2000.

326   campaign to boost Internet bandwidth . . . : This news appeared extensively in Indian newspapers in April–May 2000. The *Economist* also wrote about it on 27 May 2000 in an article called "The Wiring of India," pp. 63 and 64.

327   The head of its $100 million program . . . : Quoted in a talk by Jonathan Everett, a principal of the VIEW (Venture Investors in the Emerging World) group at the Harvard Asia Business Conference on 29 January 2000.

327   "The land of the license raj . . .": *Economist,* 27 May 2000, p. 63.

333   Edelweiss Capital . . . : References to information in this and the next paragraph are from two *Business World* articles: "Dot-com Survival: The Checklist" by Radhika Dhawan, 1 May 2000 (cover story); and "Dot-coms Adding Muscle Power" by D. N. Mukerjea, 3 July 2000, pp. 18–24.

333   The inspiration for our new economy . . . : I am grateful to Vidya Vishwanathan's seminal cover story in the 24 May 1999 issue of *Business World* for much of the data on Indians who have made good in Silicon Valley and the Nasdaq.

335   Every age has its Left Bank . . . : Dennis Cass, "Let's Go, Silicon Valley!" *Harper's Magazine,* July 2000, p. 59.

340   "No one asks you how you learned . . .": Quoted in Sugata Mitra's interview by Thane Peterson in *Business Week,* 2 March 2000.

343   Examples abound from around the world . . . : *Economist,* 24 June 2000, special survey, "Government and the Internet."

A NEW COUNTRY

345   "When old words die . . .": Rabindranath Tagore, *Gitanjali* (1912), p. 37.

345   It wrote in August 1997 . . . : *Economist,* 16 August 1997, p. 9.

348 We have seen that India . . . : We have already referred to Angus Maddison's data on India's share of world wealth in chapter 5. Angus Maddison, *Chinese Economic Performance in the Long Run* (OECD, Paris, 1998). The trade data is from Paul Bairoch (also referred to in chapter 5), "Ecarts internationaux des niveaux de vie avant la Révolution industrielle," *Annales: Economies, sociétés, civilisations,* vol. 34, no. 1 (January–February 1979).

348 It took Britain fifty-eight years . . . : World Bank, *The East Asian Miracle: Economic Growth and Public Policy* (Oxford University Press, New York, 1993). All the data in this paragraph, both on growth and on poverty, is from this source.

348 Poor countries should grow faster . . . : There is a fair amount of data to support this old hypothesis of classical economics on convergence. In my introduction, I referred to the empirical research of Jeffrey Sachs and Andrew Warner, "Economic Reform and the Process of Global Integration," *Brookings Papers on Economic Activity,* no. 1 (1995): pp. 1–118. Sachs and Warner studied eighty-four countries between 1970 and 1990 and concluded that the open economies converged and the closed ones did not. Hence, the crucial factor is that the poor countries must stay linked to the world economy. In addition, see, for example, Dan Ben David, "Equalizing Exchange: Trade Liberalization and Income Convergence," *Quarterly Journal of Economics,* vol. 108, August 1993, pp. 653–79.

349 In Indonesia the percentage of people below the poverty line . . . : The data on poverty for these countries is from World Bank, *East Asian Miracle.*

350 We are also low-cost producers of at least twelve agricultural commodities: Ashok Gulati and others, *Export Competitiveness of Selected Agricultural Commodities* (National Council of Applied Economic Research, New Delhi, 1994), pp. 286–300.

351 India's middle class was less than 10 percent . . . : All the data in this paragraph is from various studies of the National Council of Applied Economic Research. It is in turn based on the large and periodic National Sample Surveys conducted by the government. As mentioned before, the NCAER uses the term "consuming class" rather than "middle class" and the price of entry is the ownership of "middle-class goods," including education.

352 Thus, gender equity and women's empowerment . . . : Amartya Sen has been arguing in this vein over the past two decades. See especially his "Fertility Rates Drop When Women Gain Opportunities and a Voice in Society," *The Nation,* 24 July 2000, p. 16. The article provides details on the studies by Jean Dreze, Mamta Murthi, and others.

352 "Given their social structures . . .": Paul Kennedy, *Preparing for the Twenty-first Century* (Random House, New York, 1993), pp. 182–83.

353   The latest evidence . . . : David Dollar and Aart Kraay, "Growth Is Good for the Poor," World Bank Development Research Group, World Bank, Washington, D.C., 2000.

354   Lionel Trilling, the American . . . : Lionel Trilling, *The Liberal Imagination: Essays on Literature and Society* (Doubleday, New York, 1953).

355   For this reason E. M. Forster . . . : E. M. Forster, *Two Cheers for Democracy* (E. Arnold, London, 1951).

ACKNOWLEDGMENTS

This book is born out of experience. Hence, hundreds of people have contributed to it, and they are too many to thank individually. Some have been quoted in the text, but others will recognize their contributions in subtler ways. Although this is not an academic work, I did read and have quoted from a number of books. They are acknowledged under "Notes."

Soon after I ended my corporate career in 1995 and before I settled down to anything else, T. N. Ninan and P. G. Mathai suggested that I travel around India to find out if and how the country had changed after the economic reforms. I did and I found a change in the nation's mind-set. My findings appeared in a cover story entitled "A Million Reformers" in *Business World* (27 December 1995–7 January 1996). This is how this book was born and I want to thank Ninan and Mathai for having got me started.

I wish to thank a number of people for having taken the trouble to read either chapters or the entire book at various stages in its making. They are Montek and Isher Ahluwalia, André Béteille, S. Bhattacharya, Bipan Chandra, P. Chidambaram, Sumanjit Chowdhary, Puru Das, Bibek Debroy, John Elliot, Nat Glazer, David Housego, Prem Jha, Janaki Kathpalia, Edward Kern, Shiv Kumar, Rakesh Mohan, Deepak Nayyar, T. N. Ninan, Lloyd and Suzanne Rudolph, Jeff Sachs, Amartya Sen, Shunu Sen, Hardayal Singh, Jasbir Singh, Kanishka Singh, Manmohan Singh, Tom Teal, Romain Wacziarg, and Bevan Waide. I also thank Bobby Mathew and Shobha Venugopal for their patient help with word-processing the text in its different versions. My editors Krishan Chopra, at Penguin, and Robin Desser, at Knopf, lent wonderful support throughout. Finally, thanks to my publishers Knopf/Anchor Books in the US and Profile Books in the UK for permission to use the revised and updated text for this edition.

INDEX